D0206523

Birds of
India, Pakistan, Nepal, Bangladesh, Bhutan, Sri Lanka, and the Maldives

Princeton Field Guides

Rooted in field experience and scientific study, Princeton's guides to animals and plants are the authority for professional scientists and amateur naturalists alike. **Princeton Field Guides** present this information in a compact format carefully designed for easy use in the field. The guides illustrate every species in color and provide detailed information on identification, distribution, and biology.

Birds of Europe with North Africa and the Middle East, by Lars Jonsson
Coral Reef Fishes, by Ewald Lieske and Robert Myers
Birds of Kenya and Northern Tanzania: Field Guide Edition, by Dale A. Zimmerman, Donald A. Turner, and David J. Pearson
Birds of India, Pakistan, Nepal, Bangladesh, Bhutan, Sri Lanka, and the Maldives: Field Guide Edition, by Richard Grimmett, Carol Inskipp, and Tim Inskipp

Princeton University Press
http://pup.princeton.edu

Birds of
India, Pakistan, Nepal, Bangladesh, Bhutan, Sri Lanka, and the Maldives

RICHARD GRIMMETT,
CAROL INSKIPP, TIM INSKIPP

ILLUSTRATED BY CLIVE BYERS, DANIEL COLE, JOHN COX,
GERALD DRIESSENS, CARL D'SILVA, MARTIN ELLIOTT,
KIM FRANKLIN, ALAN HARRIS, PETER HAYMAN,
CRAIG ROBSON, JAN WILCZUR, AND TIM WORFOLK

Princeton University Press
Princeton, New Jersey

THE COLOUR PLATES

Clive Byers 119–127, 137–138, 141–153
Daniel Cole 1–6, 28–31, 38–39, 110–111
John Cox 32–35, 40
Gerald Driessens 26–27, 115–116
Carl D'Silva 14–25, 36–37, 78–82, 84–85, 88–95, 117–118, 139–140
Martin Elliott 52–58
Kim Franklin 61–62
Alan Harris 59, 64–67, 72–74, 96–109
Peter Hayman 41–51
Craig Robson 112–114, 128–136
Jan Wilczur 7–13, 75–77, 83, 86–87
Tim Worfolk 60, 63, 68–71

Copyright © 1999 Richard Grimmett, Carol Inskipp, and Tim Inskipp
Clive Byers, Daniel Cole, John Cox, Gerald Driessens,
Carl D'Silva, Martin Elliott, Kim Franklin, Alan Harris,
Peter Hayman, Craig Robson, Jan Wilczur, Tim Worfolk

Published in the United States, Canada, and the Philippine Islands by
Princeton University Press, 41 William Street, Princeton, New Jersey 08540

In the United Kingdom, published by Christopher Helm (Publishers) Ltd,
a subsidiary of A & C Black (Publishers) Ltd, 35 Bedford Row,
London WC1R 4JH

Library of Congress Catalog Card Number 99-63006

ISBN 0-691-04910-6 (pbk.)

http://pup.princeton.edu

Printed in Singapore

10 9 8 7 6 5 4 3 2 1

CONTENTS

THE INDIAN SUBCONTINENT

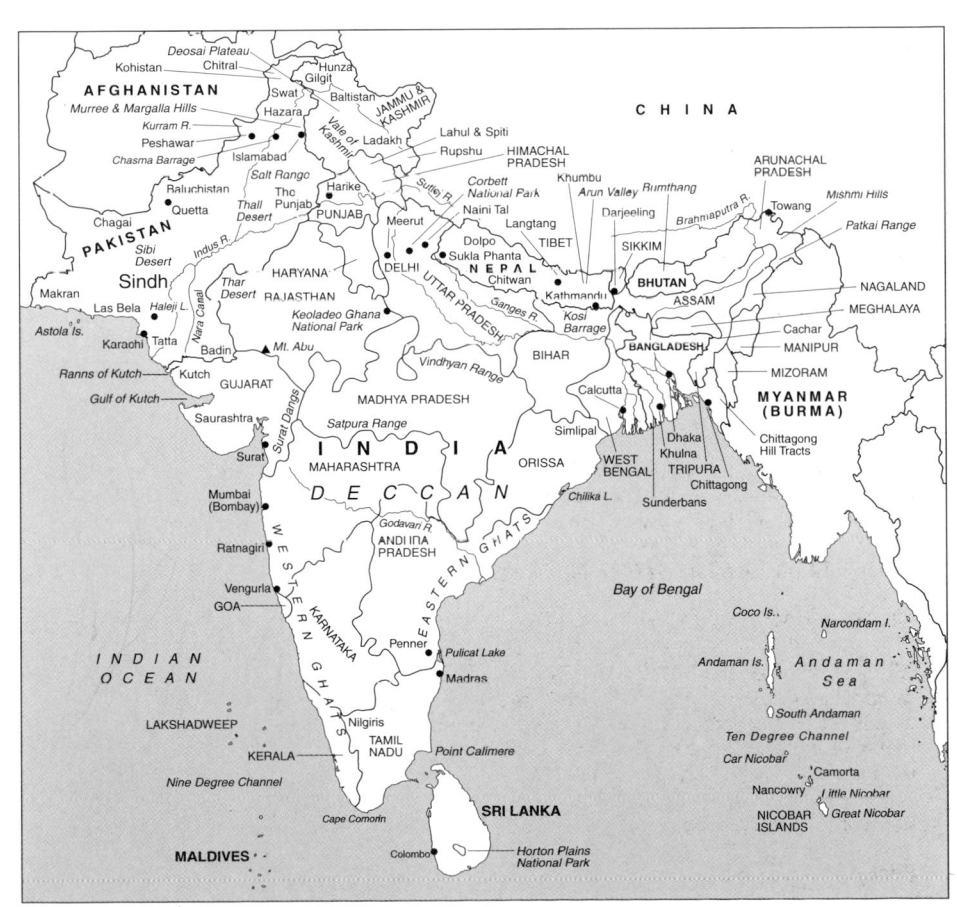

INTRODUCTION

This pocket guide is a compact edition of *Birds of the Indian Subcontinent* (1998). It provides the most essential information for identification, in a volume which is easy to carry in the field. The guide should help observers identify all of the bird species recorded in the subcontinent, and it is hoped that, once basic identification skills have been acquired, birdwatchers will record their observations and use them to expand what is known about the distribution of the birds of the region, to further the conservation of threatened species, and to learn more about birds and the environment in which they live.

The guide covers the whole of the region comprising the countries of India, Pakistan, Bangladesh, Sri Lanka, Nepal, Bhutan and the Maldives. The classic *Handbook of the Birds of India and Pakistan* by Sálim Ali and S. Dillon Ripley, which also covers the entire subcontinent and was first published in 1968–1975, lists about 1200 species. In recent years a number of additional species have been recorded in the region, and adopting the taxonomy used in *An Annotated Checklist of the Birds of the Oriental Region* (Inskipp *et al.* 1996) has produced a current total of 1295 species for the subcontinent.

Future fieldwork will certainly lead to major advances on this work, and existing published or unpublished material will undoubtedly have been missed or given insufficient attention. The authors (c/o the publishers, A & C Black) would be very grateful to receive, for use in future editions, any information which corrects or updates what is presented herein.

The book has drawn extensively from the literature, and published material up to mid 1997 has been reviewed.

Borders depicted in the maps in this book do not in any way imply an expression of opinion on the part of the authors as to the location of international or internal boundaries.

HOW TO USE THIS BOOK

Nomenclature

Taxonomy and nomenclature follow *An Annotated Checklist of the Birds of the Oriental Region* by Tim Inskipp, Nigel Lindsey and William Duckworth (1996). The sequence largely follows the same reference, although some species have been grouped out of this systematic order to enable useful comparisons to be made. In cases where differences in taxonomic opinion exist in the literature, the species limits are fully discussed in that work, to which readers requiring further information should initially refer. The sequence of species in that checklist is almost identical to that adopted in *Distribution and Taxonomy of Birds of the World* by C. G. Sibley and B. L. Monroe, Jr (1990), which was the first taxonomic sequence based on a relatively objective method of assessment. Although frequently criticised because it differs so radically from the so-called 'standard' sequence based on A. Wetmore (1930, A systematic classification for the birds of the world, *Proceedings of the United States National Museum* 76 (24): 1–8), it is undoubtedly an improvement on the latter, which was never subjected to critical review. In addition, no single sequence has ever met with universal acceptance. The English names of birds are another contentious issue, with almost as many different names for some species as there are books describing them. The names adopted here are those which, in the opinion of the authors of the *Checklist*, are the most acceptable of the various alternatives.

Species Included

All species recorded in the subcontinent up to the end of 1996 have been included, with the exception of a few reported very recently (see the list below that also includes some species found since 1996). Species with published records for the region that have since been discredited or require confirmation are included in boxed text. These include the following, which are illustrated and described: Plain-pouched Hornbill *Aceros subruficollis* (specimen now considered to be Wreathed Hornbill *A. undulatus*), Intermediate Parakeet *Psittacula intermedia* (now considered to be a hybrid), Rough-legged Buzzard *Buteo lagopus* (sight record requiring confirmation), Great-billed Heron *Ardea sumatrana* (sight records requiring confirmation), Soft-plumaged Petrel *Pterodroma mollis* (sight record requiring confirmation), Willow Warbler *Phylloscopus trochilus* (one specimen was found to be a misidentified Greenish Warbler *P. trochiloides*, and two were collected by Col. Meinertzhagen), Giant Babax *Babax waddelli* (published record requires substantiation), Small Snowfinch *Montifringilla davidiana* (collected by Meinertzhagen), and Siberian Accentor *Prunella mon-*

tanella (collected by Meinertzhagen). The following have not been included: Black-nest Swiftlet *Collocalia maxima* (specimens reidentified as Himalayan Swiftlets *C. brevirostris*), Great Black-backed Gull *Larus marinus* (specimen collected by Meinertzhagen but not preserved, and the published description is considered inadequate), Lesser Black-backed Gull *L. fuscus* (no specimens, and all sight records suspect), Mascarene Petrel *Pterodroma aterrima* (specimen lost and identification not confirmed), Eurasian Reed Warbler *Acrocephalus scirpaceus* (no definite records), and Olivaceous Warbler *Hippolais pallida* (sight records requiring confirmation). In addition, White-headed Petrel *Pterodroma lessoni* has been reported from Sri Lanka, but has not been fully accepted there.

Col. Richard Meinertzhagen collected a large number of birds in the subcontinent (and elsewhere) in the early 20th century, including several species that have not been recorded by other ornithologists. It has been demonstrated very recently that he falsified data relating to at least some of his specimens (Knox 1993; Rasmussen and Prys-Jones in prep.) and all of his records have, therefore, to be regarded as suspect.

Additional species have been recorded in recent years but are not described or illustrated here, including Elliot's Laughingthrush *Garrulax elliotii* and Brown-cheeked Laughingthrush *G. henrici* (India – Singh 1995), Nicobar Scops Owl *Otus alius* (Nicobar Islands – Rasmussen 1998), Eared Pitta *Pitta phayrei* (Bangladesh – Vestergaard 1998) and Pallas's Bunting *Emberiza pallasi* (Nepal – Hough 1998); and the following for which full details have not yet been published: Long-billed Dowitcher *Limnodromus scolopaceus* (Rajasthan, India), Pectoral Sandpiper *Calidris melanotos* (Punjab, India), Grey-faced Buzzard *Butastur indicus* (Andaman Islands), Trinidade Petrel *Pterodroma arminjoniana* (Tamil Nadu, India), Swinhoe's Minivet *Pericrocotus cantonensis* (Bangladesh), Chinese Leaf Warbler *Phylloscopus sichuanensis* (Bhutan) and Japanese Grosbeak *Eophona personata* (Arunachal Pradesh, India).

Colour Plates and Plate Captions

Whenever possible, distinctive sexual and racial variation is shown, as well as immature plumages. While the guide has aimed to be as comprehensive as possible, some plumages recognisable in the field have not been illustrated owing to space limitations.

The captions identify the figures illustrated, very briefly summarise the species' range, seasonality and habitats, and provide information on the most important identification characters, including voice where this is an important feature, and approximate body length of the species, including bill and tail, in centimetres. Length is expressed as a range when there is marked variation within the species (e.g. as a result of sexual dimorphism or racial differences). Readers are recommended to refer to the *Birds of the Indian Subcontinent* (1998) for more detailed information.

Plumage Terminology

The figures opposite illustrate the main plumage tracts and bare-part features, and are based on Grant and Mullarney (1988–1989). This terminology for bird topography has been used in the captions. Other terms have been used and are defined in the glossary. Juvenile plumage is the first plumage on fledging, and in many species it is looser, more fluffy, than subsequent plumages. In some families, juvenile plumage is retained only briefly after leaving the nest (e.g. pigeons), or hardly differs from adult plumage (e.g. many babblers), while in other groups it may be retained for the duration of long migrations or for many months (e.g. many waders). In some species (e.g. *Aquila* eagles), it may be several years before all juvenile feathers are finally moulted. The relevance of the juvenile plumage to field identification therefore varies considerably. Some species reach adult plumage after their first post-juvenile moult (e.g. larks), whereas others go though a series of immature plumages. The term 'immature' has been employed more generally to denote plumages other than adult, and is used either where a more exact terminology has not been possible or where more precision would give rise to unnecessary complexity. Terms such as 'first-winter' (resulting from a partial moult from juvenile plumage) or 'first-summer' (plumage acquired prior to the breeding season of the year after hatching) have, however, been used where it was felt that this would be useful.

Many species assume a more colourful breeding plumage, which is often more striking in the male compared with the female. This either can be realised through a partial (or in some species complete) body moult (e.g. waders) or results from the wearing-off of pale or dark feather fringes (e.g. redstarts and buntings).

DESCRIPTIVE PARTS OF A BIRD

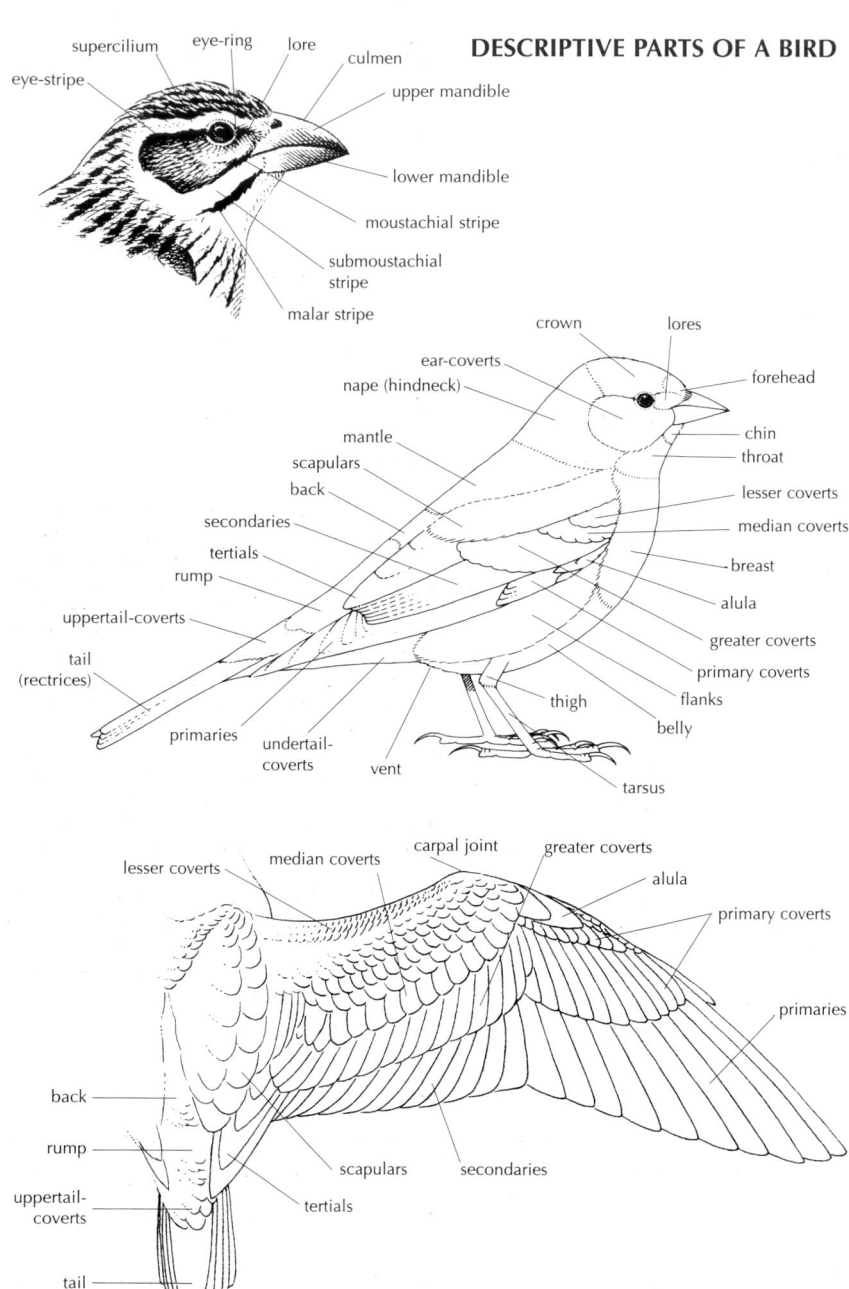

8

Key to the Maps

▪ Breeding resident	✕ Individual records
▫ Non-breeding resident	◼ Isolated or occasional breeding
▪ Winter visitor	✳ Record for a country without a specified locality
☐ Summer visitor	✚ Locality where introduced
▪ Passage visitor	✳ Location unknown/uncertain
▫ Former distribution	☐ Possible breeding
	○ Regular wintering site

CLIMATE

There are great contrasts in climate within the subcontinent. The extremes range from the almost rainless Great Indian or Thar desert to the wet evergreen forests of the Khasi Hills, Meghalaya, where an annual rainfall of 1300 cm has been recorded at Cherrapunji (one of the wettest places on Earth), and to the arctic conditions of the Himalayan peaks, where only alpine flowers and cushion plants flourish at over 4900 m. There are similar contrasts in temperature ranges. In the Thar desert, summer temperatures soar as high as 50°C while winter temperatures drop to 0°C. On the Kerala coast, the annual and daily ranges of temperature and humidity are small; the average temperature is about 27°C and the average relative humidity is 60–80%.

Despite these variations, one feature dominates the subcontinent's climate, and that is the monsoons. Most of the rain in the region falls between June and September, during the south-west-monsoon season. Typically, the monsoon begins in Kerala and the far northeast in late May or early June and moves north and west to extend over the rest of the area by the end of June, although it starts rather earlier in Sri Lanka and the Andaman Islands. In the Himalayas, the monsoon rains reach the east first and leave this area last. The monsoon begins to retreat from the northwest at the beginning of September, and usually withdraws completely by mid October.

Rain continues, however, in the southern peninsula, and in the southeast around half the annual rain falls between October and mid December. This is brought by winds coming from the northeast during the northeast monsoon. In contrast, in much of the northern part of the subcontinent there is generally clear, dry weather in October, November and early December. Low-pressure systems from the west during this season do, however, bring some light to moderate precipitation to Pakistan and northern India.

MAIN HABITATS AND BIRD SPECIES

The bird habitats of the Indian subcontinent can be roughly divided into forest, scrub, wet-lands (inland and littoral), marine, grassland, desert, and agricultural land. There is some overlap between habitats: for example, mangrove forest can also be considered as wetland, as can seasonally flooded grassland. Many bird species require mixed habitat types.

Forests
There is a great variety of forest types in the region. Tropical forest ranges from coastal man-groves to wet, dense evergreen forest, dry deciduous forest and open-desert thorn forest. In the Himalayas, temperate forest includes habitats of mixed broadleaves, moist oak and rhododendron, and dry coniferous forest of pines and firs; higher up, subalpine forest of birch, rhododendron and juniper occurs.

The forest areas of the region are vitally important for many of its birds. Over half of the bird species in the subcontinent identified by BirdLife International as globally threatened and two-thirds of the region's endemic birds are dependent on forest.

Primary tropical and subtropical broadleaved evergreen forest supports the greatest diversity of bird species. Significant areas of these forest habitats still remain in the eastern Himalayas and adjacent hills of northeast India, in the Western Ghats, in the Andaman and Nicobar Islands, and in Sri Lanka. They also contain a higher number of endemic and globally threatened species than any other habitat in the region.

Tropical deciduous forest, including moist and dry sal and teak forest, riverine forest and dry thorn forest, once covered much of the plains and lower hills of the subcontinent. Several widespread endemic species are chiefly confined to these habitats, including Plum-headed Parakeet *Psittacula cyanocephala*.

Temperate and subalpine forest grows in the Himalayas. These forest types support a relatively high proportion of species with restricted distributions, notably White-throated Tit *Aegithalos niveogularis*.

Scrub

Scrub has developed in the region where trees are unable to grow, either because soils are poor and thin, or because they are too wet, as at the edges of wetlands or in seasonally inundated floodplains. Scrub also grows naturally in extreme climatic conditions, as in semi-desert or at high altitudes in the Himalayas. In addition, there are now large areas of scrubland in the region where forest has been overexploited for fodder and fuel collection or grazing.

Relatively few birds in the subcontinent are characteristic of scrub habitats alone, but many are found in scrub mixed with grassland, in wetlands or at forest edges.

Wetlands

Wetlands are abundant in the region and support a rich array of waterfowl. As well as providing habitats for breeding resident species, they include major staging and wintering grounds for waterfowl breeding in central and northern Asia. The region possesses a wide range of wetland types, distributed almost throughout, including mountain glacial lakes, freshwater and brackish marshes, large water-storage reservoirs, village tanks, saline flats and coastal mangroves and mudflats. A total of 33 of the subcontinent's wetland bird species is globally threatened, including Spot-billed Pelican *Pelecanus philippensis*. The subcontinent's most important wetland sites include Chilika Lake, a brackish lagoon in Orissa on the east Indian coast; wetlands in the Indus valley in Pakistan; the Sunderbans in the Ganges–Brahmaputra delta in Bangladesh and India; the extensive seasonally flooded man-made lagoons of Keoladeo Ghana National Park; the vast saline flats of the Ranns of Kutch in northwest India; wetlands in the moist tropical and subtropical forest of Assam and Arunachal Pradesh; the marshes, jheels and terai swamps of the Gangetic plain; Point Calimere and Pulicat Lake on India's east coast; the Haor basin of Sylhet and east Mymensingh in northeast Bangladesh; and the Brahmaputra floodplain in the Assam lowlands. Small water-storage reservoirs or tanks are a distinctive feature in India and provide important feeding and nesting areas for a wide range of waterbirds in some places, for example on the Deccan plateau.

Grasslands

The most important grasslands for birds in the subcontinent are the seasonally flooded grassland occurring across the Himalayan foothills and in the floodplains of the Indus and Brahmaputra rivers, the arid grassland of the Thar desert, and grasslands in peninsular India, especially those in Madhya Pradesh, Maharashtra and Karnataka. These lowland grasslands support distinctive bird communities, with a number of specialist endemic species. Most of the region's endemic grassland birds are seriously at risk including Lesser Florican *Sypheotides indica*, Indian Bustard *Ardeotis nigriceps*, Bristled Grassbird *Chaetornis striatus* and Finn's Weaver *Ploceus megarhynchus*.

Desert

The Thar desert is the largest desert in the region, covering an area of 200,000 km^2 in northwest India and Pakistan. There are other extensive arid areas in Pakistan: the hot deserts of the Chagai, a vast plain west of the main mountain ranges of Baluchistan, and the Thal, Cholistan and Sibi deserts in central and eastern Pakistan. The far northern mountain regions, which the monsoon winds do not penetrate, experience a cold-desert climate. There is only one bird species, Stoliczka's Bushchat *Saxicola macrorhyncha*, which is virtually endemic to the region.

Seas

As a result of increased watching by dedicated observers, several seabirds have been added to the region's avifauna in recent years, notably the threatened Barau's Petrel *Pterodroma baraui*, which was first described for science only in 1963. Seabird breeding colonies in the subcontinent are concentrated chiefly in the Maldives and Lakshadweep.

IMPORTANCE FOR BIRDS

As many as 13% of the world's birds have been recorded in the Indian subcontinent. These include 141 endemic species, a total comprising over 10% of the region's avifauna.

New Species

New species are continually being added to the region's list. For example, recent surveys in the ornithologically poorly known state of Arunachal Pradesh revealed two laughingthrush species that were new to the subcontinent: Elliot's Laughingthrush and Brown-cheeked Laughingthrush. Both species had previously been recorded only in China. In 1991, the diminutive Nepal Wren Babbler *Pnoepyga immaculata* was first described from the Himalayan forests of Nepal (Martens and Eck 1991).

Extinct Species

Two species from the subcontinent may now be extinct. These are Pink-headed Duck *Rhodonessa caryophyllacea* and Himalayan Quail *Ophrysia superciliosa*, although some ornithologists consider that they could still survive.

Recent Rediscoveries

Two species endemic to India have been rediscovered recently. Jerdon's Courser *Rhinoptilus bitorquatus* was re-found in 1986, having last being recorded in 1900. The Forest Owlet *Athene blewitti* was located in 1997; the previous reliable record was as long ago as the 19th century.

Reasons for Species-Richness

The Indian subcontinent is rich in species. This is partly because of its wide altitudinal range, extending from sea level up to the summit of the Himalayas, the world's highest mountains. Another reason is the region's highly varied climate and associated diversity of vegetation. The other major factor contributing to the subcontinent's species-richness is its geographical position in a region of overlap between three biogeographical provinces: the Indomalayan (South and Southeast Asia), Palearctic (Europe and Northern Asia), and Afrotropical (Africa) realms. As a result, species typical of all three realms occur. Most species are Indomalayan, typified by the ioras and minivets; some are Palearctic, including the accentors; and a small number, for instance Spotted Creeper *Salpornis spilonotus*, originate in Africa.

Restricted-Range Species and Endemic Bird Areas

BirdLife International has analysed the distribution patterns of birds with restricted ranges, that is landbird species which have, throughout historical times (i.e. post-1800), had a total global breeding range of below 50,000 km^2 (about the size of Sri Lanka) (Stattersfield *et al.* 1998). A total of 99 restricted-range species breeds in the subcontinent, and a further four occur as non-breeding visitors from areas outside the region (BirdLife International 1998). BirdLife's analysis showed that restricted-range species tend to occur in places that are often islands or isolated patches of a particular habitat. These are known as centres of endemism, and are often called Endemic Bird Areas or 'conservation hotspots'. BirdLife has identified eight centres of endemism in the Indian subcontinent.

The wet lowland and montane rainforest zones of the eastern Himalayas in India, Nepal and Bhutan (also extending into Myanmar and southwest China) form an important Endemic Bird Area. Further isolated endemic-rich areas of rainforest are on the coastal flanks of the Western Ghats and in southwestern Sri Lanka. The other Endemic Bird Areas are the western Himalayas in India, Nepal and Pakistan; the central Himalayas; the Assam plains, which lie in the floodplain of the Brahmaputra in Bangladesh and India; and the Andaman and Nicobar Islands in the Bay of Bengal. Seven of the subcontinent's eight Endemic Bird Areas are largely forest areas.

More Widespread Species

The subcontinent still supports very large populations of some large waterbirds and birds of prey, such as the Painted Stork *Mycteria leucocephala* and White-rumped Vulture *Gyps bengalensis*, which are now extirpated or rare in Southeast Asia.

MIGRATION

The large majority (1006) of the 1300 or so species recorded in the region are resident, although the numbers of some of these are augmented by winter visitors breeding farther north. Some residents are sedentary throughout the year, while others undertake irregular movements, either locally or more widely within the region, depending on water conditions or food supply. Many Himalayan residents are altitudinal migrants, the level to which they descend in winter frequently depending on weather conditions; for instance, the Grandala *Grandala coelicolor* summers at up to 5500 m and winters chiefly down to 3000 m, but it has been recorded as low as 1950 m in bad weather. A number of other residents in the subcontinent breed in the Himalayas and winter farther south in the region, one example being the endemic Pied Thrush *Zoothera wardii*, which spends the winter in Sri Lanka.

Eighteen species are exclusively summer visitors to the region. Most of these, such as Lesser Cuckoo *Cuculus poliocephalus*, winter in Africa. Several species breed chiefly to the north and west of the subcontinent and extend just into Pakistan and northwest India, for instance European Bee-eater *Merops apiaster*. Some species move southeastwards, perhaps as far as Malaysia and Indonesia; White-throated Needletail *Hirundapus caudacutus* is one example.

The subcontinent attracts 159 winter visitors, some of which are also passage migrants. There is also a small number of species (19) which are known only as passage migrants. The winter visitors originate mostly in northern and central Asia.

Information on migration routes in the region is still patchy, but it is believed that many of the subcontinent's winter visitors come through Pakistan, mainly en route to India and Sri Lanka. Ringing recoveries have shown that many winter visitors enter the subcontinent via the Indus plains. There is less information about migration routes in the northeast of the region, but the Brahmaputra river and its tributaries are thought to form a flyway for birds from northeast Asia. Increasing evidence suggests that some birds breeding in the Palearctic, mainly non-passerines, migrate directly across the Himalayas to winter in the subcontinent. Other birds follow the main valleys, such as those of the Kali Gandaki, Dudh Kosi and Arun in Nepal. Birds of prey, especially *Aquila* eagles, have also been found to use the Himalayas as an east–west pathway in autumn; the wintering area of these birds is unknown. Spot-winged Starling *Saroglossa spiloptera* also undertakes east–west movements along the Himalayas, and it is possible that other species perform similar migrations.

A number of pelagic and coastal passage migrants and wintering species travel by oceanic or coastal routes. One identified coastal flyway lies on India's east coast, linking Point Calimere in Tamil Nadu with Chilika and Pulicat Lakes. Migration patterns of seabirds are particularly poorly understood, but there is now evidence that some species occur more regularly than previously thought, especially around the time of the southwest monsoon. A few species that breed outside the region and winter in East Africa migrate through Pakistan and northwest India, for example Rufous-tailed Rock Thrush *Monticola saxatilis*. As they occur mainly on autumn passage, they presumably use a different route in spring.

In addition to the subcontinent's residents, summer and winter visitors and passage migrants, nearly 100 species of vagrant have been recorded.

CONSERVATION

Religious Attitudes and Traditional Protection

The enlightened and benevolent attitudes towards wildlife of Hinduism and Buddhism have undoubtedly helped to conserve the rich natural heritage of the Indian subcontinent that still remains today.

India has a tradition of protection of all forms of animals dating from as early as 3000 years ago, when the Rig Veda mentioned the animals' right to live. Several communities, such as the Buddhists and the Jains, protect living creatures in daily life. Sacred groves, village tanks and temples where the hunting and killing of all forms of life are prohibited can be found throughout India.

Current Threats

Birds in the region are currently confronted with many threats, the most important of which are habitat loss and deterioration. Root causes of loss of and damage to habitats are complex, interlinked and often controversial. Overpopulation is often blamed for the region's environmental ills; India is predicted to take over from China as the world's most populous nation by the year 2020. Other factors are, however, important: poverty, inequitable land distribution, insecurity of tenure, lack of political will, weak government, national debt (which encourages countries to overexploit their natural resources for export), damaging international policies, high demand from overseas for resources, and misguided national policies.

Threats to Forests

Both the extent and the quality of forest resources are declining throughout much of the region. In 1997, the government estimated India's forest cover to be over 19% of the country's area, but only 11.2% of forest is dense (Forest Survey of India 1997). Only 15% of Nepal carried dense forest by 1988. Bangladesh's productive forest cover was only 6–7% in the 1990s and much of what remains is heavily degraded (Collins *et al.* 1991; Rahman 1995). Natural forest cover in Sri Lanka had dwindled to 18.9% in 1983 (Collins *et al.* 1991) and according to the United Nations Food and Agricultural Organization, only 2.8% of Pakistan's land is under forest. Bhutan, however, still retains much of its forest relatively intact, with 43% of its land area under high-density forest in 1991; the country possesses some of the best forest habitats left in the Himalayas.

The major threats to natural forest are overexploitation for fuelwood, timber and fodder, overgrazing which prevents forest regeneration, and the conversion of forest to other land uses: agriculture, notably shifting cultivation, tree plantations, urban land, and reservoirs through dam construction. The decline in Nepal's forest cover has been attributed partly to the breakdown of traditional management.

Threats to Wetlands

Wetland destruction and degradation in the region are reducing the diversity of wetlands and the population numbers of many bird species. Major threats include overexploitation of wetland resources, as local demands often exceed wetlands' ability to regenerate. Increasing hydroelectric developments are altering the characteristics and dynamics of entire river ecosystems in the region. Drainage and siltation of wetlands and intensive prawn cultivation are other major threats. Many wetlands are becoming polluted by sewage, industrial effluents and agricultural fertilisers and pesticides, although these impacts have not been quantified on a national basis.

Deforestation has resulted in habitat loss for some waterbirds. Swamp forest, which was once extensively distributed in Bangladesh, is now on the verge of disappearing. Mangrove areas, too, have also been severely damaged in many parts of India and completely wiped out in some areas.

While many of the region's natural wetlands have disappeared, new wetlands have been created. These include lakes and marshes upstream of dams and barrages on some rivers, certain of which now provide excellent habitat for waterbirds. Other wetlands have developed as a result of faulty drainage systems and overspill from irrigation canals. Rice production has also created large areas of seasonally useful habitat for some waterbirds in parts of the region, although in Bangladesh natural wetlands are being reclaimed for production of rice.

Threats to Grasslands

Grassland has been greatly reduced, fragmented and degraded by large-scale expansion of agriculture, conversion to other kinds of land use, drainage, and overgrazing. Apart from grasslands located within protected areas, practically every grass-growing tract in the region is grazed by domestic livestock. Encroachment by graziers is also increasing in protected areas. Large increases in livestock have led to widespread overgrazing, and this problem has been exacerbated as more and more grazing lands have been converted to other land uses.

Threats to Desert

The spread of irrigation has significantly reduced the habitat of desert birds. Between 1950 and 1990, the area under irrigation increased by 70% in Pakistan and by as much as 118% in India.

Threats to Agricultural Habitats

Agricultural practices have become significantly intensified in recent years in most of the region, leading to increased production. Pesticide use has also increased, including use of the organochlorines DDT and aldrin, both of which have been proved to be particularly poisonous to birds. Pesticides build up in food chains, particularly affecting species at the apex, notably birds of prey. Pesticides leached from agricultural land contaminate rivers and streams and build up in aquatic food chains, thereby affecting fish and fish-eating birds. In Europe, such factors have been shown to cause widespread declines of numerous bird species, many of which were previously common, including birds of prey, shrikes and finches (Tucker and Heath 1994). Could the same be happening in the Indian subcontinent? This seems likely, although there is little direct evidence so far.

Other Threats

Hunting is a major threat to some species in Pakistan (notably cranes and bustards) and in Bangladesh (particularly migratory waterfowl and waders). Local fishermen collect eggs of seabirds wherever they nest colonially in Pakistan and the Maldives. Persecution is so great in the Maldives that it seems doubtful whether many young of any seabird species now survive (Ash and Shafeeg 1995). Similar predation is also reported on Black-bellied Tern *Sterna acuticauda*, River Tern *S. aurantia* and Small Pratincole *Glareola lactea* along rivers in Pakistan and may well account for the relative decline in these species (Roberts 1991). In parts of India and Nepal, hunting is on the increase as traditional values wane and is significant for several species, notably threatened bustards and some pheasants.

Until very recently there was a large domestic and international bird trade in India, but since 1991 all bird trade has been banned. Recent undercover operations have, however, revealed that thousands of birds are still regularly caught and traded, both within India and for export, although in much-reduced numbers compared with those previously traded. Caged birds are popular in Pakistan. In recent years, in the Maldives, a very large trade seems to have developed in the marketing of wild birds as pets (Ash and Shafeeg 1995).

Introduced species of fauna and flora are a common threat to native birds (and other wildlife) on a worldwide scale. In the subcontinent, for example, large areas of natural habitat have been colonised by exotic plant species, such as the water hyacinth *Eichhornia*, which covers the surface of fresh waters, thus changing the habitat for many waterbirds.

Consequences

Losses and deterioration of habitats and other threats have resulted in widespread declines in bird populations, but we can only speculate on the changes that are occurring for most species. Apart from the annual waterfowl counts organised by Wetlands International and the International Waterfowl and Wetlands Research Bureau, and some studies on rare species, there is a lack of baseline data for monitoring most birds, especially common and widespread species.

In 1994, BirdLife International published a world list of 1111 bird species (11% of the world's avifauna) threatened with extinction, including 78 species which regularly occur in the Indian subcontinent (Collar *et al.* 1994). A book currently in preparation, *Threatened Birds of Asia*, will describe all Asian species at risk of extinction, highlighting the threats they face and the conservation measures proposed to save them; data are being compiled by national co-ordinators in each country.

Conservation Measures

Traditional protection, religious beliefs, legal measures and the efforts of conservation organisations have all helped to counter, albeit only partially, the threats confronting birds in the subcontinent. Without them, the region's extinct and threatened bird species would be much greater in number.

In addition to the impact of religious beliefs and traditional protection, legal conservation measures are in force in all countries in the subcontinent. The Convention on Biological Diversity has been ratified by all countries in the region. This commits member countries to conserve the variety of animals and plants within their jurisdiction and to aim to ensure that the use of biological resources is sustainable. All the subcontinent countries with major wetlands have ratified the Convention on Wetlands of International Importance, the Ramsar Convention. This requires the protection of wetlands of international importance, the promotion of wetlands and the fostering of their wise use.

There is widespread protected-area coverage. The recently revised protected-areas system in Bhutan is especially impressive, covering 22% of the country and representing all of its major ecosystems. Large proportions of Nepal (10.6%) and Sri Lanka (12.1%) are also covered by protected areas. Protected-area coverage is 4% in India, 4.7% in Pakistan and 0.8% in Bangladesh.

Local, national and international non-governmental organisations have made a major impact on bird conservation. The main national and international organisations and their activities are listed below.

NATIONAL ORGANISATIONS

INDIA
Bombay Natural History Society (BNHS), Hornbill House, Dr Salim Ali Chowk, Shaheed Bhagat Singh Road, Bombay 400 023. Publications: *Journal of the Bombay Natural History Society*; *Hornbill* magazine (quarterly).

Salim Ali Centre for Ornithology and Natural History (SACON), Kalampalayam, Coimbatore, Tamil Nadu 641 010. Publication: SACON newsletter.

Wildlife Institute of India (WII), Post Bag No. 18, Chandrabani, Dehradun 248 001.

Zoological Survey of India (ZSI), 27, Jawaharlal Nehru Road, Calcutta 700 016. Publications: *Newsletter of the Zoological Survey of India*; Annual Reports.

NEPAL
Bird Conservation Nepal (BCN), Post Box 12465, Kathmandu. Publication: *Danphe* newsletter (quarterly).

SRI LANKA
Ceylon Bird Club, Ceylon Bird Club, 39 Chatham Street, Colombo 1. Publication: *Ceylon Bird Notes* (monthly).

Field Ornithology Group of Sri Lanka (FOGSL), Department of Zoology, University of Colombo, Colombo 03. Publication: *Malkoha* (quarterly).

BHUTAN
Royal Society for the Protection of Nature (RSPN), PO Box No. 325, Thimphu. Publications: *Thrung Thrung* newsletter (half-yearly); *Rangzhin* magazine (quarterly).

PAKISTAN
Ornithological Society of Pakistan (OSP), Near Chowk Fara, Block 'D', PO Box 73, Dera Ghazi Khan 32200. Publication: *Pakistan Journal of Ornithology*.

BANGLADESH
Nature Conservation Movement (NACON), Anisuzzaman Khan (Executive Director), 125–127 (2nd floor) Nohammadia Super Market, Sobhanbag, Dhaka 1207.

Wildlife Society of Bangladesh, Department of Zoology, University of Dhaka, Dhaka.

Centre for Advanced Research in Natural Resources and Management (CARINAM), R. M. A. Rashid (President), 70 Kakrail, Dhaka 1000.

INTERNATIONAL ORGANISATIONS

BirdLife International, Wellbrook Court, Girton Road, Cambridge CB3 0NA, UK. Publication: *World Birdwatch* magazine (quarterly).

Wetlands International – Asia Pacific, Institute of Advanced Studies, University of Malaya, Lembah Pantai, 50603 Kuala Lumpur, Malaysia. Publication: *Asian Wetland News*.

World Pheasant Association South Asia (WPA–SARO), c/o WWF India, 172-B Lodi Estate, New Delhi 110 023, India. Publication: *WPA India News*.

World Wide Fund for Nature (WWF)
WWF India, 172-B Lodi Estate, New Delhi 110 023.

WWF Pakistan, UPO Box 1439, University of Peshawar, Peshawar, N.W.F.P.

WWF Nepal, PO Box 7660, Lal Durbar, Kathmandu.

WWF Bhutan, PO Box 210, Thimphu.

Oriental Bird Club (OBC), The Lodge, Sandy, Bedfordshire SG19 2DL, UK. Publications: *OBC Bulletin* (half-yearly); *Forktail* journal (annual).

REFERENCES

Ash, J. S., and Shafeeg, A. (1995) The birds of the Maldives. *Forktail* 10: 3–31.

Collar, N. J., Crosby, M. J., and Stattersfield, A. J. (1994) *Birds to Watch 2, the World List of Threatened Birds*. BirdLife International, Cambridge.

Collins, N. M., Sayer, J. A., and Whitmore, T. C. (1991) *The Conservation Atlas of Tropical Forests: Asia and the Pacific*. The World Conservation Union. Macmillan, London.

Gillham, E., and Gillham, B. (1996) *Hybrid ducks – Contribution towards an Inventory*. Privately published.

Grimmett, R., Inskipp, C. and Inskipp, T. (1998) *Birds of the Indian Subcontinent*. Christopher Helm, London.

Hough, J. (1998) Pallas's Bunting *Emberiza pallasi*: a new species for Nepal and the Indian subcontinent. *Forktail* 14: 72–73.

Inskipp, T., Lindsey, N., and Duckworth, W. (1996) *An Annotated Checklist of the Birds of the Oriental Region*. Oriental Bird Club, Sandy.

Knox, A. G. (1993) Richard Meinertzhagen – a case of fraud examined. *Ibis* 135: 320–325.

Martens, J., and Eck, S. (1995) Towards an ornithology of the Himalayas: systematics, ecology and vocalizations of Nepal birds. *Bonner Zoologische Monographien* 38: 1–445.

Ministry of Environment and Forests. (1997) *State of Forest Report 1997*. Dehra Dun: Forest Survey of India.

Rahman, S. (1995) Wildlife in Bangladesh: a diminishing resource. *TigerPaper* 22(3): 7–14.

Rasmussen, P., and Prÿs-Jones, R. (in prep.) The Asian records of Richard Meinertzhagen.

Rasmussen, P. (1998) A new scops-owl from Great Nicobar Island. *Bull. Brit. Orn. Club* 118: 141–153.

Roberts, T. J. (1991–1992) *The Birds of Pakistan*. Two vols. Oxford University Press, Karachi.

Singh, P. (1995) Recent bird records from Arunachal Pradesh, India. *Forktail* 10: 65–104.

Tucker, G., and Heath, M. (1994) *Birds in Europe: their Conservation and Status*. BirdLife International, Cambridge.

Stattersfield, A. J., Crosby, M. J., Long, A. J., and Wege, D. C. (1998) *Endemic Bird Areas of the World, Priorities for Biodiversity Conservation*. BirdLife International, Cambridge.

Vestergaard, M. (1998) Eared Pitta *Pitta phayrei*: a new species for Bangladesh and the Indian subcontinent. *Forktail* 14: 69–70.

GLOSSARY

See also figures on p.8, which cover bird topography.

Axillaries: the feathers in the armpit at the base of the underwing.

Biotope: a particular area which is substantially uniform in its environmental conditions and its flora and fauna.

Cap: a well-defined patch of colour or bare skin on the top of the head.

Carpal patch: a well-defined patch of colour on the underwing in the vicinity of the carpal joint.

Cere: a fleshy (often brightly coloured) structure at the base of the bill, containing the nostrils.

Collar: a well-defined band of colour that encircles or partly encircles the neck.

Culmen: the ridge of the upper mandible.

Edgings or edges: outer feather margins, which can frequently result in distinct paler or darker panels of colour on wings or tail.

Filoplume: a thin, hair-like feather.

Flight feathers: the primaries, secondaries and tail feathers (although not infrequently used to denote the primaries and secondaries alone).

Fringes: complete feather margins, which can frequently result in a scaly appearance to body feathers or wing-coverts.

Gape: the mouth and fleshy corner of the bill, which can extend back below the eye.

Gonys: a bulge in the lower mandible, usually distinct on gulls and terns.

Graduated tail: a tail in which the longest feathers are the central pair and the shortest the outermost, with those in between intermediate in length.

Gular pouch: a loose and pronounced area of skin extending from the throat (e.g. on pelicans or hornbills).

Gular stripe: a usually very narrow (and often dark) stripe running down the centre of the throat.

Hackles: long and pointed neck feathers that can extend across mantle and wing-coverts (e.g. on junglefowls or Nicobar Pigeon).

Hand: the outer part of the wing, from the carpal joint to the tip of the wing.

Hepatic: used with reference to the rufous-brown morph of some (female) cuckoos.

Iris (plural irides): the coloured membrane which surrounds the pupil of the eye and which can be brightly coloured.

Leading edge: the front edge of the forewing.

Local: occurring or common within a small or restricted area.

Mandible: the lower or upper half of the bill.

Mask: a dark area of plumage surrounding the eye and often covering the ear-coverts.

Morph: a distinct plumage type that occurs alongside one or more other distinct plumage types exhibited by the same species.

Nominate: the first-named race of a species, that which has its scientific racial name the same as the specific name.

Nuchal: relating to the hindneck, used with reference to a patch or collar.

Ocelli: eye-like spots of iridescent colour; a distinctive feature in the plumage of peafowls and Grey Peacock Pheasant.

Pelagic: of the open sea.

Plantation: a group of trees (usually exotic or non-native species) planted in close proximity to each other, used for timber or as a crop.

Primary projection: the extension of the primaries beyond the longest tertial on a closed wing; this can be of critical importance in identification (e.g. of larks or *Acrocephalus* warblers).

Race: subspecies, a geographical population whose members all show constant differences (e.g. in plumage or size) from those of other populations of the same species.

Rectrices (singular rectrix): the tail feathers.

Remiges (singular remex): the primaries and secondaries.

Shaft streak: a fine line of pale or dark colour in the plumage, produced by the feather shaft.

Shola: a patch of montane evergreen wet temperate forest, usually in a sheltered hill valley among rolling grassy hills from about 1500 m upwards, found in south India and Sri Lanka.

Speculum: the often glossy panel across the secondaries of, especially, dabbling ducks, often bordered by pale tips to these feathers and a greater-covert wing-bar.

Subterminal band: a dark or pale band, usually broad, situated inside the outer part of a feather or feather tract (used particularly in reference to the tail).

Terai: the undulating alluvial, often marshy strip of land 25–45 km wide lying north of the Gangetic plain, extending from Uttar Pradesh through Nepal and northern West Bengal to Assam; naturally supports tall elephant grass interspersed with dense forest, but large areas have been drained and converted to cultivation.

Terminal band: a dark or pale band, usually broad, at the tip of a feather or feather tract (especially the tail); cf. Subterminal band.

Trailing edge: the rear edge of the wing, often darker or paler than the rest of the wing; cf. Leading edge.

Vent: the area around the cloaca (anal opening), just behind the legs (should not be confused with the undertail-coverts).

Vermiculated: marked with narrow wavy lines, usually visible only at close range.

Wattle: a lobe of bare, often brightly coloured skin attached to the head (frequently at the bill-base), as on the mynas or the wattled lapwings.

Wing-linings: the entire underwing-coverts.

Wing panel: a pale or dark band across the upperwing (often formed by pale edges to the remiges or coverts), broader and generally more diffuse than a wing-bar.

Wing-bar: generally a narrow and well-defined dark or pale bar across the upperwing, and often referring to a band formed by pale tips to the greater or median coverts (or both, as in 'double wing-bar').

PLATE 1: NICOBAR SCRUBFOWL, SNOWCOCKS, PARTRIDGES AND FRANCOLINS

Maps p. 22

1 NICOBAR SCRUBFOWL *Megapodius nicobariensis* 43 cm
Adult. Resident. Nicobars. Chestnut-brown upperparts, cinnamon-brown to brownish-grey underparts, and bare red facial skin. Forest undergrowth by sandy beaches.

2 SNOW PARTRIDGE *Lerwa lerwa* 38 cm
Adult. Resident. Himalayas. Vermiculated dark brown and white upperparts, chestnut streaking on underparts, and red bill and legs. High-altitude rocky and grassy slopes with scrub.

3 SEE-SEE PARTRIDGE *Ammoperdix griseogularis* 26 cm
Male (3a) and female (3b). Resident. Pakistan. Male has white eye-stripe and chestnut and black flank stripes. Female has cream supercilium and throat, grey flecking on neck, and pinkish-buff and grey vermiculations on mantle and breast. Dry rocky foothills, sand dunes and cultivation edges.

4 TIBETAN SNOWCOCK *Tetraogallus tibetanus* 51 cm
Adult. Resident. Himalayas. White ear-covert patch, grey banding across breast, and white underparts with black flank stripes. In flight, shows only small amount of white on primaries, but extensive white in secondaries, as well as chestnut coloration on rump. High-altitude rocky slopes and alpine meadows.

5 HIMALAYAN SNOWCOCK *Tetraogallus himalayensis* 72 cm
Adult. Resident. Himalayas. Chestnut neck stripes, whitish breast contrasting with dark grey underparts, and chestnut flank stripes. In flight, shows extensive white in primaries, but little or none in secondaries, as well as greyish rump. High-altitude rocky slopes and alpine meadows.

6 BUFF-THROATED PARTRIDGE *Tetraophasis szechenyii* 64 cm
Adult. Resident. Arunachal Pradesh. Large size, white-tipped tail, buff banding across scapulars and wings, orange-buff throat, and unstreaked mantle. Subalpine forest and shrubberies.

7 CHUKAR *Alectoris chukar* 38 cm
Adult. Resident. Pakistan hills and Himalayas. Black gorget encircling throat, barring on flanks, and red bill and legs. Open rocky or grassy hills; dry terraced cultivation.

8 BLACK FRANCOLIN *Francolinus francolinus* 34 cm
Male (8a) and female (8b). Resident. N subcontinent. Male has black face with white ear-covert patch, rufous neck band, and black underparts with white spotting. Female has rufous hindneck, streaked appearance to upperparts, and heavily barred underparts. Cultivation, tall grass and scrub in plains and hills.

9 PAINTED FRANCOLIN *Francolinus pictus* 31 cm
Male (9a) and female (9b). Resident. Peninsular India and Sri Lanka. Rufous-orange face (and often throat), and bold white spotting on upperparts and underparts. Sexes rather similar. Tall grassland and cultivation with scattered trees; open thin forest.

10 CHINESE FRANCOLIN *Francolinus pintadeanus* 33 cm
Male (10a) and female (10b). Resident. Manipur. Broad black moustachial stripe, and spotted mantle; underparts heavily spotted (male) or barred (female). Dry, open broadleaved forest and scrub in hills.

11 GREY FRANCOLIN *Francolinus pondicerianus* 33 cm
Adult. Widespread resident in lowlands and low hills; unrecorded in northeast. Buffish throat with fine dark necklace. Finely barred upperparts with shaft streaking, and finely barred underparts. Dry grass and thorn scrub.

12 SWAMP FRANCOLIN *Francolinus gularis* 37 cm
Adult. Resident. From Nepal east to Assam. Rufous-orange throat, finely barred upperparts, and bold white streaking on underparts. Tall wet grassland, sugarcane fields.

13 TIBETAN PARTRIDGE *Perdix hodgsoniae* 31 cm
Adult. Resident. N Himalayas. Black patch on white face, rufous collar, and black and rufous barring on underparts. High-altitude semi-desert, rock and scrub slopes.

PLATE 2: QUAILS AND BUTTONQUAILS Maps p. 22

1 **COMMON QUAIL** *Coturnix coturnix* 20 cm
Male (1a) and female (1b). Mainly winter visitor and passage migrant, also resident. Widespread in north. Male has black 'anchor' mark on throat; some males without 'anchor' and with rufous on throat. Female probably indistinguishable from female Japanese. Crops and grassland.

2 **JAPANESE QUAIL** *Coturnix japonica* 20 cm
Male (2a) and female (2b). Winter visitor, probably breeds. Assam and Bhutan. Breeding male has rufous throat and foreneck; patterning of throat very variable on non-breeding male and, as female, probably indistinguishable from Common. Crops and grassland.

3 **RAIN QUAIL** *Coturnix coromandelica* 18 cm
Male (3a) and female (3b). Widespread resident. Male has strongly patterned head and neck, black on breast, and streaking on flanks. Female smaller than female Japanese and Common, with unbarred primaries. Crops, grassland, grass and scrub jungle.

4 **BLUE-BREASTED QUAIL** *Coturnix chinensis* 14 cm
Male (4a) and female (4b). Widespread resident; unrecorded in northwest. Small size. Male has black-and-white head pattern, slaty-blue flanks, and chestnut belly. Female has rufous forehead and supercilium, and has barred breast and flanks. Wet grassland, marshes and scrub.

5 **JUNGLE BUSH QUAIL** *Perdicula asiatica* 17 cm
Male (5a) and female (5b). Widespread resident; unrecorded in northwest and northeast. Male has barred underparts, rufous-orange throat, rufous supercilium edged with white, white moustachial stripe, brown ear-coverts, and orange-buff vent. Female has vinaceous-buff underparts, with head pattern similar to male. Rufous throat of female distinct from underparts. Dry grass and scrub, deciduous forest.

6 **ROCK BUSH QUAIL** *Perdicula argoondah* 17 cm
Male (6a) and female (6b). Resident. C and W India. Male has barred underparts, and vinaceous-buff ear-coverts and throat; lacks white moustachial stripe. Female has vinaceous-buff underparts, including throat and ear-coverts, and short whitish supercilium. Head pattern of female much plainer than in female Jungle. Dry rocky and sandy areas with thorn scrub in plains and foothills.

7 **PAINTED BUSH QUAIL** *Perdicula erythrorhyncha* 18 cm
Male (7a) and female (7b). Resident. Mainly Western and Eastern Ghats. Black spotting on upperparts and flanks, and red bill and legs. Male has white supercilium and throat, and black chin and mask. Female has rufous supercilium, ear-coverts and throat. Scrub in plains and foothills.

8 **MANIPUR BUSH QUAIL** *Perdicula manipurensis* 20 cm
Male (8a) and female (8b). Resident. NE India. Dark olive-grey upperparts, and golden-buff underparts with black cross-shaped markings. Male has chestnut forehead and throat, which are brownish-grey on female. Tall moist grassland and scrub in foothills.

9 **SMALL BUTTONQUAIL** *Turnix sylvatica* 13 cm
Male. Mainly resident. Widespread, chiefly in lowlands in India. Very small and with pointed tail. Buff edges to scapulars form prominent lines, and rufous mantle and coverts are boldly fringed buff, creating scaly appearance. Repetitive booming call. Scrub and grassland.

10 **YELLOW-LEGGED BUTTONQUAIL** *Turnix tanki* 15–16 cm
Male (10a) and female (10b). Mainly resident; summer visitor to northwest. Widespread, chiefly in lowlands. Yellow legs and bill. Comparatively uniform upperparts (lacking scaly or striped appearance), buff coverts with bold black spotting. Pattern and coloration of underparts very different from Barred. Low-pitched hoot, repeated with increasing strength, becoming human-like moan. Scrub and grassland, and crops.

11 **BARRED BUTTONQUAIL** *Turnix suscitator* 15 cm
Male (11a) and female (11b). Resident. Widespread, mainly in lowlands. Grey bill and legs, and bold black barring on sides of neck, breast and wing-coverts. Orange-rufous to orange-buff flanks and belly clearly demarcated from barred breast. Females (and some males) have black throat and centre of breast. Calls include motorcycle-like *drr-r-r-r-r*, and far-carrying *hoon-hoon-hoon-hoon*. Scrub and grassland, and open forest.

PLATE 1, p. 18

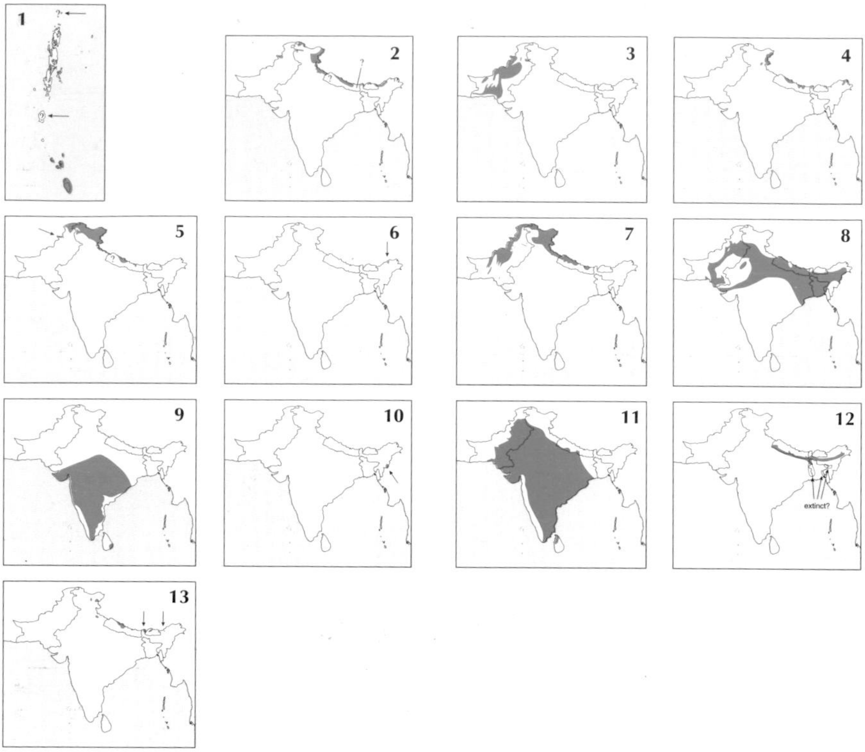

PLATE 2, p. 20

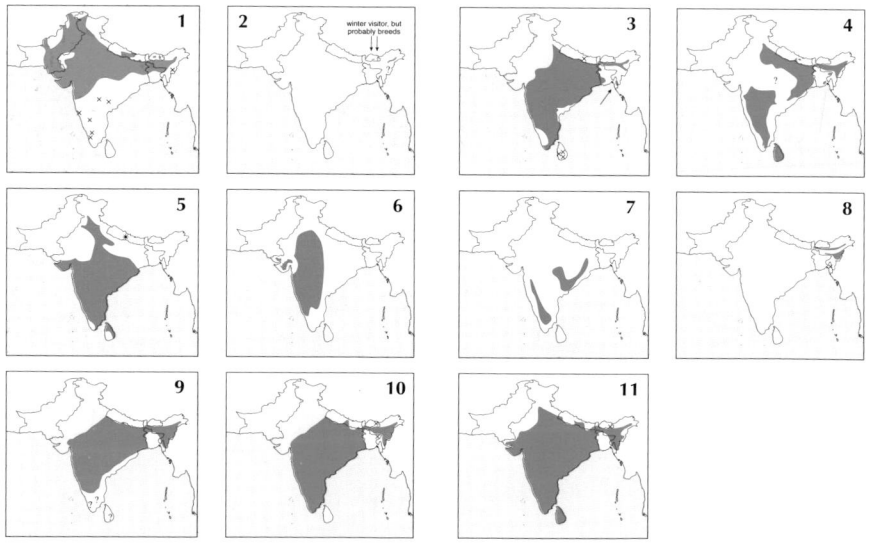

PLATE 14, p. 46

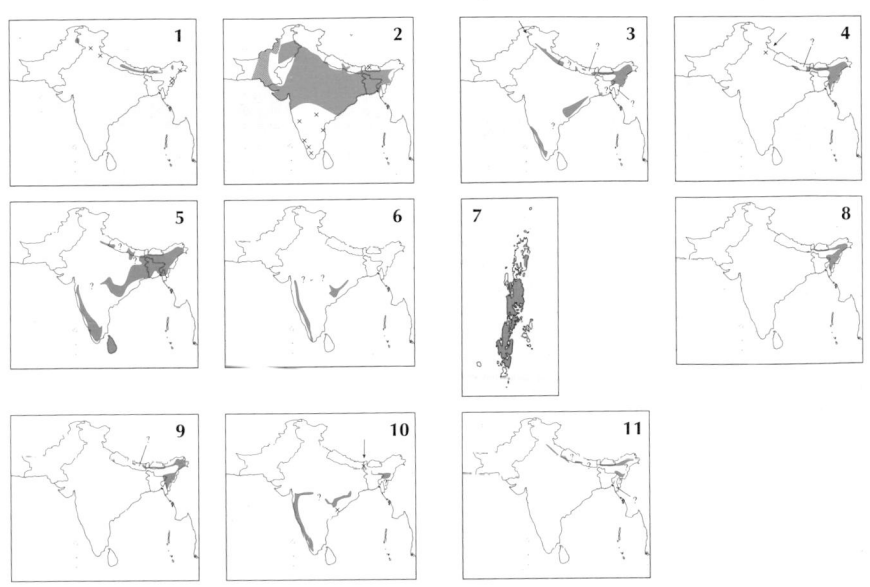

PLATE 15, p. 48

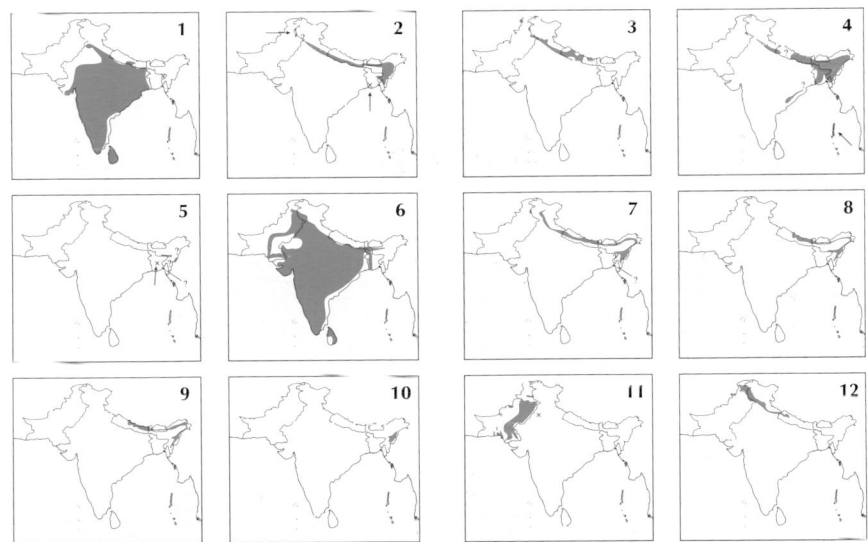

PLATE 3: PARTRIDGES AND SPURFOWL

1 HILL PARTRIDGE *Arborophila torqueola* 28 cm
Male (1a) and female (1b). Resident. Himalayas and NE India. Male has rufous crown and ear-coverts, black eye-patch and eye-stripe, white neck sides streaked with black, and white collar. Female has black barring on mantle, and lacks black border between rufous-orange foreneck and grey breast. Grey or brown legs and feet. Two or three drawn-out whistles, followed by three to six double whistles. Broadleaved forest.

2 RUFOUS-THROATED PARTRIDGE *Arborophila rufogularis* 27 cm
Male (2a) and female (2b) *A. r. rufogularis*; **male *A. r. intermedia* (2c).** Resident. Himalayas, NE India and Bangladesh. Greyish-white supercilium, diffuse white moustachial stripe, unbarred mantle, and black border between rufous-orange foreneck and grey breast. *A. r. intermedia*, occurring east and south of Brahmaputra River, has brighter orange foreneck, black throat, and lacks black border to breast. Double whistle, *wheea-whu*, repeated constantly and on ascending scale. Broadleaved forest and secondary growth.

3 WHITE-CHEEKED PARTRIDGE *Arborophila atrogularis* 28 cm
Adult. Resident. E Himalayas, NE India and Bangladesh. White cheeks, black mask and throat, barred upperparts, and orange-yellow on neck which is streaked with black. Accelerating and ascending series of *whew* notes, ending abruptly. Bamboo thickets and forest undergrowth.

4 CHESTNUT-BREASTED PARTRIDGE *Arborophila mandellii* 28 cm
Adult. Resident. E Himalayas and Assam. White half-collar, rufous-orange throat, and chestnut breast. Call starts with repetition of *prrreet*, followed by a series of *prr prr-er-it* notes, ascending to a climax. Forest undergrowth.

5 MOUNTAIN BAMBOO PARTRIDGE *Bambusicola fytchii* 35 cm
Adult. Resident. NE India and Bangladesh. Long tail, chestnut spotting on breast and upperparts, blackish spotting on flanks, and buffish supercilium. Dense grass and scrub in foothills.

6 RED SPURFOWL *Galloperdix spadicea* 36 cm
Male (6a) and female (6b) *G. s. spadicea*; **male *G. s. stewarti* (6c).** Resident. India. Red facial skin and legs/feet. Male has brownish-grey head and neck, and rufous body. Female has black mottling on upperparts, and barred underparts. Male *stewarti* of Kerala is deeper chestnut-red. Scrub, bamboo thickets and secondary growth.

7 PAINTED SPURFOWL *Galloperdix lunulata* 32 cm
Male (7a) and female (7b). Resident. India. Dark bill and legs/feet. Male has greenish-black head and neck barred with white, chestnut-red upperparts and yellowish-buff underparts with spotting and barring. Female is dark brown, with chestnut supercilium and forehead, and buff throat and malar stripe; lacks red orbital skin. Thorn scrub and bamboo thickets.

8 SRI LANKA SPURFOWL *Galloperdix bicalcarata* 34 cm
Male (8a) and female (8b). Resident. Sri Lanka. Red facial skin and legs/feet. Male is boldly streaked and spotted with white. Female has chestnut upperparts with blackish vermiculations, rufous underparts, and dark brown crown. Dense forest.

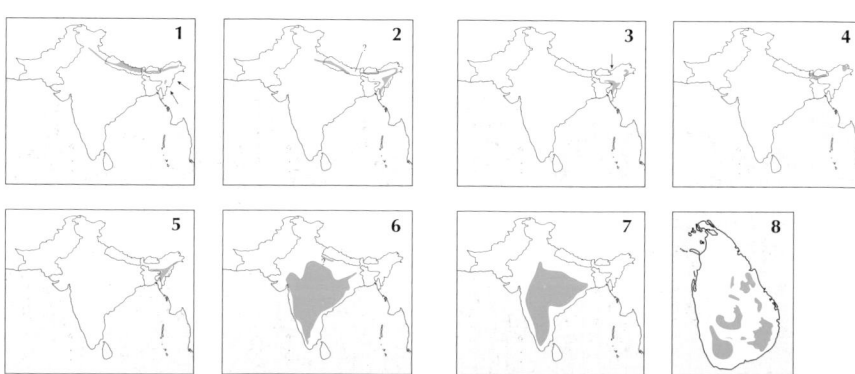

PLATE 4: HIMALAYAN QUAIL AND PHEASANTS

1 HIMALAYAN QUAIL *Ophrysia superciliosa* 25 cm
Male (1a) and female (1b). Presumed extinct. W Himalayas in India. Red bill and legs/feet.
Male has black-and-white head pattern. Female is boldly spotted and streaked with black.
Long grass and brush on steep slopes.

2 BLOOD PHEASANT *Ithaginis cruentus* 38 cm
Male (2a, 2c) and female (2b) *I. c. cruentus*; **male** *I. c. kuseri* **(2d); male** *I. c. tibetanus*
(2e). Resident. Himalayas. Crested head, and red orbital skin and legs/feet. Male has grey
upperparts streaked with white, and greenish underparts, and plumage is splashed with
red. Female has grey crest and nape, rufous-orange face, dark brown upperparts, and
rufous-brown underparts. Races vary in patterning of red and black on head of male, and
in extent of red on breast. High-altitude forest.

3 WESTERN TRAGOPAN *Tragopan melanocephalus* M 68–73 cm, F 60 cm
Male (3a) and female (3b). Resident. W Himalayas. Male has orange foreneck, blackish
underparts which are boldly spotted with white, red hindneck, and red facial skin. Female
has dark grey-brown coloration to underparts. Temperate and subalpine forest.

4 SATYR TRAGOPAN *Tragopan satyra* M 67–72 cm, F 57.5 cm
Male (4a) and female (4b). Resident. Himalayas. Male has red underparts with black-bor-
dered white spots, and olive-brown coloration to upperparts. Facial skin is blue. Female
generally has rufous tone to underparts. Temperate and subalpine forest.

5 BLYTH'S TRAGOPAN *Tragopan blythii* M 65–70 cm, F 58 cm
Male (5a) and female (5b) *T. b. blythii*; **male** *T. b. molesworthi* **(5c).** Resident. E
Himalayas and NE India. Male has sandy-grey lower breast and belly, and yellow facial
skin. Female has grey-brown underparts with indistinct spotting. Male *molesworthi*, of NE
Himalayas, has narrower red breast-band and more uniform grey underparts compared
with nominate. Broadleaved forest, dense shrubberies and bamboo.

6 TEMMINCK'S TRAGOPAN *Tragopan temminckii* M 64 cm
Male (6a) and female (6b). Resident. E Himalayas in Arunachal Pradesh. Male has grey
spotting on red underparts (spots lack black borders), and red coloration to upperparts;
blue facial skin more extensive than in male Satyr. Female has prominent white spotting
on underparts. Temperate and subalpine forest.

7 KOKLASS PHEASANT *Pucrasia macrolopha* M 58–64 cm, F 52.5–56 cm
Male (7a) and female (7b) *P. m. macrolopha*; **male (7c)** *P. m. nipalensis.* Resident. W
Himalayas. Male has bottle-green head and ear-tufts, chestnut on breast, and streaked
appearance to body. Female has white throat, short buff ear-tufts, and streaked body. Both
sexes have wedge-shaped tail. Races illustrated from eastern part of range; those to west
show more chestnut on upperparts and underparts. Temperate and subalpine forest.

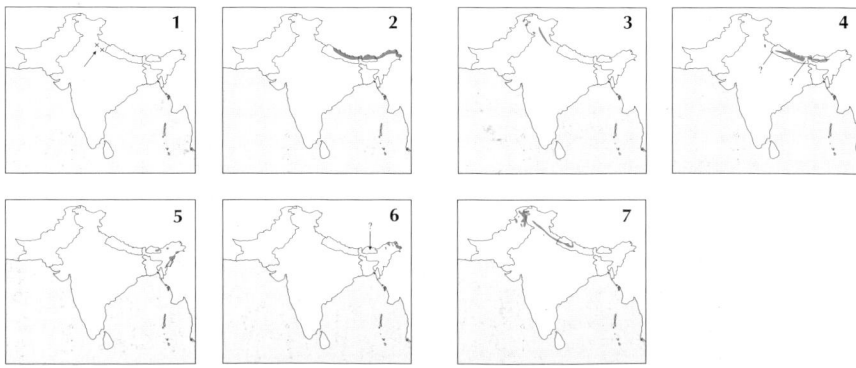

PLATE 5: PHEASANTS

1 HIMALAYAN MONAL *Lophophorus impejanus* M 70 cm, F 63.5 cm
Male (1a) and female (1b). Resident. Himalayas. Male is iridescent green, copper and purple, with white patch on back and cinnamon-brown tail, and spatulate-tipped crest. Female has white throat, short crest, boldly streaked underparts, white crescent on upper-tail-coverts, and narrow white tip to tail. Summers on rocky and grass-covered slopes; winters in forest.

2 SCLATER'S MONAL *Lophophorus sclateri* M 68 cm, F 63 cm
Male (2a) and female (2b). Resident. E Himalayas in Arunachal Pradesh. Male has tufted crest, white lower back and rump/uppertail-coverts, and broad white tip to the cinnamon-brown tail. Female has greyish-white rump/uppertail-coverts, and broad white tip to tail. Underparts of female are more uniform and lack bold splashes of white compared with female Himalayan. Fir forest.

3 RED JUNGLEFOWL *Gallus gallus* M 65–75 cm, F 42–46 cm
Male (3a) and female (3b). Resident. Himalayas, NE and E India, and Bangladesh. Male has orange and golden-yellow neck hackles, blackish-brown underparts, and rufous-orange panel on secondaries. Male has eclipse plumage (not illustrated) which lacks neck hackles and elongated central tail feathers. Female has black-streaked golden 'shawl', and rufous-brown underparts streaked with buff. Forest undergrowth and scrub.

4 GREY JUNGLEFOWL *Gallus sonneratii* M 70–80 cm, F 38 cm
Male (4a) and female (4b). Resident. Peninsular India. Male has 'shawl' of white and pale yellow spotting, and golden-yellow spotting on scapulars. Eclipse male (not illustrated) lacks neck hackles and elongated tail feathers. Female has white streaking on underparts. Forest undergrowth, secondary growth, bamboo thickets.

5 SRI LANKA JUNGLEFOWL *Gallus lafayetii* M 66–72.5 cm, F 35 cm
Male (5a) and female (5b). Resident. Sri Lanka. Male has orange-red underparts, yellow spot on comb, elongated orange feathers covering entire mantle, and purplish-black wings and tail. Apparently does not have eclipse plumage. Female has white streaking on breast, and black-and-white patterning to belly. Forest.

6 KALIJ PHEASANT *Lophura leucomelanos* M 65–73 cm, F 50–60 cm
Male (6a) and female (6b) *L. l. hamiltonii*; male *L. l. leucomelanos* **(6c)**; male *L. l. melan-ota* **(6d)**; male *L. l. lathami* **(6e).** Resident. Himalayas, NE India and Bangladesh. Both sexes have red facial skin and downcurved tail. Male has blue-black upperparts, and variable amounts of white on rump and underparts. Male *hamiltonii*, of W Himalayas, has whitish crest. Female varies from dull brown to reddish-brown, with greyish-buff fringes producing scaly appearance. Forest with dense undergrowth.

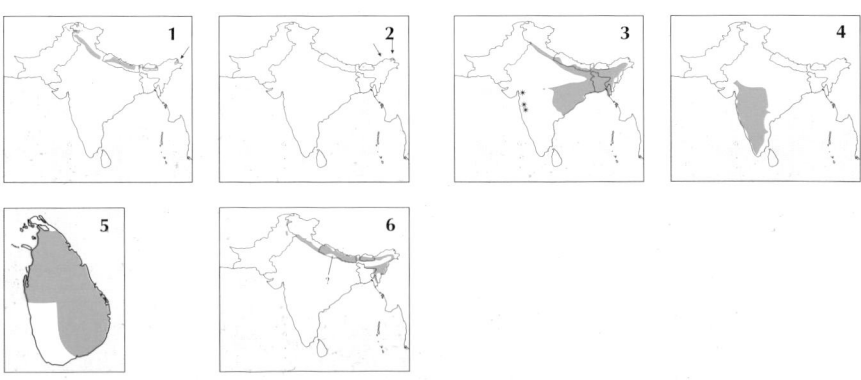

PLATE 6: PHEASANTS

1 TIBETAN EARED PHEASANT *Crossoptilon harmani* 72 cm
Adult. Resident. Himalayas in NE Arunachal Pradesh. Blue-grey, with white throat and white nape band. Red facial skin. Long, broad and slightly downcurved tail. Sexes similar. High-altitude forest.

2 CHEER PHEASANT *Catreus wallichii* M 90–118 cm, F 61–76 cm
Male (2a, 2c) and female (2b). Resident. W Himalayas. Long, broadly barred tail, pronounced crest, and red facial skin. Male is more cleanly and strongly marked than female, with pronounced barring on mantle, unmarked neck, and broader barring across tail. Steep, craggy hillsides with scrub, secondary growth.

3 MRS HUME'S PHEASANT *Syrmaticus humiae* M 90 cm, F 60 cm
Male (3a, 3c) and female (3b, 3d). Resident. NE India. Male is chestnut and blue-black, with white banding along scapulars and across wings, and has strongly barred tail. Female has narrow whitish wing-bars, and white tips to tail feathers. Both sexes have long graduated tail and red facial skin. Steep rocky slopes with forest and scrub.

4 GREY PEACOCK PHEASANT *Polyplectron bicalcaratum* M 64 cm, F 48 cm
Male (4a) and female (4b). Resident. E Himalayas and Bangladesh. Male has prominent purple and green ocelli, particularly on wing-coverts and tail; tail is long and broad, and has short tufted crest. Female is smaller, with shorter tail and smaller and duller ocelli. Undergrowth in tropical and subtropical forest.

5 INDIAN PEAFOWL *Pavo cristatus* M 180–230 cm, F 90–100 cm
Male (5a) and female (5b). Resident. India, SE Pakistan, Nepal and Bhutan. Male has blue neck and breast, and spectacular glossy green train of elongated uppertail-covert feathers with numerous ocelli. Female lacks elongated uppertail-coverts; has whitish face and throat and white belly. Primaries of female are brown (chestnut in male), although this is not depicted on plate. Forest undergrowth in wild; villages and cultivation where semi-feral.

6 GREEN PEAFOWL *Pavo muticus* M 180–300 cm, F 100–110 cm
Male (6a) and female (6b). Former resident? NE India and Bangladesh. Male has erect tufted crest, and is mainly green, with long green train of elongated uppertail-covert feathers with numerous ocelli. Female lacks long train; otherwise is similar to male, but upperparts are browner. Dense forest.

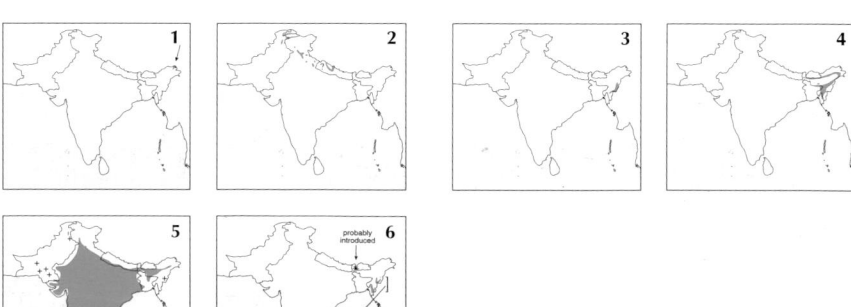

PLATE 7: GEESE AND SWANS

1 **MUTE SWAN** *Cygnus olor* 125–155 cm
Adult (1a) and juvenile (1b). Vagrant. Pakistan and India. Adult has orange bill with black base and knob. Juvenile is mottled sooty-brown, and has grey bill with black base. Large rivers and lakes.

2 **WHOOPER SWAN** *Cygnus cygnus* 140–165 cm
Adult (2a) and juvenile (2b). Vagrant. Pakistan, Nepal and India. Adult has yellow of bill extending as wedge towards tip. Juvenile is smoky-grey, with pinkish bill. Longer neck and more angular head shape than Tundra. Large rivers and lakes.

3 **TUNDRA SWAN** *Cygnus columbianus* 115–140 cm
Adult (3a) and juvenile (3b). Vagrant. Pakistan, Nepal and India. Adult has yellow of bill typically as oval-shaped patch. Juvenile is smoky-grey, with pinkish bill. Smaller in size, and with shorter neck and more rounded head, compared with Whooper. Lakes.

4 **BEAN GOOSE** *Anser fabalis* 66–84 cm
Adult (4a, 4b). Vagrant. Nepal, India and Bangladesh. Black bill with orange band, and orange legs. Has slimmer neck and smaller, more angular head than Greylag; head, neck and upperparts are darker and browner. Juvenile (not illustrated) is similar to adult, although head and neck not so dark, and with less distinct fringes to upperparts. In flight, lacks pale grey forewing of Greylag. Open country.

5 **GREATER WHITE-FRONTED GOOSE** *Anser albifrons* 66–86 cm
Adult (5a, 5b) and juvenile (5c). Winter visitor. Pakistan, N India and Bangladesh. Adult has white band at front of head, black barring on belly, orange-pink bill, and orange legs and feet. Upperwing more uniform than in Greylag. Juvenile lacks frontal band and belly barring. Large rivers and lakes.

6 **LESSER WHITE-FRONTED GOOSE** *Anser erythropus* 53–66 cm
Adult (6a, 6b) and juvenile (6c). Winter visitor. Pakistan and NE India. Smaller and more compact, with squarer head and stouter bill, compared with Greater White-fronted. White frontal band of adult extends onto forehead. Both adult and juvenile have yellow eye-ring, and darker head and neck than Greater. Wet grassland and lakes.

7 **GREYLAG GOOSE** *Anser anser* 75–90 cm
Adult (7a, 7b) and juvenile (7c). Winter visitor. N subcontinent. Large grey goose with pink bill and legs. Shows pale grey forewing in flight. Grassland, crops, lakes and large rivers.

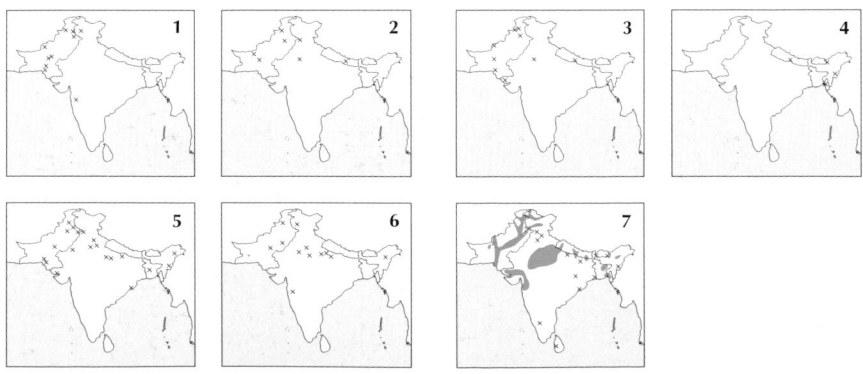

PLATE 8: GEESE, WHISTLING-DUCKS, AND SHELDUCKS

1 BAR-HEADED GOOSE *Anser indicus* 71–76 cm
Adult (1a, 1b) and juvenile (1c). Breeds in Ladakh; widespread winter visitor. Yellowish legs and black-tipped yellow bill. Adult has white head with black banding, and white line down grey neck. Juvenile has white face and dark grey crown and hindneck. Plumage paler steel-grey, with more uniform pale grey forewing, compared with Greylag. Breeds by high-altitude lakes; winters near large rivers and lakes.

2 SNOW GOOSE *Anser caerulescens* 65–84 cm
Adult white morph (2a, 2b). Vagrant. India. All white, with black wing-tips and pink bill and legs. Also occurs as 'blue' morph with white head and neck and dark grey body. Grass by reservoirs.

3 RED-BREASTED GOOSE *Branta ruficollis* 53–55 cm
Adult. Vagrant. India. Reddish-chestnut cheek patch and foreneck/breast, and black-and-white body pattern. Habitat in subcontinent unknown.

4 FULVOUS WHISTLING-DUCK *Dendrocygna bicolor* 51 cm
Adult (4a, 4b) and juvenile (4c). Resident. Mainly NE India and Bangladesh. Larger than Lesser, with bigger, squarer head and larger bill. Adult from adult Lesser by warmer rufous-orange head and neck, dark blackish line down hindneck, dark striations on neck, more prominent streaking on flanks, indistinct chestnut-brown patch on forewing, and white band across uppertail-coverts. Freshwater wetlands.

5 LESSER WHISTLING-DUCK *Dendrocygna javanica* 42 cm
Adult (5a, 5b) and juvenile (5c). Widespread resident. Smaller than Fulvous. Adult from adult Fulvous by greyish-buff head and neck, dark brown crown, lack of well-defined dark line down hindneck, bright chestnut patch on forewing, and chestnut uppertail-coverts. Freshwater wetlands.

6 RUDDY SHELDUCK *Tadorna ferruginea* 61–67 cm
Male (6a, 6b) and female (6c). Breeds in Himalayas; widespread winter visitor. Rusty-orange, with buff to orange head; white upperwing- and underwing-coverts contrast with black remiges in flight. Breeding male has black neck band. Freshwater wetlands.

7 COMMON SHELDUCK *Tadorna tadorna* 58–67 cm
Male (7a, 7b), female (7c) and juvenile (7d, 7e). Has bred Baluchistan; widespread winter visitor. Adult has greenish-black head and neck, and largely white body with chestnut breast-band and black scapular stripe. Female is duller than male and lacks knob on bill. Juvenile lacks breast-band and has sooty-brown upperparts. White upperwing- and underwing-coverts contrast with black remiges in flight. Freshwater and coastal wetlands.

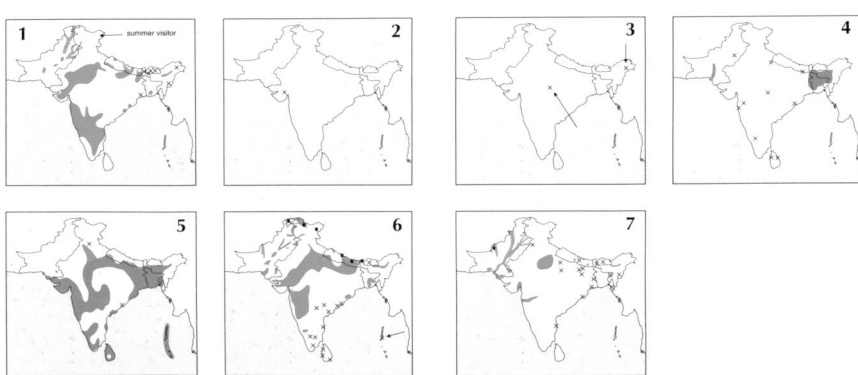

PLATE 9: MISCELLANEOUS WATERFOWL

1 WHITE-WINGED DUCK *Cairina scutulata* 66–81 cm
Male (1a, 1b); variant male (1c). Resident. NE India and Bangladesh. Large size. White upperwing- and underwing-coverts, and white head variably speckled with black. Head, neck and breast can be mainly white on some. Sexes similar, although female duller with more heavily speckled head. Small freshwater wetlands in tropical forest.

② COMB DUCK *Sarkidiornis melanotos* 56–76 cm
Male (2a, 2b), female (2c) and juvenile (2d). Resident. Widespread in India, also Nepal lowlands and Bangladesh. Whitish head, speckled with black, and whitish underparts with incomplete narrow breast-band. Upperwing and underwing blackish. Male has fleshy comb. Comb lacking in female and she is much smaller with duller upperparts. Juvenile has pale supercilium, buff scaling on upperparts, and rufous-buff underparts with dark scaling on sides of breast. Freshwater wetlands in well-wooded country.

③ COTTON PYGMY-GOOSE *Nettapus coromandelianus* 30–37 cm
Male (3a, 3b), eclipse male (3c), female (3d, 3e) and juvenile (3f). Widespread resident. Small size. Male has broad white band across wing, and female has white trailing edge to wing. Male has white head and neck, black cap, and black breast-band. Eclipse male, female and juvenile have dark stripe through eye. Vegetation-covered freshwater wetlands.

4 MANDARIN DUCK *Aix galericulata* 41–49 cm
Male (4a, 4b) and female (4c, 4d). Vagrant. Nepal, India and Bangladesh. Male has reddish bill, orange 'mane' and 'sails', and white stripe behind eye. Female and eclipse male have white 'spectacles' and white spotting on breast and flanks; eclipse male has reddish (not greyish) bill. In flight, shows dark upperwing and underwing, with white trailing edge, and white belly. Freshwater wetlands.

5 WHITE-HEADED DUCK *Oxyura leucocephala* 43–48 cm
Male (5a) and female (5b). Winter visitor. Pakistan and N India. Swollen base to bill, and pointed tail which is often held erect. Male has blue bill, white head with black cap. Female has grey bill and striped head. Large fresh waters, lakes and brackish lagoons.

6 PINK-HEADED DUCK *Rhodonessa caryophyllacea* 60 cm
Male (6a) and female (6b). Probably extinct. Mainly NE India. Male has pink head and bill and dark brown body. Female has greyish-pink head and duller brown body. In flight, pale fawn secondaries contrast with dark forewing, and pinkish underwing contrasts with dark body. Pools and marshes in elephant-grass jungle.

7 MARBLED DUCK *Marmaronetta angustirostris* 39–42 cm
Adult (7a, 7b). Breeds in Pakistan; winter visitor to N subcontinent. Shaggy hood, dark mask, and diffusely spotted body. Upperwing rather uniform and underwing very pale. Shallow freshwater lakes and ponds.

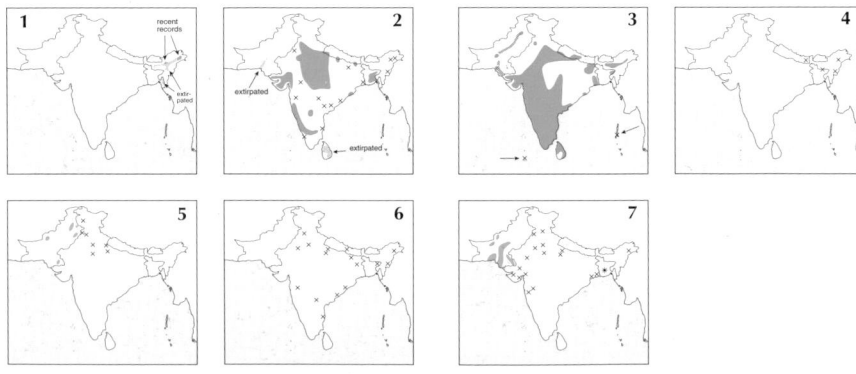

PLATE 10: DABBLING DUCKS

1 GADWALL *Anas strepera* 39–43 cm
Male (1a, 1b) and female (1c, 1d). Widespread winter visitor. White patch on inner secondaries in all plumages. Male is mainly grey, with white belly and black rear end; bill is dark grey. Female has orange sides to dark bill and clear-cut white belly; otherwise similar to female Mallard. Freshwater wetlands.

2 FALCATED DUCK *Anas falcata* 48–54 cm
Male (2a, 2b) and female (2c, 2d). Winter visitor. N subcontinent. Male has bottle-green head with maned hindneck, and elongated black-and-grey tertials; shows pale grey forewing in flight. Female has rather plain greyish head, a dark bill, dark spotting and scalloping on brown underparts, and greyish-white fringes to exposed tertials; shows greyish forewing and white greater-covert bar in flight, but does not show striking white belly (as in female Eurasian Wigeon). Lakes and large rivers.

3 EURASIAN WIGEON *Anas penelope* 45–51 cm
Male (3a, 3b) and female (3c, 3d). Widespread winter visitor. Male has yellow forehead and forecrown, chestnut head, and pinkish breast; shows white forewing in flight. Female has rather uniform head, breast and flanks. In all plumages, shows white belly and rather pointed tail in flight. Male has distinctive whistled *wheeooo* call. Freshwater and coastal wetlands.

4 MALLARD *Anas platyrhynchos* 50–65 cm
Male (4a, 4b) and female (4c, 4d). Breeds in Himalayas; widespread winter visitor. In all plumages, has white-bordered purplish speculum. Male has yellow bill, dark green head and purplish-chestnut breast. Female is pale brown and boldly patterned with dark brown. Bill variable, patterned mainly in dull orange and dark brown. Freshwater wetlands.

5 SPOT-BILLED DUCK *Anas poecilorhyncha* 58–63 cm
Male (5a, 5b) and female (5c) *A. p. poecilorhyncha*; **male** *A. p. zonorhyncha* **(5d, 5e).** Widespread resident. Yellow tip to bill, dark crown and eye-stripe, and spotted breast. Nominate has red loral spot, and boldly scalloped flanks; white tertials and green speculum. *A. p. zonorhyncha*, which occurs in NE India, is more uniform sooty-black on upperparts and flanks; has mainly dark grey tertials, blue speculum and dark cheek stripe. Freshwater wetlands.

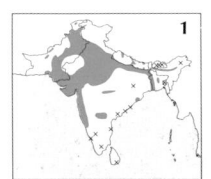 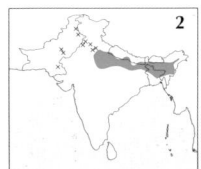 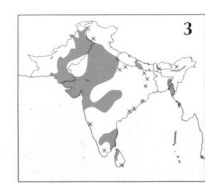 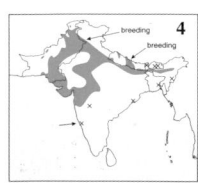

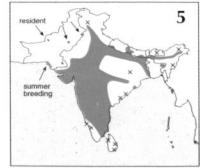

PLATE 11: DABBLING DUCKS

1 BAIKAL TEAL *Anas formosa* 39–43 cm
Male (1a, 1b) and female (1c, 1e). Winter visitor. N subcontinent. Grey forewing and broad white trailing edge to wing in flight (recalling Northern Pintail). Male has striking head pattern, black-spotted pinkish breast, black undertail-coverts, and chestnut-edged scapulars. Female has dark-bordered white loral spot and buff supercilium that is broken above eye by dark crown; some females have white half-crescent on cheeks. Large rivers.

2 COMMON TEAL *Anas crecca* 34–38 cm
Male (2a, 2b) and female (2c, 2d). Widespread winter visitor. Male has chestnut head with green band behind eye, white stripe along scapulars, and yellowish patch on undertail-coverts. Female has rather uniform head, lacking pale loral spot and dark cheek bar of female Garganey, and with less prominent supercilium; further, bill often shows orange at base, and has prominent white streak at sides of undertail-coverts. In flight, both sexes have broad white band along greater coverts, and green speculum with narrow white trailing edge; forewing of female is brown. Freshwater wetlands and brackish waters.

3 SUNDA TEAL *Anas gibberifrons* 37–47 cm
Male (3a, 3b) and female (3c). Resident. Andamans. Brown, with variable white markings on head. Head can be rather uniform with prominent eye-ring. In flight, shows white axillaries and broad white band across greater coverts. Freshwater wetlands and tidal creeks.

4 GARGANEY *Anas querquedula* 37–41 cm
Male (4a, 4b) and female (4c, 4d). Widespread winter visitor. Male has white stripe behind eye, and brown breast contrasting with grey flanks; shows blue-grey forewing in flight. Female has more patterned head than female Common Teal, with pale supercilium, whitish loral spot, pale line below dark eye-stripe, and dark cheek-bar; shows pale grey forewing and broad white trailing edge to wing in flight. Freshwater wetlands and coastal lagoons.

5 NORTHERN PINTAIL *Anas acuta* 51–56 cm
Male (5a, 5b) and female (5c, 5d). Widespread winter visitor. Long neck and pointed tail. Male has chocolate-brown head, with white stripe down sides of neck. Female has comparatively uniform buffish head, slender grey bill, and (as male) shows white trailing edge to secondaries and greyish underwing in flight. Freshwater wetlands and brackish lagoons.

6 NORTHERN SHOVELER *Anas clypeata* 44–52 cm
Male (6a, 6b) and female (6c, 6d). Widespread winter visitor. Long spatulate bill and bluish forewing. Male has dark green head, white breast, chestnut flanks, and blue forewing. Female recalls female Mallard in plumage, but has greyish-blue forewing. Freshwater wetlands.

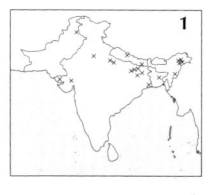 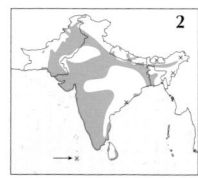  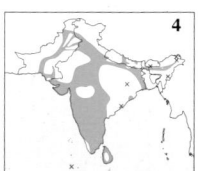

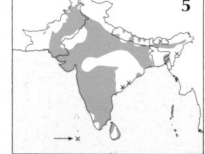 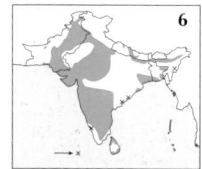

PLATE 12: DIVING DUCKS

1 RED-CRESTED POCHARD *Rhodonessa rufina* 53–57 cm
Male (1a, 1b) and female (1c, 1d). Widespread winter visitor; unrecorded in Sri Lanka. Large, with square-shaped head. Shape at rest and in flight more like dabbling duck. Male has rusty-orange head, black neck and breast, and white flanks. Female has pale cheeks contrasting with brown cap. Both sexes have largely white flight feathers on upperwing, and whitish underwing. Large lakes and rivers.

2 COMMON POCHARD *Aythya ferina* 42–49 cm
Male (2a, 2b), female (2c, 2d) and immature male (2e). Widespread winter visitor; unrecorded in Sri Lanka. Large, with domed head. Pale grey flight feathers and grey forewing result in different upperwing pattern from other *Aythya*. Male has chestnut head, black breast, and grey upperparts and flanks. Female has brownish head and breast contrasting with paler brownish-grey upperparts and flanks; lacks white undertail-coverts. Eye of female is dark and bill has grey central band. Lakes and reservoirs.

3 FERRUGINOUS POCHARD *Aythya nyroca* 38–42 cm
Male (3a, 3b) and female (3c). Breeds in Baluchistan, Kashmir and Ladakh; widespread winter visitor. Smallest *Aythya* duck, with dome-shaped head. Chestnut head, breast and flanks and white undertail-coverts. Female is duller than male with dark iris. In flight, shows extensive white wing-bar and white belly. Freshwater pools, coastal lagoons.

4 BAER'S POCHARD *Aythya baeri* 41–46 cm
Male (4a, 4b), immature male (4c) and female (4d). Winter visitor. Mainly NE India and Bangladesh. Greenish cast to dark head and neck, which contrast with chestnut-brown breast. White patch on foreflanks visible above water. Female and immature male have duller head and breast than adult male. Female has dark iris and pale and diffuse chestnut-brown loral spot. Large rivers and lakes.

5 TUFTED DUCK *Aythya fuligula* 40–47 cm
Male (5a, 5b), immature male (5c), female (5d, 5e) and female with scaup-like head (5f). Widespread winter visitor. Breeding male is glossy black, with prominent crest and white flanks. Eclipse/immature males are duller, with greyish flanks. Female is dusky brown, with paler flanks; some females may show scaup-like white face patch, but they usually also show tufted nape and squarer head. Note female also has yellow iris unlike female Common, Ferruginous and Baer's Pochards. Lakes and reservoirs.

6 GREATER SCAUP *Aythya marila* 40–51 cm
Male (6a, 6b), immature male (6c), female (6d, 6e) and immature female (6f). Winter visitor. N subcontinent. Larger and stockier than Tufted, and lacking any sign of crest. Male has grey upperparts contrasting with black rear end. Immature male is duller. Female has broad white face patch, which is less extensive on juvenile/immature. Female usually has greyish-white vermiculations ('frosting') on upperparts and flanks. Large lakes and rivers.

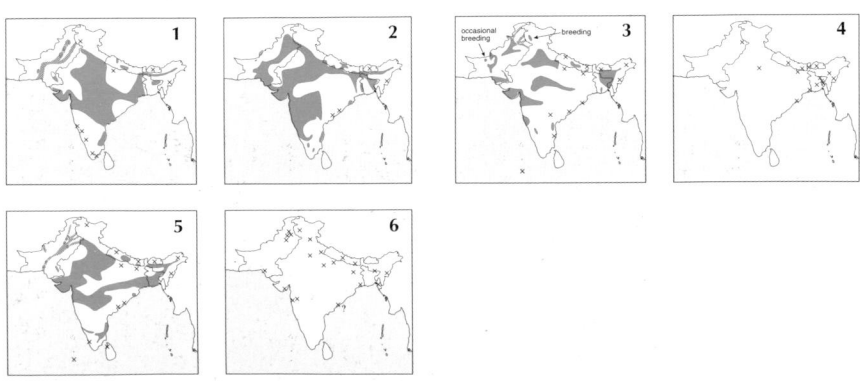

PLATE 13: MISCELLANEOUS DUCKS

1 LONG-TAILED DUCK *Clangula hyemalis* 36–47 cm
Winter male (1a, 1b) and winter female (1c, 1d). Vagrant. Pakistan, Nepal and India. Small, stocky, with stubby bill and pointed tail. Swims low in water and partially opens wings before diving. Both sexes show dark upperwing and underwing in flight. Winter male has dark cheek patch and breast, long white scapulars, and long tail. Female and immature male variable, but usually with dark crown, cheek patch and breast. Lakes and large rivers.

2 WHITE-WINGED SCOTER *Melanitta fusca* 51–58 cm
Male (2a, 2b) and female (2c). Vagrant. Pakistan. Both sexes show white secondaries in flight. Male black, with yellow on bill and white crescent below eye. Immature male is duller and lacks white eye-crescent. Female brown, with pale patch on lores and another on ear-coverts. Coastal waters.

3 COMMON GOLDENEYE *Bucephala clangula* 42–50 cm
Male (3a, 3b) and female (3c, 3d). Winter visitor. N subcontinent. Stocky, with bulbous head. Male has dark green head, with large white patch on lores. Female and immature male have brown head, indistinct whitish collar, and grey body, with white wing patch usually visible at rest. Swims with body flattened, and partially spreads wings when diving. In flight, both sexes show distinctive white patterning on wing. Lakes and large rivers.

4 SMEW *Mergellus albellus* 38–44 cm
Male (4a, 4b) and female (4c, 4d). Winter visitor. N subcontinent. Much smaller than the mergansers. Male is mainly white, with black markings. Immature male and female have chestnut cap, with white throat and lower ear-coverts. Lakes, rivers and streams.

5 RED-BREASTED MERGANSER *Mergus serrator* 52–58 cm
Male (5a, 5b) and female (5c, 5d). Winter visitor. Mainly Pakistan, also India and Nepal. Male has spiky crest, white collar, ginger breast, and grey flanks. Female and immature male have chestnut head which merges with grey of neck. Slimmer than Common Merganser, and with finer bill; chestnut of head and upper neck contrasts less with grey lower neck than in Common Merganser. In flight, white wing patch is broken by black bar, unlike on Common. Coastal waters, large rivers and lakes.

6 COMMON MERGANSER *Mergus merganser* 58–72 cm
Male (6a, 6b) and female (6c, 6d). Breeds in Ladakh; winters mainly in N subcontinent. Male has dark green head, and whitish breast and flanks (with variable pink wash). Female and immature male have chestnut head and greyish body. Lakes, rivers and streams.

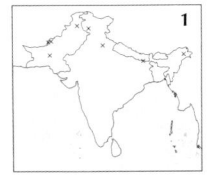 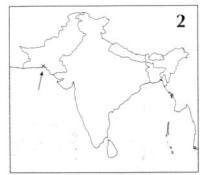 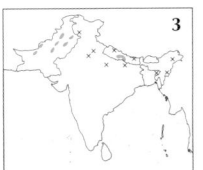 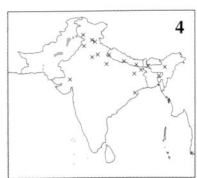

 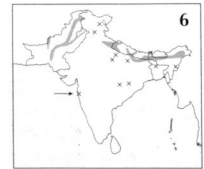

PLATE 14: YELLOW-RUMPED HONEYGUIDE AND WOODPECKERS

Maps p. 23

1 YELLOW-RUMPED HONEYGUIDE *Indicator xanthonotus* 15 cm
Male (1a) and female (1b). Resident. Himalayas and NE India. Golden-yellow forehead, back and rump, streaked underparts, and square blackish tail. Inner edge of tertials are white, forming parallel lines down back. Male has pronounced yellow malar stripes. Near Giant Rock Bee nests on cliffs, and adjacent forest.

2 EURASIAN WRYNECK *Jynx torquilla* 16–17 cm
Adult. Breeds in NW Himalayas; widespread in winter; unrecorded in Sri Lanka. Cryptically patterned with grey, buff and brown. Has dark stripe down nape and mantle, and long, barred tail. Summers in open forest; winters in open scrub, and cultivation edges.

3 SPECKLED PICULET *Picumnus innominatus* 10 cm
Male (3a) and female (3b). Resident. Himalayas, hills of SW, E and NE India, and Bangladesh. Tiny size. Whitish underparts with black spotting, black ear-covert patch and malar stripe, and white in black tail. Male has orange on forehead, barred with black; this lacking in female. Bushes and bamboo in forest and secondary growth.

4 WHITE-BROWED PICULET *Sasia ochracea* 9–10 cm
Male (4a) and female (4b). Resident. Himalayas, NE India and Bangladesh. Tiny size. Rufous underparts, and white supercilium behind eye. Male has golden-yellow on forehead which is lacking in female. Bushes and bamboo in forest and secondary growth.

5 RUFOUS WOODPECKER *Celeus brachyurus* 25 cm
Male (5a) and female (5b). Resident. Himalayas, NE, E and W India, Bangladesh and Sri Lanka. Short black bill and shaggy crest. Rufous-brown, with prominent black barring. Male has scarlet patch on ear-coverts. Forest and secondary growth.

6 WHITE-BELLIED WOODPECKER *Dryocopus javensis* 48 cm
Male (6a) and female (6b). Resident. Western and Eastern Ghats. Large black woodpecker with white belly. Male has red crown and moustachial stripe; red restricted to hindcrown on female. In flight, shows white rump, white underwing-coverts, and small white patch at base of primaries. Forest and secondary growth with tall trees.

7 ANDAMAN WOODPECKER *Dryocopus hodgei* 38 cm
Male (7a) and female (7b). Resident. Andaman Is. Large blackish woodpecker. Male has red crown and moustachial stripe; red restricted to hindcrown on female. Forest.

8 PALE-HEADED WOODPECKER *Gecinulus grantia* 25 cm
Male (8a), female (8b) and juvenile male (8c). Resident. Himalayas, NE India and Bangladesh. Pale bill, golden-olive head, pinkish-buff barring to primaries, and crimson to cromson-brown upperparts. Male has crimson-pink on crown. Bamboo jungle.

9 BAY WOODPECKER *Blythipicus pyrrhotis* 27 cm
Male (9a), female (9b) and juvenile male (9c). Resident. Himalayas, NE India and Bangladesh. Long pale bill, and rufous upperparts with dark brown barring. Male has red on sides of neck. Juvenile has streaked crown, and barring on underparts. Dense broadleaved forest and secondary growth.

10 HEART-SPOTTED WOODPECKER *Hemicircus canente* 16 cm
Male (10a), female (10b) and juvenile (10c). Resident. Mainly hills of NE and E India. Prominent crest; very short tail. Black-and-white plumage, with heart-shaped black spots on tertials. Male has black crown, female has white crown, and juvenile has black spotting on white crown. Broadleaved forest and coffee plantations.

11 GREAT SLATY WOODPECKER *Mulleripicus pulverulentus* 51 cm
Male (11a) and female (11b). Resident. Himalayas, NE India and Bangladesh. Huge, slate-grey woodpecker with long bill and long neck and tail. Male has pinkish-red moustachial patch. Mature trees in tropical forest and forest clearings.

1 BROWN-CAPPED PYGMY WOODPECKER *Dendrocopos nanus* 13 cm
Male (1a) and female (1b) *D. n. nanus*; **male** *D. n. gymnopthalmus* **(1c).** Resident. Widespread; unrecorded in Pakistan. Very small. Has brown crown and eye-stripe, brown coloration to upperparts, greyish-to brownish-white underparts (streaked with brown), and white spotting on central tail feathers. In Sri Lanka, *gymnopthalmus* has dark brown crown and upperparts and whiter underparts. Light forest and secondary growth.

2 GREY-CAPPED PYGMY WOODPECKER *Dendrocopos canicapillus* 14 cm
Male (2a) and female (2b). Resident. Himalayas, NE India and Bangladesh. Very small. Has grey crown, blackish eye-stripe, blackish coloration to upperparts, diffuse blackish malar stripe, and dirty fulvous underparts streaked with black. Throughout most of range, lacks white spotting on central tail feathers (present in nominate of NE, which also has whiter underparts). Forest, and trees in cultivation.

3 BROWN-FRONTED WOODPECKER *Dendrocopos auriceps* 19–20 cm
Male (3a) and female (3b). Resident. Hills of Baluchistan and Himalayas. Brownish forehead and forecrown, yellowish central crown, white-barred upperparts, prominent black moustachial stripe, well-defined blackish streaking on underparts, pink undertail-coverts, and unbarred central tail feathers. Subtropical and temperate forest.

4 FULVOUS-BREASTED WOODPECKER *Dendrocopos macei* 18–19 cm
Male (4a) and female (4b) *D. m. macei*; **male** *D. m. andamanensis* **(4c).** Resident. Himalayas, NE and E India, and Bangladesh. White barring on upperparts, diffusely streaked buffish underparts, buff wash to sides of head and neck. Upper mantle usually barred white. Andaman race has black spotting on breast, pale bill. Forest edges, open forest.

5 STRIPE-BREASTED WOODPECKER *Dendrocopos atratus* 21–22 cm
Male (5a) and female (5b). Resident. NE Indian hills and Bangladesh. White barring on upperparts, prominently streaked underparts, white sides of head and neck, and olive-yellow wash to underparts. Upper mantle lacks white barring; also has larger bill and more red on forehead in male, compared with Fulvous-breasted. Open forest.

6 YELLOW-CROWNED WOODPECKER *Dendrocopos mahrattensis* 17–18 cm
Male (6a) and female (6b). Resident. Widespread east of Indus R. Yellowish forehead and forecrown, white-spotted upperparts, poorly defined moustachial stripe, dirty underparts with heavy but diffuse streaking, red patch on lower belly, and white barring on central tail feathers. Open woodland, open country with scattered trees.

7 RUFOUS-BELLIED WOODPECKER *Dendrocopos hyperythrus* 20 cm
Male (7a) and female (7b). Resident. Himalayas, NE India and Bangladesh. Whitish face and rufous underparts. Lacks white 'shoulder' patch. Juvenile has barred underparts. Subtropical and temperate forest.

8 CRIMSON-BREASTED WOODPECKER *Dendrocopos cathpharius* 18 cm
Male (8a) and female (8b) *D. c. cathpharius*; **male** *D. c. pyrrhothorax* **(8c).** Resident. Himalayas, NE India. Small white wing patch, streaked underparts, and variable crimson patch on breast. Male has extensive red on nape and hindneck. Broadleaved forest.

9 DARJEELING WOODPECKER *Dendrocopos darjellensis* 25 cm
Male (9a) and female (9b). Resident. Himalayas, NE India. Small white wing patch, black streaking on yellowish-buff underparts, and yellow patch on side of neck. Forest.

10 GREAT SPOTTED WOODPECKER *Dendrocopos major* 24 cm
Male (10a) and female (10b). Resident. NE Indian hills. Extensive white 'shoulder' patch, unstreaked underparts, and black of moustachial stripe extending down side of breast. Male has black crown and crimson patch on nape. Oak and pine forest.

11 SIND WOODPECKER *Dendrocopos assimilis* 20–22 cm
Male (11a) and female (11b). Resident. Widespread in Pakistan. Unstreaked underparts, and black moustachial stripe joining hindneck. Lacks black border to rear of ear-coverts of Himalayan; also has larger white shoulder patch and forehead, whiter underparts, broader white barring on wings and paler pink vent. Dry forest and plantations.

12 HIMALAYAN WOODPECKER *Dendrocopos himalayensis* 23–25 cm
Male (12a) and female (12b) *D. h. himalayensis*; *D. h. albescens* **(12c).** Resident. W Himalayas. White 'shoulder' patch, unstreaked underparts, and black rear border to ear-coverts. Forest.

1b 1a 1c 2b 2a 3b 3a 4b 4a 4c 5b 5a 7a 7b 6a 6b 8b 8a 8c 9a 9b 10a 10b 11a 11b 12b 12a 12c

C.D'S

PLATE 16: WOODPECKERS   Maps p. 54

1 **LESSER YELLOWNAPE** *Picus chlorolophus* 27 cm
Male (1a) and female (1b) *P. c. chlorolophus*; male *P. c. chlorigaster* of peninsula **(1c)**. Resident. Himalayas, hills of India, Bangladesh and Sri Lanka. Tufted yellow nape, scarlet and white markings on head, and barring or spotting on underparts. Smaller, with less prominent crest and smaller bill, compared with Greater Yellownape. Forest, secondary growth, plantations.

2 **GREATER YELLOWNAPE** *Picus flavinucha* 33 cm
Male (2a) and female (2b). Resident. Himalayas, NE and E India, and Bangladesh. Tufted yellow nape, yellow or rufous-brown throat, dark foreneck streaking, unbarred underparts, and rufous barring on secondaries. Forest and forest edges.

3 **LACED WOODPECKER** *Picus vittatus* 30–33 cm
Male (3a) and female (3b). Recorded once in Bangladesh. Scaling on belly and flanks. From Streak-throated by unscaled olive-yellow foreneck and breast, broad black moustachial stripe, finer white supercilium, black tail, and reddish eye. Mangroves.

4 **STREAK-THROATED WOODPECKER** *Picus xanthopygaeus* 30 cm
Male (4a) and female (4b). Widespread resident; unrecorded in Pakistan. Scaling on lower breast, belly and flanks. Smaller than Scaly-bellied, with dark bill and pale eye, streaked throat and upper breast, and indistinct barring on tail. Forest, secondary growth and plantations.

5 **SCALY-BELLIED WOODPECKER** *Picus squamatus* 35 cm
Male (5a) and female (5b). Resident. Hills of Baluchistan and Himalayas. Scaling on belly and flanks. Larger than Streak-throated, with pale bill, reddish eye and prominent black eye-stripe and moustachial. Unstreaked throat and upper breast (except juvenile), and barred tail. Forest, scrub, and open country with large trees.

6 **GREY-HEADED WOODPECKER** *Picus canus* 32 cm
Male (6a) and female (6b). Resident. Himalayas, NE and E India, and Bangladesh. Plain grey face, black nape and moustachial, and uniform greyish-green underparts. Forest.

7 **HIMALAYAN FLAMEBACK** *Dinopium shorii* 30–32 cm
Male (7a) and female (7b). Resident. Himalayas, NE India, and locally in hills of peninsula and Bangladesh. Smaller bill than Greater, with unspotted black hindneck, and brownish-buff centre of throat (and breast on some), with black spotting forming irregular border. Centre of divided moustachial stripe is brownish-buff (with touch of red on some males). Crown of female is streaked with white. Breast less heavily marked with black than on Common Flameback. Mature forest.

8 **COMMON FLAMEBACK** *Dinopium javanense* 28–30 cm
Male (8a) and female (8b). Resident. Hills of SW and NE India and Bangladesh. Smaller size and smaller bill than Greater, with unspotted black hindneck, and irregular line of black spotting down centre of throat. Smaller size and bill compared with Himalayan; moustachial stripe lacks clear dividing line (usually solid black, although can appear divided on some and similar to Himalayan). Crown of female is finely spotted with white. Forest.

9 **BLACK-RUMPED FLAMEBACK** *Dinopium benghalense* 26–29 cm
Male (9a) and female (9b) *D. b. benghalense*; male *D. b. psarodes* **(9c).** Widespread resident. Black eye-stripe and throat (lacking dark moustachial stripe), spotting on wing-coverts, and black rump. Sri Lankan *psarodes* has crimson upperparts. Light forest, plantations, groves and trees in open country.

10 **GREATER FLAMEBACK** *Chrysocolaptes lucidus* 33 cm
Male (10a) and female (10b) *C. l. guttacristatus*; male *C. l. stricklandi* **(10c).** Resident. Himalayas, hills of India, Bangladesh and Sri Lanka. White or black-and-white spotted hindneck and upper mantle, large size, and long bill. Moustachial stripe is clearly divided. Female has prominent white spotting on crown and crest. Sri Lankan race *stricklandi* has crimson upperparts. Forest and groves.

11 **WHITE-NAPED WOODPECKER** *Chrysocolaptes festivus* 29 cm
Male (11a) and female (11b). Resident. Widespread in India, also W Nepal and Sri Lanka. White hindneck and mantle, and black scapulars and back forming V-shape. Moustachial stripe is clearly divided. Rump is black. Female has yellow crown. Light forest, scrub and scattered trees.

C.D'S

1 GREAT BARBET *Megalaima virens* 33 cm
Adult. Resident. Himalayas, NE India and Bangladesh. Large yellow bill, bluish head, brown breast and mantle, olive-streaked yellowish underparts, and red undertail-coverts. Call is an incessant and far-reaching *piho piho*. Mainly subtropical and temperate forest.

2 BROWN-HEADED BARBET *Megalaima zeylanica* 27 cm
Adult *M. z. caniceps* (2a) and adult *M. z. inornata* (2b). Widespread resident; unrecorded in Pakistan. Fine streaking on brown head and breast, brown throat, orange circumorbital skin and bill (when breeding), and white-spotted wing-coverts. Streaking almost absent on belly and flanks. Call is a monotonous *kutroo, kutroo, kutroo* or *kutruk, kutruk, kutruk*. Forest, wooded areas and trees near habitation.

LARGE GREEN

3 LINEATED BARBET *Megalaima lineata* 28 cm
Adult (3a) and paler variant (3b). Resident. Himalayan foothills, NE and E India, and Bangladesh. Bold white streaking on head and breast, uniform unspotted wing-coverts and whitish throat. Less extensive circumorbital skin than Brown-headed (which is usually separated from bill). Note range differences compared with Brown-headed. A monotonous *kotur, kotur, kotur,* slightly mellower and softer than Brown-headed. Open forest and well-wooded areas.

4 WHITE-CHEEKED BARBET *Megalaima viridis* 23 cm
Adult (4a) and juvenile (4b). Resident. Western Ghats and hills of Tamil Nadu. Brownish bill. White supercilium and cheeks contrasting with brown crown and nape. Whitish throat, and bold white streaking on breast. Call is a *pucock, pucock, pucock*. Wooded areas, gardens, groves.

5 YELLOW-FRONTED BARBET *Megalaima flavifrons* 21 cm
Adult. Resident. Sri Lanka. Yellow forehead and malar stripe, blue ear-coverts and throat, scaled appearance to breast, and dark legs and feet. Call is a rolling, ascending *kowowowowowo*. Forest and well-wooded gardens.

6 GOLDEN-THROATED BARBET *Megalaima franklinii* 23 cm
Adult. Resident. Himalayas, NE India and Bangladesh. Yellow centre of crown and throat, greyish-white cheeks and lower throat, and broad black mask. Call is a wailing, repetitive *peeyu, peeyu*, recalling Great but higher-pitched. Subtropical and temperate forest.

7 BLUE-THROATED BARBET *Megalaima asiatica* 23 cm
Adult (7a) and juvenile (7b). Resident. Himalayas, NE India and Bangladesh. Blue 'face' and throat, red forehead and hindcrown, and black band across crown. Juvenile has duller head pattern. Call is a loud *took-a-rook, took-a-rook*. Open forest, groves and gardens.

8 BLUE-EARED BARBET *Megalaima australis* 17 cm
Adult (8a) and juvenile (8b). Resident. E Himalayan foothills, NE India and Bangladesh. Small size, blue throat and ear-coverts, black malar stripe, and red patches on side of head. Juvenile lacks head patterning, but shows traces of blue on side of head and throat. Call is a disyllabic, repetitive *tk-trrt* etc. Dense evergreen forest.

9 CRIMSON-FRONTED BARBET *Megalaima rubricapilla* 17 cm
Adult *M. r. malabarica* (9a); adult (9b) and juvenile (9c) *M. r. rubricapilla*. Resident. Western Ghats and Sri Lanka. Small size. Both races have blue band down side of head and breast, and unstreaked green belly and flanks. In Western Ghats, *malabarica* has crimson cheeks, throat and breast. In Sri Lanka, *rubricapilla* has orange cheeks and throat. Juveniles are duller, but show traces of adult head pattern. Call is very similar to Coppersmith, although possibly softer and quicker, a fast-delivered *poop, poop, poop* etc. Open wooded country.

10 COPPERSMITH BARBET *Megalaima haemacephala* 17 cm
Adult (10a) and juvenile (10b). Resident. Widespread east of Indus R. Small size, crimson forehead and breast patch, yellow patches above and below eye, yellow throat, and streaked underparts. Juvenile lacks red on head and breast. Call is a repetitive *tuk, tuk, tuk* etc. Open wooded country and groves.

PLATE 16, p. 50

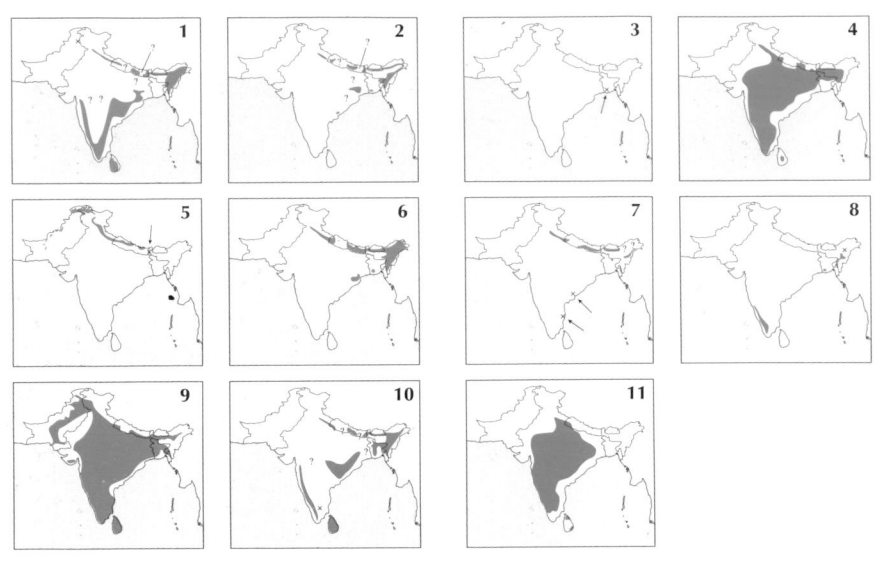

PLATE 17, p. 52

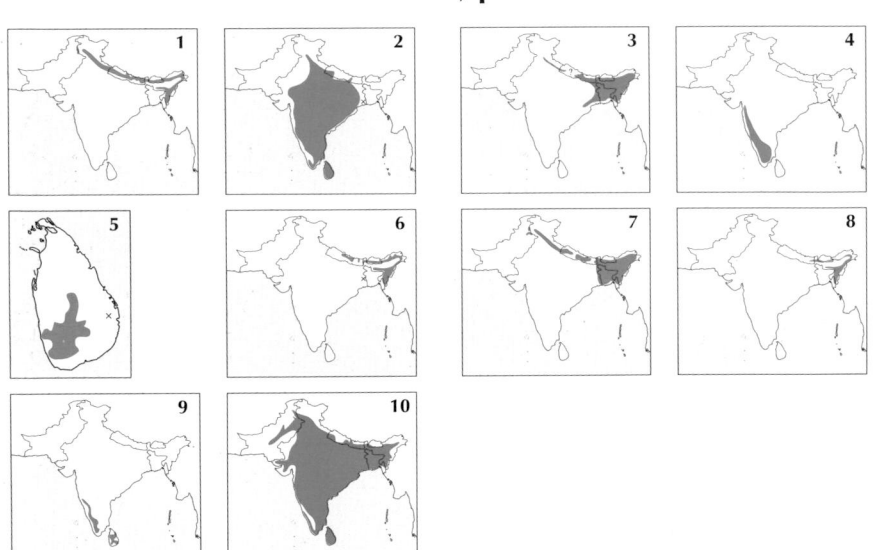

PLATE 21, p. 62

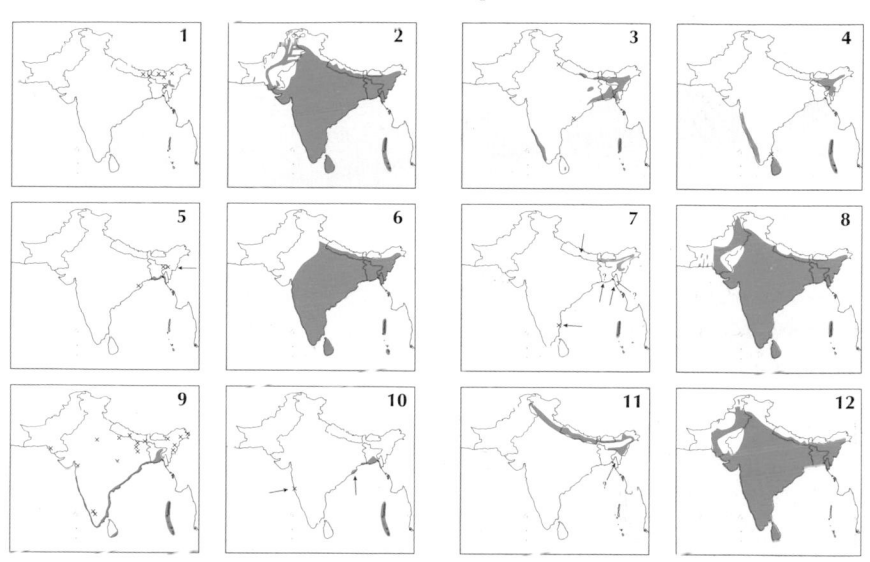

PLATE 23, p. 66

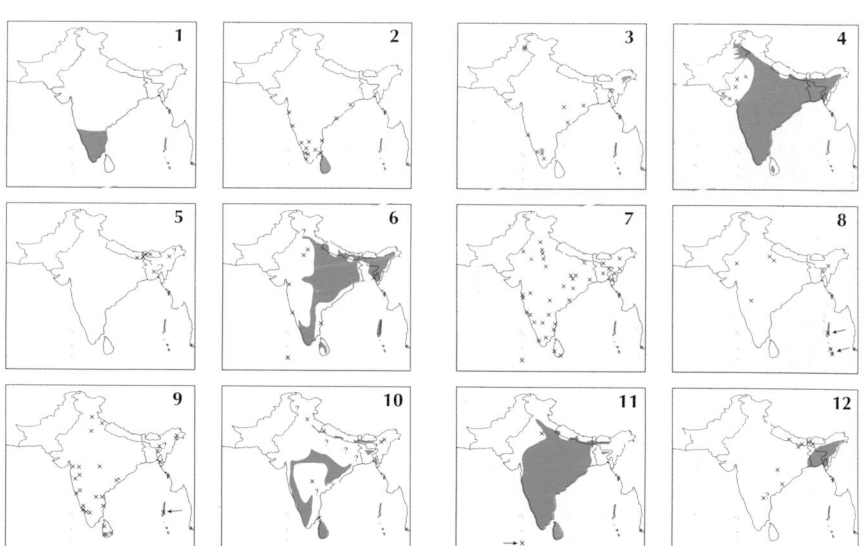

PLATE 18: SMALL AND MEDIUM-SIZED HORNBILLS

1 MALABAR GREY HORNBILL *Ocyceros griseus* 45 cm
Male (1a, 1b), female (1c) and immature (1d). Resident. Western Ghats. Orange or yellowish bill, lacking casque, and broad greyish-white supercilium. Darker grey upperparts than Indian Grey, with pale streaking to crown and sides of head, shorter, darker grey tail, and rufous undertail-coverts. Female has black patch at base of lower mandible. Immature has rufous fringes to upperparts. Open forest.

2 SRI LANKA GREY HORNBILL *Ocyceros gingalensis* 45 cm
Male (2a, 2b), female (2c) and immature (2d). Resident. Sri Lanka. White underparts contrasting with grey upperparts. Lacks prominent supercilium and has brownish crown. Male has cream-coloured bill with black patch at base. Female has mainly black bill with cream stripe along cutting edge. Older birds have white outer tail feathers (but otherwise are dark grey with white tips). Forest and well-wooded areas.

3 INDIAN GREY HORNBILL *Ocyceros birostris* 50 cm
Male (3a, 3b) and immature (3c). Widespread resident; unrecorded in Sri Lanka. Prominent black casque and extensive black at base of bill. Paler sandy brownish-grey upperparts than Malabar Grey, with longer tail that has dark subterminal band and elongated central feathers. Has white trailing edge to wings. Female similar to male, but with smaller bill and casque. Open forest and wooded areas with fruiting trees.

4 MALABAR PIED HORNBILL *Anthracoceros coronatus* 65 cm
Male (4a, 4b), female (4c) and immature (4d). Resident. Western Ghats, E India and Sri Lanka. Compared with Oriental has axe-shaped casque with large black patch along upper ridge, white outer tail feathers (immatures have black at base, but not so extensive as in Oriental), broader white trailing edge to wing, and pink throat patches. Orbital skin is blue-black on male, pinkish on female. Female's casque similar in shape and patterning to male's, although lacks black at posterior end; bill of female lacks black at tip. Open forest and large fruit trees near villages.

5 ORIENTAL PIED HORNBILL *Anthracoceros albirostris* 55–60 cm
Male (5a, 5b), female (5c) and immature (5d). Resident. Himalayan foothills, NE India and E India, and Bangladesh. Cylindrical casque with black patch at tip, mainly black tail with white tips to outer feathers, indistinct white trailing edge to wing, and pale blue throat patch. Unlike Malabar, there is marked sexual dimorphism in casque shape: female has smaller and more rounded casque, with black at posterior end, and black at tip of bill. Open forest, groves and large fruit trees near villages.

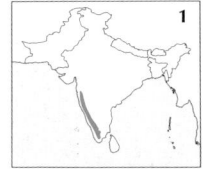  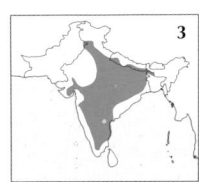 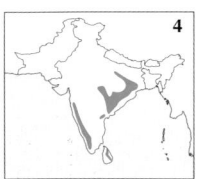

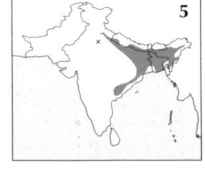

PLATE 19: LARGE HORNBILLS

1 GREAT HORNBILL *Buceros bicornis* 95–105 cm
Male (1a, 1b). Resident. Himalayas, NE India, Bangladesh and Western Ghats. Huge size, massive yellow casque and bill, and white tail with black subterminal band. Has white neck, wing-bars and trailing edge to wing which are variably stained with yellow. Sexes alike, although female has white iris and lacks black at ends of casque. Mature forest.

2 BROWN HORNBILL *Anorrhinus tickelli* 60–75 cm
Male (2a, 2b) and female (2c, 2d). Resident. NE India. Medium-sized brown hornbill with stout yellowish bill. Male has white cheeks, throat and upper breast; rest of underparts rufous; in flight, has white tips to tail (except central feathers) and to primaries. Female is uniformly brown on underparts, and lacks white tips to flight feathers and tail. Broadleaved evergreen forest.

3 RUFOUS-NECKED HORNBILL *Aceros nipalensis* 90–100 cm
Male (3a, 3b), female (3c) and immature (3d). Resident. Himalayas, NE India and Bangladesh. White terminal band to tail and white wing-tips. Red pouch. Male and immature have rufous head and neck. Female has black head and neck. Broadleaved evergreen forest.

4 WREATHED HORNBILL *Aceros undulatus* 75–85 cm
Male (4a, 4b), female (4c) and immature (4d). Resident. E Himalayan foothills, NE India and Bangladesh. White tail and all-black wings. Has bill corrugations (except immature) and bar across pouch. Male has whitish head and neck and yellow pouch. Female has black head and neck with blue pouch. Broadleaved evergreen forest.

5 NARCONDAM HORNBILL *Aceros narcondami* 45–50 cm
Male (5a, 5b), female (5c) and immature (5d). Resident. Narcondam I, Andamans. Small size. White tail and all-black wings. Bluish-white pouch. Male and immature have rufous head and neck. Female has black head and neck. High forest.

6 PLAIN-POUCHED HORNBILL *Aceros subruficollis* 65–70 cm
Male (6a, 6b) and female (6c). [No definite records, but may possibly occur in the northeast. Very similar to Wreathed, but smaller; as that species has white tail and all-black wings. Lacks corrugations on bill, and has plain pouch. Mature forest.]

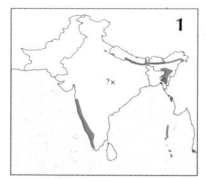 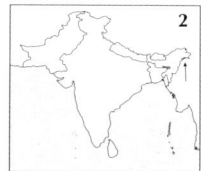 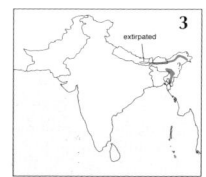 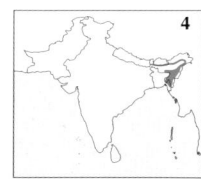

PLATE 20: COMMON HOOPOE, TROGONS AND ROLLERS

1 COMMON HOOPOE *Upupa epops* 31 cm
Adult (1a, 1b). Summer visitor to far north; resident and winter visitor to much of rest of subcontinent. Rufous-orange or orange-buff, with black-and-white wings and tail and black-tipped fan-like crest. Open country, cultivation and villages.

2 MALABAR TROGON *Harpactes fasciatus* 31 cm
Male (2a), female (2b) and immature (2c) *H. f. malabaricus*; male *H. f. fasciatus* (2d). Resident. Western Ghats, hills of W Tamil Nadu, and Sri Lanka (*H. f. fasciatus*). Male has black or dark grey head and breast, pink underparts, and black-and-grey vermiculated wing-coverts. Female has dark cinnamon head and breast, pale cinnamon underparts, and brown-and-buff vermiculated coverts. Immature male has blackish or grey head and breast, and cinnamon underparts; coverts are vermiculated with grey on older birds. Dense broadleaved forest.

3 RED-HEADED TROGON *Harpactes erythrocephalus* 35 cm
Male (3a), female (3b) and immature (3c). Resident. Himalayas, NE India and Bangladesh. Male has crimson head and breast, pink underparts, and black-and-grey vermiculated wing-coverts. Female has dark cinnamon head and breast, and brown-and-buff vermiculated coverts. Immature male has whitish underparts; older immatures resemble female, but have black-and-grey vermiculated coverts. Call is a descending sequence of notes, *tyaup, tyaup, tyaup, tyaup, tyaup*. Dense broadleaved forest.

4 WARD'S TROGON *Harpactes wardi* 38 cm
Male (4a) and female (4b). Resident. E Himalayas in Bhutan and Arunachal Pradesh. Large trogon. Male is maroon, with deep pink forehead, supercilium and underparts; bill is also deep pink. Female is browner, with yellow forehead, supercilium and underparts. Call is a rapid series of mellow *klew* notes, often slightly accelerating and dropping in pitch towards end. Broadleaved evergreen forest.

5 EUROPEAN ROLLER *Coracias garrulus* 31 cm
Adult (5a, 5b) and juvenile (5c). Summer visitor to W Pakistan, Jammu and Kashmir; passage migrant in Pakistan and NW India. Turquoise head and underparts, and rufous-cinnamon mantle. Has black flight feathers and tail corners. Juvenile is much duller, and has whitish streaking on throat and breast; patterning of wings and tail helps separate from Indian Roller. Open woodland and cultivation.

6 INDIAN ROLLER *Coracias benghalensis* 33 cm
Adult (6a, 6b) and immature (6c) *C. b. benghalensis*; adult *C. b. affinis* (6d). Widespread resident. Rufous-brown on nape and underparts, white streaking on ear-coverts and throat, and greenish mantle. Has turquoise band across primaries and dark blue terminal band to tail. Juvenile is duller than adult. *C. b. affinis*, of NE subcontitnent, has purplish-brown underparts, blue streaking on throat, and dark corners to tail instead of dark terminal band. Cultivation, open woodland, gardens.

7 DOLLARBIRD *Eurystomus orientalis* 28 cm
Adult (7a, 7b) and juvenile (7c). Resident and partial migrant. Himalayas, NE and SW India, Bangladesh and Sri Lanka. Dark greenish, appearing black at distance, with red bill and eye-ring. In flight, shows turquoise patch on primaries. Tropical forest and forest clearings.

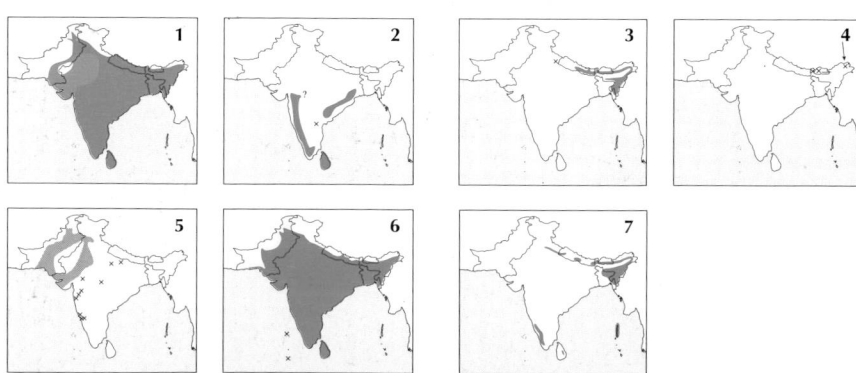

1a

1b

2a

2b

2d

3c

3a

3b

2c

4b

5c

4a

5b

5a

7b

6b

6d

7a

7c

6c

6a

C.D'S

PLATE 21: KINGFISHERS

1 BLYTH'S KINGFISHER *Alcedo hercules* 22 cm
Adult. Resident. Mainly NE India. Large size with huge bill. Dark greenish-blue ear-coverts. Has dark greenish-blue on head, scapulars and wings, with turquoise spotting. Shaded streams in dense tropical and subtropical forest.

(2) COMMON KINGFISHER *Alcedo atthis* 16 cm
Adult. Widespread resident. Orange ear-coverts. Greenish-blue on head, scapulars and wings, and turquoise line down back. Fresh waters in open country, also mangroves and seashore in winter.

3 BLUE-EARED KINGFISHER *Alcedo meninting* 16 cm
Adult (3a) and juvenile (3b). Resident. Himalayan foothills, NE, E and SW India, Bangladesh and Sri Lanka. Blue ear-coverts (except on juvenile). Lacks green tones to blue of head, scapulars and wings, and has deeper blue line down back and deeper orange underparts compared with Common. Mainly streams in dense forest.

4 ORIENTAL DWARF KINGFISHER *Ceyx erithacus* 13 cm
Adult (4a) and juvenile (4b) *C. e. erithacus*; **adult** *C. e. rufidorsa* **(4c).** Resident. Himalayan foothills, NE and SW India, and Bangladesh. Tiny size. Orange head with violet iridescence, and black upperparts with variable blue streaking. Juvenile duller, with whitish underparts (with orange breast-band) and orange-yellow bill. Vagrant *C. e. rufidorsa* has rufous-orange upperparts with violet iridescence. Shady streams in moist broadleaved forest.

5 BROWN-WINGED KINGFISHER *Halcyon amauroptera* 36 cm
Adult. Resident. E India and Bangladesh. Brownish-orange head and underparts. Brown mantle, wings and tail, and turquoise rump. Coastal wetlands.

6 STORK-BILLED KINGFISHER *Halcyon capensis* 38 cm
Adult *H. c. capensis* **(6a)** and *H. c. intermedia* **(6b).** Widespread resident; unrecorded in Pakistan and NW India. Brown cap. Orange-buff collar and underparts, and blue upperparts. Cap lacking or poorly defined in Andaman and Nicobar Is; *intermedia* of Nicobars has dark blue upperparts. Shaded lakes and running waters.

7 RUDDY KINGFISHER *Halcyon coromanda* 26 cm
Adult (7a) and juvenile (7b). Resident. E Himalayan foothills, NE India and Bangladesh. Adult is rufous-orange with violet iridescence on upperparts; bill is red and rump turquoise. Juvenile has browner upperparts.

(8) WHITE-THROATED KINGFISHER *Halcyon smyrnensis* 28 cm
Adult. Widespread resident. White throat and centre of breast, brown head and most of underparts, and turquoise upperparts. White wing patch. Cultivation, forest edges, gardens, and freshwater and coastal wetlands.

9 BLACK-CAPPED KINGFISHER *Halcyon pileata* 30 cm
Adult (9a) and juvenile (9b). Resident. Mainly coasts of India and Bangladesh. Black cap, white collar, purplish-blue upperparts, and pale orange underparts. Shows white wing patch in flight. Chiefly coastal wetlands.

10 COLLARED KINGFISHER *Todiramphus chloris* 24 cm
Adult (10a) and juvenile (10b) *T. c. humii*; **adult** *T. c. davisoni* of Andamans **(10c); adult** *T. c. occipitalis* **(10d)** of Nicobars. Resident. Locally in E and W India, and Bangladesh. Dark bill, blue-green upperparts, and white or buff underparts with white or buff collar. Birds in Nicobar Is (*occipitalis*) have broad rufous-buff supercilium. Mainly coastal wetlands.

(11) CRESTED KINGFISHER *Megaceryle lugubris* 41 cm
Adult. Resident. Himalayas, NE India and Bangladesh. Much larger than Pied, with evenly barred wings and tail. Lacks supercilium, and has spotted breast (sometimes mixed with rufous). Mountain rivers, large rivers in foothills.

(12) PIED KINGFISHER *Ceryle rudis* 31 cm
Male (12a) and female (12b) *C. r. leucomelanura*; **adult male** *C. r. travancoreensis* of SW peninsula **(12c).** Widespread resident. Smaller than Crested, with white supercilium, white patches on wings, and black band(s) across breast. Female has single breast-band (double in male). Still fresh waters, slow-moving rivers and streams, also tidal creeks and pools.

PLATE 22: BEE-EATERS

1 BLUE-BEARDED BEE-EATER *Nyctyornis athertoni* 31–34 cm
Adult. Resident. Himalayan foothills, NE and E India, Western Ghats, hills of W Tamil Nadu and Bangladesh. Large size, square-ended tail, and blue 'beard'. Has yellowish-buff belly and flanks with greenish streaking. Juvenile has blue beard, even when very young. Edges of broadleaved forest.

2 GREEN BEE-EATER *Merops orientalis* 16–18 cm
Adult (2a, 2b) and juvenile (2c) *M. o. beludschicus* of NW subcontinent; *M. o. orientalis* **(2d);** *M. o. ferrugeiceps* of NE subcontinent **(2e).** Widespread resident and summer visitor. Small size. Blue cheeks, with black gorget, and golden to rufous coloration to crown. Green tail with elongated central feathers. Juvenile has square-ended tail; crown and mantle are green, lacks black gorget, and throat is pale yellowish- or bluish-green. Open country.

3 BLUE-CHEEKED BEE-EATER *Merops persicus* 24–26 cm
Adult (3a, 3b). Summer visitor and passage migrant. Pakistan and NW India. Chestnut throat, whitish forehead, turquoise-and-white supercilium, and turquoise-and-green ear-coverts. Green upperparts, underparts and tail, although may show touch of turquoise on rump, belly and tail-coverts. Near water in arid areas.

4 BLUE-TAILED BEE-EATER *Merops philippinus* 23–26 cm
Adult (4a, 4b) and juvenile (4c). Breeds in N and NE subcontinent; winters in peninsula and Sri Lanka. Blue rump, tail and undertail-coverts. Chestnut throat. Forehead and supercilium are mainly green, and concolorous with crown, with touch of blue on supercilium. Chestnut of throat extends onto ear-coverts, and blue streak below black mask is less extensive than in Blue-cheeked, and lacks green in lower ear-coverts. Green upperparts and underparts washed with brown and blue. Juvenile differs from juvenile Blue-cheeked in having strong blue cast to tail and more extensive rufous throat. Near water in wooded country.

5 EUROPEAN BEE-EATER *Merops apiaster* 23–25 cm
Adult (5a, 5b, 5c) and juvenile (5d). Summer visitor to Vale of Kashmir and N and W Pakistan mountains; passage migrant chiefly in Pakistan. Yellow throat, black gorget, blue underparts, chestnut crown and mantle, and golden-yellow scapulars. Juvenile is duller than adult, but still shows chestnut on crown and well-defined yellowish throat. Open country.

6 CHESTNUT-HEADED BEE-EATER *Merops leschenaulti* 18–20 cm
Adult (6a, 6b) and juvenile (6c) *M. l. leschenaulti; M. l. andamanensis* of Andaman Is **(6d).** Resident and partial migrant. Himalayas, NE, E, SW and SE India, Bangladesh and Sri Lanka. Chestnut crown, nape and mantle, and yellow throat with diffuse black gorget. Tail has slight fork. Juvenile washed-out version of adult, but crown and nape dark green on some; has rufous wash to lower throat, diffuse black gorget and turquoise rump. Near streams in deciduous forest.

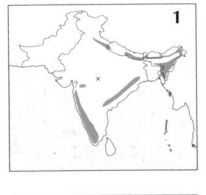 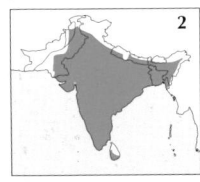 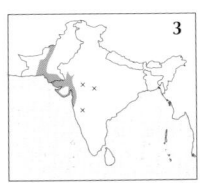 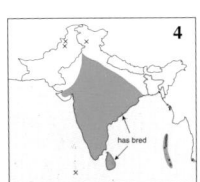

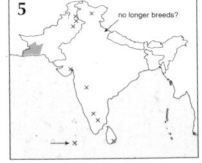 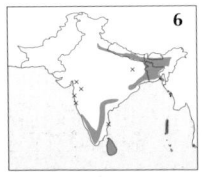

1 PIED CUCKOO *Clamator jacobinus* 33 cm
Adult (1a) and juvenile (1b). Widespread resident and partial migrant. Black and white with crest. Upperparts browner, underparts more buffish on juvenile. A metallic *piu...piu...pee-pee piu, pee-pee piu*. Forest, well-wooded areas, also bushes in semi-desert.

2 CHESTNUT-WINGED CUCKOO *Clamator coromandus* 47 cm
Adult (2a) and immature (2b). Breeds in Himalayas, NE India and Bangladesh; passage migrant in India; winter visitor to Sri Lanka. Prominent crest, whitish collar, and chestnut wings. Immature has rufous fringes to upperparts. A series of double metallic whistles, *breep breep*. Broadleaved forest.

3 LARGE HAWK CUCKOO *Hierococcyx sparverioides* 38 cm
Adult (3a) and juvenile (3b). Breeds in Himalayas and NE India; scattered winter records in subcontinent. Larger than Common Hawk Cuckoo, with browner upperparts, strongly barred underparts, and broader tail banding. Juvenile has barred flanks and broad tail banding; head dark grey on older immatures. A shrill *pee-pee-ah...pee-pee-ah*, which rises in pitch to an hysterical crescendo. Broadleaved forest.

4 COMMON HAWK CUCKOO *Hierococcyx varius* 34 cm
Adult (4a) and juvenile (4b). Widespread resident and partial migrant. Smaller than Large Hawk Cuckoo, with grey upperparts, more rufous on underparts, indistinct barring on belly and flanks, and narrow tail banding. Juvenile has spotted flanks and narrow tail banding. Call as Large, but more shrill and manic. Well-wooded country.

5 HODGSON'S HAWK CUCKOO *Hierococcyx fugax* 29 cm
Adult (5a) and juvenile (5b). Resident or summer visitor. Mainly E Himalayas and NE Indian hills. Stouter bill than Common Hawk Cuckoo; typically darker slate-grey above, and underparts are more rufous and lack barring. Underparts of juvenile have broad spotting. Call is a shrill *gee-whiz...*etc. Broadleaved evergreen and moist deciduous forest.

6 INDIAN CUCKOO *Cuculus micropterus* 33 cm
Male (6a) and juvenile (6b). Breeds in Himalayas and E subcontinent. Brown coloration to upperparts and tail, broad barring on underparts, and pronounced white tail markings. Juvenile has broad white tips to feathers of crown, nape, scapulars and wing-coverts. A descending whistle, *kwer-kwah...kwah-kurh*. Forest and well-wooded country.

7 EURASIAN CUCKOO *Cuculus canorus* 32–34 cm
Male (7a) and hepatic female (7b). Breeds in hills of Pakistan, Himalayas, and N, NE and C India; scattered winter records. Finer barring on whiter underparts than Oriental and call a *cuck-oo...cuck-oo*. Forest and well-wooded country.

8 ORIENTAL CUCKOO *Cuculus saturatus* 30–32 cm
Male (8a) and hepatic female (8b). Breeds in Himalayas and NE India; winter visitor to Andamans and Nicobars. Broader barring on buffish-white underparts compared with Eurasian, and upperparts are a shade darker, with paler head. Hepatic female slightly more heavily barred than Eurasian. A resonant *ho..ho..ho..ho*. Forest and well-wooded country.

9 LESSER CUCKOO *Cuculus poliocephalus* 25 cm
Male (9a) and hepatic female (9b). Breeds in Himalayas and NE India; passage migrant in peninsula and Sri Lanka. Smaller than Oriental; hepatic female can be bright rufous and indistinctly barred on crown and nape. A strong, cheerful *pretty-peel-lay-ka-beet*. Forest and well-wooded country.

10 BANDED BAY CUCKOO *Cacomantis sonneratii* 24 cm
Adult. Widespread resident; unrecorded in Pakistan. White supercilium, finely barred white underparts, and fine and regular dark barring on upperparts. A shrill, whistled *pi-pi-pew-pew*. Forest and wooded country.

11 GREY-BELLIED CUCKOO *Cacomantis passerinus* 23 cm
Adult (11a), hepatic female (11b) and juvenile (11c). Summers in Himalayas; widespread resident or winter visitor farther south; unrecorded in northwest. Grey adult is grey with white vent and undertail-coverts. On hepatic female, base colour of underparts is mainly white, upperparts are bright rufous with crown and nape only sparsely barred, and tail is unbarred. Juvenile is either grey with pale barring on underparts, or similar to hepatic female, or intermediate. A clear *pee-pipee-pee...pipee-pee*. Wooded country.

12 PLAINTIVE CUCKOO *Cacomantis merulinus* 23 cm
Adult (12a), hepatic female (12b) and juvenile (12c). Resident. NE India and Bangladesh. Adult has orange underparts. On hepatic female, base colour of underparts is pale rufous, and upperparts and tail are strongly barred. Juvenile has bold streaking on rufous-orange head and breast. A mournful *tay...ta...tee*. Forest and wooded country.

1 ASIAN EMERALD CUCKOO *Chrysococcyx maculatus* 18 cm
Male (1a), female (1b) and juvenile (1c). Summer visitor, mainly to E Himalayas, NE India and Bangladesh; winter visitor to Andamans and Nicobars. Male has emerald-green upperparts. Female has rufous-orange crown and nape and unbarred bronze-green mantle and wings. Juvenile has unbarred rufous-orange crown and nape, rufous-orange barring on mantle and wing-coverts, and rufous-orange wash to barred throat and breast. Loud descending *kee-kee-kee-kee*. Evergreen forest.

2 VIOLET CUCKOO *Chrysococcyx xanthorhynchus* 17 cm
Male (2a), female (2b) and juvenile (2c). Resident or summer visitor, mainly to NE Indian hills. Male has purple upperparts. Female has uniform bronze-brown upperparts, with only slight greenish tinge, and white underparts with brownish-green barring. Juvenile has extensive dark barring on crown and nape, and lacks rufous-orange wash to throat. A disyllabic and repeated *che-wick*, particularly in flight, and an accelerating trill. Secondary evergreen forest and orchards.

3 DRONGO CUCKOO *Surniculus lugubris* 25 cm
Adult (3a) and juvenile (3b). Summer visitor to Himalayas; resident farther south. Himalayas, NE, W, S and SE India, and Sri Lanka. Black, with white-barred undertail-coverts. Bill fine and downcurved, and tail has indentation. Juvenile is spotted with white. An ascending series of whistles, broken off and quickly repeated. Forest and well-wooded areas.

4 ASIAN KOEL *Eudynamys scolopacea* 43 cm
Male (4a) and female (4b). Mainly resident. Widespread. Male is greenish-black, with green bill. Female is spotted and barred with white. Open woodland, gardens and cultivation.

5 GREEN-BILLED MALKOHA *Phaenicophaeus tristis* 38 cm
Adult. Resident. Himalayas, NE India and Bangladesh. Greyish-green coloration, green and red bill, red eye-patch, white-streaked supercilium, and white-tipped tail. Dense forest and thickets.

6 BLUE-FACED MALKOHA *Phaenicophaeus viridirostris* 39 cm
Adult. Resident. Peninsular India and Sri Lanka. Greenish coloration, green bill, blue eye-patch, and bold white tips to tail. Scrub and secondary growth.

7 SIRKEER MALKOHA *Phaenicophaeus leschenaultii* 42 cm
Adult. Widespread resident; unrecorded in northeast and parts of northwest. Sandy coloration, yellow-tipped red bill, dark mask with white border, and bold white tips to tail. Thorn scrub.

8 RED-FACED MALKOHA *Phaenicophaeus pyrrhocephalus* 46 cm
Adult (8a) and juvenile (8b). Resident. Sri Lanka. Green bill, red face patch, black breast, white malar stripe and underparts. Juvenile duller. Dense, tall, mainly evergreen forest.

9 GREATER COUCAL *Centropus sinensis* 48 cm
Adult (9a) and juvenile (9b). Widespread resident. Larger than Lesser, with brighter and more uniform chestnut wings, and black underwing-coverts. Juvenile is heavily barred. Tall grassland, scrub and groves.

10 BROWN COUCAL *Centropus andamanensis* 48 cm
Adult (10a) and juvenile (10b). Resident. Andamans. Fawn-brown head and body, with chestnut wings. Juvenile is diffusely barred. Forest edges, gardens and cultivation.

11 LESSER COUCAL *Centropus bengalensis* 33 cm
Adult breeding (11a), adult non-breeding (11b) and immature (11c). Resident. Himalayas, NE, E and SW India, and Bangladesh. Smaller than Greater, with duller chestnut wings (including browner tertials and primary tips), and chestnut underwing-coverts; often with buff streaking on scapulars and wing-coverts. Non-breeding has pronounced buff shaft streaking on head and body, chestnut wings and black tail. Immature similar to non-breeding adult, but has barred wings and tail. Tall grassland, reedbeds and shrubberies.

12 GREEN-BILLED COUCAL *Centropus chlororhynchus* 43 cm
Adult. Resident. Sri Lanka. Green bill. Wings are maroon-brown, and contrast less with head and body than on Greater. Tall forest with dense undergrowth.

PLATE 25: HANGING PARROTS AND PARAKEETS   Maps p. 72

1 **VERNAL HANGING PARROT** *Loriculus vernalis* 14 cm
Male (1a) and immature (1b). Resident. Mainly NE and E India, Western Ghats and Bangladesh. Small green parrot. Adult with red bill and red rump. Broadleaved forest.

2 **SRI LANKA HANGING PARROT** *Loriculus beryllinus* 14 cm
Male (2a) and immature (2b). Resident. Sri Lanka. Adult has crimson crown, and orange cast to mantle. Broadleaved forest.

3 **ALEXANDRINE PARAKEET** *Psittacula eupatria* 53 cm
Male (3a) and female (3b). Widespread resident; unrecorded in W Pakistan. Very large, with maroon shoulder patch. Male has black chin stripe and pink collar. Forest and well-wooded areas.

4 **ROSE-RINGED PARAKEET** *Psittacula krameri* 42 cm
Male (4a) and female (4b). Widespread resident. Green head and blue-green tip to tail. Male has black chin stripe and pink collar. Forest, wooded areas and cultivation.

5 **SLATY-HEADED PARAKEET** *Psittacula himalayana* 41 cm
Male (5a), female (5b) and immature (5c). Resident. Himalayas. Dark grey head, red-and-yellow bill, dark green upperparts, and yellow-tipped tail. Forest and well-wooded areas.

6 **GREY-HEADED PARAKEET** *Psittacula finschii* 36 cm
Male (6a), female (6b) and immature (6c). Resident. NE India and Bangladesh. Grey head, red-and-yellow bill, yellowish-green upperparts, and yellow-cream tip to tail. Hill forest and cultivation.

7 **INTERMEDIATE PARAKEET** *Psittacula intermedia* 36 cm
Male (7a) and female (7b). [Probably a hybrid. Trapped in Uttar Pradesh. Slaty-purple head with rufous-purple on forehead and around eye. Red upper mandible, and yellowish-white tip to tail. Habitat unknown.]

8 **PLUM-HEADED PARAKEET** *Psittacula cyanocephala* 36 cm
Male (8a), female (8b) and immature (8c). Widespread resident; unrecorded in northwest and parts of northeast. Head is plum-red on male, pale grey on female. Yellow upper mandible, and white-tipped blue-green tail. Head of female is paler grey than in Slaty-headed, and lacks black chin stripe and half-collar; has yellow collar and upper breast. Forest and well-wooded areas.

9 **BLOSSOM-HEADED PARAKEET** *Psittacula roseata* 36 cm
Male (9a), female (9b) and immature (9c). Resident. Mainly NE Indian hills and Bangladesh. Head is pinkish on male, pale greyish-blue on female. Yellow upper mandible, and yellow-tipped tail. Head of female is paler greyish-blue than in Grey-headed and lacks black chin stripe and half-collar. Well-wooded areas and open forest.

10 **MALABAR PARAKEET** *Psittacula columboides* 38 cm
Male (10a), female (10b) and immature (10c). Resident. Western Ghats. Blue-grey head, breast and mantle. Blue primaries, yellow tip to tail. Female lacks blue-green collar of male. Evergreen and moist deciduous forest.

11 **LAYARD'S PARAKEET** *Psittacula calthropae* 31 cm
Male (11a), female (11b) and immature (11c). Resident. Sri Lanka. Blue-grey head and mantle, green collar and underparts. Yellow tip to tail. Forest edges, plantations and gardens.

12 **DERBYAN PARAKEET** *Psittacula derbiana* 46 cm
Male (12a) and female (12b). Resident. Arunachal Pradesh. Large size, and violet-grey head and underparts. Female has black bill. Conifer forest and cultivation.

13 **RED-BREASTED PARAKEET** *Psittacula alexandri* 38 cm
Male (13a), female (13b) and immature (13c). Resident. Himalayan foothills, NE India and Bangladesh. Lilac-grey head and pink underparts. Open forest and secondary growth.

14 **NICOBAR PARAKEET** *Psittacula caniceps* 61 cm
Male (14a) and female (14b). Resident. Nicobars. Large size, buffish-grey head. Tall forest.

15 **LONG-TAILED PARAKEET** *Psittacula longicauda* 46–48 cm
Male (15a) and immature (15b) P. l. tytleri; male (15c) and female (15d) P. l. nicobarica. Resident. Andamans and Nicobars. Pinkish-red cheeks. *P. l. tytleri* of Andamans has extensive lilac wash to upperparts. Cultivation, gardens and forest.

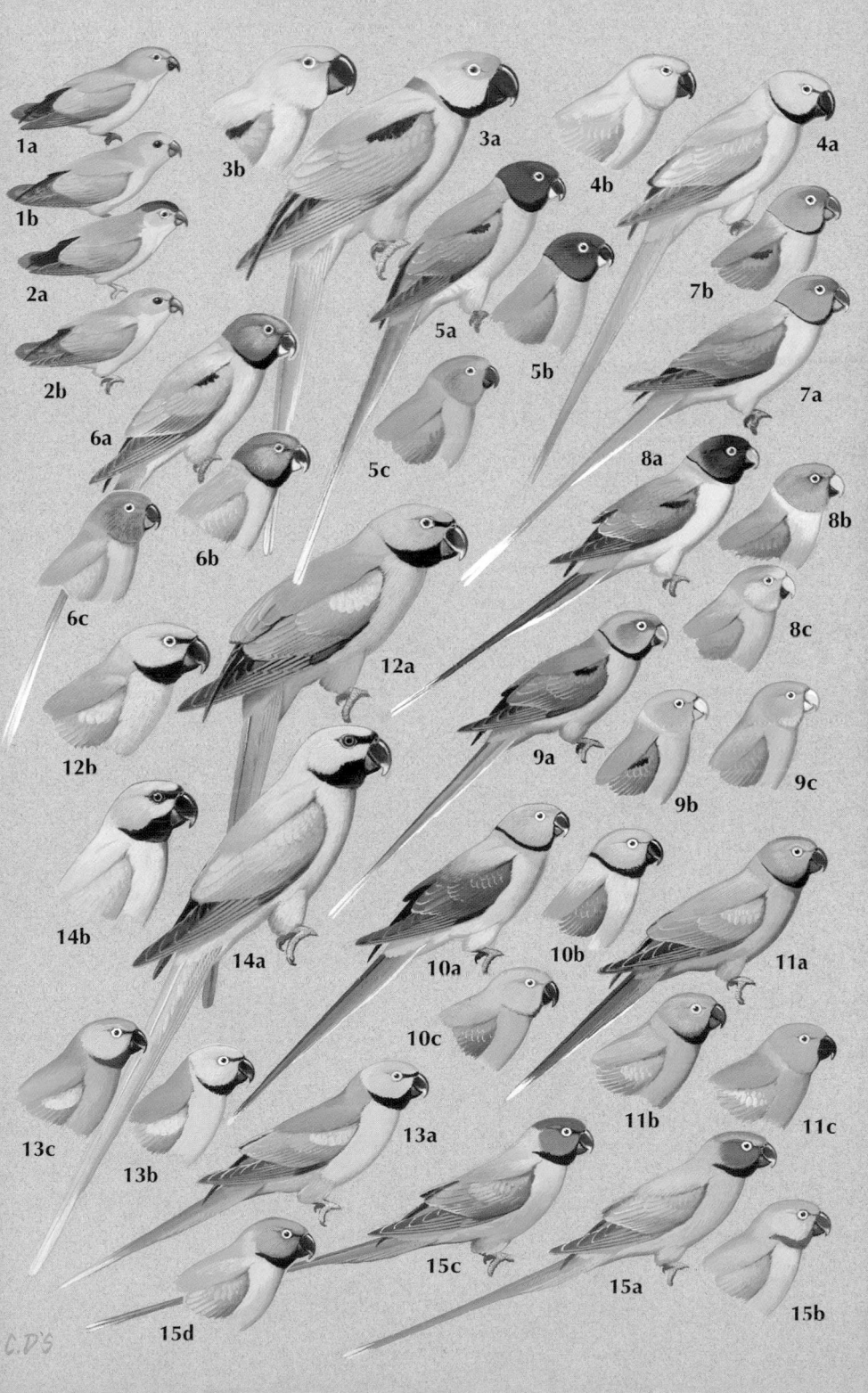

1a 1b 2a 2b 3a 3b 4a 4b 5a 5b 5c 6a 6b 6c 7a 7b 8a 8b 8c 9a 9b 9c 10a 10b 10c 11a 11b 11c 12a 12b 13a 13b 13c 14a 14b 15a 15b 15c 15d

C.D's

PLATE 24, p. 68

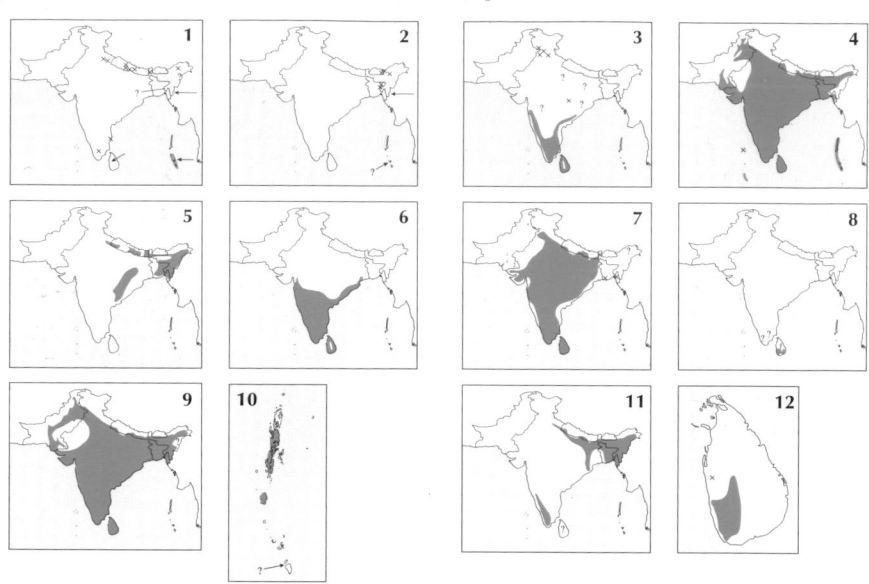

PLATE 25, p. 70

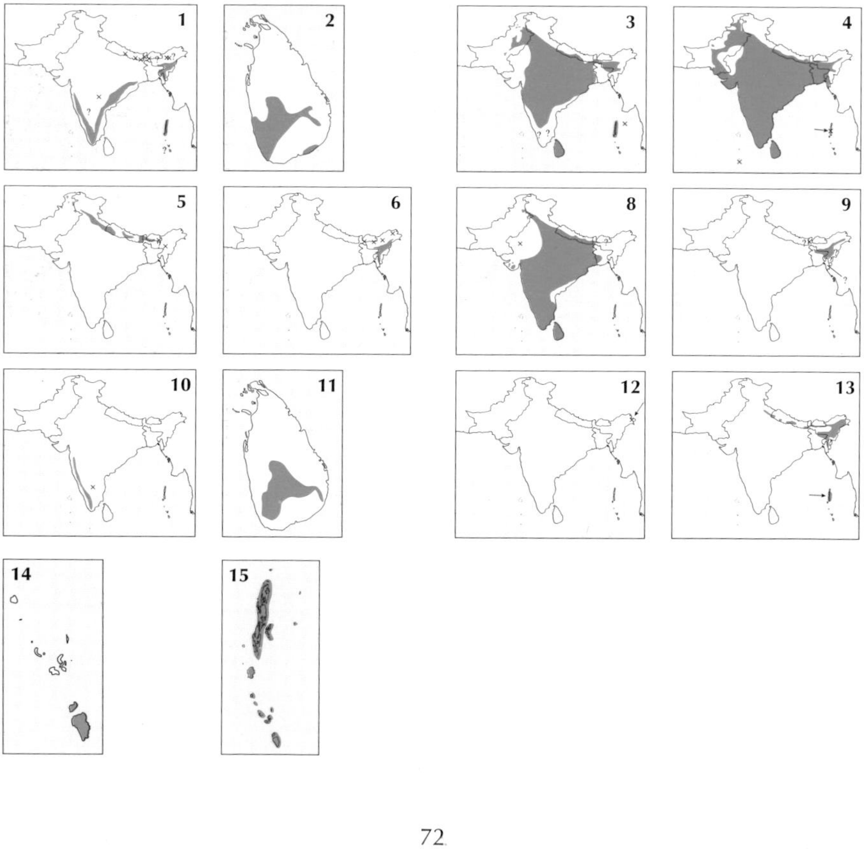

72

PLATE 28, p. 78

PLATE 29, p. 80

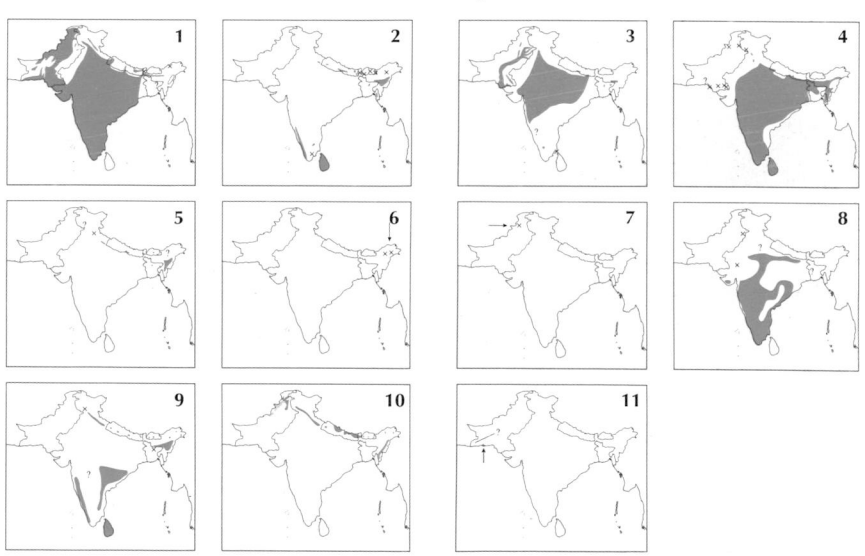

PLATE 26: SWIFTLETS AND NEEDLETAILS

1 **GLOSSY SWIFTLET** *Collocalia esculenta* 10 cm
Adult (1a, 1b). Resident. Andamans and Nicobars. Small size, square-ended tail, glossy upperparts and breast, and white belly. Around habitation.

2 **INDIAN SWIFTLET** *Collocalia unicolor* 12 cm
Adult (2a, 2b). Resident. Western Ghats, islets on Malabar coast, Sri Lanka. Uniform upperparts, with indistinct indentation to tail. Hills.

3 **HIMALAYAN SWIFTLET** *Collocalia brevirostris* 14 cm
Adult (3a, 3b). Resident. Himalayas and NE India. Greyish rump band, and distinct indentation to tail. Open areas near forest.

4 **EDIBLE-NEST SWIFTLET** *Collocalia fuciphaga* 12 cm
Adult (4a, 4b). Resident. Andamans and Nicobars. Narrow greyish rump band. Upperparts blacker and tail indentation narrower than on Himalayan. Coast and around habitation.

5 **WHITE-RUMPED NEEDLETAIL** *Zoonavena sylvatica* 11 cm
Adult (5a, 5b). Resident. Himalayas, NE, E and SW India, and Bangladesh. Small size, white rump, and whitish belly and undertail-coverts. Wing shape and flight action different from House Swift; lacks white throat of that species. Broadleaved forest.

6 **WHITE-THROATED NEEDLETAIL** *Hirundapus caudacutus* 20 cm
Adult (6a, 6b). Summer visitor. Himalayas and NE India. Well-defined white throat, prominent pale 'saddle', and white patch on tertials. Ridges, cliffs, upland grassland and river valleys.

7 **SILVER-BACKED NEEDLETAIL** *Hirundapus cochinchinensis* 20 cm
Adult (7a, 7b). Resident. Hills of NE India and Bangladesh, Western Ghats and Sri Lanka. Poorly defined pale throat, prominent pale 'saddle', and dark lores. Lacks white on inner web of tertials (shown by White-throated), although tertials have pale grey inner web which can be visible in field. Smaller and less powerful than Brown-backed and tends to show shorter, square-ended tail and less distinct tail 'spines'. Broadleaved forest.

8 **BROWN-BACKED NEEDLETAIL** *Hirundapus giganteus* 23 cm
Adult (8a, 8b). Resident. Hills of NE India and Bangladesh, Western Ghats and Sri Lanka. Large size, brown throat, indistinct 'saddle', and white lores. Pointed tail with prominent 'needles'. Broadleaved forest.

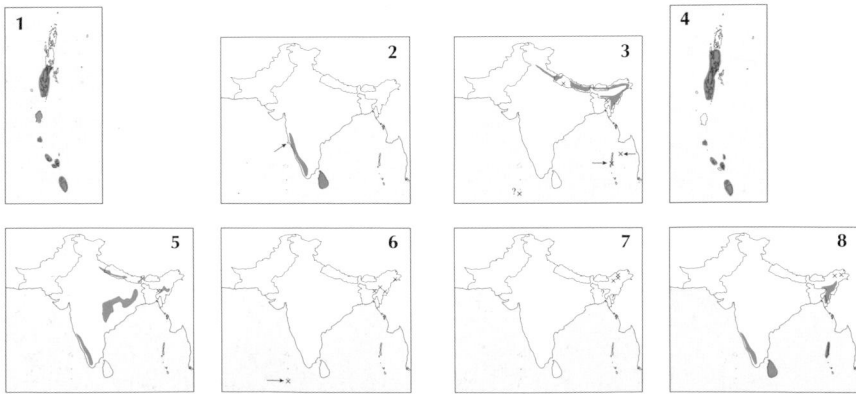

# G. Driessens '95

PLATE 27: SWIFTS

1 COMMON SWIFT *Apus apus* 17 cm
Adult (1a, 1b) and juvenile (1c, 1d). Mainly summer visitor. Baluchistan, Himalayas and Maldives. Uniform dark brown upperparts, lacking any contrast on upperwing. No white rump. Chiefly mountains.

2 PALLID SWIFT *Apus pallidus* 17 cm
Adult (2a, 2b). Winter visitor. Pakistan. Pale grey-brown upperparts and underparts with darker eye-patch, and has more extensive pale throat than Common. Shows contrast between dark outer primaries and inner wing-coverts and paler rest of wing. Underparts more distinctly scaled than in Common, and has dark-saddled, pale-headed appearance. Coastal areas.

3 ASIAN PALM SWIFT *Cypsiurus balasiensis* 13 cm
Adult (3a, 3b). Resident. Widespread; unrecorded in Pakistan. Small size and long, forked tail (usually held closed). Brown underbody with paler throat. Open country and cultivation with palms.

4 HOUSE SWIFT *Apus affinis* 15 cm
Adult A. a. affinis (4a, 4b); adult A. a. nipalensis (4c, 4d). Widespread resident; unrecorded in parts of northwest. Stocky shape and comparatively short wings. Tail has square end or slight fork. White rump. *A. a. nipalensis,* of Himalayas and NE India, has narrower white rump band, and tail has slight fork, compared with three other races which are known as 'Little Swift'. Habitation, cliffs and ruins.

5 FORK-TAILED SWIFT *Apus pacificus* 15–18 cm
Adult (5a, 5b). Breeds in Himalayas and NE India; scattered winter records in peninsula. White rump, slimmer-bodied and longer wings, deeply forked tail, and white scaling on underparts are useful features from House Swift. Open ridges and hilltops.

6 DARK-RUMPED SWIFT *Apus acuticauda* 17 cm
Adult (6a, 6b). Resident. Meghalaya, Bhutan, and Mizoram? Blackish upperparts, including rump. Lacks distinct pale throat, and has whitish scaling on underparts. Rocky cliffs and gorges.

7 ALPINE SWIFT *Tachymarptis melba* 22 cm
Adult (7a, 7b). Resident? Locally in subcontinent. Large size, white throat and brown breast-band, and white patch on belly. Mainly hills and mountains.

8 CRESTED TREESWIFT *Hemiprocne coronata* 23 cm
Adult male (8a, 8b), female (8c, 8d), and juvenile (8e). Widespread resident; unrecorded in Pakistan. Large size and long, forked tail. Blue-grey upperparts and paler underparts, becoming whitish on belly and vent. Male has dull orange ear-coverts (dark grey in female). Well-wooded areas and forest.

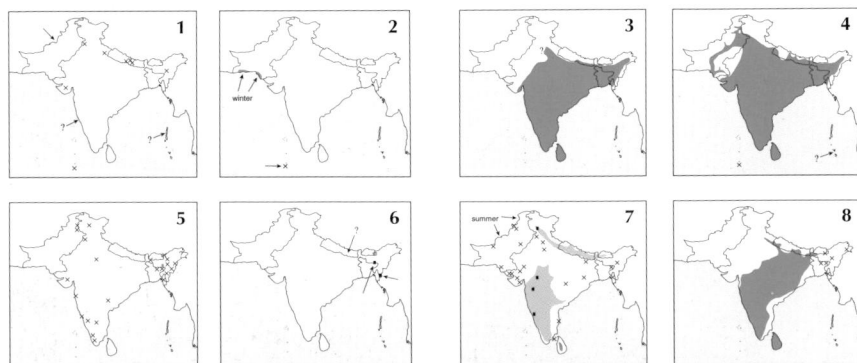

1 BARN OWL *Tyto alba* 36 cm
Adult *T. a. stertens* (**1a**); adult *T. a. deroepstorffi* (**1b**). Widespread resident. Unmarked white face, whitish underparts, and golden-buff and grey upperparts. In Andamans, *deroepstorffi* has rufous face and darker upperparts (upperparts heavily marked with rufous and dark brown). Habitation and cultivation.

2 GRASS OWL *Tyto capensis* 36 cm
Adult (**2a, 2b**). Resident. NE and SW India, and S Nepal. Whitish face and underparts, dark barring on flight feathers, golden-buff patch at base of primaries, and dark-barred tail. Upperparts are heavily marked with dark brown. Mottled, rather than streaked upperparts, lack of prominent streaking on breast and black eyes are useful features from Short-eared Owl which may be found in similar habitats. Tall grassland.

3 ORIENTAL BAY OWL *Phodilus badius* 29 cm
Adult. Resident. NE and SW India, and Sri Lanka. Oblong-shaped, vinaceous-pinkish facial discs. Underparts vinaceous-pink, spotted with black; upperparts chestnut and buff, spotted and barred with black. Call is a series of eerie, upward-inflected whistles. Dense broadleaved forest.

4 ANDAMAN SCOPS OWL *Otus balli* 19 cm
Adult. Resident. Andamans. Unstreaked dark rufous-brown upperparts with indistinct buff and dark brown markings; underparts finely vermiculated and spotted with dark brown and buff. Call is an abrupt *hoot...hoot-coorroo*. Cultivation and habitation.

5 MOUNTAIN SCOPS OWL *Otus spilocephalus* 20 cm
Adult *O. s. spilocephalus* (**5a**); adult *O. s. huttoni* of W Himalayas (**5b**). Resident. Himalayas, NE India and Bangladesh. Lacks prominent ear-tufts. Upperparts mottled with buff and brown; underparts indistinctly spotted with buff and barred with brown. Call is a double whistle, *toot-too*. Dense broadleaved forest.

6 PALLID SCOPS OWL *Otus brucei* 22 cm
Adult (**6a**) and juvenile (**6b**). Resident. Pakistan and NW India. Pale, grey and rather uniform. Compared with grey morph Eurasian Scops, has less distinct scapular spots, and narrow dark streaking on underparts, which lack pale horizontal panels. Shows fewer pale bars on tail (2–4, rather than 5–7 on central rectrices) compared with Eurasian; facial disc usually paler and plainer with black border finer and stronger. Tips of primaries do not project beyond tail (usually slightly projecting on Eurasian). Call is a resonant *whoop-whoop-whoop...*. Stony foothills in semi-desert.

7 EURASIAN SCOPS OWL *Otus scops* 19 cm
Adult brown (**7a**) and grey (**7b**) morphs. Summer visitor to N and W Pakistan mountains; winters in S Pakistan and NW India. Prominent white spots on scapulars, and streaked underparts with pale horizontal bands. Longer primary projection than Oriental Scops. Call is plaintive bell-like whistle. Scrub in dry rocky hills and valleys.

8 ORIENTAL SCOPS OWL *Otus sunia* 19 cm
Adult *O. s. sunia* rufous (**8a**) and brown (**8b**) morphs; rufous specimen from Nicobars (**8c**). Resident. Himalayas, NE, W and S India, and Sri Lanka. Prominent ear-tufts. Prominent white scapular spots, streaked underparts and upperparts, and lacks prominent nuchal collar. Rufous morph distinct from Eurasian Scops; otherwise not distinguishable on plumage, although Oriental has shorter primary projection (4–5, rather than 6–7, primaries extend beyond tertials). Call is frog-like *wut-chu-chraaii*. Forest, wooded areas and habitation.

9 COLLARED SCOPS OWL *Otus bakkamoena* 23–25 cm
Adult *O. b. gangeticus* grey morph (**9a**); adult *O. b. plumipes* rufous-brown morph (**9b**). Widespread resident; unrecorded in parts of northwest and northeast. Larger than other scops owls, with buff nuchal collar, finely streaked underparts, and indistinct buffish scapular spots. Iris dark orange or brown. Call is a subdued, frog-like *whuk*, repeated at irregular intervals. Forest and well-wooded areas.

1 EURASIAN EAGLE OWL *Bubo bubo* 56–66 cm
Adult *B. b. hemachalana* (1a); adult *B. b. bengalensis* (1b). Widespread resident; unrecorded in parts of northwest, northeast and Sri Lanka. Very large, with upright ear-tufts. Upperparts mottled dark brown and tawny-buff; underparts heavily streaked. In NW subcontinent, *hemachalana* is larger and paler. Call is a resonant *tu-whooh*. Cliffs, rocky hills, ravines and wooded areas.

2 SPOT-BELLIED EAGLE OWL *Bubo nipalensis* 63 cm
Adult (2a) and immature (2b). Resident. Himalayas, NE India, Western Ghats and Bangladesh. Very large, with bold chevron-shaped spots on underparts. Upperparts dark brown, barred with buff. Call is a deep hoot and a mournful scream. Dense forest.

3 DUSKY EAGLE OWL *Bubo coromandus* 58 cm
Adult. Widespread resident; unrecorded in Sri Lanka. Large grey owl with prominent ear-tufts. Underparts greyish-white with brown streaking. Call is a deep, resonant *wo, wo, wo, wo-o-o-o-o*. Well-watered areas with extensive tree cover.

4 BROWN FISH OWL *Ketupa zeylonensis* 56 cm
Adult. Widespread resident; unrecorded in Pakistan. Compared with other fish owls, has close dark barring on dull buff underparts, which also show finer streaking, and upperparts are duller brown with finer streaking. Calls include a soft, deep *hup-hup-hu* and a wild *hu-hu-hu-hu...hu ha*. Forest and well-wooded areas near water.

5 TAWNY FISH OWL *Ketupa flavipes* 61 cm
Adult. Resident. Himalayas, NE India and Bangladesh. Pale orange upperparts with bold black streaking, bold orange-buff barring on wing-coverts and flight feathers, whitish patch on forehead, broad black streaking on pale rufous-orange underparts (which lack fine dark cross-barring). Call is a deep *whoo-hoo* and a cat-like mewing. Banks of streams and rivers in dense broadleaved forest.

6 BUFFY FISH OWL *Ketupa ketupu* 50 cm
Adult. Resident? Told from much larger Tawny Fish Owl by finer streaking on underparts, duller buffish-white to greyish-white barring on flight feathers and tail, and tendency towards heavier and more diffuse streaking on crown and nape. Rufous-orange coloration with heavier black streaking, and white forehead, help separate it from Brown Fish Owl. Call is monotonous *bup-bup-bup-bup-bup-bup-bup....* Forested streams in plains.

7 SNOWY OWL *Nyctea scandiaca* 53–66 cm
Male (7a) and female (7b). Vagrant. Pakistan. Mainly white, with variable dark markings. Open country.

8 MOTTLED WOOD OWL *Strix ocellata* 48 cm
Adult. Resident. Peninsular India. Concentric barring on facial discs, and white, rufous and dark brown mottling on upperparts; dark brown barring mixed with rufous on whitish underparts. Call is a spooky, quavering *whaa-aa-aa-aa-ah*. Open wooded areas, groves around villages and cultivation.

9 BROWN WOOD OWL *Strix leptogrammica* 47–53 cm
Adult *S. l. newarensis* (9a); adult *S. l. indranee* (9b). Resident. Himalayas, NE India, Eastern and Western Ghats, Bangladesh and Sri Lanka. Facial discs lack black concentric barring, uniform brown upperparts with fine white barring on scapulars, and buffish-white underparts with fine brown barring. In peninsula, smaller *indranee* has rufous facial discs. Calls include a *hoo-hoohoohoo(hoo)* and a loud eerie scream. Dense broadleaved forest.

10 TAWNY OWL *Strix aluco* 45–47 cm
Adult *S. a. nivicola* (10a); adult *S. a. biddulphi* (10b). Resident. N Baluchistan, Himalayas and NE India. Heavily streaked underparts, white markings on scapulars, dark centre to crown, and pale forecrown stripes. In W Himalayas, *biddulphi* has greyer upperparts (which are streaked rather than barred) and whiter underparts compared with *nivicola*. Call is a *too-tu-whoo*. Temperate forest.

11 HUME'S OWL *Strix butleri* 37–38 cm
Adult. Resident. Makran coast, Pakistan. Dark forehead dividing pale facial discs, white scapular spots, buff and brown barring on flight feathers and tail, buff underparts with dark barring, and orange eyes. Call is a *whooo woohoo-woohoo*. Rocky gorges.

1a, 1b, 2a, 2b, 3, 4, 5, 6, 7a, 7b, 8, 9a, 9b, 10a, 10b, 11

Dan Cole 85.

1 COLLARED OWLET *Glaucidium brodiei* 17 cm
Adult. Resident. Himalayas, NE India and Bangladesh. Very small and heavily barred. Spotted crown, streaking on flanks, and owl-face pattern on upper mantle. Call is a pleasant *toot..tootoot..toot.* Subtropical and temperate forest.

2 ASIAN BARRED OWLET *Glaucidium cuculoides* 23 cm
Adult (2a) and immature (2b) *G. c. cuculoides;* adult *G. c. rufescens* of NE subcontinent **(2c).** Resident. Himalayas, NE India and Bangladesh. Small and heavily barred. Buff barring on wing-coverts and flight feathers, and streaked flanks. Call is a continuous bubbling whistle. Tropical, subtropical and temperate forest.

3 JUNGLE OWLET *Glaucidium radiatum* 20 cm
Adult *G. r. radiatum* **(3a); adult** *G. r. malabaricum* **(3b).** Widespread resident; unrecorded in most of northeast. Small, heavily barred. Smaller than Asian Barred, with more closely barred upperparts and underparts. Rufous barring on wing-coverts and flight feathers, and barred flanks. Birds in Malabar coastal strip are more rufous on breast and upperparts. Call is a loud *kao..kao..kao* followed by *kao..kuk,* and notes similar to Asian Barred's. Note range differences from Asian Barred. Open tropical and subtropical forest.

4 CHESTNUT-BACKED OWLET *Glaucidium castanonotum* 19 cm
Adult. Resident. Sri Lanka. Small and heavily barred. Back and wing-coverts are bright chestnut, diffusely barred with brown and some buff. Belly and flanks streaked. Call is a slow *kraw...kraw....* Dense forest.

5 LITTLE OWL *Athene noctua* 23 cm
Adult. Resident. Baluchistan and trans-Himalayas. Sandy-brown, with streaked breast and flanks, and streaked crown. Call is a plaintive *quew,* repeated every few seconds, and a soft barking. Cliffs and ruins in semi-desert.

6 SPOTTED OWLET *Athene brama* 21 cm
Adult *A. b. indica* **(6a); adult** *A. b. brama* of S India **(6b).** Widespread resident. White spotting on upperparts, including crown, and diffuse brown spotting or barring on underparts. Pale facial discs and nuchal collar. Call is a harsh, screechy *chirurr-chirurr-chirurr...* followed by/alternated with *cheevak, cheevak, cheevak.* Habitation and cultivation.

7 FOREST OWLET *Athene blewitti* 23 cm
Adult. Resident. C India. Compared with Spotted Owlet has rather dark grey-brown crown and nape, only faintly spotted with white, and lacks prominent white collar of Spotted. Wings (apart from inner coverts) and tail broadly banded blackish-brown and white, with white-tipped remiges and a broad white tail-tip Breast dark brown, and barring on upper flanks is broader and more prominent; rest of underparts white, much cleaner than on Spotted. Deciduous forest.

8 BOREAL OWL *Aegolius funereus* 24–26 cm
Adult. Rare resident? NW Pakistan and NW India. Greyish facial discs bordered with black, and with angular upper edge. Call is a soft *po-po-po....* Subalpine scrub.

9 BROWN HAWK OWL *Ninox scutulata* 32 cm
Adult *N. s. lugubris* **(9a); adult** *N. s. obscura* of Andamans and Nicobars **(9b).** Resident. Himalayas, NE, E and W India, Bangladesh and Sri Lanka. Hawk-like profile. Dark face, and rufous-brown streaking on underparts. Has dark brown underparts in Andamans. Call is a soft, pleasant *oo..ok, oo..ok,....* Forest and well-wooded areas.

10 ANDAMAN HAWK OWL *Ninox affinis* 28 cm
Adult. Resident. Andamans. Rufous spotting on white underparts. Call is a loud *craw.* Mangrove forest.

11 LONG-EARED OWL *Asio otus* 35–37 cm
Adult (11a, 11b). Mainly winter visitor to Pakistan and NW India; has bred. Long ear-tufts, orange-brown facial discs and orange eyes. Additional differences from Short-eared are more heavily streaked belly and flanks, orange-buff base coloration to primaries and tail feathers, and lack of white trailing edge to wing. Stunted trees and poplar plantations in winter.

12 SHORT-EARED OWL *Asio flammeus* 37–39 cm
Adult (12a, 12b). Widespread winter visitor and passage migrant. Streaked underparts and short ear-tufts. Buffish facial discs and yellow eyes. Open country.

PLATE 31: FROGMOUTHS AND NIGHTJARS   Maps p. 86

1 SRI LANKA FROGMOUTH *Batrachostomus moniliger* 23 cm
Male (1a) and female (1b). Resident. Western Ghats and Sri Lanka. Smaller and shorter-tailed than Hodgson's, with bigger-looking head and bill. Male brownish-grey; female more rufous and less heavily marked. Song is a series of loud liquid chuckles. Dense tropical and subtropical evergreen forest.

2 HODGSON'S FROGMOUTH *Batrachostomus hodgsoni* 27 cm
Male (2a) and female (2b). Resident. E Himalayas, NE India and Bangladesh. Larger, longer-tailed and more evenly proportioned than Sri Lanka Frogmouth. Male more rufous than male Sri Lanka, with underparts more heavily and irregularly marked with black, white and rufous. Female more uniform rufous than male. Song is a series of soft *gwaa* notes. Subtropical evergreen forest.

3 GREAT EARED NIGHTJAR *Eurostopodus macrotis* 40–41 cm
Adult (3a, 3b). Resident. Mainly NE India, Bangladesh and Western Ghats. Very large and richly coloured, with prominent ear-tufts. Fine rufous barring on black ear-coverts and throat, dark brown barring on buff underparts, and tail broadly banded with golden-buff and dark brown. Lacks pale spots on wings or tail. Song is a clear, wailing *pee-wheeeu*. Broadleaved moist forest and secondary growth.

4 GREY NIGHTJAR *Caprimulgus indicus* 27–32 cm Table p. 361
Male (4a, 4b) and female (4c). Widespread resident; unrecorded in parts of northwest. Grey to grey-brown, and heavily marked with black. Lacks pale rufous-brown nuchal collar and buff or rufous edges to scapulars. Song is a loud, resonant *chunk-chunk-chunk-chunk....* Forest clearings and scrub-covered slopes.

5 EURASIAN NIGHTJAR *Caprimulgus europaeus* 25 cm Table p. 361
Male (5a, 5b) and female (5c). Mainly summer visitor and passage migrant. Pakistan and NW Gujarat. Medium-sized, grey nightjar with regular, bold lanceolate streaking on crown, nape and scapulars (latter with buffish outer edges). Song is a continuous churring; soft *quoit quoit* in flight. Rocky slopes with scattered bushes.

6 EGYPTIAN NIGHTJAR *Caprimulgus aegyptius* 25 cm Table p. 361
Male (6a, 6b). Summer visitor. SW Pakistan. Medium-sized, sandy nightjar with finely streaked crown, black 'inverted anchor-shaped' marks on scapulars, unbroken narrow white throat crescent; never shows any white on wings or tail. Song is a *kowrr..kowrr..kowrr...*; guttural *tuk-l tuk-l* in flight. Semi-desert.

7 SYKES'S NIGHTJAR *Caprimulgus mahrattensis* 23 cm Table p. 361
Male (7a, 7b) and female (7c). Resident. Breeds in Pakistan and parts of NW India; winters south to C India. Small, grey nightjar. Has finely streaked crown, black 'inverted anchor-shaped' marks on scapulars, large white patches on sides of throat, and irregular buff spotting on nape forming indistinct collar. Has continuous churring song; low, soft *chuck-chuck* in flight. Breeds in semi-desert; wide variety of habitats in winter.

8 LARGE-TAILED NIGHTJAR *Caprimulgus macrurus* 33 cm Table p. 361
Male (8a, 8b) and female (8c). Resident. Himalayas south to Bangladesh and C India. More warmly coloured and strongly patterned than Grey, with longer and broader tail. Has diffuse pale rufous-brown nuchal collar, well-defined buff edges to scapulars, buff tips to black-centred wing-coverts. Song is a series of loud, resonant calls: *chaunk-chaunk-chaunk*, repeated at the rate of about 100 per minute. Edges of tropical and subtropical forest.

9 JERDON'S NIGHTJAR *Caprimulgus atripennis* 28 cm Table p. 361
Male (9a, 9b). Resident. C and S peninsula and Sri Lanka. More warmly coloured and strongly patterned than Grey. Has rufous band across nape/upper mantle, well-defined buff edges to scapulars, and broad, buff tips to black-centred coverts forming wing-bars. Song is a series of liquid, tremulous calls: *ch-wo-wo*, repeated at the rate of 13–20 per minute. Edges of moist forest and secondary growth.

10 INDIAN NIGHTJAR *Caprimulgus asiaticus* 24 cm Table p. 361
Adult (10a, 10b). Widespread resident; unrecorded in most of northeast. Small. Has boldly streaked crown, rufous-buff nuchal collar, bold black centres and broad buff edges to scapulars, and relatively unmarked central tail feathers. Song is a far-carrying *chuk-chuk-chuk-chuk-tukaroo*; short sharp *qwit-qwit* in flight. Open wooded country in plains and foothills.

11 SAVANNA NIGHTJAR *Caprimulgus affinis* 23 cm Table p. 361
Male (11a, 11b) and female (11c). Widespread resident; unrecorded in Sri Lanka. Crown and mantle finely vermiculated, scapulars edged with rufous-buff; male has largely white outer tail feathers (although this may be difficult to see). Song is a strident *dheet*. Open forest, stony areas with scrub.

84

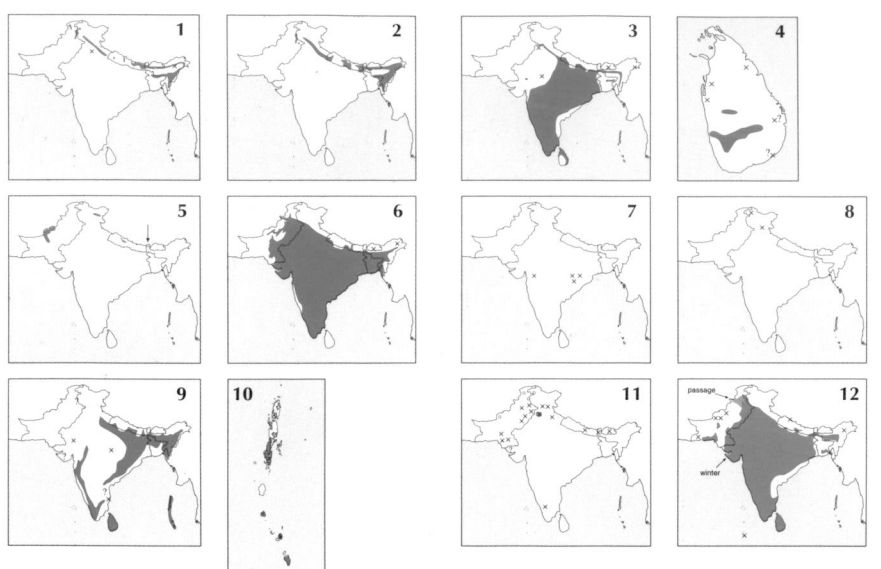

PLATE 34, p. 92

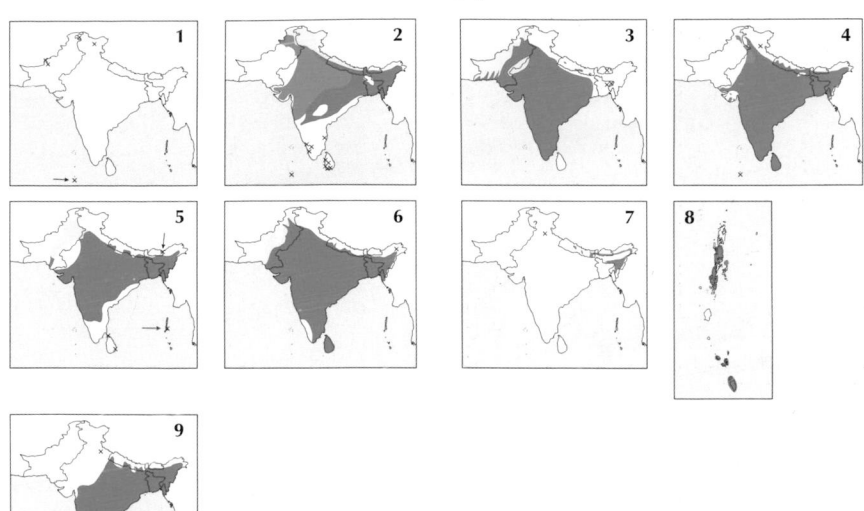

PLATE 38, p. 100

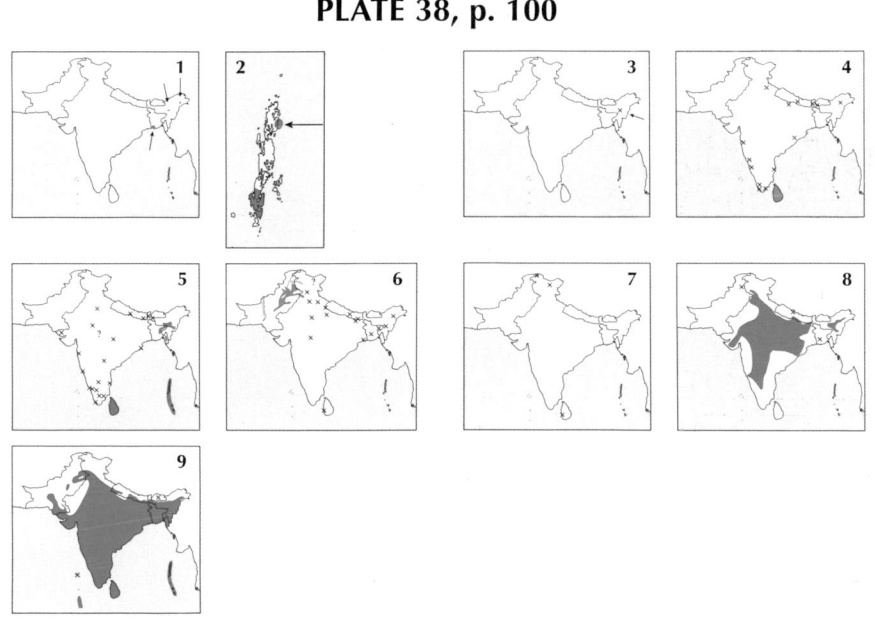

PLATE 32: PIGEONS

1 ROCK PIGEON *Columba livia* 33 cm
Adult *C. l. neglecta* (1a, 1b); adult *C. l. intermedia* (1c, 1d). Widespread resident; unrecorded in parts of northwest and northeast. Grey tail with blackish terminal band, and broad black bars across greater coverts and tertials/secondaries. Northern race *neglecta* has whitish back. Feral populations differ considerably in coloration and patterning. Feral birds live in villages and towns; wild birds around cliffs and ruins.

2 HILL PIGEON *Columba rupestris* 33 cm
Adult (2a, 2b, 3c). Resident. Himalayas. Similar to Rock, but has white band across tail contrasting with blackish terminal band. High-altitude villages and cliffs, mainly in Tibetan plateau country.

3 SNOW PIGEON *Columba leuconota* 34 cm
Adult (3a, 3b, 3c). Resident. Himalayas. Slate-grey head, creamy-white collar and underparts, fawn-brown mantle, and white band across black tail. Cliffs and gorges in mountains with plentiful rainfall.

4 YELLOW-EYED PIGEON *Columba eversmanni* 30 cm
Adult (4a, 4b). Winter visitor and passage migrant. Pakistan and N India. Smaller than Rock, with narrower and shorter black wing-bars. Yellow orbital skin and iris, brownish cast to upperparts, purplish cast to grey crown and nape, and extensive greyish-white back and upper rump. Also slight differences in tail pattern from Rock: dark terminal band is less clear cut and shows diffuse paler grey subterminal band. Plains cultivation.

5 COMMON WOOD PIGEON *Columba palumbus* 43 cm
Adult (5a, 5b). Resident. Baluchistan and Himalayas east to Nepal. White wing patch and dark tail-band, buff neck patch, and deep vinous underparts. In flight, from below, shows greyish-white band across tail and grey undertail-coverts are concolorous with base of tail. Scrub-covered and wooded hillsides.

6 SPECKLED WOOD PIGEON *Columba hodgsonii* 38 cm
Male (6a) and female (6b). Resident. Himalayas and NE Indian hills. Speckled underparts, white spotting on wing-coverts, and lacks buff patch on neck. Male has maroon mantle and maroon on underparts, replaced by grey on female. In flight, from below, shows dark grey undertail-coverts and underside to tail. Mainly oak-rhododendron forest.

7 ASHY WOOD PIGEON *Columba pulchricollis* 36 cm
Adult (7a, 7b). Resident. Himalayas and NE Indian hills. Buff collar, slate-grey breast, becoming buff on belly and undertail-coverts, and uniform slate-grey upperparts. In flight, from below, creamy buff undertail-coverts contrast with dark underside to tail. Broadleaved forest.

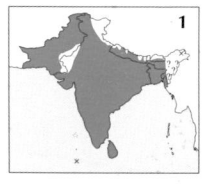 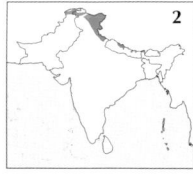 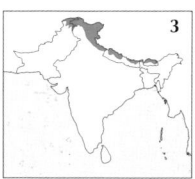 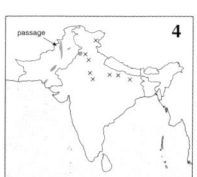

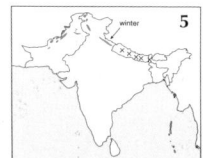 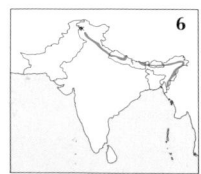 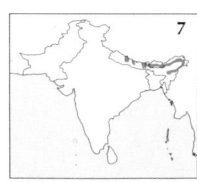

PLATE 33: PIGEONS

1 NILGIRI WOOD PIGEON *Columba elphinstonii* 42 cm
Adult (1a, 1b). Resident. Western Ghats. Checkerboard pattern on neck, maroon-brown upperparts, uniform slate-grey tail. Moist evergreen forest.

2 SRI LANKA WOOD PIGEON *Columba torringtoni* 36 cm
Adult (2a, 2b). Resident. Sri Lanka. Checkerboard pattern on neck, slate-grey upperparts, including tail, and lilac- to purplish-grey underparts with grey undertail-coverts. Mainly hill forest.

3 PALE-CAPPED PIGEON *Columba punicea* 36 cm
Adult (3a, 3b) and juvenile (3c). Resident. Eastern Ghats, NE India and Bangladesh. Pale cap, vinous-chestnut underparts, and maroon-brown mantle and wing-coverts with green-and-purple gloss. Juvenile initially lacks cap; upperparts browner, with chestnut fringes, and underparts mixed grey and rufous-buff. Tropical and subtropical forest and secondary growth.

4 ANDAMAN WOOD PIGEON *Columba palumboides* 41 cm
Adult (4a, 4b). Resident. Andamans and Nicobars. Dark slate-grey upperparts and grey underparts including undertail-coverts, with paler head and neck, latter with indistinct checkerboard patterning. Reddish cere, base of bill and eye patch. Dense evergreen forest.

5 GREEN IMPERIAL PIGEON *Ducula aenea* 43–47 cm
Adult (5a, 5b). Resident. Mainly Western Ghats, E and NE India, Bangladesh and Sri Lanka. Large size, metallic green upperparts and tail, and maroon undertail-coverts (darker than belly). *D. a. nicobarica* (not illustrated) from Nicobar Is. has dark and more bluish or purplish upperparts than other races in subcontinent, and undertail-coverts are brown or grey. Moist tropical broadleaved forest.

6 MOUNTAIN IMPERIAL PIGEON *Ducula badia* 43–51 cm
Adult (6a, 6b). Resident. Himalayas, NE Indian hills and Western Ghats. Large size, brownish upperparts, dark brown band across base of tail, and pale buff undertail-coverts (which are paler, not darker, than belly and vent). Tall evergreen forest.

7 PIED IMPERIAL PIGEON *Ducula bicolor* 41 cm
Adult (7a, 7b). Resident. Mainly Nicobars. Creamy-white, with black flight feathers and black terminal band to tail. Evergreen broadleaved forest.

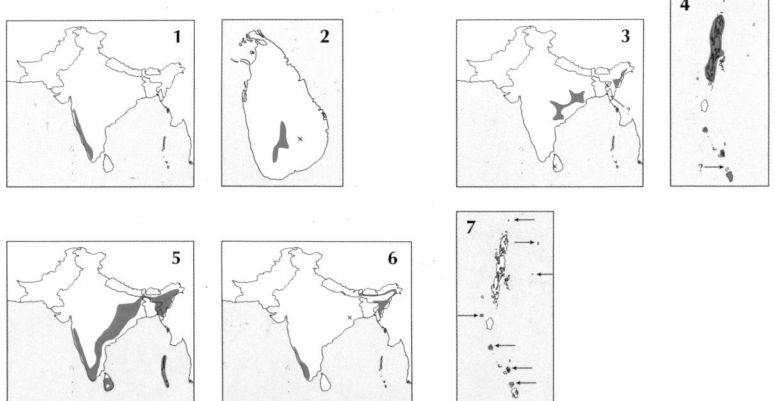

PLATE 34: DOVES

1 EUROPEAN TURTLE DOVE *Streptopelia turtur* 33 cm
Adult (1a, 1b) and juvenile (1c). Vagrant. Pakistan, India and Maldives. Has white sides and tip to tail. Told from *meena* race of Oriental Turtle by smaller size and slimmer build; broader, paler rufous-buff fringes to scapulars and wing-coverts; more buffish- or brownish-grey rump and uppertail-coverts; and greyish-pink breast, becoming whitish on belly and undertail-coverts. Juvenile lacks neck-barring. Cultivation in drier mountains and valleys.

2 ORIENTAL TURTLE DOVE *Streptopelia orientalis* 33 cm
Adult *S. o. meena* of W Himalayas **(2a, 2b); adult (2c, 2d) and juvenile (2e) *S. o. agricola*** of E Himalayas and NE India; **adult *S. o. erythrocephala*** of the peninsula **(2f).** Resident and winter visitor. Himalayas, NE India and Bangladesh south to C peninsular India, except arid northwest. Rufous-scaled scapulars and wing-coverts, brownish-grey to dusky maroon-pink underparts, and black and bluish-grey barring on neck sides. In all but one Indian race (*meena*), has grey sides and tip to tail. Juvenile lacks neck-barring. Open forest.

3 LAUGHING DOVE *Streptopelia senegalensis* 27 cm
Adult (3a, 3b). Widespread resident; unrecorded in most of Himalayas, the northeast and Sri Lanka. Slim, small, with fairly long tail. Brownish-pink head and underparts, uniform upperparts, and black stippling on upper breast. Dry cultivation and scrub-covered hills.

4 SPOTTED DOVE *Streptopelia chinensis* 30 cm
Adult *S. c. suratensis* (4a, 4b); adult *S. c. tigrina* of NE subcontinent **(4c).** Widespread resident; unrecorded in most of northwest and N Himalayas. Spotted upperparts, and black-and-white chequered patch on neck sides. *S. c. tigrina* of NE subcontinent has buff scaling on upperparts. Cultivation, habitation and open forest.

5 RED COLLARED DOVE *Streptopelia tranquebarica* 23 cm
Male (5a) and female (5b). Widespread resident; unrecorded in most of northwest, N Himalayas, S India and Sri Lanka. Male has blue-grey head with black half-collar, pinkish-maroon upperparts, and pink underparts. Compared with Eurasian Collared, female has darker buffish-grey underparts, darker fawn-brown upperparts, greyer underwing-coverts, and is much smaller and more compact. Light woodland and trees in open country.

6 EURASIAN COLLARED DOVE *Streptopelia decaocto* 32 cm
Adult (6a, 6b). Widespread resident; unrecorded in W Pakistan, most of Himalayas and SW India. Sandy-brown with black half-collar. Larger and longer-tailed than Red Collared Dove, with paler upperparts and underparts and white underwing-coverts. Open dry country with cultivation and groves.

7 BARRED CUCKOO DOVE *Macropygia unchall* 41 cm
Male (7a) and female (7b). Resident. Himalayas and NE Indian hills. Long, graduated tail, slim body and small head. Upperparts and tail rufous, barred with dark brown. Male has unbarred head and neck with extensive purple-and-green gloss. Female is heavily barred on head, neck and underparts. Dense broadleaved forest.

8 ANDAMAN CUCKOO DOVE *Macropygia rufipennis* 41 cm
Male (8a) and female (8b). Resident. Andamans and Nicobars; only cuckoo dove in these islands. Long, graduated tail, slim body and small head. Feathers of brown upperparts are fringed with rufous. Male has brown barring across breast and belly, and unmarked rufous head. Female has black mottling on crown and nape, and unbarred underparts. Dense forest.

9 EMERALD DOVE *Chalcophaps indica* 27 cm
Male (9a) and female (9b, 9c). Widespread resident; unrecorded in most of northwest. Stout and broad-winged, with very rapid flight. Green upperparts and black-and-white banding on back. Male has grey crown and white shoulder patch. Moist tropical and subtropical broadleaved forest.

92

PLATE 35: GREEN PIGEONS

1 NICOBAR PIGEON *Caloenas nicobarica* 41 cm
Male (1a, 1b). Resident. Mainly Nicobars. Stocky, metallic green pigeon with long metallic green and copper neck hackles, and short white tail. Juvenile has blackish tail. Dense evergreen forest.

2 ORANGE-BREASTED GREEN PIGEON *Treron bicincta* 29 cm
Male (2a) and female (2b). Resident. Himalayas, hills of India, Bangladesh and Sri Lanka. Central tail feathers of both sexes are grey. Male has orange breast, bordered above by lilac band, and green mantle. Female has yellow cast to breast and belly, and grey hind-crown and nape. Subtropical moist broadleaved forest.

3 POMPADOUR GREEN PIGEON *Treron pompadora* 28 cm
Male (3a) and female (3b) *T. p. phayrei;* male *T. p. affinis* of S India **(3c);** male *T. p. pompadora* of Sri Lanka **(3d);** male *T. p. chloroptera* **(3e)** of Andaman and Nicobar Is. Resident. Himalayas, hills of NE and SW India, Bangladesh and Sri Lanka. Both sexes told from Thick-billed Green by thin blue-grey bill (without prominent red base) and lack of prominent greenish orbital skin. Male has maroon mantle; where range overlaps with Thick-billed's, has diffuse orange patch on breast, greenish-yellow throat, and uniform chestnut undertail-coverts. Female lacks maroon mantle; tail shape and pattern help separate it from female Orange-breasted and Wedge-tailed Green. Larger *chloroptera* has less extensive patch of maroon on upperparts and different patterning on undertail-coverts. Tropical and subtropical moist broadleaved forest and well-wooded areas.

4 THICK-BILLED GREEN PIGEON *Treron curvirostra* 27 cm
Male (4a) and female (4b). Resident. E Himalayas, NE India and Bangladesh. Both sexes told from Pompadour Green by thick bill with red base, prominent greenish orbital skin and barred appearance to undertail-coverts. Male has maroon mantle, and green breast without orange wash. Tropical and subtropical forest and well-wooded areas.

5 YELLOW-FOOTED GREEN PIGEON *Treron phoenicoptera* 33 cm
Adult *T. p. phoenicoptera* (5a); adult *T. p. chlorigaster* (5b, 5c). Widespread resident; unrecorded in most of Himalayas and northwest. Large size, broad olive-yellow collar, pale greyish-green upperparts, mauve shoulder patch, yellowish band at base of tail, and yellow legs and feet. Populations in peninsular India and Sri Lanka (*T. p. chlorigaster*) have greenish-yellow belly and flanks. Deciduous forest and fruiting trees around villages and cultivation.

6 PIN-TAILED GREEN PIGEON *Treron apicauda* 42 cm
Male (6a) and female (6b). Resident. Himalayas, NE India and Bangladesh. Both sexes have pointed central tail feathers, grey tail, green mantle, and lime-green rump. Male has pale orange wash to breast. Tall tropical and subtropical forest.

7 WEDGE-TAILED GREEN PIGEON *Treron sphenura* 33 cm
Male (7a) and female (7b). Resident. Himalayas, NE India and Bangladesh. Both sexes have long wedge-shaped tail, indistinct yellow edges to wing-coverts and tertials, and dark green rump and tail. Male has maroon patch on upperparts (less extensive than on Pompadour Green) and orange wash to crown and breast. Female has uniform green head (lacking grey crown of female Pompadour where ranges overlap). Subtropical and temperate broadleaved forest.

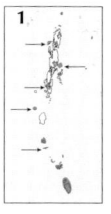 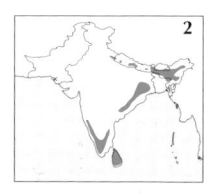 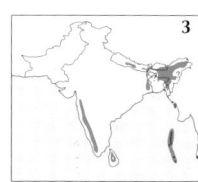 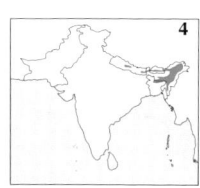
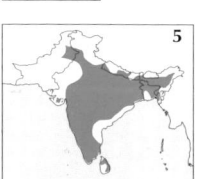 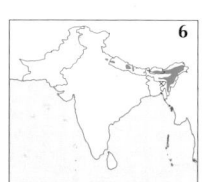 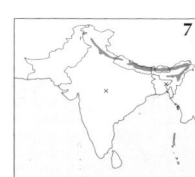

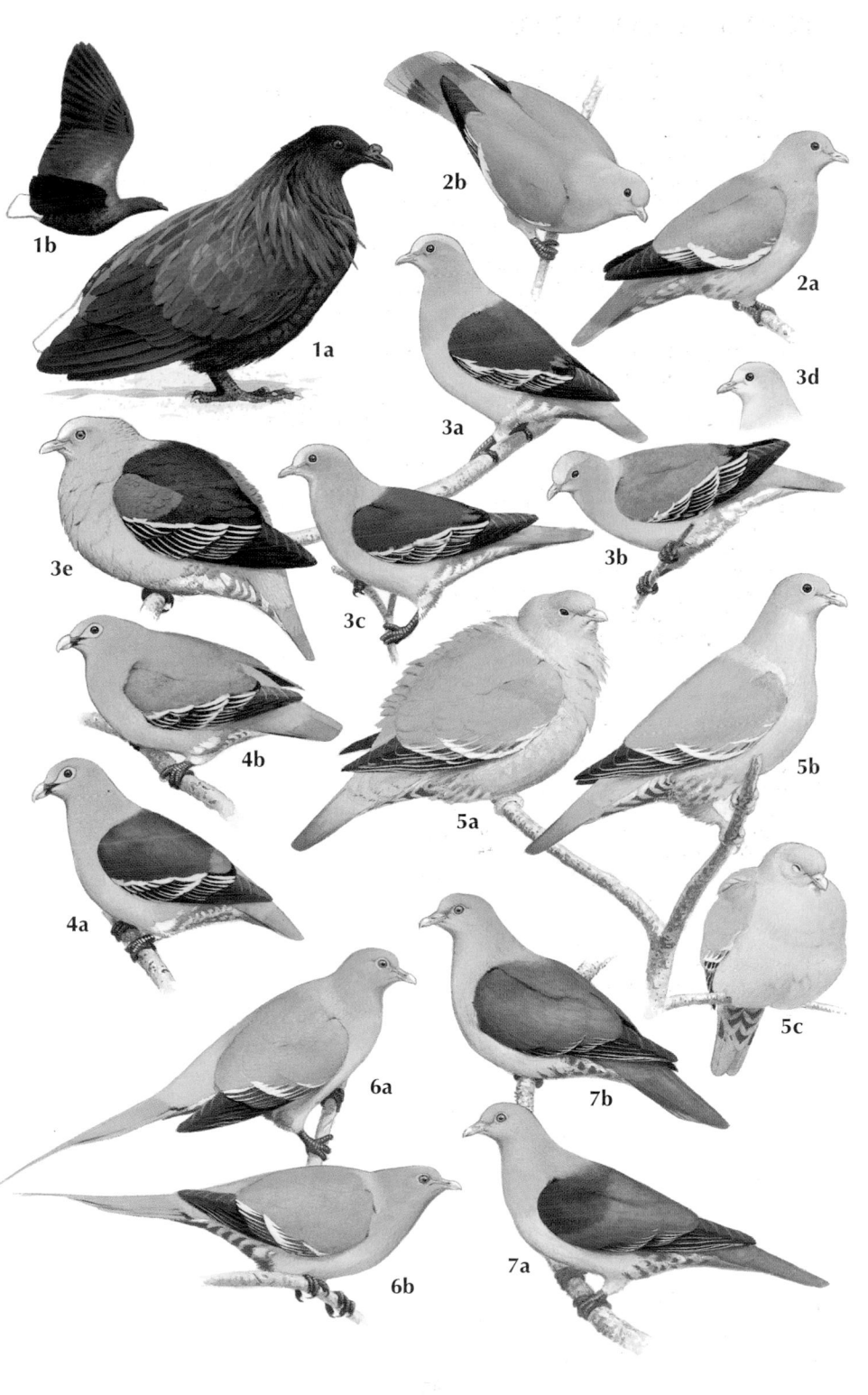

PLATE 36: BUSTARDS

1 LITTLE BUSTARD *Tetrax tetrax* 40–45 cm
Male breeding (1a, 1b), male non-breeding (1c) and female (1d, 1e). Winter visitor. Pakistan and N India. Small, stocky bustard with white panel across secondaries and inner primaries. Non-breeding male less heavily marked on upperparts and whiter on underparts compared with female, and shows more white on wing. Breeding male has grey face, and black-and-white pattern on neck and breast. Grassland and short crops.

2 GREAT BUSTARD *Otis tarda* 75–105 cm
Male breeding (2a, 2b) and female (2c, 2d). Vagrant. Pakistan. Very large, stocky bustard. In all plumages, has greyish head and upper neck, cinnamon lower neck, cinnamon upperparts with bold black barring, and white underparts. Patterning of white on wing differs from that of other bustards. Male larger than female, with thicker neck, and with more extensive white on wing (tertials and wing-coverts show more white). Short-grass plains.

3 INDIAN BUSTARD *Ardeotis nigriceps* 92–122 cm
Male (3a, 3b) and female (3c). Resident. India. Very large bustard. In all plumages, has greyish or white neck, black crown and crest, uniform brown upperparts, and white-spotted black wing-coverts. Upperwing lacks extensive area of white. Male huge, with black breast-band, and with almost white neck only very finely vermiculated with dark grey. Female smaller; neck appears greyer owing to profuse dark grey vermiculations, and typically lacks black breast-band. Dry grassland with bushes.

4 MACQUEEN'S BUSTARD *Chlamydotis macqueeni* 55–65 cm
Male (4a, 4b) and juvenile (4c). Mainly winter visitor to Pakistan and NW India; also breeds in S Pakistan. Medium-sized bustard. In all plumages, shows dark vertical stripe down neck. In flight, extensive white patch on outer primaries. Sexes similar, but female is smaller and lacks whitish panel across greater coverts. Juvenile very similar to female, but lacks black-tipped crest, neck stripe is finer, and white on wing is washed with buff and less prominent. Semi-desert with scattered shrubs and sandy grassland.

5 BENGAL FLORICAN *Houbaropsis bengalensis* 66 cm
Male (5a, 5b) and female (5c, 5d). Resident. Lowlands in N India and S Nepal. Larger and stockier than Lesser Florican, with broader head and thicker neck. Male has black head, neck and underparts, and in flight wings are entirely white except for black tips. Female and immature are buff-brown to sandy-rufous, and have buffish-white wing-coverts with fine dark barring. First-summer male resembles adult male, but reverts to female-like plumage in second winter; full adult male plumage acquired by second summer. Tall grassland with scattered bushes.

6 LESSER FLORICAN *Sypheotides indica* 46–51 cm
Male breeding (6a, 6b), male non-breeding (6c) and female (6d, 6e). Resident. Breeds in NW India; winters south to SE India; also summers in Nepal. Small, slim, long-necked bustard. Male breeding has spatulate-tipped head plumes, black head/neck and underparts, and white collar across upper mantle; white wing-coverts show as patch on closed wing, but has less white on wing than Bengal Florican. Non-breeding male similar to female, but has white wing-coverts. Female and immature are sandy or cinnamon-buff; separated from female/immature Bengal Florican by smaller size and slimmer appearance, heavily marked wing-coverts, and rufous rather than buff background coloration to barred flight feathers. Dry grassland and crops.

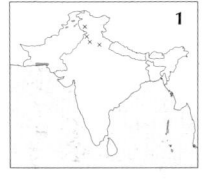 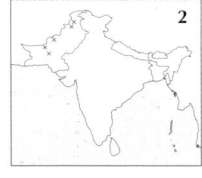 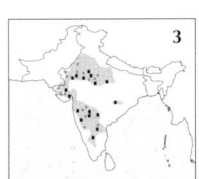 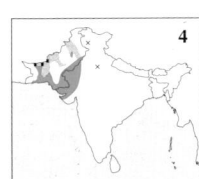

 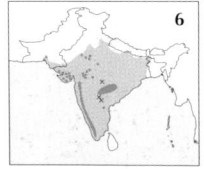

PLATE 37: CRANES

1 SIBERIAN CRANE *Grus leucogeranus* 120–140 cm
Adult (1a, 1b) and immature (1c). Winter visitor. Mainly Keoladeo Ghana Bird Sanctuary. Adult is white, with bare red face, pinkish-red legs, and noticeably downcurved reddish bill. Immature has brownish bill and fully feathered head at first and is strongly marked with cinnamon-brown on head, neck, mantle and wings, with some white body feathers by first winter; by third winter, red mask is apparent and body feathers are mainly white. In flight, both adult and immature show black primaries which contrast with rest of wing. Freshwater marshes.

2 SARUS CRANE *Grus antigone* 156 cm
Adult (2a, 2b) and immature (2c) *G. a. antigone*; **adult** *G. a. sharpii* **(2d).** Resident. Mainly NW India and W Nepal. Adult is grey, with bare red head and upper neck and bare ashy-green crown. In flight, black primaries contrast with rest of wing. Immature has rusty-buff feathering to head and neck, and upperparts are marked with brown; older immatures are similar to adult but have dull red head and upper neck and lack greenish crown of adult. *G. a. sharpii*, which occurs in NE subcontinent, is darker grey than nominate, with elongated tertials concolorous with rest of upperparts. Cultivation in well-watered country.

3 DEMOISELLE CRANE *Grus virgo* 90–100 cm
Adult (3a, 3b) and immature (3c). Winter visitor. Mainly W India; passage migrant in Pakistan. Small crane. Adult has black head and neck with white tuft behind eye, and grey crown; black neck feathers extend as a point beyond breast, and elongated tertials project as shallow arc beyond body, giving rise to distinctive shape. Immature similar to adult, but head and neck are dark grey, tuft behind eye is grey and less prominent, elongated feathers of foreneck and tertials are shorter and protrude less, and has grey-brown cast to upperparts. In flight, Demoiselle is best separated at a distance from Common by black breast. Cultivation, large rivers and reservoirs.

4 COMMON CRANE *Grus grus* 110–120 cm
Adult (4a, 4b) and immature (4c). Winter visitor. Mainly NW India. Adult has mainly black head and foreneck, with white stripe behind eye extending down side of neck. Immature has brown markings on upperparts with buff or grey head and neck; adult head pattern apparent on some by first winter and as adult by second winter. Crops, lakes and reservoirs.

5 HOODED CRANE *Grus monacha* 97 cm
Adult (5a, 5b) and immature (5c). Vagrant. India. Small crane. Adult is uniform dark grey, with white head and upper neck and black forehead; red patch on forecrown visible at close range. Immature has strong cinnamon wash to greyish-white head and neck. In flight, has almost uniform slate-grey upperwing and underwing. Plains and marshes.

6 BLACK-NECKED CRANE *Grus nigricollis* 139 cm
Adult (6a, 6b) and immature (6c). Breeds in Ladakh; winters mainly in Bhutan. Adult is pale grey with contrasting black head, upper neck and bunched tertials; shows more contrast between black flight feathers and pale grey coverts than Common, and has black tail-band. Immature has buff or brownish head, neck, mantle and mottling to wing-coverts. As adult by second winter. Summers by high-altitude lakes; winters in fallow cultivation and marshes.

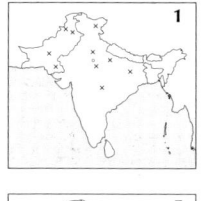 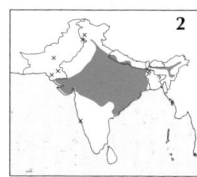 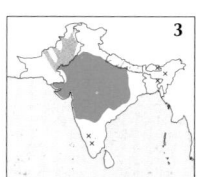 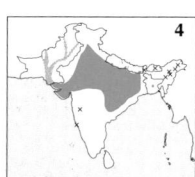

 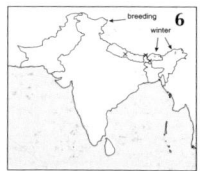

PLATE 38: MASKED FINFOOT, RAILS AND CRAKES   Maps p. 87

1 MASKED FINFOOT *Heliopais personata* 56 cm
Male (1a) and female (1b). Resident? Assam and Bangladesh. Large size, with yellow bill and green legs and feet. Female has whitish throat and foreneck (black in male). Pools in dense forest and mangrove creeks.

2 ANDAMAN CRAKE *Rallina canningi* 34 cm
Adult (2a) and juvenile (2b). Resident. Andamans. Green bill and legs/feet. Lacks white throat and barring on wing-coverts. Adult has chestnut upperparts and black-and-white barred underparts. Juvenile duller, with less pronounced barring on underparts. Forest marshes.

3 RED-LEGGED CRAKE *Rallina fasciata* 23 cm
Adult (3a) and juvenile (3b). Resident. Assam. Broad black-and-white barring on underparts. Adult told from Slaty-legged by red legs, white or buff barring on wings, rufous-brown upperparts, and indistinct whitish to rufous-buff throat. Juvenile from juvenile Slaty-legged by red legs, conspicuous barring on wings, and warmer brown coloration to upperparts, head and breast. Marshes and paddy-field edges.

4 SLATY-LEGGED CRAKE *Rallina eurizonoides* 25 cm
Adult (4a) and juvenile (4b). Resident. Mainly India and Sri Lanka. Black-and-white barring on underparts. Adult told from Red-legged by greenish or grey legs, lack of barring on wings, olive-brown mantle contrasting with rufous neck and breast, narrower and more numerous white barring on underparts, and prominent white throat. Juvenile from juvenile Red-legged by leg colour and lack of barring on wings. Marshes in well-wooded country.

5 SLATY-BREASTED RAIL *Gallirallus striatus* 27 cm
Adult male (5a) and juvenile (5b) *G. s. albiventer.* Widespread resident; unrecorded in Pakistan. Straightish, longish bill with red at base. Legs olive-grey. Adult has chestnut crown and nape, slate-grey foreneck and breast, white barring and spotting on upperparts, and barred flanks and undertail-coverts. Juvenile has rufous-brown crown and nape, and white barring on wing-coverts. Marshes, mangroves and paddy-fields.

6 WATER RAIL *Rallus aquaticus* 23–28 cm
Adult (6a) and juvenile (6b) *R. a. korejewi.* Breeds in Kashmir; winter visitor, mainly to N subcontinent. Slightly downcurved bill with red at base. Legs pinkish. Adult has dark-streaked olive-brown upperparts, grey underparts, black-and-white barring on flanks, and white undertail-coverts. Juvenile has buff underparts, with blackish flank barring and rufous-buff undertail-coverts. Marshes.

7 CORN CRAKE *Crex crex* 27–30 cm
Adult. Vagrant. Pakistan, India and Sri Lanka. Stout pinkish bill and legs. Rufous-chestnut on wings, and rufous-brown and white barring on flanks. Juvenile has buffish, rather than grey, neck and breast. Grassland and crops.

8 BROWN CRAKE *Amaurornis akool* 28 cm
Adult. Resident. N and C subcontinent. Olive-brown upperparts, grey underparts, and olive-brown flanks and undertail-coverts; underparts lack barring. Has greenish bill and pinkish-brown to purple legs. Juvenile has dull iris but is otherwise similar to adult. Marshes and vegetation bordering watercourses.

9 WHITE-BREASTED WATERHEN *Amaurornis phoenicurus* 32 cm
Adult (9a) and juvenile (9b). Widespread resident. Adult has grey upperparts, and white face, foreneck and breast; undertail-coverts rufous-cinnamon. Juvenile has greyish face, foreneck and breast, and olive-brown upperparts. Thick cover close to fresh waters.

PLATE 39: CRAKES AND OTHER RALLIDS   Maps p. 106

1 BLACK-TAILED CRAKE *Porzana bicolor* 25 cm
Adult. Resident. Himalayas and NE India. Red legs. Sooty-grey head and underparts, rufescent olive-brown upperparts, and sooty-black tail and undertail-coverts. Juvenile has dull iris. Forest pools and marshes, paddy-field edges.

2 LITTLE CRAKE *Porzana parva* 20–23 cm
Male (2a), female (2b) and juvenile (2c). Winter visitor and passage migrant. Pakistan, India and Bangladesh. Longer wings than Baillon's (primaries extending noticeably beyond tertials at rest), with less extensive barring on flanks, and pronounced pale edges to scapulars and tertials (features for all plumages). Adult also with red at base of bill. Female has buff underparts. Juvenile has more extensive barring on flanks than adult (but less than on Baillon's). Marshes.

3 BAILLON'S CRAKE *Porzana pusilla* 17–19 cm
Adult (3a) and juvenile (3b). Breeds in Indian Himalayas; widespread winter visitor and passage migrant. Adult has rufous-brown upperparts (brighter than in male Little) extensively marked with white; barring on flanks extends farther forward than on Little, and bill is all green. Juvenile has buff underparts; compared with Little, wings are shorter, barring on underparts more extensive, has more extensive white flecking to warmer brown upperparts, and lacks pronounced pale fringes to tertials and scapulars. Marshes, edges of lakes and pools, and paddy-fields.

4 RUDDY-BREASTED CRAKE *Porzana fusca* 22 cm
Adult (4a) and juvenile (4b). Widespread resident. Red legs, chestnut underparts, and black-and-white barring restricted to rear flanks and undertail-coverts. Juvenile dark olive-brown, with white-barred undertail-coverts and fine greyish-white mottling/barring on rest of underparts. Marshes, paddy-fields and canals.

5 SPOTTED CRAKE *Porzana porzana* 22–24 cm
Adult (5a) and juvenile (5b). Widespread winter visitor; unrecorded in E India. Profuse white spotting on head, neck and breast. Stout bill, barred flanks, and unmarked buff undertail-coverts. Adult has yellowish bill with red at base, and grey head and breast. Juvenile has buffish-brown head and breast, and bill is brown. Marshes and lakes.

6 WATERCOCK *Gallicrex cinerea* M 43 cm, F 36 cm
Male breeding (6a), juvenile male (6b), 1st-summer male (6c) and female (6d). Widespread resident. Male is mainly greyish-black, with yellow-tipped red bill and red shield and horn. First-summer male has broad rufous-buff fringes to plumage. Non-breeding male and female have buff underparts with fine barring, and buff fringes to dark brown upperparts. Juvenile has uniform rufous-buff underparts, and rufous-buff fringes to upperparts. Male is much larger than female. Marshes and flooded fields.

(7) PURPLE SWAMPHEN *Porphyrio porphyrio* 45–50 cm
Adult (7a) and juvenile (7b). Widespread resident. Large size, purplish-blue coloration, and huge red bill and red frontal shield. Juvenile greyer, with duller bill. Large marshes.

(8) COMMON MOORHEN *Gallinula chloropus* 32–35 cm
Adult (8a) and juvenile (8b). Widespread resident and winter visitor. White lateral undertail-coverts and usually white line along flanks. Breeding adult has red bill with yellow tip and red shield; non-breeding adult has duller bill and legs. Juvenile has dull green bill, and is mainly brown. Freshwater wetlands.

(9) COMMON COOT *Fulica atra* 36–38 cm
Adult (9a) and juvenile (9b). Widespread resident and winter visitor. Blackish, with white bill and shield. Immature duller with whitish throat. Juvenile grey-brown, with whitish throat and breast. Standing fresh waters.

PLATE 40: SANDGROUSE Maps p. 106

1 TIBETAN SANDGROUSE *Syrrhaptes tibetanus* 48 cm
Male (1a, 1b) and female (1c). Resident. NW Indian Himalayas. Large and pin-tailed. Black spotting on upperparts, finely barred breast and white belly. In flight, black flight feathers contrast with sandy coverts on upperwing, and underwing is mainly black except for white lesser coverts and trailing edge to primaries. Female has barred upperparts. Semi-desert in Tibetan plateau country.

2 PALLAS'S SANDGROUSE *Syrrhaptes paradoxus* 30–41 cm
Male (2a, 2b) and female (2c). Vagrant. India. Pin-tailed and elongated outer primaries. Black patch on belly, largely white underwing, and pale upperside to primaries. Male has narrow black gorget across breast and unbarred wing-coverts. Arid plains and uplands.

3 PIN-TAILED SANDGROUSE *Pterocles alchata* 31–39 cm
Male breeding (3a, 3b) and female (3c, 3d). Probably breeds; winter visitor to Pakistan and NW India. Pin-tailed. White belly, with two (male) or three (female) narrow black bands across neck and breast. Largely white underwing and pale grey upperside to primaries. Male in breeding plumage has greenish upperparts with yellowish spotting; buff and barred with black in non-breeding plumage. Desert and semi-desert.

4 CHESTNUT-BELLIED SANDGROUSE *Pterocles exustus* 31–33 cm
Male (4a, 4b) and female (4c, 4d). Widespread resident; unrecorded in Himalayas, the northeast and Sri Lanka. Pin-tailed, with dark underwing, blackish-chestnut belly, and black breast line. Female has buff banding across upperwing-coverts and lacks black gorget across throat, which are useful distinctions at rest from Black-bellied. Desert and sparse thorn scrub.

5 SPOTTED SANDGROUSE *Pterocles senegallus* 30–35 cm
Male (5a, 5b) and female (5c). Breeds in S Pakistan and Rajasthan; winters in Pakistan and NW India. Pin-tailed. Rather pale upperwing with dark trailing edge, and whitish belly with black line down centre. Underwing lacks Crowned's strong contrast between black remiges and whitish coverts. Female is spotted on upperparts and breast. Sandy desert and arid foothills.

6 BLACK-BELLIED SANDGROUSE *Pterocles orientalis* 33–35 cm
Male (6a, 6b) and female (6c). Breeds in Baluchistan; winters in Pakistan and NW India. Stocky and short-tailed. Has black belly, and white underwing-coverts contrast with black flight feathers. Male has black and chestnut throat and grey neck and breast. Female is very heavily marked. Semi-desert.

7 CROWNED SANDGROUSE *Pterocles coronatus* 27–29 cm
Male (7a, 7b) and female (7c). Resident. Mainly Pakistan. Small, compact and short-tailed. Blackish flight feathers contrast with coverts on both surfaces of wing. Male has bold buff spotting on scapulars and upperwing-coverts, and black-and-white markings on head. Female uniformly barred and spotted, including on belly, and has orange-buff throat. Desert.

8 PAINTED SANDGROUSE *Pterocles indicus* 28 cm
Male (8a, 8b) and female (8c). Resident. N Pakistan and India. Small, stocky, and heavily barred. Underwing dark grey. Male has chestnut, buff and black bands across breast, and unbarred orange-buff neck and inner wing-coverts. Female heavily barred all over, with yellowish face and throat. Arid low hills.

9 LICHTENSTEIN'S SANDGROUSE *Pterocles lichtensteinii* 24–26 cm
Male (9a, 9b) and female (9c). Resident. SW Pakistan. Small, stocky, and heavily barred. Underwing dark grey. Male has buff and black bands across breast and barred neck. Female heavily barred all over, including on face and throat. Stony hills in desert.

PLATE 39, p. 102

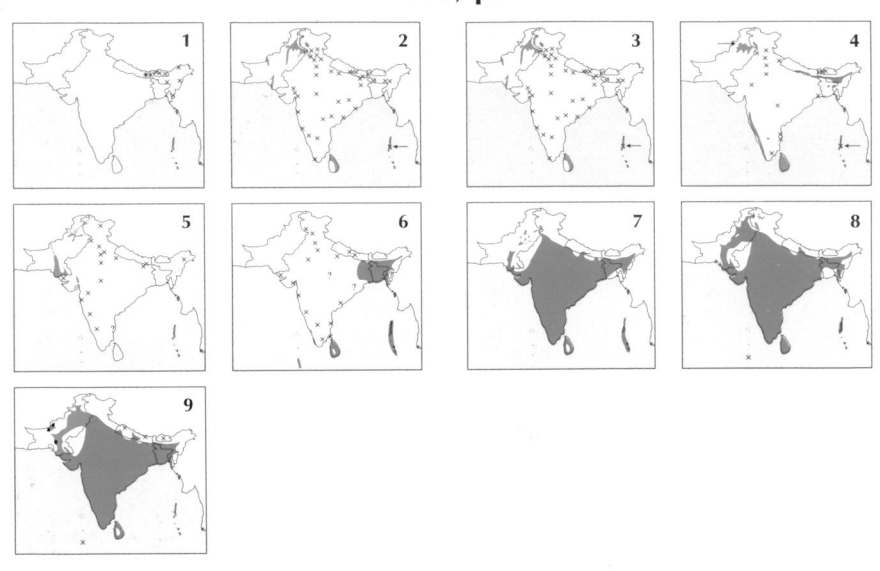

PLATE 40, p. 104

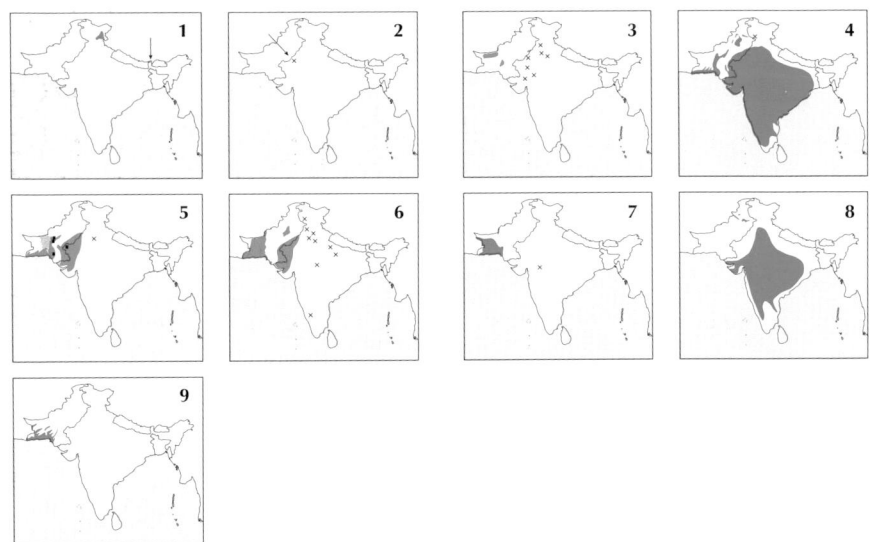

PLATE 47, p. 120

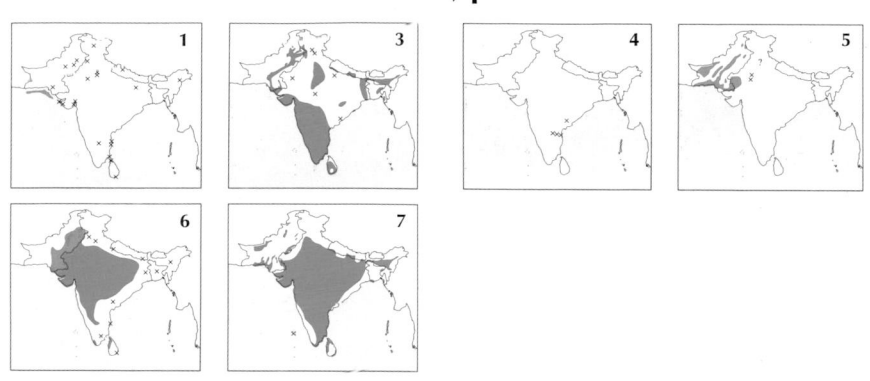

PLATE 48, p. 122

PLATE 41: EURASIAN WOODCOCK AND SNIPES

1 EURASIAN WOODCOCK *Scolopax rusticola* 33–35 cm
Adult (1a, 1b). Breeds in Pakistan hills and Himalayas; winters in Himalayas, Indian hills and Sri Lanka. Bulky and rufous-brown with broad, rounded wings. Crown and nape banded black and buff; lacks sharply defined mantle and scapular stripes. Dense, moist forest, also plantations in S India.

2 SOLITARY SNIPE *Gallinago solitaria* 29–31 cm
Adult (2a, 2b). Resident and winter visitor. Baluchistan, Himalayas and NE India. Large, dull-coloured snipe with long bill. Compared with Wood Snipe is colder-coloured and less boldly marked; also has less striking head pattern, white spotting on ginger-brown breast, rufous barring on mantle and scapulars (finer white mantle and scapular stripes). Wings longer and narrower than in Wood. Note, legs should be yellowish. High-altitude marshes and streams.

3 WOOD SNIPE *Gallinago nemoricola* 28–32 cm
Adult (3a, 3b). Breeds in Himalayas and NE India; winters in Himalayas, S Indian hills and Sri Lanka. Large, with heavy and direct flight and broad wings. Bill relatively short and broad-based. More boldly marked than Solitary, with buff and blackish head stripes, broad buff stripes on blackish mantle and scapulars, and warm buff neck and breast with brown streaking. Legs greenish. Breeds in alpine meadows and dwarf scrub; winters in forest marshes.

4 PINTAIL SNIPE *Gallinago stenura* 25–27 cm
Adult (4a), juvenile (4b), flight (4c, 4d) and tail (4e). Widespread winter visitor; unrecorded in parts of the northwest and northeast and Himalayas. Compared with Common, has more rounded wings, and slightly slower and more direct flight. Lacks well-defined white trailing edge to secondaries, and has densely barred underwing-coverts and pale (buff-scaled) upperwing-covert panel (more pronounced than shown). Feet project noticeably beyond tail in flight. At rest, shows little or no tail projection beyond closed wings; usually shows bulging supercilium in front of eye. Marshes.

5 SWINHOE'S SNIPE *Gallinago megala* 25–27 cm
Adult (5a), juvenile (5b), flight (5c, 5d) and tail (5e). Winter visitor. Mainly NE subcontinent and S India. Very similar to Pintail. In flight, is heavier, with longer bill and more pointed wings, and feet only just project beyond tail. Some birds quite dusky on neck, breast and flanks, unlike Pintail. Marshes.

6 GREAT SNIPE *Gallinago media* 27–29 cm
Adult (6a), juvenile (6b), flight (6c, 6d) and tail (6e). Winter visitor. S India and Sri Lanka. Medium-sized, bulky snipe, with broader wings than Common, and slower and more direct flight. Heavily barred underwing, narrow but distinct white wing-bars, and prominent white at sides of tail (latter two features less pronounced in juvenile). Marshes.

7 COMMON SNIPE *Gallinago gallinago* 25–27 cm
Adult (7a), juvenile (7b), flight (7c, 7d) and tail (7e). Breeds in NW Himalayas; widespread winter visitor. Compared with Pintail, wings are more pointed, and has faster and more erratic flight; shows prominent white trailing edge to wing and white banding on underwing-coverts. Marshes and paddy stubbles.

8 JACK SNIPE *Lymnocryptes minimus* 17–19 cm
Adult (8a, 8b, 8c). Widespread winter visitor. Small, with short bill. Flight weaker and slower than that of Common, with rounded wing-tips. Has divided supercilium but lacks pale crown-stripe. Mantle and scapular stripes very prominent. Marshes and paddy stubbles.

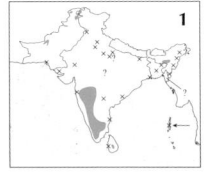 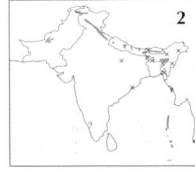 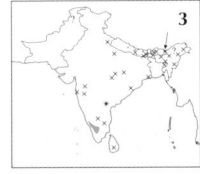 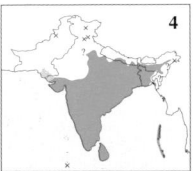

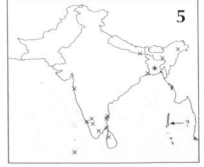 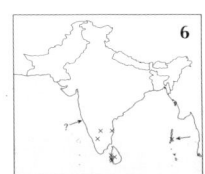 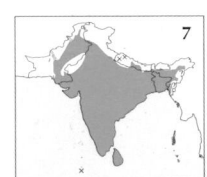 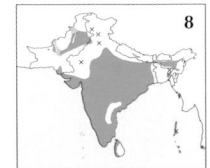

PLATE 42: GODWITS AND CURLEWS

(1) BLACK-TAILED GODWIT *Limosa limosa* 36–44 cm
Male breeding (1a), female breeding (1b), non-breeding (1c), juvenile (1d) and flight (1e, 1f) L. l. limosa; non-breeding L. l. melanuroides (1g). Widespread winter visitor. White wing-bars and white tail-base with black tail band. At rest, appears lankier with longer neck, legs and bill compared with Bar-tailed. In breeding plumage, has blackish barring on underparts and white belly. In non-breeding plumage, is more uniform on upperparts and breast than Bar-tailed. Juvenile has cinnamon underparts and cinnamon fringes to dark-centred upperparts. Eastern *L. l. melanuroides* has narrower wing-bar. Mainly fresh waters.

2 BAR-TAILED GODWIT *Limosa lapponica* 37–41 cm
Male breeding (2a), female breeding (2b), non-breeding (2c), juvenile (2d) and flight (2e, 2f). Widespread winter visitor, mainly to coasts. Lacks wing-bar, has barred tail and white V on back. Breeding male has chestnut-red underparts. Breeding female has pale chestnut or cinnamon underparts, although many as non-breeding. Non-breeding has dark streaking on breast and streaked appearance to upperparts. Juvenile similar to non-breeding, but with buff wash to underparts and buff edges to mantle/scapulars. See plate 44 for comparison with Asian Dowitcher. Estuaries and lagoons.

3 WHIMBREL *Numenius phaeopus* 40–46 cm
Adult N. p. phaeopus (3a, 3b, 3c); adult N. p. variegatus (3d, 3e). Widespread winter visitor, mainly to coasts. Smaller than both curlews, with shorter bill. Distinctive head pattern, with whitish supercilium and crown-stripe, dark eye-stripe, and dark sides of crown. Eastern *N. p. variegatus* has barred underwing-coverts and mainly brown rump and back. Flight call distinctive, *he-he-he-he-he-he-he*. Estuaries, tidal creeks and mangroves.

(4) EURASIAN CURLEW *Numenius arquata* 50–60 cm
Adult N. a. orientalis (4a, 4b, 4c). Widespread winter visitor, mainly to coasts. Large size and long, curved bill. Rather plain head. Underwing-coverts are white and rump/back mainly white; white ground colour to belly and vent. Has distinctive mournful *cur-lew* call. Estuaries, tidal creeks and mangroves.

5 EASTERN CURLEW *Numenius madagascariensis* 60–66 cm
Adult (5a, 5b, 5c). Vagrant. Bangladesh. Mainly coastal. Large size and very long, curved bill. Dark back and rump and heavily barred underwing-coverts and axillaries. Underparts washed with buff in adult breeding and juvenile (ground colour of Eurasian's breast and belly is whiter), although underbody in non-breeding adult is paler and more like Eurasian.

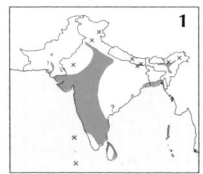 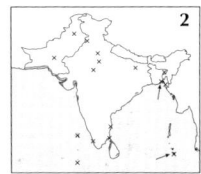 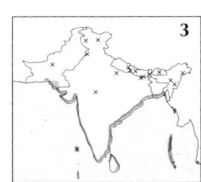 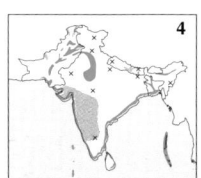

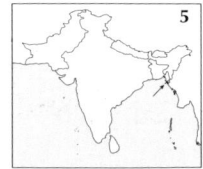

PLATE 43: *TRINGA* SANDPIPERS

(1) SPOTTED REDSHANK *Tringa erythropus* 29–32 cm
Adult breeding (1a), adult non-breeding (1b, 1c, 1d), and juvenile (1e). Widespread winter visitor. Red at base of bill, and red legs. Longer bill and legs than Common Redshank, and upperwing comparatively uniform. Non-breeding plumage is paler grey above and whiter below than Common. Underparts black in breeding plumage. Juvenile has grey barring on underparts. *Tu-ick* flight call. Mainly fresh waters, also coastal waters.

(2) COMMON REDSHANK *Tringa totanus* 27–29 cm
Adult breeding (2a), adult non-breeding (2b, 2c, 2d) and juvenile (2e). Breeds in NW Himalayas; widespread winter visitor. Orange-red at base of bill, orange-red legs, and broad white trailing edge to wing. Non-breeding plumage is grey-brown above, with grey breast. Neck and underparts heavily streaked in breeding plumage; upperparts with variable dark brown and cinnamon markings. Juvenile has brown upperparts with buff spotting and fringes. Anxious *teu-hu-hu* flight call. Fresh and coastal waters.

(3) MARSH SANDPIPER *Tringa stagnatilis* 22–25 cm
Adult breeding (3a), adult non-breeding (3b, 3c, 3d). Widespread winter visitor. Smaller and daintier than Common Greenshank, with proportionately longer legs and finer bill. Legs greenish or yellowish. Upperparts are grey and foreneck and underparts white in non-breeding plumage. In breeding plumage, foreneck and breast streaked and upperparts blotched and barred. Juvenile has dark-streaked upperparts with buff fringes. Abrupt, dull *yup* flight call. Mainly freshwater wetlands.

(4) COMMON GREENSHANK *Tringa nebularia* 30–34 cm
Adult breeding (4a) and non-breeding (4b, 4c, 4d). Widespread winter visitor. Stocky, with long, stout bill and long, stout greenish legs. Upperparts grey and foreneck and underparts white in non-breeding plumage. In breeding plumage, foreneck and breast streaked, upperparts untidily streaked. Juvenile has dark-streaked upperparts with fine buff or whitish fringes. Loud, ringing *tu-tu-tu* flight call. Wide range of freshwater and saltwater wetlands.

5 NORDMANN'S GREENSHANK *Tringa guttifer* 29–32 cm
Adult breeding (5a), adult non-breeding (5b, 5c) and juvenile (5d). Winter visitor. India, Bangladesh and Sri Lanka. Stockier than Common Greenshank, with shorter, yellowish legs, and deeper bill with blunt tip. Breeding adult has black spotting on breast and prominent white notching on scapulars and tertials. Non-breeding has paler and more uniform upperparts than Common. Juvenile has rather uniform upperparts, with paler fringes to wing-coverts, and strongly bicoloured bill. Flight call is *kwork* or *gwaak*, very different from Common Greenshank. Freshwater and coastal wetlands.

6 GREEN SANDPIPER *Tringa ochropus* 21–24 cm
Adult breeding (6a) and non-breeding (6b, 6c, 6d). Widespread winter visitor. White rump, and very dark upperwing lacks wing-bar. Greenish legs. Compared with Wood Sandpiper, has indistinct (or non-existent) supercilium behind eye and darker upperparts. In flight, underwing very dark. Ringing *tluee-tueet* flight call. Mainly freshwater wetlands.

(7) WOOD SANDPIPER *Tringa glareola* 18–21 cm
Adult breeding (7a), adult non-breeding (7b, 7c, 7d) and juvenile (7e). Widespread winter visitor. White rump and dark upperwing lacks wing-bar. Yellowish legs, prominent supercilium, and heavily spotted upperparts. Soft *chiff-if-if* flight call. Freshwater and coastal wetlands.

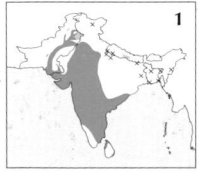 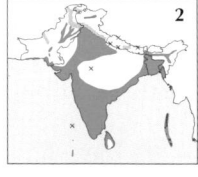 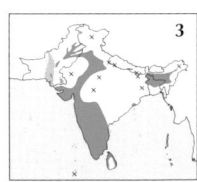 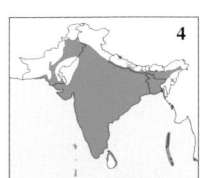

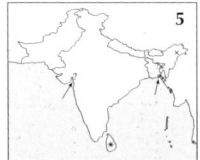 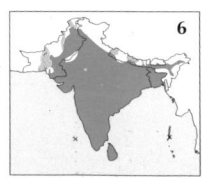 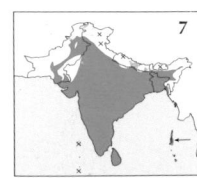

PLATE 44: MISCELLANEOUS WADERS

1 TEREK SANDPIPER *Xenus cinereus* 22–25 cm
Adult breeding (1a, 1b), adult non-breeding (1c, 1d) and juvenile (1e). Widespread winter visitor, mainly to coasts, also inland. Longish, upturned bill and short yellowish legs. In flight, shows prominent white trailing edge to secondaries and grey rump and tail. Adult breeding has blackish scapular lines. Flight call is pleasant *hu-hu-hu*. Mainly coastal wetlands.

2 COMMON SANDPIPER *Actitis hypoleucos* 19–21 cm
Adult breeding (2a, 2b) and juvenile (2c, 2d). Breeds in Himalayas; widespread winter visitor. Horizontal stance and constant bobbing action distinctive. White wing-bar and brown rump and centre of tail in flight. In breeding plumage, has irregular dark streaking and barring on upperparts, lacking in non-breeding. Juvenile has buff fringes and dark subterminal crescents to upperparts. Flight call is anxious *wee-wee-wee*. Breeds by mountain streams and rivers; winters at freshwater and coastal wetlands.

3 GREY-TAILED TATTLER *Heteroscelus brevipes* 24–27 cm
Adult breeding (3a), adult non-breeding (3b, 3c, 3d) and juvenile (3e). Vagrant. Bangladesh. Uniform grey upperparts including rump/tail and grey underwing. Stocky, with short yellow legs. Prominent supercilium, usually extending beyond eye; primaries extend to tail-tip. Adult breeding has barring on breast and flanks. Adult non-breeding uniform grey on upperparts and breast. Juvenile has indistinct white spotting on upperparts. Coastal wetlands.

4 RUDDY TURNSTONE *Arenaria interpres* 23 cm
Adult breeding (4a), adult non-breeding (4b, 4c, 4d) and juvenile (4e). Widespread winter visitor to coasts. Short bill and orange legs. In flight, shows white stripes on wings and back and black tail. In breeding plumage, has complex black-and-white neck and breast pattern and much chestnut-red on upperparts; duller and less strikingly patterned in non-breeding plumage. Juvenile has buff fringes to upperparts, and blackish breast. Rocky coasts and tidal mudflats.

5 ASIAN DOWITCHER *Limnodromus semipalmatus* 34–36 cm
Adult breeding (5a), adult non-breeding (5b, 5c) and juvenile (5d). Winter visitor to coasts of India, Bangladesh and Sri Lanka. Slightly smaller than Bar-tailed Godwit. Broad-based black bill with swollen tip, and square-shaped head. Shows diffuse pale wing-bar and grey tail in flight. Underparts brick-red in breeding plumage. Upperparts and underparts heavily streaked in non-breeding plumage. Juvenile has buff fringes to upperparts and wash to breast. Intertidal mudflats and mudbanks.

6 GREAT KNOT *Calidris tenuirostris* 26–28 cm
Adult breeding (6a), adult non-breeding (6b, 6c, 6d) and juvenile (6e). Winter visitor, chiefly to coasts. Larger than Red Knot, and often with slightly downcurved bill. Adult breeding heavily marked with black on breast and flanks, with chestnut patterning to scapulars. Adult non-breeding typically more heavily streaked on upperparts and breast than Red Knot, and juvenile is more strongly patterned than that species. Intertidal flats and tidal creeks.

7 RED KNOT *Calidris canutus* 23–25 cm
Adult breeding (7a), adult non-breeding (7b, 7c, 7d) and juvenile (7e). Winter visitor, chiefly to coasts. Stocky, with short, straight bill. Adult breeding is brick-red on underparts. Adult non-breeding whitish on underparts and uniform grey on upperparts. Juvenile has buff fringes and dark subterminal crescents to upperparts. Mainly intertidal mudflats.

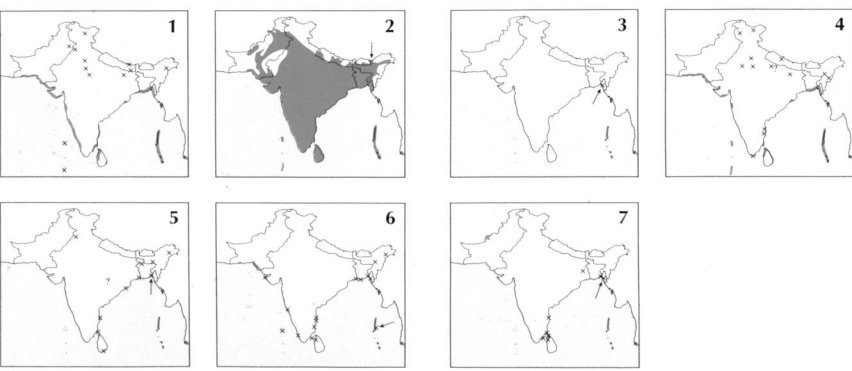

PLATE 45: STINTS AND SANDERLING

1 **SANDERLING** *Calidris alba* 20 cm
Adult breeding (1a, 1b), adult non-breeding (1c, 1d, 1e) and juvenile (1f). Winter visitor, mainly to coasts. Stocky, with short bill. Very broad white wing-bar. Adult breeding usually shows some rufous on sides of head, breast and upperparts. Non-breeding is pale grey above and very white below. Juvenile chequered black-and-white above. Sandy beaches.

2 **LITTLE STINT** *Calidris minuta* 13–15 cm
Adult breeding fresh (2a) and worn (2b), adult non-breeding (2c, 2d) and juvenile (2e, 2g, dull variant 2f). Widespread winter visitor. More rotund and upright than Temminck's, with dark legs. In flight, shows grey sides to tail; has weak *pi-pi-pi* flight call. Adult breeding has pale mantle V, rufous wash to face, neck sides and breast, and rufous fringes to upperpart feathers. Non-breeding has untidy, mottled/streaked appearance, with grey breast sides. Juvenile has whitish mantle V, greyish nape, prominent white supercilium which typically splits above eye (not shown in plate), and rufous fringes to upperparts. Freshwater and coastal wetlands.

3 **RED-NECKED STINT** *Calidris ruficollis* 13–16 cm
Adult breeding fresh (3a) and worn (3b), adult non-breeding (3c, 3d) and juvenile (3e, 3g, dull variant 3f). Winter visitor. India, Bangladesh and Sri Lanka. Very similar to Little. Adult breeding typically has unstreaked rufous-orange throat, foreneck and breast, white sides of lower breast with dark streaking, and greyish-centred tertials and wing-coverts (with greyish-white fringes); lacks prominent mantle V. Juvenile lacks prominent mantle V; has different coloration and patterning to lower scapulars (grey with dark subterminal marks with whitish or buffish fringes; typically blackish with rufous fringes in Little), and grey-centred, whitish- or buffish-edged tertials (usually blackish with rufous edges in Little); supercilium does not usually split in front of eye. Call much as Little. Mainly coastal.

4 **TEMMINCK'S STINT** *Calidris temminckii* 13–15 cm
Adult breeding (4a, 4b), adult non-breeding (4c, 4d) and juvenile (4e, 4f). Widespread winter visitor. More elongated than Little, and with more horizontal stance. In flight, shows white sides to tail; flight call a purring trill. Legs yellowish. In all plumages, lacks mantle V and is usually rather uniform, with complete breast-band and indistinct supercilium. Adult breeding has irregular dark markings on upperparts and juvenile regular buff fringes (patterning very different from Little). Freshwater and coastal wetlands.

5 **LONG-TOED STINT** *Calidris subminuta* 13–15 cm
Adult breeding (5a), adult non-breeding (5b, 5c, 5d) and juvenile (5e). Winter visitor. Mainly E subcontinent. Long and yellowish legs, longish neck, and upright stance. In all plumages, has prominent supercilium and heavily streaked foreneck and breast. Adult breeding and juvenile have prominent rufous fringes to upperparts; juvenile has very striking mantle V. In winter, upperparts more heavily marked than Little's. Call is a soft *prit* or *chirrup*. Freshwater and coastal wetlands.

6 **SHARP-TAILED SANDPIPER** *Calidris acuminata* 17–21 cm
Adult breeding (6a), adult non-breeding (6b) and juvenile (6c, 6d, 6e). Vagrant. Pakistan and Sri Lanka. Rufous crown (indistinct in winter) and prominent white supercilium. Adult non-breeding is greyish with breast-band of fine streaking. Adult breeding has dark markings over entire underparts, with arrow-head markings on flanks. Juvenile has buff wash to lightly streaked breast. Freshwater and coastal wetlands.

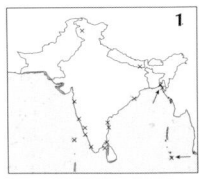 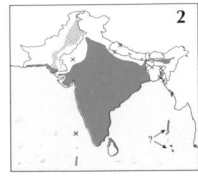 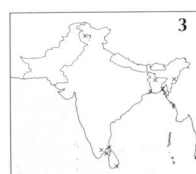 

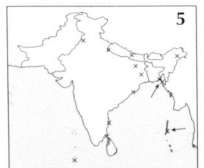 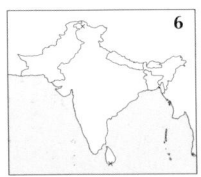

PLATE 46: MISCELLANEOUS WADERS

1 DUNLIN *Calidris alpina* 16–22 cm
Adult breeding (1a, 1b), adult non-breeding (1c, 1d) and juvenile (1e). Winter visitor, mainly to coasts, also inland. Shorter legs and bill compared with Curlew Sandpiper, and with dark centre to rump. Adult breeding has black belly. Adult non-breeding darker grey-brown than Curlew Sandpiper, with less distinct supercilium. Juvenile has streaked belly, rufous fringes to mantle and scapulars, and buff mantle V. Flight call is a slurrred *screet*. Mainly coastal wetlands, also flooded fields.

2 CURLEW SANDPIPER *Calidris ferruginea* 18–23 cm
Adult breeding (2a, 2b), adult non-breeding (2c, 2d) and juvenile (2e, 2f). Winter visitor, mainly to coasts, also inland. White rump. More elegant than Dunlin, and with longer, more downcurved bill, and longer legs. Adult breeding has chestnut-red head and underparts. Adult non-breeding paler grey than Dunlin, with more distinct supercilium. Juvenile has strong supercilium, buff wash to breast, and buff fringes to upperparts. Flight call is a low, purring *prrriit*. Mainly coastal wetlands, also inland waters.

3 BUFF-BREASTED SANDPIPER *Tryngites subruficollis* 18–20 cm
Adult (3a) and juvenile (3b, 3c, 3d). Vagrant. India and Sri Lanka. Small size and short bill. Face and underparts buff. Upperparts neatly fringed with buff. Short grass, mud and seashore.

4 SPOON-BILLED SANDPIPER *Calidris pygmea* 14–16 cm
Adult breeding (4a), adult non-breeding (4b, 4c) and juvenile (4d). Winter visitor. India, Bangladesh and Sri Lanka. Stint-sized. Spatulate tip to bill. Adult winter has paler grey upperparts than Little Stint, with more pronounced white supercilium, forehead and cheeks; underparts appear cleaner and whiter. Adult breeding more uniform rufous-orange on face and breast compared with Little (recalling Red-necked). Juvenile very similar to Little Stint, but shows more white on face and darker eye-stripe and ear-coverts (masked appearance). Flight call is a quiet *preep*. Intertidal mudflats.

5 BROAD-BILLED SANDPIPER *Limicola falcinellus* 16–18 cm
Adult breeding (5a, 5b), adult non-breeding (5c, 5d) and juvenile (5e, 5f). Winter visitor to coasts. Distinctive shape: stockier than Dunlin with legs set well back and downward-kinked bill. In all plumages, has more prominent supercilium than Dunlin, with 'split' before eye, and contrasting with dark eye-stripe. Adult breeding has bold streaking on neck and breast contrasting with white belly. Non-breeding has dark patch at bend of wing (sometimes obscured by breast feathers) and strong streaking on breast; dark inner wing-coverts show as dark leading edge to wing in flight. Juvenile has buff mantle/scapular lines and streaked breast. Flight call is a buzzing *chrrreet*. Intertidal mudflats and tidal creeks.

6 RUFF *Philomachus pugnax* M 26–32 cm, F 20–25 cm
Male breeding (6a, 6b, 6c), female breeding (6d), adult male non-breeding (6e, 6f), juvenile female (6g, 6h) and juvenile male (6i). Widespread winter visitor and passage migrant. Distinctive shape, with long neck, small head and short, slightly downcurved bill. Non-breeding and juvenile have neatly fringed upperparts, juvenile with buff underparts. Breeding birds typically have black and chestnut markings on upperparts, male with striking ruff. Freshwater wetlands and intertidal mudflats.

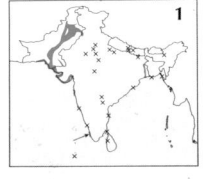 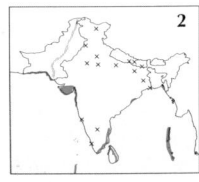 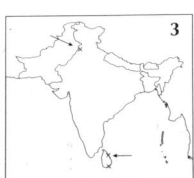 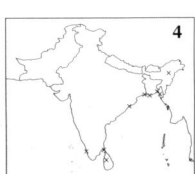

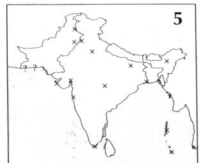 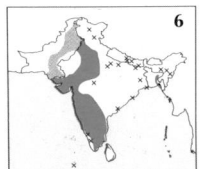

PLATE 47: PHALAROPES, COURSERS AND EURASIAN THICK-KNEE

Maps p. 107

1 RED-NECKED PHALAROPE *Phalaropus lobatus* 18–19 cm
Adult breeding (1a), adult non-breeding (1b, 1c) and juvenile (1d). Winter visitor, mainly in offshore waters of Pakistan, NW and SE India and Sri Lanka. Typically seen swimming. More delicately built than Red Phalarope, with fine bill. Adult breeding has white throat and red stripe down side of grey neck. Adult non-breeding has darker grey upperparts than Red, with white edges to mantle and scapular feathers, forming fairly distinct lines (poorly depicted in plate). Juvenile has dark grey upperparts with orange-buff mantle and scapular lines. Winters at sea.

2 RED PHALAROPE *Phalaropus fulicaria* 20–22 cm
Adult breeding (2a), adult non-breeding (2b, 2c) and juvenile (2d). Vagrant. India. Typically seen swimming. Stockier than Red-necked Phalarope, with stouter bill that is often pale or yellowish at base. Adult breeding has red neck and underparts and white face patch. Adult non-breeding has more uniform and paler grey mantle, scapulars and rump than Red-necked. Juvenile has dark upperparts evenly fringed with buff (lacking mantle and scapular stripes of Red-necked). Habitat not recorded in subcontinent.

3 GREATER PAINTED-SNIPE *Rostratula benghalensis* 25 cm
Adult male (3a), adult female (3b) and juvenile (3c). Widespread resident. Rail-like wader, with broad, rounded wings and longish, downcurved bill. White or buff 'spectacles' and 'braces'. Adult female has maroon head and neck and dark greenish wing-coverts. Adult male and juvenile duller, and have buff spotting on wing-coverts. Freshwater marshes, vegetated pools and mangroves.

4 JERDON'S COURSER *Rhinoptilus bitorquatus* 27 cm
Adult (4a, 4b). Resident. Andhra Pradesh. Huge eye, and short yellow bill with black tip. Broad supercilium, and brown and white bands across breast. Thin scrub forest in rocky foothills.

5 CREAM-COLOURED COURSER *Cursorius cursor* 21–24 cm
Adult (5a, 5b) and juvenile (5c). Resident and winter visitor. Pakistan and NW India. Pale sandy upperparts and underparts. Adult has sandy-rufous forehead, grey nape and pale lores. Juvenile has buffish crown and dark scaling on upperparts. Sand dunes and stony desert.

6 INDIAN COURSER *Cursorius coromandelicus* 23 cm
Adult (6a, 6b). Widespread resident in plains. Grey-brown upperparts and orange underparts, with dark belly, chestnut crown, and dark eye-stripe. In flight, shows white band across uppertail-coverts, and has broad, rounded wings. Juvenile has brown barring on chestnut-brown underparts. Open dry country and dry river beds.

7 EURASIAN THICK-KNEE *Burhinus oedicnemus* 40–44 cm
Adult (7a, 7b, 7c) and juvenile (7d). Widespread resident. Sandy-brown and streaked. Short yellow-and-black bill, striking yellow eye, and long yellow legs. Desert, stony hills, open dry forest and fields.

PLATE 48: MISCELLANEOUS WADERS, JACANAS   Maps p. 107

1 EURASIAN OYSTERCATCHER *Haematopus ostralegus* 40–46 cm
Adult breeding (1a, 1b) and non-breeding (1c). Winter visitor to coasts. Black and white, with broad white wing-bar. Bill reddish. White collar in non-breeding plumage. Sandy and rocky coasts, and coral reefs.

2 IBISBILL *Ibidorhyncha struthersii* 38–41 cm
Adult (2a, 2b) and juvenile (2c). Resident. Himalayas. Adult has black face, downcurved dark red bill, and black and white breast-bands. Juvenile has brownish upperparts with buff fringes, faint breast-band, and dull legs and bill. Mountain streams and rivers with shingle beds.

3 BLACK-WINGED STILT *Himantopus himantopus* 35–40 cm
Adult (3a, 3b) and immature (3c). Widespread resident. Slender appearance, long pink-ish legs, and fine straight bill. Upperwing black and legs extend a long way behind tail in flight. Juvenile has browner upperparts with buff fringes. Freshwater wetlands, brackish marshes and saltpans.

4 PIED AVOCET *Recurvirostra avosetta* 42–45 cm
Adult (4a, 4b) and juvenile (4c). Breeds in Pakistan and Kutch; widespread winter visitor and passage migrant. Upward kink to black bill. Distinctive black-and-white patterning. Juvenile has brown and buff mottling on mantle and scapulars. Alkaline and brackish ponds, and coastal wetlands.

5 CRAB-PLOVER *Dromas ardeola* 38–41 cm
Adult (5a, 5b) and juvenile (5c). Winter visitor to coasts; breeds in Sri Lanka. Black-and-white plumage, with stout black bill and very long blue-grey legs. Juvenile like washed-out version of adult. Intertidal mudflats, coral reefs and coastal rocks.

6 PHEASANT-TAILED JACANA *Hydrophasianus chirurgus* 31 cm
Adult breeding (6a, 6b) and non-breeding (6c). Widespread resident. Extensive white on upperwing, and white underwing. Yellowish patch on sides of neck. Adult breeding has brown underparts and long tail. Adult non-breeding and juvenile have white underparts, with dark line down side of neck and dark breast-band (which are too distinct in plate). Freshwater wetlands.

7 BRONZE-WINGED JACANA *Metopidius indicus* 28–31 cm
Adult (7a, 7b) and immature (7c). Widespread resident; largely absent from Pakistan and Sri Lanka. Dark upperwing and underwing. Adult has white supercilium, bronze-green upperparts, and blackish underparts. Juvenile has orange-buff wash on breast, short white supercilium, and yellowish bill. Freshwater wetlands.

8 GREAT THICK-KNEE *Esacus recurvirostris* 49–54 cm
Adult (8a, 8b). Widespread resident. Upturned black-and-yellow bill, and white forehead and 'spectacles'. In flight, shows grey mid-wing panel and black secondaries. Stony banks of larger rivers and lakes; coastal wetlands.

9 BEACH THICK-KNEE *Esacus neglectus* 53–57 cm
Adult (9a, 9b). Resident. Andamans. Stouter and straighter bill than Great Thick-knee. Forehead and lores mainly black. In flight, shows grey secondaries and white inner primaries. Sandy and muddy shores and coral reefs.

PLATE 49: PRATINCOLES AND PLOVERS

1 **COLLARED PRATINCOLE** *Glareola pratincola* 16–19 cm
Adult breeding (1a, 1b, 1c), adult non-breeding (1d) and juvenile (1e). Breeds in Pakistan; winter visitor to India and Sri Lanka. White trailing edge to secondaries (although this can be difficult to see). Pronounced fork to tail, with tail-tip reaching tips of closed wings on adult at rest. Juvenile has shorter outer tail feathers, and upperpart feathers are fringed with buff with dark subterminal marks; white trailing edge is best feature from juvenile Oriental. Dry bare ground around wetlands.

2 **ORIENTAL PRATINCOLE** *Glareola maldivarum* 23–24 cm
Adult breeding (2a, 2b, 2c), adult non-breeding (2d) and juvenile (2e). Widespread resident; no recent records for Pakistan. Lacks white trailing edge to secondaries. Only shallow tail-fork, tail-tip falling well short of wing-tip at rest. Often with strong peach-orange wash on underparts in breeding plumage. Adult breeding has cream throat bordered by black gorget; with gorget of faint streaking in non-breeding plumage (these features are also shown by Collared). Dry bare ground around wetlands, and lowland fields.

3 **SMALL PRATINCOLE** *Glareola lactea* 16–19 cm
Adult breeding (3a, 3b, 3c) and non-breeding (3d). Widespread resident. Small size, with sandy-grey coloration, and square-ended tail (or with shallow fork). White panel across secondaries, blackish underwing-coverts and black tail band in flight. Adult breeding has black lores and buff wash to throat; non-breeding lacks these features and has streaked throat. Juvenile has indistinct buff fringes and brown subterminal marks to upperparts. Large rivers and lakes with sand or shingle banks.

4 **EUROPEAN GOLDEN PLOVER** *Pluvialis apricaria* 26–29 cm
Adult breeding (4a, 4b) and non-breeding (4c, 4d). Vagrant. Pakistan and India. Stockier than Pacific Golden, with shorter and stouter bill and shorter legs. Underwing-coverts and axillaries largely white. In flight, toes do not project beyond tail (noticeable projection on Pacific). In non-breeding plumage, supercilium is usually less distinct and is rather plain-faced. Grassland and mud on lakeshores and in estuaries.

5 **PACIFIC GOLDEN PLOVER** *Pluvialis fulva* 23–26 cm
Adult breeding (5a, 5b), adult non-breeding (5c, 5d). Widespread winter visitor. Golden-yellow markings on upperparts, and dusky grey underwing-coverts and axillaries. Slimmer-bodied, longer-necked and longer-legged than Grey Plover, and with narrower white wing-bar and dark rump. Mudbanks of wetlands, ploughed fields and grassland.

6 **GREY PLOVER** *Pluvialis squatarola* 27–30 cm
Adult breeding (6a), adult non-breeding (6b, 6c, 6d) and juvenile (6e). Winter visitor, mainly to coasts. White underwing, and black axillaries. Stockier, with stouter bill and shorter legs, than Pacific Golden. Whitish rump and prominent white wing-bar. Has extensive white spangling to upperparts in breeding plumage; upperparts mainly grey in non-breeding (in all plumages lacking golden spangling of Pacific Golden). Sandy shores, mudflats and tidal creeks.

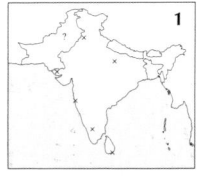 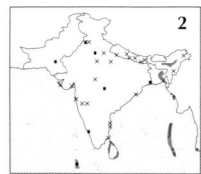 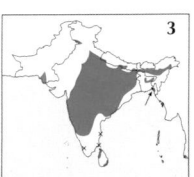 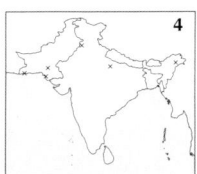

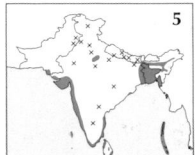 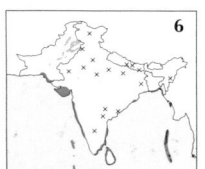

PLATE 50: PLOVERS Maps p. 128

1 COMMON RINGED PLOVER *Charadrius hiaticula* 18–20 cm
Adult breeding (1a) and non-breeding (1b, 1c). Widespread winter visitor. Prominent breast-band and white hindcollar. Prominent wing-bar in flight. Adult breeding has orange legs and bill-base (duller in non-breeding; more olive-yellow in juvenile). Non-breeding and juvenile have prominent whitish supercilium and forehead compared with Little Ringed. Flight call is a soft *too-li*, or *too weep* when alarmed. Mudbanks of freshwater and coastal wetlands.

2 LONG-BILLED PLOVER *Charadrius placidus* 19–21 cm
Adult breeding (2a) and non-breeding (2b, 2c). Winter visitor, mainly to N subcontinent; unrecorded in Pakistan. Like a large Little Ringed, but has longer tail with clearer dark subterminal bar, and more prominent white wing-bar; ear-coverts never black, and has less distinct eye-ring than Little Ringed. White forehead and supercilium more prominent in non-breeding compared with Little Ringed. Flight call is a clear *piwee*. Shingle banks of large rivers.

3 LITTLE RINGED PLOVER *Charadrius dubius* 14–17 cm
Adult breeding (3a) and non-breeding (3b, 3c). Widespread resident and winter visitor. Small size, elongated and small-headed appearance, and uniform upperwing with only a very narrow wing-bar. Legs yellowish or pinkish. Adult breeding has striking yellow eye-ring. Adult non-breeding and juvenile have less distinct head pattern. Flight call is a descending *pee-oo* or short *peeu*. Freshwater and coastal wetlands.

4 KENTISH PLOVER *Charadrius alexandrinus* 15–17 cm
Adult male breeding (4a) and non-breeding (4b, 4c) *C. a. alexandrinus*; breeding *C. a. seebohmi* (4d). Breeds locally in Pakistan, India and Sri Lanka; widespread winter visitor. Small size and stocky appearance. White hindcollar and usually small, well-defined patches on sides of breast. Male of widespread nominate race has rufous cap and black eye-stripe and forecrown; male *seebohmi*, of Sri Lanka and S India, generally lacks these features, and often has whitish lores. Flight call is a soft *pi..pi..pi*, or a rattling trill. Sandy seashores, sandy banks of freshwater wetlands and saltpans.

5 LESSER SAND PLOVER *Charadrius mongolus* 19–21 cm
Male breeding (5a), female breeding (5b) and adult non-breeding (5c, 5d). Breeds in N Himalayas, India; winters on coasts of subcontinent. Larger and longer-legged than Kentish, lacking white hindcollar. Told from Greater Sand by smaller and stouter bill (with blunt tip), and shorter dark grey or dark greenish legs. In flight, feet do not usually extend beyond tail and white wing-bar is narrower across primaries. Breeding male typically shows full black mask and forehead and more extensive rufous on breast compared with Greater Sand (although variation exists in these characters). Flight call is a hard *chitik* or *chi-chi-chi*. Breeds in Tibetan plateau country; winters on coastal wetlands.

6 GREATER SAND PLOVER *Charadrius leschenaultii* 22–25 cm
Male breeding (6a), female breeding (6b) and adult non-breeding (6c, 6d). Winter visitor to coasts. Larger and lankier than Lesser Sand, with longer and larger bill, usually with pronounced gonys and more pointed tip. Longer legs are paler, with distinct yellowish or greenish tinge. In flight, feet project beyond tail and has broader white wing-bar across primaries. Flight call is a trilling *prrrirt*, softer than that of Lesser. Coastal wetlands.

7 CASPIAN PLOVER *Charadrius asiaticus* 18–20 cm
Male breeding (7a) and adult non-breeding (7b, 7c, 7d). Winter visitor. India, Sri Lanka and Maldives. Slim bill, slender appearance and complete breast-band. White underwing-coverts and greenish or brownish legs best distinctions from Oriental. Breeding male has dark crown and eye-stripe. Mudflats and coast.

8 ORIENTAL PLOVER *Charadrius veredus* 22–25 cm
Male breeding (8a), adult non-breeding (8b, 8c, 8d). Vagrant. India and Sri Lanka. Larger than Caspian, with very long yellowish or pinkish legs. Has brown underwing-coverts. Breeding male has mainly whitish head and neck. Mudflats and coast.

9 BLACK-FRONTED DOTTEREL *Elseyornis melanops* 16–18 cm
Adult breeding. Not to scale. Vagrant. India. Short, black-tipped red bill; black stripe through eye, black breast-band, and purplish scapular patch. Mainly stony beds of rivers and streams.

PLATE 50, p. 126

PLATE 54, p. 136

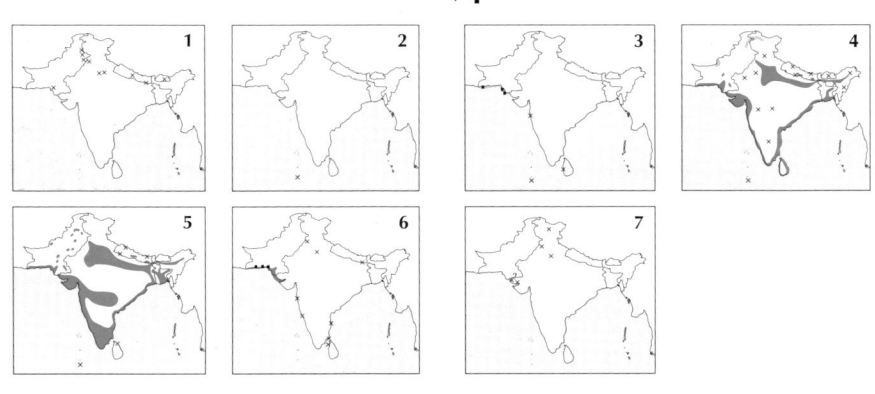

PLATE 68, p. 164

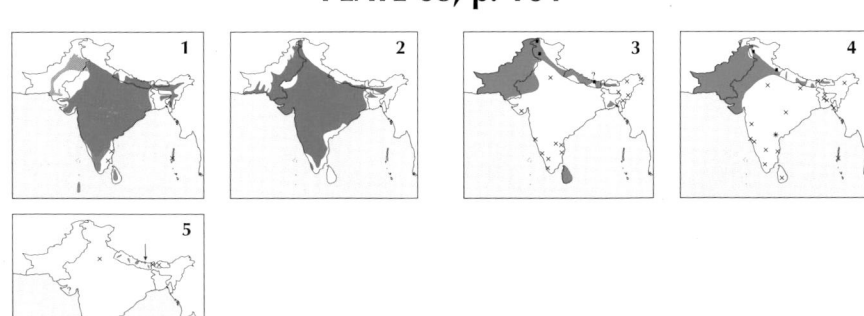

PLATE 71, p. 170

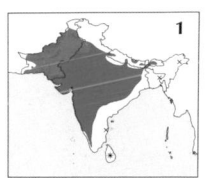

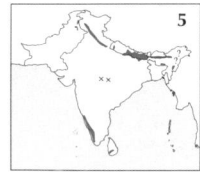

PLATE 88, p. 204

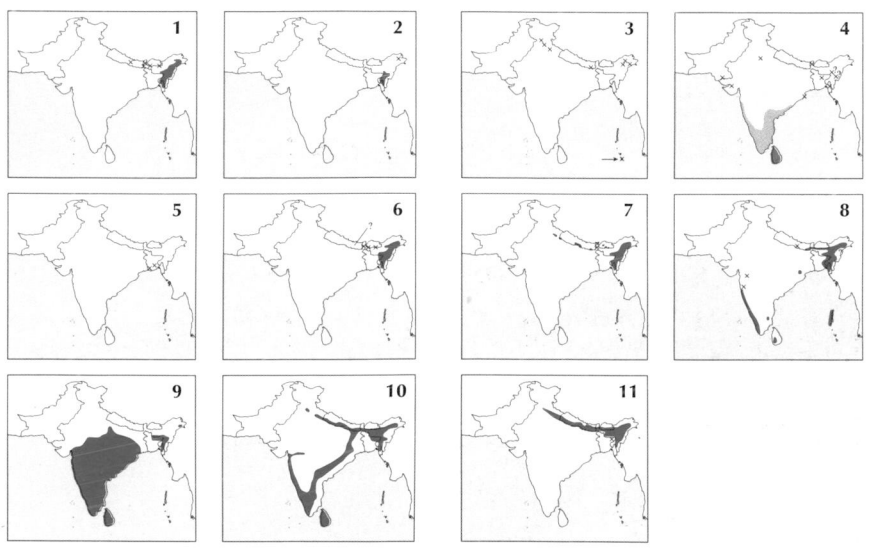

PLATE 51: LAPWINGS

1 NORTHERN LAPWING *Vanellus vanellus* 28–31 cm
Adult male breeding (1a) and adult non-breeding (1b, 1c). Winter visitor to N subcontinent. Black crest, white (or buff) and black face pattern, black breast-band, and dark green upperparts. Has very broad, rounded wing-tips. Shows whitish rump and blackish tail band in flight. Wet grassland, marshes, fallow fields, and wetland edges.

2 YELLOW-WATTLED LAPWING *Vanellus malarbaricus* 26–28 cm
Adult (2a, 2b) and juvenile (2c). Resident. Mainly in India. Yellow wattles and legs. White supercilium, dark cap, and brown breast-band. Open dry ground.

3 RIVER LAPWING *Vanellus duvaucelii* 29–32 cm
Adult (3a, 3b). Resident. N subcontinent; unrecorded in Pakistan. Black cap and throat, grey sides to neck, and black bill and legs. Black patch on belly. Mainly sandbanks and shingle banks of rivers, also estuaries.

4 GREY-HEADED LAPWING *Vanellus cinereus* 34–37 cm
Adult non-breeding (4a, 4b) and juvenile (4c). Winter visitor. Nepal, mainly NE India, and Bangladesh. Yellow bill with black tip, and yellow legs. Grey head, neck and breast, latter with diffuse black border, and black tail-band. Secondaries are white. River banks, marshes and wet fields.

5 RED-WATTLED LAPWING *Vanellus indicus* 32–35 cm
Adult (5a) and juvenile (5b) *V. i. indicus*; **adult** *V. i. atronuchalis* **(5c, 5d).** Widespread resident. Black cap and breast, red bill with black tip, and yellow legs. *V. i. atronuchalis*, of E India, has black head, neck and breast, with white patch on ear-coverts. Open flat ground near water.

6 SOCIABLE LAPWING *Vanellus gregarius* 27–30 cm
Adult breeding (6a, 6b) and non-breeding (6c). Winter visitor, now mainly to Pakistan and N and NW India. Dark cap, with white supercilia which join at nape. Adult breeding has yellow wash to sides of head, and black-and-maroon patch on belly. Non-breeding and immature have duller head pattern, white belly and streaked breast. Dry fallow fields and scrub desert.

7 WHITE-TAILED LAPWING *Vanellus leucurus* 26–29 cm
Adult (7a, 7b) and juvenile (7c). Breeds in Baluchistan; winters in N subcontinent. Blackish bill, and very long yellow legs. Plain head. Tail all white, lacking black band of other *Vanellus* plovers. Freshwater marshes and marshy lake edges.

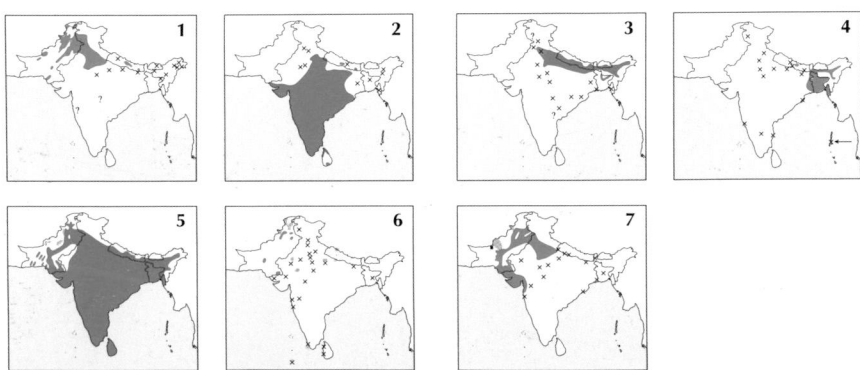

PLATE 52: SKUAS

1 BROWN SKUA *Catharacta antarctica* 63 cm
Adult (1a) and juvenile (1b). Visitor. India, Sri Lanka and Maldives. Larger and more powerful than South Polar, with broader-based wings and larger bill. Usually darker, lacking contrast between pale head and underbody and darker upperbody; can be very similar to South Polar in general colour and appearance, but upperparts of adult are more heavily and irregularly splashed with pale markings. Juvenile warmer, more rufous-brown, in coloration, and upperparts more uniform (lacking pronounced pale splashes of adult). Coastal waters.

2 SOUTH POLAR SKUA *Catharacta maccormicki* 53 cm
Adult pale morph (2a), adult intermediate (2b), adult dark morph (2c) and juvenile (2d). Visitor. India, Sri Lanka and Maldives. Slightly smaller and slighter than Brown Skua, with finer bill. Pale morph distinctive: pale sandy-brown head and underbody contrasting with dark brown mantle and upperwing- and underwing-coverts. Dark morph lacks heavy pale streaking/mottling of Brown, and usually has pale forehead, dark cap/head and paler hindneck; uniform (unbarred) underwing-coverts, axillaries and uppertail- and undertail-coverts are best distinctions from dark juvenile Pomarine Jaeger. Intermediates also occur. Juvenile has pale to mid grey head and underparts, and dark grey upperparts. Coastal waters.

3 POMARINE JAEGER *Stercorarius pomarinus* 56 cm
Adult dark morph breeding (3a), adult pale morph breeding (3b), adult pale morph non-breeding (3c), juvenile pale morph (3d) and juvenile dark morph (3e, 3f). Visitor. Pakistan, India and Sri Lanka. Larger and stockier than Parasitic Jaeger, with heavier bill and broader-based wings. Adult breeding has long, broad central tail feathers twisted at end to form swollen tip (although tips can be broken off). Occurs in both pale and dark morphs. Adult non-breeding (pale morph) has indistinct cap, and barring to breast and upper- and undertail-coverts; uniform dark underwing-coverts distinguish it from birds in first- and second-winter plumage. Broader round-tipped central tail feathers best distinction from Parasitic. Juvenile variable, typically dark brown with broad pale barring on uppertail- and undertail-coverts and underwing-coverts; head, neck and underparts never appear rufous-coloured as on some juvenile Parasitic (although others appear virtually identical to Pomarine); note also the second pale crescent at base of primary coverts on underwing on most birds (in addition to pale base to underside of primaries), diffuse vermiculations (never streaking) on nape and neck, and blunt-tipped or almost non-existent projection of central tail feathers (more prominent and pointed in juvenile Parasitic). Coastal waters.

4 PARASITIC JAEGER *Stercorarius parasiticus* 45 cm
Adult dark morph breeding (4a), adult pale morph breeding (4b), adult pale morph non-breeding (4c), juvenile pale morph (4d), juvenile intermediate morph (4e) and juvenile dark morph (4f). Visitor to coasts, mainly Pakistan. Smaller and more lightly built than Pomarine Jaeger, with slimmer bill and narrower-based wings. Adult breeding has pointed tip to elongated central tail feathers. Occurs in both pale and dark morphs. Adult non-breeding is as Pomarine but has more pointed tail-tip. Juvenile more variable than juvenile Pomarine, ranging from grey and buff with heavy barring to completely blackish-brown, and many have rusty-orange to cinnamon-brown cast to head and nape (not found on Pomarine); except for all-dark juveniles, further distinctions from Pomarine are dark streaking on head and neck and pale tips to primaries. Coastal waters.

 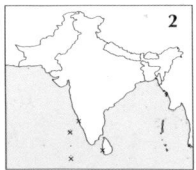 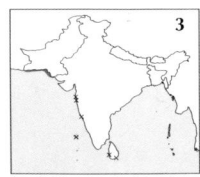 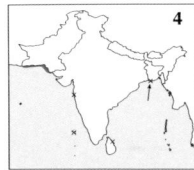

PLATE 53: LARGE GULLS

1 YELLOW-LEGGED GULL *Larus cachinnans* 55–65 cm
Adult non-breeding (1a), 1st-winter (1b) and 2nd-winter (1c) *L. c. cachinnans*; **adult non-breeding** *L. c. barabensis* **(1d).** Widespread winter visitor. Much larger and broader-winged than Mew Gull. Adult has paler grey upperparts than Heuglin's; may show faint streaking on head in non-breeding plumage. Juvenile and first-year told from Heuglin's by paler inner primaries, and much paler underwing-coverts with dark barring; diffusely barred tail, dark greater-covert bar, and lack of distinct mask and patch of mottling on breast help separate it from juvenile Pallas's; brown mottling on mantle best distinction from first-winter Pallas's. Second-year has paler grey mantle than second-year Heuglin's; diffusely barred tail, dark greater-covert bar, and lack of distinct mask help separate it from first-year Pallas's. *L. c. barabensis* may occur in region; adult has darker upperparts than nominate, and usually more black and less white on primaries. Coasts and inland waters.

2 HEUGLIN'S GULL *Larus heuglini* 58–65 cm
Adult non-breeding (2a), 1st-winter (2b) and 2nd-winter (2c) *L. h. taimyrensis*; **adult non-breeding (2d), 1st-winter (2e) and 2nd-winter (2f)** *L. h. heuglini.* Winter visitor, mainly to coasts. Darkest large gull of region. Adult has darker grey upperparts than Yellow-legged; head more heavily streaked in non-breeding plumage than in that species. Juvenile and first-year told from Yellow-legged by dark inner primaries and darker under-wing-coverts, and usually broader dark tail-band; mainly dark tail, dark greater-covert bar, dark underwing, and lack of distinct mask help separate it from juvenile Pallas's; brown mottling on mantle further distinction from first-winter Pallas's. Second-year has darker grey mantle and darker upperwing and underwing than second-year Yellow-legged. *L. h. taimyrensis* bulkier and broader-winged than *L. h. heuglini*, and upperparts of adult are a shade paler. Coasts and inland waters.

3 PALLAS'S GULL *Larus ichthyaetus* 69 cm
Adult breeding (3a), adult non-breeding (3b), 1st-winter (3c), 2nd-winter (3d) and 3rd-summer (3e). Widespread winter visitor. Angular head with gently sloping forehead, crown peaking behind eye. Bill large, 'dark-tipped', with bulging gonys. Adult breeding has black hood with bold white eye-crescents, and yellow bill with red tip and black subterminal band; white tips to primaries contrasting with black subterminal marks, and white wedge-shaped patch on outer wing contrasting with pale grey coverts. Adult non-breeding has largely white head with variable black mask (and white eye-crescents). First-winter has grey mantle and scapulars; told from second-winter Yellow-legged by head pattern (as adult non-breeding), absence of dark greater-covert bar, and more pronounced dark tail-band. Second-winter has largely grey upperwing, with dark lesser-covert bar and extensive black on primaries and primary coverts. Third-winter as adult non-breeding, but with more black on primaries. Coasts and inland lakes and large rivers.

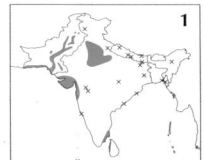  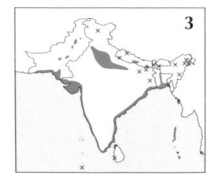

1b

1c

1a

2f

1d

2d

2e

2a

2b

2c

3b

3d

3c

3e

3a

1 MEW GULL *Larus canus* 43 cm
Adult non-breeding (1a), 1st-winter (1b), 1st-summer (1c) and 2nd-winter (1d). Visitor. N subcontinent. Smaller and daintier than Yellow-legged, with shorter and finer bill. Adult has darker grey mantle than Yellow-legged, with more black on wing-tips; bill yellowish-green, with dark subterminal band in non-breeding plumage, and dark iris. Head and hindneck heavily marked in non-breeding (unlike adult non-breeding Yellow-legged). First-winter/first-summer have uniform grey mantle; unbarred greyish greater coverts forming mid-wing panel, narrow black subterminal tail-band, and well-defined dark tip to greyish/pinkish bill best distinctions (in addition to structural differences) from second-year Yellow-legged (which also has grey mantle). Second-winter has black on primary coverts. Lakes and large rivers in region, also coasts elsewhere.

2 WHITE-EYED GULL *Larus leucophthalmus* 39 cm
Adult breeding (2a) and 1st-winter (2b). Vagrant. Maldives. Dark mantle and upperwing, and blackish underwing. Slim, dark bill. Prominent crescents above and below eye. Smaller and slimmer than Sooty. Adult has black hood, and grey mantle and upperwing; bill is reddish. First-year has grey-brown mantle and upperwing, and dark ear-coverts and nape. Fishing ports and harbours.

3 SOOTY GULL *Larus hemprichii* 45 cm
Adult breeding (3a), 1st-winter (3b) and 2nd-winter (3c). Breeds in Pakistan; visitor to coasts elsewhere. Dark upperwing and underwing. Heavy, long, two-toned bill. Adult has brown hood, and greyish-brown mantle and upperwing; bill yellow with black-and-red tip. First-winter and second-winter have rather uniform brownish head and breast, and dark tail-band; bill initially greyish with black tip, becoming similar to adult during second winter. Coasts.

4 BROWN-HEADED GULL *Larus brunnicephalus* 42 cm
Adult breeding (4a), adult non-breeding (4b), 1st-winter (4c) and juvenile (4d). Breeds in Ladakh; widespread winter visitor and passage migrant. Slightly larger than Black-headed, with more rounded wing-tips, and broader bill. Adult has broad black wing-tips (broken by white 'mirrors') and white patch on outer primaries and primary coverts; underside to primaries largely black and underwing-coverts greyer compared with Black-headed; iris pale yellow (rather than brown as in adult Black-headed). In breeding plumage, hood paler brown (especially on face) than Black-headed's. Juvenile and first-winter have broad black wing-tips contrasting with white patch on primary coverts and base of primaries. Coasts and large inland lakes and rivers.

5 BLACK-HEADED GULL *Larus ridibundus* 38 cm
Adult breeding (5a), adult non-breeding (5b) and 1st-winter (5c). Widespread winter visitor and passage migrant. Smaller than Brown-headed Gull, with finer bill and narrower and more pointed wings. Distinctive white 'flash' on primaries/primary coverts of upperwing; black on wing-tips and upperwings is much less extensive than in Brown-headed in all plumages. Bill blackish-red and hood uniform dark brown in breeding plumage. In non-breeding and first-winter plumages, bill tipped black and head largely white with dark ear-covert patch. Coasts and large inland lakes and rivers.

6 SLENDER-BILLED GULL *Larus genei* 43 cm
Adult breeding (6a), adult non-breeding (6b) and 1st-winter (6c). Resident in Pakistan; winter visitor to Nepal, India and Sri Lanka. Head white throughout year, although may show grey ear-covert spot in winter. Gently sloping forehead, longish neck, and larger bill compared with Black-headed. Iris pale, except in juvenile. In first-winter plumage also has paler orange bill (with dark tip smaller or absent) and more extensive white 'flash' on outer primaries compared with Black-headed. Adult has variable pink flush on underparts. Coastal waters.

7 LITTLE GULL *Larus minutus* 27 cm
Adult breeding (7a), adult non-breeding (7b), 1st-winter (7c) and 2nd-winter (7d). Vagrant. India. Small gull, with short legs, blackish bill, and buoyant flight. Adult has dark grey underwing, and lacks black on upperwing. Blackish head in breeding plumage; blackish rear crown and spot behind eye in adult non-breeding and immature plumages. Black M-mark across upperwing when immature. Coastal and inland waters.

PLATE 55: LARGE TERNS

1 **GULL-BILLED TERN** *Gelochelidon nilotica* 35–38 cm
Adult breeding (1a, 1b), adult non-breeding (1c), 1st-winter (1d) and juvenile (1e).
Breeds locally in Pakistan and N India; widespread in winter. Stout, gull-like black bill and more gull-like appearance than Sandwich Tern. Grey rump and tail concolorous with back. Black half-mask in non-breeding and immature plumages (lacking black 'U' across hindcrown of Sandwich). Juvenile less heavily marked on upperparts than juvenile Sandwich. Coastal and freshwater wetlands.

2 **CASPIAN TERN** *Sterna caspia* 47–54 cm
Adult breeding (2a, 2b), adult non-breeding (2c) and juvenile (2d). Breeds in Pakistan, Gujarat and Sri Lanka; widespread in winter. Large size and broad-winged/short-tailed appearance. Huge red bill and black underside to primaries. Upperwing pattern poorly defined in immature plumages (compared with the crested terns). Coastal and large inland waters.

3 **RIVER TERN** *Sterna aurantia* 38–46 cm
Adult breeding (3a, 3b), adult non-breeding (3c), 1st-winter (3d) and juvenile (3e).
Widespread resident; unrecorded in Sri Lanka. Adult breeding has orange-yellow bill, black cap, greyish-white underparts, and long greyish-white outer tail feathers. In non-breeding plumage elongated outer tail feathers are missing, when has blackish mask and mainly grey crown. Large size, stocky appearance and stout yellow bill (with dark tip) help separate adult non-breeding and immature from Black-bellied. Large inland waters.

4 **LESSER CRESTED TERN** *Sterna bengalensis* 35–37 cm
Adult breeding (4a, 4b), adult non-breeding (4c), 1st-winter (4d) and juvenile (4e).
Occurs offshore almost all year; breeds in Pakistan. Orange to orange-yellow bill, smaller and slimmer than Great Crested's, with paler grey upperparts (adult) and usually less boldly patterned upperwing (immatures). Mainly offshore waters; also tidal creeks and harbours.

5 **GREAT CRESTED TERN** *Sterna bergii* 46–49 cm
Adult breeding (5a, 5b), adult non-breeding (5c), 1st-winter (5d) and juvenile (5e) S. b. velox; adult non-breeding S. b. cristata (5f). Resident. Coasts of subcontinent. Lime-green to cold yellow bill. Larger and stockier than Lesser Crested, with darker grey upperparts (adult) or darker and usually more strongly patterned upperwing (immatures). S. b. cristata, with paler grey upperparts, has not been recorded, but may be the race occurring in the Nicobar Islands. Mainly offshore waters; also tidal channels.

6 **SANDWICH TERN** *Sterna sandvicensis* 36–41 cm
Adult breeding (6a, 6b), adult non-breeding (6c) and 1st-winter (6d). Visitor. Mainly W coasts. Slim black bill with yellow tip, and more rakish appearance than Gull-billed. White rump and tail contrast with greyer back. U-shaped black crest in non-breeding and first-winter/first-summer plumages. Juvenile more heavily marked than juvenile Gull-billed, and has black rear crown and nape. Coasts, tidal creeks and open sea.

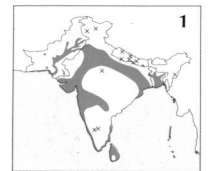 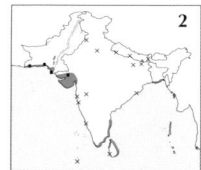 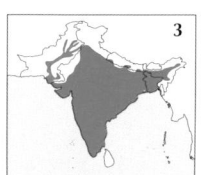 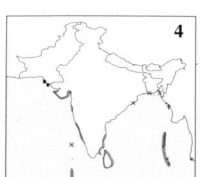

 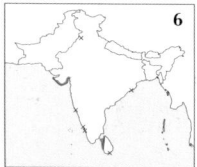

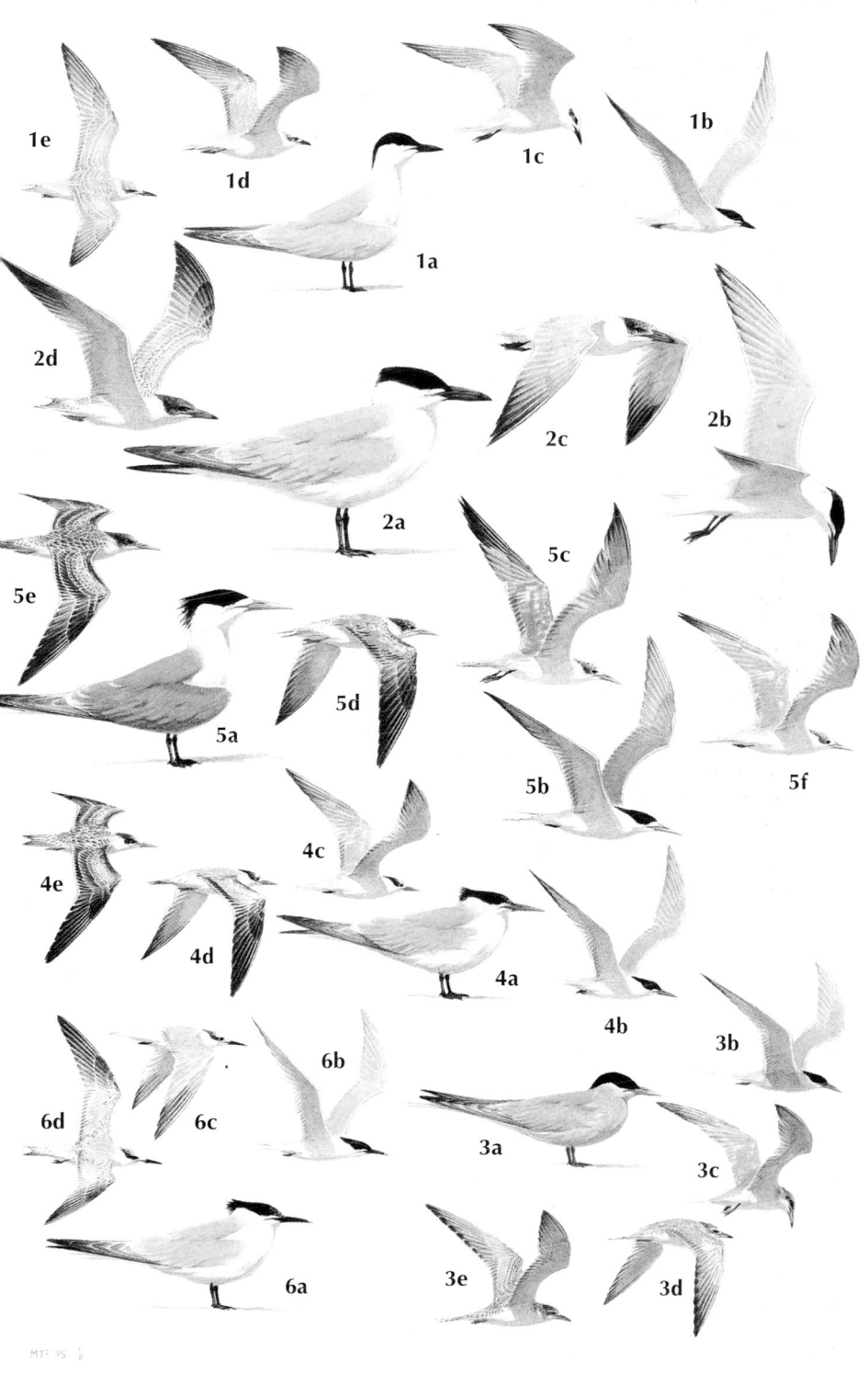

1e
1d
1c
1b
1a
2d
2c
2b
2a
5e
5c
5a
5d
5b
5f
4e
4c
4d
4a
4b
3b
6d
6c
6b
3a
3c
6a
3e
3d

MTF 95

PLATE 56: SMALL TERNS

1 **ROSEATE TERN** *Sterna dougallii* 33–38 cm
Adult breeding (1a, 1b), adult non-breeding (1c), 1st-summer (1d), 1st-winter (1e) and juvenile (1f). Resident and summer visitor. India, Sri Lanka and Maldives. Pale grey upperparts and rump concolorous with back, long tail with white outer feathers, broad white trailing edge to wing, and rather stiff and rapid flight action. In breeding plumage, has more black at bill-tip than Common Tern, and pink flush to underparts. Juvenile has black bill and legs, black subterminal marks to upperpart feathers, and largely black crown. Flight call is different from Common and Black-naped, a disyllabic *chu-vee*. Coastal waters and offshore islands.

2 **BLACK-NAPED TERN** *Sterna sumatrana* 35 cm
Adult breeding (2a), adult non-breeding (2b), 2nd-winter (2c) and juvenile (2d). Resident. Mainly Maldives, Andamans and Nicobars. Adult very pale greyish-white, with black bill and legs, and black mask and nape band. Black nape band not so clear cut in non-breeding plumage. Juvenile has black subterminal marks to upperpart feathers, and head pattern similar to adult but with black streaking on crown; shows less black on crown than juvenile Roseate but is otherwise very similar in plumage. Inshore waters around islands and lagoons.

3 **COMMON TERN** *Sterna hirundo* 31–35 cm
Adult breeding (3a, 3b), adult non-breeding (3c), 1st-winter (3d) and juvenile (3e) S. h. hirundo; adult breeding S. h. longipennis (3f, 3g). Breeds in Ladakh; widespread winter visitor, mainly to coasts. Grey mantle contrasts with white rump and uppertail-coverts (compare with Roseate and White-cheeked), although contrast may be less apparent in non-breeding birds. In breeding plumage, compared with Roseate, has orange-red bill with less black at tip, pale grey wash to underparts, dark trailing edge to underside of primaries and dark outer wedge to upperside, and shorter tail streamers which do not extend beyond tail at rest. In non-breeding and first winter has darker grey upperparts, shorter tail with grey outer webs to feathers, and narrower white trailing edge to wing compared with Roseate. Upperparts, underparts and bill darker in *longipennis*. Juvenile has orange legs and bill-base. Mainly coastal waters, also large inland waters.

4 **ARCTIC TERN** *Sterna paradisaea* 33–35 cm
Adult breeding (4a, 4b), adult non-breeding (4c) and juvenile (4d). Vagrant. India. Uniform translucent primaries, and shorter legs than Common. In breeding plumage, has dark red bill normally lacking black tip. Juvenile has white secondaries which form white trailing edge to wing. Recorded inland in region, but usually found on coasts.

5 **WHITE-CHEEKED TERN** *Sterna repressa* 32–34 cm
Adult breeding (5a, 5b), adult non-breeding (5c) and juvenile (5d). Breeds off Maharashtra coast; offshore waters of Pakistan, W India, Lakshadweep and Maldives in non-breeding season. Smaller than Common, with darker grey upperparts and uniform grey rump and tail concolorous with back; underwing has darker trailing edge and pale central panel. In breeding plumage, darker grey on underparts than Common, and with white cheeks; from adult breeding Whiskered by longer bill, paler grey underparts, and longer tail streamers. Offshore waters.

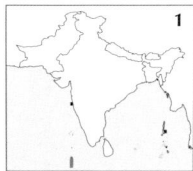 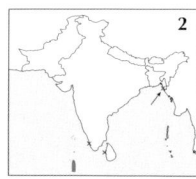 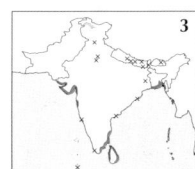 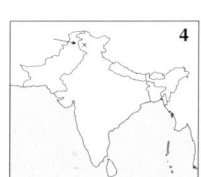

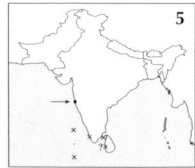

PLATE 57: SMALL TERNS

1 **LITTLE TERN** *Sterna albifrons* 22–24 cm
Adult breeding (1a, 1b), adult non-breeding (1c) and juvenile (1d) *S. a. albifrons*; **adult breeding** *S. a. sinensis* **(1e).** Resident; breeds locally, widespread in non-breeding season. Fast flight with rapid wingbeats, long bill, and narrow-based wings. Adult breeding has white forehead and black-tipped yellow bill. Adult non-breeding and immature have blackish bill, and black mask and nape band. Juvenile has dark subterminal marks to upperpart feathers. *S. a. sinensis*, of W coast of peninsula and Sri Lanka, has longer tail and white primary shafts. Mainly freshwater lakes and rivers, also coastal waters.

2 **SAUNDERS'S TERN** *Sterna saundersi* 23 cm
Adult breeding (2a, 2b) and 1st-winter (2c). Breeds in Pakistan, Gujarat, Sri Lanka and Maldives?; in non-breeding season on W and S Indian coasts. Adult breeding as Little Tern, but more rounded white forehead patch (lacking short white supercilium), and shorter reddish-brown to brown legs (orange on Little), broader black outer edge to primaries, and grey rump and centre of tail (can be grey on some Little, e.g. *S. a. sinensis*). There are no sure features for separating other plumages, although darker grey upperparts including rump and dark bar on secondaries may be useful. Coastal waters.

3 **BLACK-BELLIED TERN** *Sterna acuticauda* 33 cm
Adult breeding (3a, 3b), adult non-breeding (3c) and juvenile (3d). Widespread resident; unrecorded in Sri Lanka. Smaller than River Tern, with orange bill (with variable black tip) in all plumages. Adult breeding has grey breast, black belly and vent, and long outer tail feathers. Adult non-breeding and immatures have white underparts, and black mask and streaking on crown. Breeds on large rivers; also other inland waters in winter.

4 **WHISKERED TERN** *Chlidonias hybridus* 23–25 cm
Adult breeding (4a, 4b), adult non-breeding (4c, 4d), 1st-winter (4e) and juvenile (4f). Breeds in Kashmir and Assam; widespread in winter. In breeding plumage, white cheeks contrast with black cap and grey underparts. In non-breeding and juvenile plumage, from White-winged by larger bill, grey rump concolorous with back and tail, and different head pattern. Compared with White-winged, juvenile generally lacks pronounced dark lesser-covert and secondary bars and has black and buff markings on mantle/scapulars that appear more chequered (more uniformly dark in White-winged). Inland and coastal waters.

5 **WHITE-WINGED TERN** *Chlidonias leucopterus* 20–23 cm
Adult breeding (5a), adult non-breeding (5b, 5c), 1st-summer (5d) and juvenile (5e). Widespread winter visitor. In breeding plumage, black head and body contrast with pale upperwing-coverts, and has black underwing-coverts. In non-breeding and juvenile plumage, smaller bill, whitish rump contrasting with grey tail, and different head pattern are distinctions from Whiskered. Black ear-covert patch is bold and drops below eye, and usually has well-defined black line down nape. Mainly freshwater wetlands, also coasts.

6 **BLACK TERN** *Chlidonias niger* 22–24 cm
Adult breeding (6a), adult non-breeding (6b, 6c), 1st-winter (6d) and juvenile (6e). Passage migrant/vagrant. India and Sri Lanka. In breeding plumage, black head and underbody and uniform grey upperwing and underwing. Non-breeding and juvenile have dark patch on side of breast; from juvenile White-winged by less contrast between mantle and upperwing-coverts and by grey rump and tail. Marshes, pools and lakes.

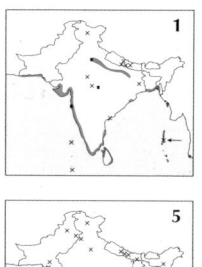
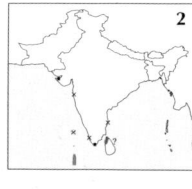
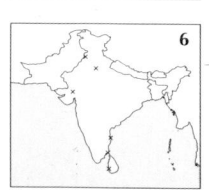
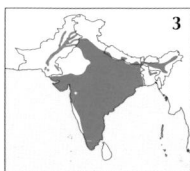
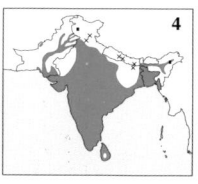

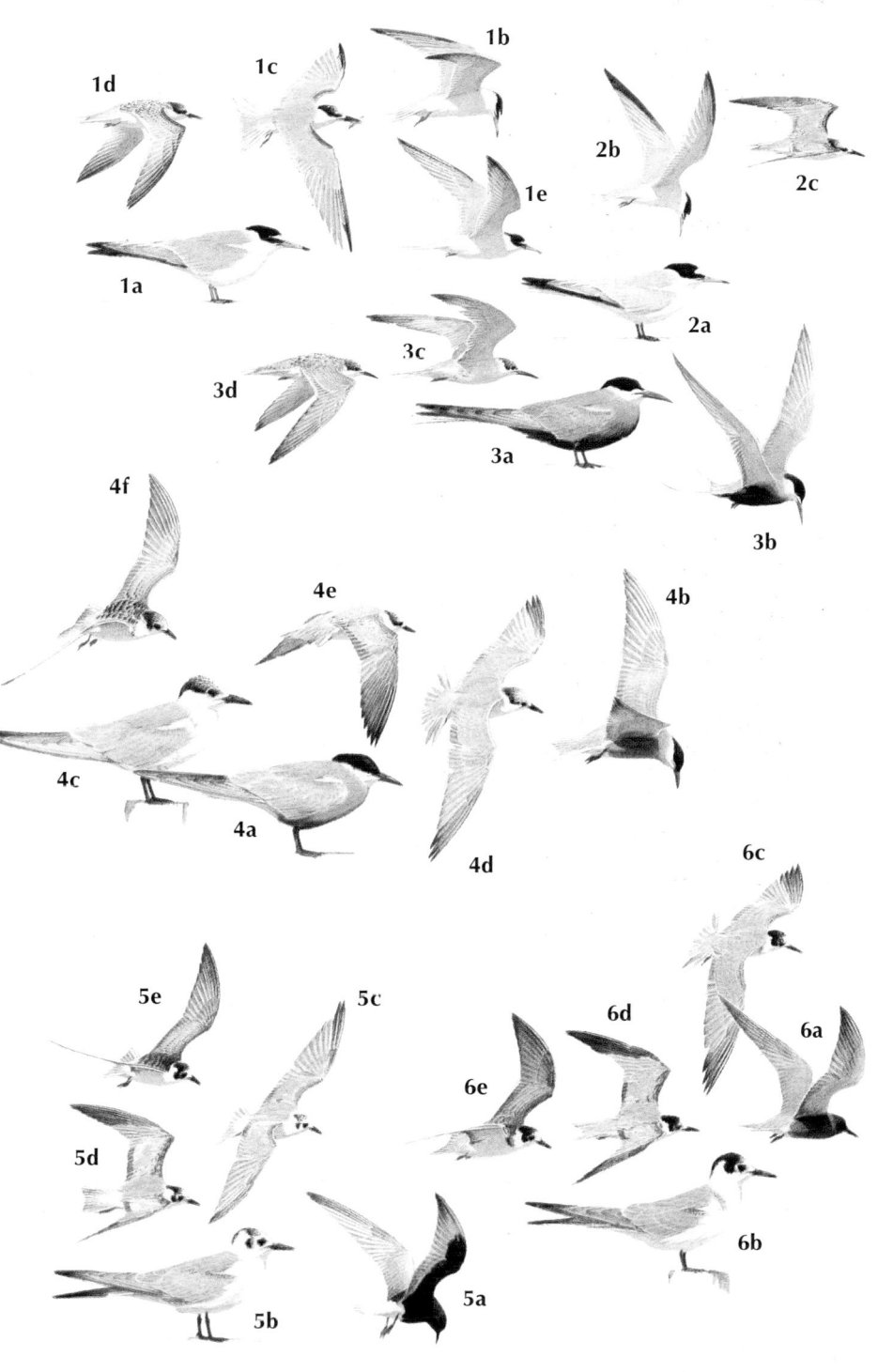

PLATE 58: TERNS, NODDIES AND INDIAN SKIMMER

1 WHITE TERN *Gygis alba* 30 cm
Adult (1a, 1b, 1c) and juvenile (1d). Breeds on Maldives. Adult all white, with beady black eye and upturned bill. Juvenile has buff and brown barring and spotting on upperparts. Pelagic, except when breeding.

2 BRIDLED TERN *Sterna anaethetus* 30–32 cm
Adult breeding (2a, 2b), adult non-breeding (2c) and juvenile (2d, 2e). Breeds off Maharashtra coast, Lakshadweep and Maldives?; offshore waters of Pakistan, W India and Sri Lanka in non-breeding season. Smaller and more elegant than Sooty Tern. In breeding plumage, white forehead patch extends over eye as broad white supercilium, and has brownish-grey mantle and wings. Juvenile has greyish-white crown, dark mask and white forehead and supercilium (shadow-pattern of adult), buffish fringes to mantle and wing-coverts, and brownish patch on side of breast. Mainly offshore waters.

3 SOOTY TERN *Sterna fuscata* 33–36 cm
Adult (3a, 3b), 1st-summer (3c) and juvenile (3d, 3e). Breeds off Maharashtra coast, Lakshadweep and Maldives?; seas adjacent to breeding islands in non-breeding season. Larger and more powerful than Bridled Tern, with blacker upperparts, more extensive blackish underside to primaries (contrasting with white underwing-coverts), and white forehead patch not extending over eye. Juvenile has sooty-black head and breast contrasting with whitish lower belly, bold white spotting on mantle, scapulars and upperwing-coverts, and pale underwing-coverts. Pelagic, except when breeding.

4 BROWN NODDY *Anous stolidus* 42 cm
Adult (4a, 4b, 4c) and juvenile (4d, 4e). Breeds in Lakshadweep and Maldives; also recorded off other coasts. Brown, with coverts paler than flight feathers, pale panel across upperwing-coverts. Bill stouter, proportionately shorter and noticeably downcurved compared with Black and Lesser. Juvenile has browner forehead and crown. Pelagic, except when breeding.

5 BLACK NODDY *Anous minutus* 34 cm
Adult (5a, 5b). Vagrant. India and Sri Lanka. Blacker than Brown Noddy, with all-dark upperwing and underwing. Paler and greyer centre of tail contrasts with darker upperparts. Slim, straight bill longer than head. Pelagic.

6 LESSER NODDY *Anous tenuirostris* 32 cm
Adult (6a, 6b). Breeds on Maldives; vagrant to India and Sri Lanka. Long, slim bill as Black Noddy. Pale greyish lores contrasting with black patch in front of eye. Upperwing-coverts slightly paler than remiges, underwing-coverts concolorous with remiges, and paler and greyer tail centre contrasting with darker upperparts. Pelagic, except when breeding.

7 INDIAN SKIMMER *Rynchops albicollis* 40 cm
Adult (7a) and juvenile (7b). Resident. N and C subcontinent. Adult has large, drooping orange-red bill, black cap, and black mantle and wings contrasting with white underparts. Juvenile has whitish fringes to mantle and upperwing-coverts, diffuse cap, and dull orange bill with black tip. Mainly larger rivers.

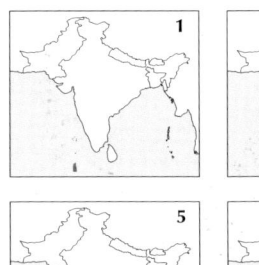 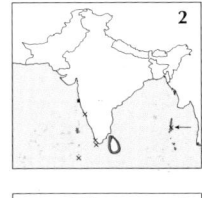 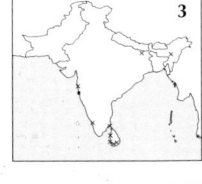 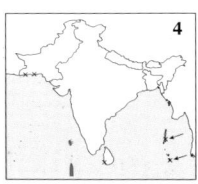

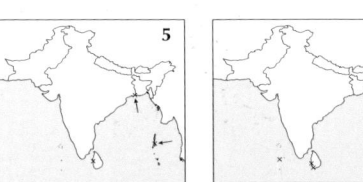 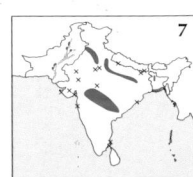

PLATE 59: KITES, BAZAS AND OSPREY

1 OSPREY *Pandion haliaetus* 55–58 cm
Adult (1a, 1b). Breeds in Himalayas; widespread in winter. Long wings, typically angled at carpals, and short tail. Has whitish head with black stripe through eye, white under-body and underwing-coverts, and black carpal patches. Large inland waters and coastal waters.

2 JERDON'S BAZA *Aviceda jerdoni* 46 cm
Adult (2a, 2b) and juvenile (2c, 2d). Resident. E Himalayas, hills of India, Bangladesh and Sri Lanka. Long and erect, white-tipped crest. Long, broad wings (pinched in at base) and fairly long tail. Pale rufous head, indistinct gular stripe, rufous-barred underparts and underwing-coverts, and bold barring across primary tips. At rest, closed wings extend well down tail. Juvenile has whitish head, and narrower dark barring on tail. Broadleaved evergreen forest.

3 BLACK BAZA *Aviceda leuphotes* 33 cm
Adult (3a, 3b, 3c). Resident. Himalayan foothills, NE and S India, Bangladesh and Sri Lanka. Largely black, with long crest, white breast-band, and greyish underside to primaries contrasting with black underwing-coverts. Broadleaved evergreen forest.

4 BLACK-SHOULDERED KITE *Elanus caeruleus* 31–35 cm
Adult (4a, 4b, 4c) and juvenile (4d). Widespread resident; unrecorded in parts of north-west and northeast. Small size. Grey and white with black 'shoulders'. Flight buoyant, with much hovering. Juvenile has brownish-grey upperparts with pale fringes, with less distinct shoulder patch. Grassland with cultivation and open scrub.

5 RED KITE *Milvus milvus* 60–66 cm
Adult (5a, 5b, 5c). Vagrant. Nepal and India. Long and deeply forked rufous-orange tail. Wings long, and usually sharply angled. Rufous underparts and underwing-coverts, whitish head, pale band across upperwing-coverts, and striking whitish patches at base of primaries on underwing. Recorded in region in semi-desert.

6 BLACK KITE *Milvus migrans* 55–68.5 cm
Adult (6a, 6b, 6c) and juvenile (6d, 6e) *M. m. lineatus;* **adult (6f) and juvenile (6g)** *M. m. govinda.* Widespread resident and winter visitor. Shallow tail-fork. Much manoeuvring of arched wings and twisting of tail in flight. Dark rufous-brown, with variable whitish crescent at primary bases on underwing, and pale band across median coverts on upperwing. Juvenile has broad whitish or buffish streaking on head and underparts. *M. m. lineatus* larger than *govinda*, with broader wings and generally more prominent whitish primary patch. Mainly around habitation, also mountains.

7 BRAHMINY KITE *Haliastur indus* 48 cm
Adult (7a, 7b) and juvenile (7c, 7d). Widespread resident; unrecorded in parts of north-west and northeast. Small size and kite-like flight. Wings usually angled at carpals. Tail rounded. Adult mainly chestnut, with white head, neck and breast. Juvenile mainly brown, with pale streaking on head, mantle and breast, large whitish patches at bases of primaries, and cinnamon-brown tail. Inland and coastal waters.

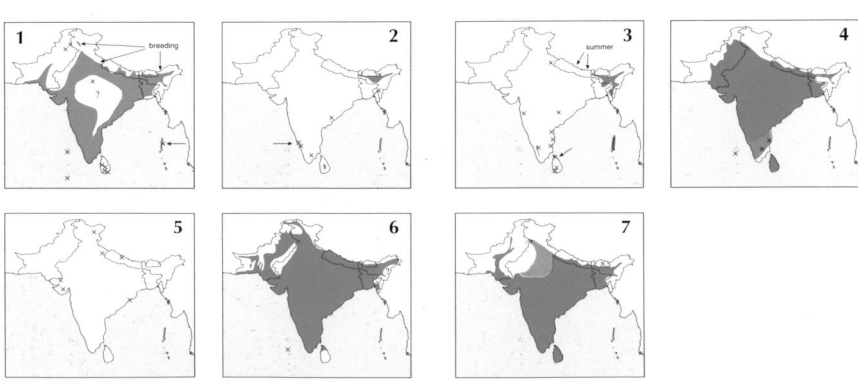

PLATE 60: SEA EAGLES AND FISH EAGLES

1 WHITE-BELLIED SEA EAGLE *Haliaeetus leucogaster* 66–71 cm
Adult (1a, 1b), juvenile (1c, 1d) and immature (1e). Resident. Mainly coasts and offshore islands. Soars and glides with wings pressed forward and in pronounced V. Distinctive shape, with slim head, bulging secondaries, and short wedge-shaped tail. Adult has white head and underparts, grey upperparts, white underwing-coverts contrasting with black remiges, and mainly white tail. Juvenile has pale head, whitish tail with brownish subterminal band and pale wedge on inner primaries. Immatures show mixture of juvenile and adult features. Mainly coastal habitats.

2 PALLAS'S FISH EAGLE *Haliaeetus leucoryphus* 76–84 cm
Adult (2a, 2b), juvenile (2c, 2d) and immature (2e). Resident. N subcontinent. Soars and glides with wings flat. Long, broad wings and protruding head and neck. Adult has pale head and neck, dark brown upperwing and underwing, and mainly white tail with broad black terminal band. Juvenile less bulky, looks slimmer-winged, longer-tailed and smaller-billed than juvenile White-tailed; has dark mask, pale band across underwing-coverts, pale patch on underside of inner primaries, all-dark tail, and pale crescent on uppertail-coverts. Older immatures have whitish tail with mottled band. Mainly larger rivers and lakes, also tidal creeks.

3 WHITE-TAILED EAGLE *Haliaeetus albicilla* 70–90 cm
Adult (3a, 3b), juvenile (3c, 3d) and immature (3e). Widespread winter visitor. Huge, with broad wings, short wedge-shaped tail, and protruding head and neck. Soars and glides with wings level. Adult has large yellow bill, pale head, and white tail. Juvenile has whitish centres to tail feathers, pale patch on axillaries, and variable pale band across underwing-coverts. Bill becomes yellow with age. Coasts, large lakes and rivers.

4 GREY-HEADED FISH EAGLE *Ichthyophaga ichthyaetus* 69–74 cm
Adult (4a, 4b) and juvenile (4c, 4d). Widespread resident; unrecorded in Pakistan. Adult told from Lesser Fish Eagle by largely white tail with broad black subterminal band, darker and browner upperparts, and rufous-brown breast. Juvenile has pale supercilium, boldly streaked head and underparts, diffuse brown tail barring, and whitish underwing with pronounced dark trailing edge. Slow-running waters, lakes and tidal lagoons in wooded country.

5 LESSER FISH EAGLE *Ichthyophaga humilis* 64 cm
Adult (5a, 5b) and juvenile (5c, 5d). Resident. Himalayas. Adult differs from Grey-headed in smaller size, greyish tail, paler grey upperparts, white patch at base of outer primaries on underwing, and greyer underparts. Juvenile browner than adult, with paler underwing and paler base to tail; lacks prominent streaking of juvenile Grey-headed, and has clear-cut white belly and different tail pattern. Forested streams and lakes.

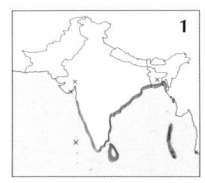 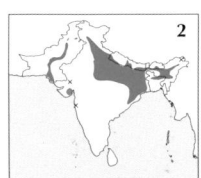 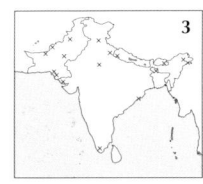 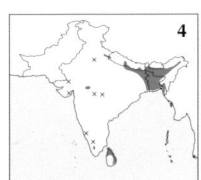

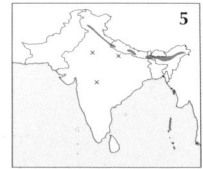

PLATE 61: VULTURES

1 LAMMERGEIER *Gypaetus barbatus* 100–115 cm
Adult (1a, 1b), juvenile (1c) and immature (1d). Resident. Pakistan and Himalayas. Huge size, long and narrow pointed wings, and large wedge-shaped tail. Adult has blackish upperparts, wings and tail, and cream or rufous-orange underparts contrasting with black underwing-coverts. Juvenile has blackish head and neck and grey-brown underparts. Mountains.

2 EGYPTIAN VULTURE *Neophron percnopterus* 60–70 cm
Adult (2a, 2b, 2c), immature (2d, 2e) and juvenile (2f). Resident. Widespread in Pakistan, Nepal and India, except the northeast. Small vulture with long, pointed wings, small and pointed head, and wedge-shaped tail. Adult mainly dirty white, with bare yellowish face and black flight feathers. Juvenile blackish-brown with bare grey face. With maturity, tail, body and wing-coverts become whiter and face yellower. Around habitation.

3 WHITE-RUMPED VULTURE *Gyps bengalensis* 75–85 cm
Adult (3a, 3b, 3c) and juvenile (3d, 3e, 3f). Widespread resident; unrecorded in Sri Lanka. Smallest of the *Gyps* vultures. Adult mainly blackish, with white rump and back, and white underwing-coverts. Key features of juvenile are dark brown coloration, streaking on underparts and upperwing-coverts, dark rump and back, whitish head and neck, and all-dark bill: in flight, underbody and lesser underwing-coverts distinctly darker than on Long-billed, while whitish panel on underwing narrower than on Eurasian Griffon; similar in coloration to juvenile Himalayan, but much smaller and less heavily built, with narrower-looking wings and shorter tail, underparts less heavily streaked, and lacks prominent streaking on mantle and scapulars. Around habitation.

4 LONG-BILLED VULTURE *Gyps indicus* 80–95 cm
Adult (4a, 4b, 4c) and juvenile (4d, 4e) *G. i. indicus*; adult *G. i. tenuirostris* (4f). Widespread resident; unrecorded in Sri Lanka. Adult has pale sandy-brown body and upperwing-coverts, blackish head and neck, white downy ruff, comparatively slim bill, and pale cere, and lacks pale streaking on underparts; in flight, lacks broad whitish band across median underwing-coverts shown by Eurasian Griffon, and has whiter rump and back. Much smaller and less heavily built than Himalayan Griffon, with slimmer bill. Juvenile has blackish bill (yellowish/greenish on adult nominate), blackish cere, feathery buff neck ruff, and some whitish down on head and neck (except in *tenuirostris*): distinguished from juvenile Eurasian Griffon by darker brown upperparts with more pronounced pale streaking, paler and less rufescent underparts with less distinct pale streaking, and pale pinkish culmen (possibly not shown by very young birds, and juvenile *tenuirostris* has all-dark bill); best distinctions from juvenile White-rumped are paler and less clearly streaked underparts, paler underwing-coverts, paler lesser and median upperwing-coverts (owing to heavy streaking), and whitish rump and back. *G. i. tenuirostris*, which occurs north of the Gangetic plain, completely lacks white down on grey head and neck (both adult and immature); bill appears longer and slimmer than on nominate, and adult and sub-adult have blackish bill and cere with pinkish culmen (i.e. as juvenile of nominate). Around habitation.

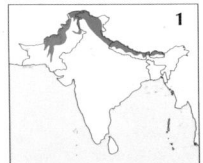 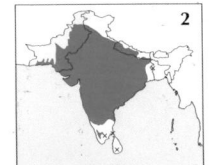 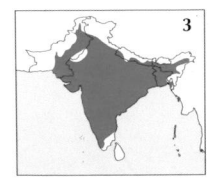 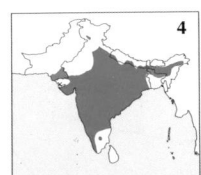

KHEF

PLATE 62: VULTURES

1 HIMALAYAN GRIFFON *Gyps himalayensis* 115–125 cm
Adult (1a, 1b, 1c) and juvenile (1d, 1e, 1f). Resident. Himalayas. Larger than Eurasian Griffon, with broader body and slightly longer tail. Wing-coverts and body pale buffish-white, contrasting strongly with dark flight feathers and tail; underparts lack pronounced streaking; legs and feet pinkish with dark claws, and has yellowish cere. Immature has brown feathered ruff, with bill and cere initially black (yellowish on adult), and has dark brown body and upperwing-coverts boldly and prominently streaked with buff (wing-coverts almost concolorous with flight feathers), and back and rump also dark brown; streaked upperparts and underparts and pronounced white banding across underwing-coverts are best distinctions from Cinereous Vulture; very similar in plumage to juvenile White-rumped Vulture, but much larger and more heavily built, with broader wings and longer tail, underparts more heavily streaked, and streaking on mantle and scapulars. Mountains.

2 EURASIAN GRIFFON *Gyps fulvus* 95–105 cm
Adult (2a, 2b, 2c) and juvenile (2d, 2e, 2f). Resident. Breeds in hills of Pakistan and Himalayas; winters south to plains of Pakistan, N and NW India. Larger than Long-billed, with stouter bill. Key features of adult are blackish cere, whitish head and neck, rufescent-buff upperparts, rufous-brown underparts and thighs with prominent pale streaking, and dark grey legs and feet; rufous-brown underwing-coverts usually show prominent whitish banding (especially across medians). Immature richer rufous-brown on upperparts and upperwing-coverts (with prominent pale streaking) than adult; has rufous-brown feathered neck ruff, more whitish down covering grey head and neck, blackish bill (yellowish on adult), and dark iris (pale yellowish-brown in adult). Semi-desert, dry open plains and hills.

3 CINEREOUS VULTURE *Aegypius monachus* 100–110 cm [BLACK handwritten above]
Adult (3a, 3b) and juvenile (3c). Breeds in Pakistan; winters mainly in Pakistan and Himalayas. Very large vulture with broad, parallel-edged wings. Soars with wings flat. At a distance appears typically uniformly dark, except for pale areas on head and bill. Adult blackish-brown with paler brown ruff; may show paler band across greater underwing-coverts, but underwing darker and more uniform than on *Gyps* species. Juvenile blacker and more uniform than adult. Breeds in mountains; forages in wide range of habitats.

4 RED-HEADED VULTURE *Sarcogyps calvus* 85 cm [KING handwritten above]
Adult (4a, 4b, 4c) and immature (4d, 4e, 4f). Resident. Mainly Nepal and India. Comparatively slim and pointed wings. Adult has bare reddish head and cere, white patches at base of neck and upper thighs, and reddish legs and feet; in flight, greyish-white bases to secondaries show as broad panel. Juvenile has white down on head; pinkish coloration to head and feet, white patch on upper thighs, and whitish undertail-coverts are best features. Open country near habitation, and well-wooded hills.

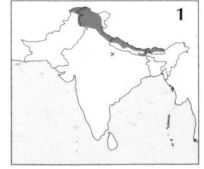 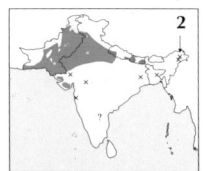 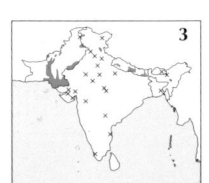 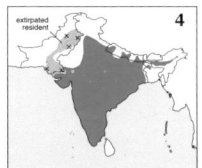

PLATE 63: SHORT-TOED SNAKE EAGLE, SERPENT EAGLES AND BLACK EAGLE

1 SHORT-TOED SNAKE EAGLE *Circaetus gallicus* 62–67 cm
Pale phase (1a, 1b, 1c), dark phase (1d), gliding (1e) and soaring (1f). Resident. Pakistan, S Nepal and India. Long and broad wings, pinched in at base, and rather long tail. Head broad and rounded. Soars with wings flat or slightly raised; frequently hovers. Pattern variable, often with dark head and breast, barred underbody, dark trailing edge to underwing, and broad subterminal tail-band; can be very pale on underbody and underwing. Open dry plains and hills.

2 CRESTED SERPENT EAGLE *Spilornis cheela* 56–74 cm
Adult (2a, 2b) and juvenile (2c, 2d) *S. c. cheela*; adult (2e) *S. c. davisoni*; soaring (2f). Widespread resident; unrecorded in most of northwest and northeast. Broad, rounded wings. Soars with wings held forward and in pronounced V. Adult has broad white bands across wings and tail; hooded appearance at rest, with yellow cere and lores, and white spotting on brown underparts. Juvenile has blackish ear-coverts, yellow cere and lores, whitish head and underparts, narrower barring on tail (than adult), and largely white underwing with fine dark barring and dark trailing edge. *S. c. davisoni*, of Andamans and Nicobars, is small, with buff underparts and underwing-coverts, and narrower white banding on wings and tail. Forest and well-wooded country.

3 SMALL SERPENT EAGLE *Spilornis minimus* 46–48 cm
Adult (3a, 3b) and juvenile (3c, 3d) *S. m. minimus*; adult *S. m. klossi* (3e, 3f). Resident. Nicobars. Very small. *S. m. minimus*, of central Nicobars, has white scaling on black crest, cinnamon-grey underparts with white barring, broad grey central band across uppertail, and broad white central band and some white at base on undertail. Juvenile *minimus* has buff tips to crown, crest and upperparts, and full second pale band across uppertail. *S. m. klossi*, of Great Nicobar, has cinnamon scaling on black crest, blackish gular stripe, plain cinnamon underparts, and narrow black banding on white undertail. Forest near rivers.

4 ANDAMAN SERPENT EAGLE *Spilornis elgini* 50 cm
Adult (4a, 4b) and juvenile (4c, 4d). Resident. S Andaman Is. Adult has dark brown underparts and underwing-coverts with white spotting, brownish-grey banding on uppertail, narrow greyish-white barring on underside of remiges, and two narrow greyish-white bands across undertail. Juvenile paler brown, with white fringes to feathers of crown and nape, dark ear-covert patch, and more prominent banding on underside of wings and tail. Open forest and forest clearings.

5 BLACK EAGLE *Ictinaetus malayensis* 69–81 cm
Adult (5a, 5b, 5e) and juvenile (5c, 5d). Resident. Himalayas, hills of India, Bangladesh and Sri Lanka. Distinctive wing shape, and long tail. Flies with wings raised in V, with primaries upturned. At rest, long wings extend to tip of tail. Adult dark brownish-black, with striking yellow cere and feet; in flight, shows whitish barring on uppertail-coverts, and faint greyish barring on tail and underside of remiges (cf. dark morph of Changeable Hawk Eagle, Plate 71). Juvenile has dark-streaked buffish head, underparts and underwing-coverts. Broadleaved forest in hills and mountains.

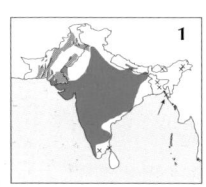 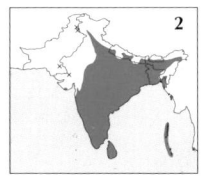 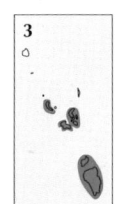 

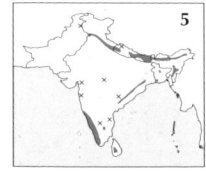

1a · 1b · 1c · 1d · 1e · 1f

2c · 2a · 2b · 2c · 2d · 2e · 2f

3c · 3e · 3a · 3b · 3d · 3f

4a · 4c · 4b · 4d

5c · 5a · 5b · 5d · 5e

Tim Worfolk

PLATE 64: HARRIERS

1 EURASIAN MARSH HARRIER *Circus aeruginosus* 48–58 cm
Adult male (1a, 1b, 1c), adult female (1d, 1e, 1f) and juvenile (1g) *C. a. aeruginosus;* **adult male (1h, 1i, 1j, 1k), immature male (1l), adult female (1m, 1n, 1o) and juvenile (1p, 1q)** *C. a. spilonotus.* Widespread winter visitor; unrecorded in parts of W Pakistan and NE India. Broad-winged and stocky. Glides and soars with wings in noticeable V. Male of widespread *aeruginosus* has pale head, brown mantle and upperwing-coverts contrasting with grey secondaries/inner primaries; female mainly dark brown, except for cream on head and on leading edge of wing. Male *spilonotus*, which has been recorded in NE subcontinent, has blackish or streaked head, and black mantle and median coverts with feathers boldly edged with white; larger and stouter than Pied, with broader wings, and never so cleanly marked. Female *spilonotus* has white uppertail-coverts, dark-barred greyish flight feathers and tail, cream head and breast with dark streaking, and diffuse rufous streaking on underparts. Juvenile *spilonotus* is rather dark, with pale breast-band and pale patch at base of underside of primaries; head usually mainly cream, with variable dark streaking (paler than shown). Reedbeds, marshes, lakes and coastal lagoons.

2 PIED HARRIER *Circus melanoleucos* 41–46.5 cm
Adult male (2a, 2b, 2c), adult female (2d, 2e, 2f), immature male (2g) and juvenile (2h, 2i, 2j). Breeds in Assam; winter visitor mainly to NE subcontinent, Western Ghats and Sri Lanka. Male has black head, upperparts and breast, white underbody and forewing, and black median-covert bar. Female has white uppertail-covert patch, dark-barred greyish remiges and rectrices, pale leading edge to wing, pale underwing, and whitish belly. Juvenile has pale markings on head, rufous-brown underbody, white uppertail-covert patch, and dark underwing with pale patch on primaries. Open grassland and cultivation.

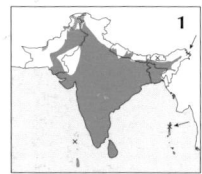 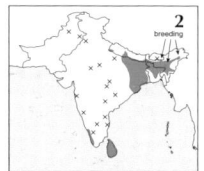

PLATE 65: HARRIERS

1 HEN HARRIER *Circus cyaneus* 44–52 cm
Adult male (1a, 1b, 1c), female (1d, 1e, 1f) and immature male (1g). Winter visitor. Mainly Pakistan, Himalayas and NW India. Comparatively broad-winged and stocky. Male has dark grey upperparts, extensive black wing-tips, lacks black secondary bars, and has dark trailing edge to underwing. Female has broad white band across uppertail-coverts, narrow pale neck-collar, and rather plain head pattern (usually lacking dark ear-covert patch). Juvenile has streaked underparts as female, but with rufous-brown coloration. Open country in plains and foothills.

2 PALLID HARRIER *Circus macrourus* 40–48 cm
Adult male (2a, 2b, 2c), female (2d, 2e, 2f), immature male in flight (2g) and juvenile (2h, 2i). Widespread winter visitor; unrecorded in parts of northeast and W Pakistan. Slim-winged and fine-bodied, with buoyant flight. Folded wings fall short of tail-tip, and legs longer than on Montagu's. Male has pale grey upperparts, dark wedge on primaries, very pale grey head and underbody, and lacks black secondary bars. Immature male may show rusty breast-band and juvenile facial markings. Female has distinctive underwing pattern: pale primaries, irregularly barred and lacking dark trailing edge, contrast with darker secondaries which have pale bands narrower than on female Montagu's and tapering towards body (although first-summer Montagu's more similar in this respect), and lacks prominent barring on axillaries. Typically, female has stronger head pattern than Montagu's, with more pronounced pale collar, dark ear-coverts and dark eye-stripe, and upperside of flight feathers darker and lacking banding; told from female Northern by narrower wings with more pointed hand, stronger head pattern, and patterning of underside of primaries. Juvenile has unstreaked orange-buff underparts and underwing-coverts; on underwing, primaries evenly barred (lacking pronounced dark fingers), without dark trailing edge, and usually with pale crescent at base; head pattern more pronounced than Montagu's, with narrower white supercilium, more extensive dark ear-covert patch, and broader pale collar contrasting strongly with dark neck sides. Open country in plains and foothills.

3 MONTAGU'S HARRIER *Circus pygargus* 43–47 cm
Adult male (3a, 3b, 3c), female (3d, 3e, 3f), immature male (3g) and juvenile (3h, 3i). Widespread winter visitor. Folded wings reach tail-tip, and legs shorter than on Pallid. Male has black band across secondaries, extensive black on underside of primaries, and rufous streaking on belly and underwing-coverts. Female differs from female Pallid in distinctly and evenly barred underside to primaries with dark trailing edge, broader and more pronounced pale bands across secondaries, barring on axillaries, less pronounced head pattern, and distinct dark banding on upperside of remiges. Juvenile has unstreaked rufous underparts and underwing-coverts, and darker secondaries than female; differs from juvenile Pallid in having broad dark fingers and dark trailing edge to hand on underwing, and paler face with smaller dark ear-covert patch and less distinct collar. Open country in plains and foothills.

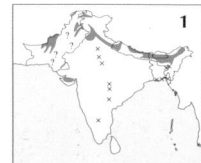 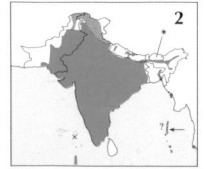 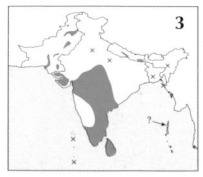

PLATE 66: ACCIPITERS

1 CRESTED GOSHAWK *Accipiter trivirgatus* 30–46 cm
Male (1a, 1b) and juvenile (1c, 1d) *A. t. indicus.* Resident. Mainly Himalayas, NE and SW India, and Sri Lanka. Larger size and crest are best distinctions from Besra. Short and broad wings, pinched in at base. Wing-tips barely extend beyond tail-base at rest. Male has dark grey crown and paler grey ear-coverts, black submoustachial and gular stripes, and rufous-brown streaking on breast and barring on belly and flanks. Female has browner crown and ear-coverts, and browner streaking and barring on underparts. Juvenile has rufous or buffish fringes to crown, crest and nape feathers, streaked ear-coverts, and buff/rufous wash to streaked underparts (barring restricted to lower flanks and thighs). Dense broadleaved tropical and subtropical forest.

2 SHIKRA *Accipiter badius* 30–36 cm
Male (2a, 2b), female (2c, 2d) and juvenile (2e, 2f) *A. b. dussumieri.* Widespread resident, except in parts of northwest. Adults paler than Besra and Eurasian Sparrowhawk. Underwing pale, with fine barring on remiges, and slightly darker wing-tips. Male has pale blue-grey upperparts, indistinct grey gular stripe, fine brownish-orange barring on underparts, unbarred white thighs, and unbarred or only lightly barred central tail feathers. Female has upperparts more brownish-grey. Juvenile has pale brown upperparts, more prominent gular stripe, and streaked underparts; told from juvenile Besra by paler upperparts and narrower tail barring, and from Eurasian Sparrowhawk by streaked underparts. Open woods and groves.

3 NICOBAR SPARROWHAWK *Accipiter butleri* 30–34 cm
Male (3a, 3b) and juvenile (3c, 3d) *A. b. butleri*; juvenile (3e, 3f) from Great Nicobar. Resident. Nicobars. Very short primary projection. Male has pale blue-grey upperparts, mainly whitish underparts and underwing-coverts, indistinct gular stripe, and unbarred tail with narrow diffuse terminal band. Female slightly browner on upperparts, with marginally stronger barring on breast. Juvenile of nominate race has rufous upperparts with dark brown feather centres, rufous-buff underparts with browner streaking, and dark banding on rufous-cinnamon secondaries and tail. The single juvenile specimen from Great Nicobar has much browner and darker upperparts and may represent an undescribed race. Tall trees.

4 CHINESE SPARROWHAWK *Accipiter soloensis* 25–30 cm
Adult (4a, 4b) and juvenile (4c, 4d). Winter visitor. Nicobars. Narrow and pointed wings, with long primary projection at rest. Adult has blue-grey head and upperparts, indistinct grey gular stripe, and rufous-orange breast; distinctive underwing pattern, with unbarred remiges and coverts, blackish wing-tips and dark grey trailing edge. Sub-adults show some dark barring on underside of flight feathers. Juvenile has dark brown upperparts, pronounced dark gular stripe, and rufous-brown spotting and barring on underparts; compared with juvenile Japanese Sparrowhawk, crown is a darker slate-grey than mantle, lacks distinct supercilium, and has distinctive underwing pattern (dark grey wing-tips and trailing edge, largely unmarked greyish-brown to pale rufous coverts). Forest and wooded country.

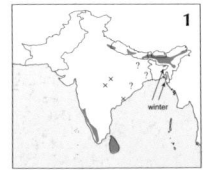 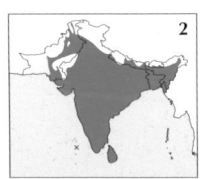 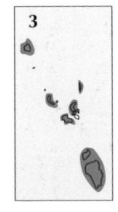 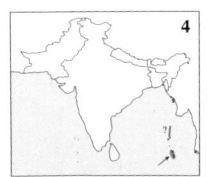

PLATE 67: ACCIPITERS

1 JAPANESE SPARROWHAWK *Accipiter gularis* 25–31.5 cm
Male (1a, 1b), female (1c, 1d) and juvenile (1e, 1f). Winter visitor. Locally in India. Very small. Long primary projection. In all plumages, pale bars on tail generally broader than dark bars (reverse on Besra). Underpart patterning of adults rather different from Besra; juveniles more similar. Male has dark bluish-grey upperparts, pale rufous to pale grey underparts (some with fine grey barring), and dark crimson iris. Female has browner upperparts, whitish underparts with distinct barring, indistinct gular stripe, and yellow iris. Juvenile has brown to rufous streaking and barring on underparts. Probably forest.

2 BESRA *Accipiter virgatus* 29–36 cm
Adult male (2a, 2b), female (2c, 2d) and juvenile (2e, 2f) ***A. v. virgatus.*** Resident. Himalayas, NE and SW India, Bangladesh and Sri Lanka. Small, with short primary projection. Upperparts darker than Shikra (Plate 66), and prominent gular stripe and streaked breast should separate it from Eurasian Sparrowhawk; underwing strongly barred compared with Shikra. In all plumages, resembles Crested Goshawk (Plate 66), but considerably smaller, lacks crest, and has longer and finer legs. Male has dark slate-grey upperparts, broad blackish gular stripe, and bold rufous streaking on breast and barring on belly. Female browner on upperparts, with blackish crown and nape. Juvenile told from juvenile Shikra by darker, richer brown upperparts, broader gular stripe, and broader tail barring. Breeds in dense broadleaved forest; also open wooded country in winter.

3 EURASIAN SPARROWHAWK *Accipiter nisus* 31–36 cm
Male (3a, 3b), female (3c, 3d) and juvenile (3e, 3f) ***A. n. melaschistos.*** Resident and winter visitor. Breeds in Baluchistan and Himalayas; winters in Himalayan foothills and south to S India. Upperparts of adult darker than Shikra (Plate 66), with prominent tail barring, and uniform barring on underparts and absence of prominent gular stripe should separate it from Besra; underwing strongly barred compared with Shikra. Male has dark slate-grey upperparts and reddish-orange barring on underparts. Female dark brown on upperparts, with dark brown barring on underparts. Juvenile has dark brown upperparts and barred underparts. Well-wooded country and open forest.

4 NORTHERN GOSHAWK *Accipiter gentilis* 50–61 cm
Male (4a), female (4b, 4c) and juvenile (4d, 4e). Winter visitor and resident? Mainly Pakistan and Himalayas. Very large, with heavy, deep-chested appearance. Wings comparatively long, with bulging secondaries. Male has grey upperparts (greyer than female Eurasian Sparrowhawk), white supercilium, and finely barred underparts. Female considerably larger, with browner upperparts. Juvenile has heavy streaking on buff-coloured underparts. Forest.

 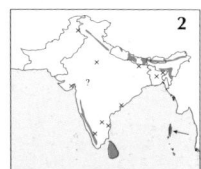 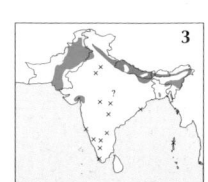 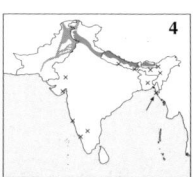

PLATE 68: BUZZARDS AND ORIENTAL HONEY-BUZZARD
Maps p. 128

1 ORIENTAL HONEY-BUZZARD *Pernis ptilorhyncus* 57–60 cm
Male (1a, 1b, 1c), female (1d), juvenile (1e) and soaring (1f). Widespread resident; absent in parts of NW and NE subcontinent and SE India. Wings and tail long and broad, and has narrow neck and small head. Soars with wings flat. Has small crest. Very variable in plumage, with underparts and underwing-coverts ranging from dark brown through rufous to white, and unmarked, streaked or barred; often shows dark moustachial stripe and gular stripe, and gorget of streaking across lower throat. Lacks dark carpal patch. Male has grey face, greyish-brown upperparts, two black tail-bands, usually three black bands across underside of remiges, and dark brown iris. Female has browner face and upperparts, three black tail-bands, four narrower black bands across remiges, and yellow iris. Juvenile has finer and less distinct banding across underside of remiges, three or more tail-bands, and extensive dark tips to primaries; cere yellow (grey on adult) and iris dark. Well-wooded country.

2 WHITE-EYED BUZZARD *Butastur teesa* 43 cm
Adult (2a, 2b, 2c), juvenile (2d, 2e) and soaring (2f). Widespread resident; absent in parts of the northwest, northeast and south. Longish, rather slim wings, long tail, and buzzard-like head. Pale median-covert panel. Flight *Accipiter*-like. Adult has black gular stripe, white nape patch, barred underparts, dark wing-tips, and rufous tail; iris yellow. Juvenile has buffish head and breast streaked with dark brown, with moustachial and throat stripes indistinct or absent; rufous uppertail more strongly barred; iris brown. Dry open country.

3 COMMON BUZZARD *Buteo buteo* 51–56 cm
Adult *B. b. japonicus* (3a, 3b, 3c, 3d); adult *B. b. refectus* (3e, 3f); soaring (3g). Breeds in Himalayas; widespread in winter. Stocky, with broad rounded wings and moderate-length tail. Most compact *Buteo* in region. Plumage variable; some much as Long-legged and Upland. *B. b. japonicus*, a winter visitor, typically has rather pale head and underparts, with variable dark streaking on breast and brown patch on belly/thighs; tail dark-barred grey-brown. *B. b. refectus*, resident in the Himalayas, dark brown to rufous-brown, with variable amounts of white on underparts; tail dull brown with some dark barring, or uniform sandy-brown. *B. b. vulpinus* (not illustrated), a winter visitor, is extremely variable, although usually has rufous tail (and is similar to Long-legged; see that species). Open-country habitats.

4 LONG-LEGGED BUZZARD *Buteo rufinus* 61 cm
Adult (4a, 4b, 4c, 4d), juvenile (4e, 4f) and soaring (4g). Breeds in Himalayas; winters in Pakistan, Himalayas, Assam and Bangladesh. Larger and longer-necked than Common, with longer wings and tail (appears more eagle-like); soars with wings in deeper V. Variable in plumage. Most differ from Common in having combination of paler head and upper breast, rufous-brown lower breast and belly, more uniform rufous underwing-coverts, more extensive black carpal patches, larger pale primary patch on upperwing, and unbarred pale orange uppertail. Rufous and black morphs much as some plumages of Common. Juvenile generally less rufous, with narrower and more diffuse trailing edge to wing, and lightly barred tail which on many is pale greyish-brown; best distinguished from similar-plumaged Common by larger size, different structure, and more prominent carpal patches and dark belly. Breeds in forested hills; winters in open-country habitats.

5 UPLAND BUZZARD *Buteo hemilasius* 71 cm
Adult (5a, 5b, 5c, 5d), juvenile (5e, 5f) and gliding (5g). Breeds in Nepal?; winters in Himalayas and N India. Larger, longer-winged and longer-tailed than Common (appearing more eagle-like); soars with wings in deeper V. Tarsus always at least three-quarters feathered (often entirely feathered; half feathered or less on Common and Long-legged). Plumage variable. 'Classic' pale morph has combination of large white primary patch on upperwing, greyish-white tail (with fine bars towards tip), whitish head and underparts with dark brown streaking, brown thighs forming dark U-shape, and extensive black carpal patches (*japonicus* race of Common can be very similar); never has rufous tail or rufous thighs as in many Long-legged. 'Blackish morph' probably not distinguishable on plumage from those of Common/Long-legged. Juvenile has narrower and more diffuse trailing edge to wing, and more prominently barred tail. Open country in hills and mountains.

6 ROUGH-LEGGED BUZZARD *Buteo lagopus* 50–60 cm
Adult (6a, 6b), juvenile (6c) and gliding (6d). [One published record; confirmation desirable. Long wings and tail. Adult has black tail band, dark belly, and whitish underwing-coverts with large black carpal patches. Juvenile lacks clear-cut black tail-band.]

PLATE 69: AQUILA EAGLES

1 LESSER SPOTTED EAGLE *Aquila pomarina* 60–65 cm
Adult (1a, 1b, 1c), juvenile (1d, 1e, 1f), immature (1g) and gliding (1h). Resident. N subcontinent; largely unrecorded in Pakistan. Stocky, medium-sized eagle with rather short and broad wings, buzzard-like head and smallish bill; rather short tail. Wings angled down at carpals when gliding and soaring. Told from Greater Spotted by slightly narrower wings and longer tail, pale buff-brown upperwing- and underwing-coverts contrasting with dark flight feathers (although some Greater Spotted can be similar), and double whitish carpal crescent on underwing. In some plumages can resemble Steppe (Plate 70), but shows prominent double whitish carpal crescents, lacks distinct barring on underside of primaries, and has dark chin; also smaller, with less protruding head and smaller bill, shorter wings with less deep-fingered tips, and smaller trousers exposing long, thin-looking feathered tarsus. Wooded areas in lowlands.

2 GREATER SPOTTED EAGLE *Aquila clanga* 65–72 cm
Adult (2a, 2b, 2c), juvenile (2d, 2e, 2f), juvenile '*fulvescens*' (2g, 2h) and gliding (2i). Breeds in NW subcontinent; winters mainly in N subcontinent. Medium-sized eagle with rather short and broad wings, stocky head, and short tail. Wings distinctly angled down at carpals when gliding, almost flat when soaring. Heavier than Lesser Spotted, with broader wings and squarer hand, and shorter tail; dark brown upperwing- and underwing-coverts show little contrast with flight feathers (although some can be similar to Lesser Spotted), and usually lacks second whitish carpal crescent on underwing. Compared with Steppe Eagle (Plate 70), has less protruding head in flight, with shorter wings and less deep-fingered wing-tips; at rest, trousers less baggy, and bill smaller with rounded (rather than elongated) nostril and shorter gape; lacks adult Steppe's barring on underside of flight and tail feathers, dark trailing edge to wing, and has dark chin. Pale variant '*fulvescens*' distinguished from juvenile Imperial Eagle (Plate 70) by structural differences, lack of prominent pale wedge on inner primaries on underwing, and unstreaked underparts. Juvenile has bold whitish tips to dark brown coverts. Mainly inland waters.

3 GOLDEN EAGLE *Aquila chrysaetos* 75–88 cm
Adult (3a, 3b, 3c), juvenile (3d, 3e), sub-adult (3f) and gliding (3g). Resident. Baluchistan and Himalayas. Large, with long and broad wings (with pronounced curve to trailing edge), long tail, and distinctly protruding head and neck. Wings clearly pressed forward and raised (with upturned fingers) in pronounced V when soaring. Adult has pale panel across upperwing-coverts, gold crown and nape, and two-toned tail. Juvenile has white base to tail and white patch at base of flight feathers. Rugged mountains above treeline.

 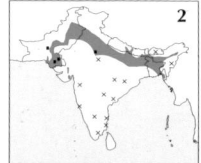 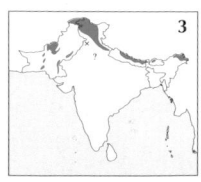

PLATE 70: AQUILA EAGLES

1 TAWNY EAGLE *Aquila rapax* 63–71 cm
Adult (1a, 1b, 1c, 1d, 1e), juvenile (1f, 1g), sub-adult (1h) and gliding (1i). Widespread resident; unrecorded in the northeast and Sri Lanka. Compared with Steppe, hand of wing does not appear so long and broad, tail slightly shorter, and looks smaller and weaker at rest; gape-line ends level with centre of eye (extends to rear of eye in Steppe), and adult has yellowish iris. Differs from the spotted eagles (Plate 69) in more protruding head and neck in flight, baggy trousers, yellow iris, and oval nostril. Adult extremely variable, from dark brown through rufous to pale cream, and unstreaked or streaked with rufous or dark brown. Dark morph very similar to adult Steppe (which shows much less variation); distinctions include less pronounced barring and dark trailing edge on underwing, dark nape, and dark throat. Rufous to pale cream Tawny uniformly pale from uppertail-coverts to back, with undertail-coverts same colour as belly (contrast often apparent on similar species). Pale adults also lack prominent whitish trailing edge to wing, tip to tail and greater-covert bar (present on immatures of similar species). Characteristic, if present, is distinct pale inner-primary wedge on underwing. Juvenile also variable, with narrow white tips to unbarred secondaries; otherwise as similar-plumaged adult. Many (possibly all) non-dark Tawny have distinctive immature/sub-adult plumage: dark throat and breast contrasting with pale belly, and can show dark banding across underwing-coverts; whole head and breast may be dark. Desert, semi-desert and cultivation.

2 STEPPE EAGLE *Aquila nipalensis* 76–80 cm
Adult (2a, 2b, 2c), juvenile (2d, 2e, 2f), immature (2g, 2h) and gliding (2i). Widespread winter visitor to N and C subcontinent. Broader and longer wings than Greater and Lesser Spotted (Plate 69), with more pronounced and spread fingers, and more protruding head and neck; wings flatter when soaring, and less distinctly angled down at carpals when gliding. When perched, clearly bigger and heavier, with heavier bill and baggy trousers. Adult separated from adult spotted eagles by underwing pattern (dark trailing edge, distinct barring on remiges, indistinct/non-existent pale crescents in carpal region), pale rufous nape patch and pale chin. Juvenile has broad white bar across underwing, double white bar on upperwing, and white crescent across uppertail-coverts; prominence of bars on upperwing and underwing much reduced on older immatures, and such birds are very similar to some Lesser Spotted (see that species). Wooded hills, open country and lakes.

3 IMPERIAL EAGLE *Aquila heliaca* 72–83 cm
Adult (3a, 3b, 3c), juvenile (3d, 3e, 3f), sub-adult (3g, 3h) and gliding (3i). Winter visitor. Mainly Pakistan and NW India. Large, stout-bodied eagle with long and broad wings, longish tail, and distinctly protruding head and neck. Wings flat when soaring and gliding. Adult has almost uniform upperwing, small white scapular patches, golden-buff crown and nape, and two-toned tail. Juvenile has pronounced curve to trailing edge of wing, pale wedge on inner primaries, streaked buffish body and wing-coverts, uniform pale rump and back (lacking distinct pale crescent shown by other species, except Tawny), and white tips to median and greater upperwing-coverts. Open country in plains, deserts and around wetlands.

 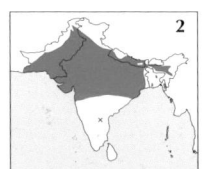 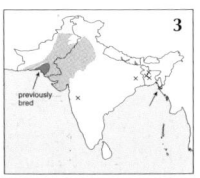

Tim Worfolk

1 BONELLI'S EAGLE *Hieraaetus fasciatus* 65–72 cm
Adult (1a, 1b, 1c), juvenile (1d, 1e, 1f) and soaring (1g). Widespread resident; unrecorded in most of northeast, east and Sri Lanka. Medium-sized eagle with long and broad wings, distinctly protruding head, and long square-ended tail. Soars with wings flat. Adult has pale underbody and forewing, blackish band along underwing-coverts, whitish patch on mantle, and pale greyish tail with broad dark terminal band. Juvenile has ginger-buff to reddish-brown underbody and underwing-coverts (with variable dark band along greater underwing-coverts), uniform upperwing, and pale crescent on uppertail-coverts and patch on back. Well-wooded country in plains and hills.

2 BOOTED EAGLE *Hieraaetus pennatus* 45–53 cm
Pale morph (2a, 2b, 2c), dark morph (2d, 2e) and soaring (2f). Breeds in Baluchistan and Himalayas; widespread in winter, but unrecorded in parts of northwest, northeast and east. Smallish eagle with long wings and long square-ended tail. Glides and soars with wings flat or slightly angled down at carpal. Always shows white shoulder patches, pale median-covert panel, pale wedge on inner primaries, white crescent on uppertail-coverts, and greyish undertail with darker centre and tip. Head, body and wing-coverts whitish, brown or rufous respectively in pale, dark and rufous morphs.

3 RUFOUS-BELLIED EAGLE *Hieraaetus kienerii* 53–61 cm
Adult (3a, 3b), juvenile (3c, 3d) and soaring (3e). Resident. Himalayas, hills of NE and SW India, Bangladesh and Sri Lanka. Smallish, with buzzard-shaped wings and tail. At rest, wing-tips extend well down tail. Glides and soars with wings flat. Adult has blackish hood and upperparts, white throat and breast, and (black-streaked) rufous rest of underparts. Juvenile has white underparts and underwing-coverts, dark mask and white supercilium, and dark patches on breast and flanks. Moist broadleaved forest.

4 CHANGEABLE HAWK EAGLE *Spizaetus cirrhatus* 61–72 cm
Adult pale morph (4a, 4b), dark morph (4c, 4d) and juvenile (4e, 4f) *S. c. limnaetus;* **adult** *S. c. cirrhatus* **(4g, 4h); soaring (4i).** Resident. Widespread in subcontinent; unrecorded in Pakistan. Narrower, more parallel-edged wings than Mountain Hawk Eagle. Soars with wings flat (except in display, when both wings and tail raised). Adult *limnaetus*, of N subcontinent, lacks prominent crest, and has boldly streaked underparts (with barring confined to flanks, thighs and undertail-coverts) and narrower tail barring compared with Mountain; dark morph told from Black Eagle (Plate 63) by structural differences, greyish undertail with diffuse dark terminal band, and extensive greyish bases to underside of remiges. Juvenile generally whiter on head than juvenile Mountain. Nominate *cirrhatus*, of peninsular India and Sri Lanka, best told from *kelaarti* race of Mountain by wing shape, patterning of breast and underwing-coverts, and dark vent and undertail-coverts. Broadleaved forest and well-wooded country.

5 MOUNTAIN HAWK EAGLE *Spizaetus nipalensis* 70–72 cm
Adult (5a, 5b) and juvenile (5c, 5d) *S. n. nipalensis;* **adult** *S. n. kelaarti* **(5e); soaring (5f).** Resident. Himalayas, hills of India and Sri Lanka. Prominent crest. Wings broader than on Changeable, with more pronounced curve to trailing edge. Soars with wings in shallow V. Distinguished from Changeable by extensive barring on underparts, whitish-barred rump, and stronger dark barring on tail. Juvenile told from juvenile Changeable by more extensive dark streaking on crown and sides of head, white-tipped black crest (useful in N subcontinent only), buff-barred rump, and fewer, more prominent tail-bars. *S. n. kelaarti*, of Sri Lanka and SW India, is smaller, with rufous barring on underparts, and underwing-coverts buff and almost unmarked. Forested hills and mountains.

PLATE 72: FALCONETS AND FALCONS

1 **COLLARED FALCONET** *Microhierax caerulescens* 18 cm
Adult (1a, 1b, 1c) and juvenile (1d). Resident. Himalayas and NE Orissa. Very small. Rather shrike-like when perched. Flies with rapid beats interspersed with long glides. Adult has white collar, black crown and eye-stripe, and rufous-orange underparts. Juvenile has rufous-orange on forehead and supercilium, and white throat. Edges of broadleaved tropical forest.

2 **PIED FALCONET** *Microhierax melanoleucos* 20 cm
Adult (2a, 2b, 2c). Resident. E Himalayas and NE India. Larger than Collared Falconet. Adult has white underparts and lacks white hindcollar. Forest clearings and wooded foothills.

3 **LESSER KESTREL** *Falco naumanni* 29–32 cm
Male (3a, 3b, 3c), immature male (3d, 3e) and female (3f, 3g, 3h). Widespread passage migrant. Slightly smaller and slimmer than Common Kestrel. Flapping shallower and stiffer. Claws whitish (black on Common). Male has uniform blue-grey head (without dark moustachial stripe), unmarked rufous upperparts, blue-grey greater coverts, and almost plain orange-buff underparts. In flight, underwing whiter with more clearly pronounced darker tips to primaries; tail often looks more wedge-shaped. First-year male more like Common; best distinguished by structural differences and unmarked rufous mantle and scapulars. Female and juvenile have less distinct moustachial stripe than Common, and lack any suggestion of dark eye-stripe; underwing tends to be cleaner and whiter, with primary bases unbarred (or only lightly barred) and coverts less heavily spotted, and dark primary tips more pronounced. Open grassland and cultivation.

4 **COMMON KESTREL** *Falco tinnunculus* 32–35 cm
Male (4a, 4b, 4c) and female (4d, 4e, 4f). Resident in mountains of Pakistan, Himalayas and Western Ghats and Sri Lanka; widespread winter visitor. Long, rather broad tail; wing-tips more rounded than on most falcons. Frequently hovers. Male has greyish head with diffuse dark moustachial stripe, rufous upperparts heavily marked with black, and grey tail with black subterminal band. Female and juvenile have rufous crown and nape streaked with black, diffuse and narrow dark moustachial stripe, rufous upperparts heavily barred and spotted with black, and dark barring on rufous tail; underwing more heavily barred than male's. Open country.

5 **RED-NECKED FALCON** *Falco chicquera* 31–36 cm
Adult (5a, 5b, 5c) and juvenile (5d). Widespread resident; unrecorded in most of the northeast, W Pakistan and Sri Lanka. Powerful falcon with pointed wings and longish tail. Flight usually fast and dashing. Adult has rufous crown and nape, pale blue-grey upperparts, white underparts finely barred with black, and grey tail with broad black subterminal band. Juvenile has lightly streaked crown, and rufous fringes and more extensive dark barring on upperparts. Open country with trees.

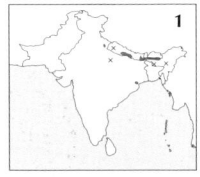 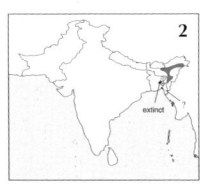 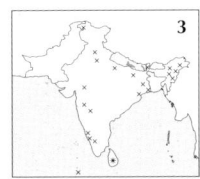 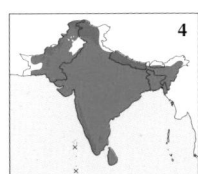

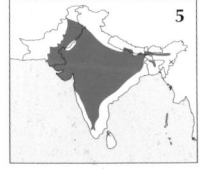

PLATE 73: FALCONS

1 AMUR FALCON *Falco amurensis* 28–31 cm
Male (1a, 1b), female (1c, 1d), immature male (1e, 1f) and juvenile (1g). Widespread passage migrant; unrecorded in Pakistan. In all plumages, has red to pale orange cere, eye-ring, legs and feet. Frequently hovers. Male dark grey, with rufous thighs and under-tail-coverts and white underwing-coverts. First-year male shows mixture of adult male and juvenile characters. Female has dark grey upperparts, short moustachial stripe, whitish underparts with some dark barring and spotting, and orange-buff thighs and undertail-coverts; uppertail barred; underwing white with strong dark barring. Juvenile has rufous-buff fringes to upperparts, rufous-buff streaking on crown, and boldly streaked underparts. Open country.

2 SOOTY FALCON *Falco concolor* 33–36 cm
Adult (2a, 2b) and juvenile (2c, 2d). Summer visitor. Makran coast, Pakistan. Slim, with very long wings and tail (latter wedge-shaped at tip). Adult entirely pale grey with black-ish flight feathers; older males can be almost black. Juvenile has narrow buff fringes to upperparts, and yellowish-brown underparts and underwing-coverts which are diffusely streaked. Rocky areas and desert.

3 MERLIN *Falco columbarius* 25–30 cm
Male (3a, 3b) and female (3c, 3d). Winter visitor. N subcontinent. Small and compact, with short, pointed wings. Flight typically swift, with rapid beats interspersed with short dashing glides, when wings often closed into body. Male has blue-grey upperparts, broad black subterminal tail-band, weak moustachial stripe, and diffuse patch of rufous-orange on nape. Female and juvenile have weak moustachial stripe, brown upperparts with variable rufous/buff markings, and strongly barred uppertail. Open country.

4 EURASIAN HOBBY *Falco subbuteo* 30–36 cm
Adult (4a, 4b) and juvenile (4c, 4d). Breeds in Himalayas; widespread winter visitor; unrecorded in Sri Lanka. Slim, with long pointed wings and medium-length tail. Hunting flight swift and powerful, with stiff beats interspersed with short glides. Adult has broad black moustachial stripe, cream underparts with bold blackish streaking, and rufous thighs and undertail-coverts. Juvenile has dark brown upperparts with buffish fringes, pale buff-ish underparts which are more heavily streaked, and lacks rufous thighs and undertail-coverts. Well-wooded areas; also open country in winter.

5 ORIENTAL HOBBY *Falco severus* 27–30 cm
Adult (5a, 5b) and immature (5c, 5d). Resident. Mainly Himalayas and NE India. Similar to Eurasian Hobby in structure, flight action and appearance, although slightly stockier, with shorter tail. Adult has complete blackish hood, bluish-black upperparts, and unmarked rufous underparts and underwing-coverts. Juvenile has browner upperparts, and heavily streaked rufous-buff underparts. Open wooded hills.

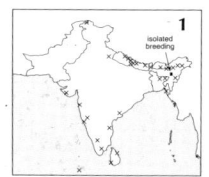 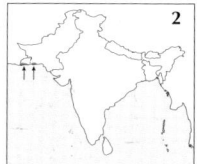 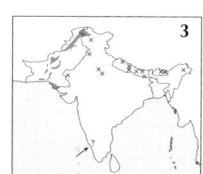 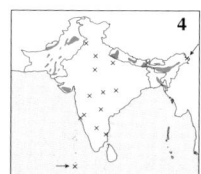

PLATE 74: LARGE FALCONS

1 LAGGAR FALCON *Falco jugger* 43–46 cm
Adult (1a, 1b, 1c) and juvenile (1d, 1e). Widespread resident; unrecorded in parts of northeast and east and Sri Lanka. Large falcon, although smaller, slimmer-winged and less powerful than Saker. Adult has rufous crown, fine but prominent dark moustachial stripe, dark brown upperparts, and rather uniform uppertail; underparts and underwing-coverts vary, can be largely white or heavily streaked, but lower flanks and thighs usually wholly dark brown; may show dark panel across underwing-coverts. Juvenile similar to adult, but crown duller and underparts very heavily streaked, and has greyish bare parts; differs from juvenile Peregrine in paler crown, finer moustachial stripe, and unbarred uppertail. Open arid country and cultivation in plains and low hills.

2 SAKER FALCON *Falco cherrug* 50–58 cm
***F. c. cherrug* (2a, 2b, 2c, 2d); *F. c. milvipes* (2e).** Winter visitor. Mainly Pakistan, Gujarat and Nepal. Large falcon with long wings and long tail. Wingbeats slow in level flight, with lazier flight action than Peregrine. At rest, tail extends noticeably beyond closed wings (wings fall just short of tail-tip on Laggar and are equal to tail on Peregrine). Adult has paler crown, less clearly defined moustachial stripe and paler rufous-brown upperparts than Laggar; underparts generally not so heavily marked as on Laggar, with flanks and thighs usually clearly streaked and not appearing wholly brown (although some overlap exists); outer tail feathers more prominently barred. Juvenile (not illustrated) has greyish cere, and greyish legs and feet; otherwise similar to adult, but crown more heavily marked, moustachial stripe stronger, underparts more heavily streaked, and upperparts darker brown. *F. c. milvipes*, a rare winter visitor (and race recorded in Nepal) has broad orange-buff barring on upperparts. Desert and semi-desert, mainly in hills and mountains.

3 PEREGRINE FALCON *Falco peregrinus* 38–48 cm
Adult (3a, 3b) and juvenile (3c, 3d) *F. p. peregrinator;* adult (3e, 3f) and juvenile (3g, 3h) *F. p. babylonicus;* adult *F. p. calidus* (3i, 3j). Widespread resident and winter visitor. Heavy-looking falcon with broad-based and pointed wings and short, broad-based tail. Flight strong, with stiff, shallow beats and occasional short glides. *F. p. calidus*, a winter visitor throughout the subcontinent, has slate-grey upperparts, broad and clean-cut black moustachial stripe, and whitish underparts with narrow blackish barring; juvenile *calidus* (not illustrated) has browner upperparts, heavily streaked underparts, broad moustachial stripe, and barred uppertail. *F. p. peregrinator*, resident throughout subcontinent, has dark grey upperparts with more extensive black hood (and less pronounced moustachial stripe), and rufous underparts with dark barring on belly and thighs; juvenile *peregrinator* has darker brownish-black upperparts than adult, and paler underparts with heavy streaking. *F. p. babylonicus* ('Barbary Falcon'), confined as a breeder to N and W Pakistan and wintering east to NW India, has pale blue-grey upperparts, buffish underparts with only sparse streaking and barring, rufous on crown and nape, and a narrower dark moustachial stripe; juvenile *babylonicus* has darker brown upperparts with narrow rufous-buff fringes, heavily streaked underparts and underwing-coverts, and only a trace of rufous on forehead and supercilium. Breeds in hills, mountains and stony semi-desert; winters around inland and coastal wetlands.

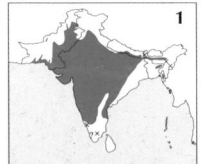 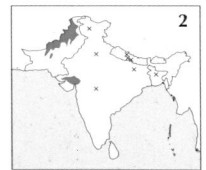 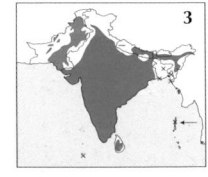

PLATE 75: GREBES AND LOONS

(1) LITTLE GREBE *Tachybaptus ruficollis* 25–29 cm
Adult breeding (1a) and non-breeding (1b, 1c). Widespread resident; unrecorded in parts of northwest and northeast. Small size, often with puffed-up rear end. In breeding plumage, has rufous cheeks and neck sides and yellow patch at base of bill. In non-breeding plumage, has brownish-buff cheeks and flanks. Juvenile is similar to non-breeding but has brown stripes across cheeks. Mainly freshwater wetlands.

2 RED-NECKED GREBE *Podiceps grisegena* 40–50 cm
Adult breeding (2a) and non-breeding (2b, 2c). Winter visitor. N Pakistan, N and NW India. Slightly smaller than Great Crested with stouter neck, squarer head, and stockier body which is often puffed-up at rear end. Black-tipped yellow bill. Black crown extends to eye, and has dusky cheeks and foreneck in non-breeding plumage. White cheeks and reddish foreneck in breeding plumage. Lakes.

(3) GREAT CRESTED GREBE *Podiceps cristatus* 46–51 cm
Adult breeding (3a) and non-breeding (3b, 3c). Breeds in NW subcontinent; winter visitor to N subcontinent. Large and slender-necked, with pinkish bill. Black crown does not extend to eye, and has white cheeks and foreneck in non-breeding plumage. Rufous-orange ear-tufts and white cheeks and foreneck in breeding plumage. Lakes, reservoirs and coastal waters.

4 HORNED GREBE *Podiceps auritus* 31–38 cm
Adult breeding (4a) and non-breeding (4b, 4c). Winter visitor. Pakistan and India. Bill is stouter and does not appear upturned as it does in Black-necked. Has two white patches on upperwing, with white patch on wing-coverts, usually lacking on Black-necked. Triangular-shaped head, with crown peaking at rear. White cheeks contrasting with black crown and white foreneck in non-breeding plumage. Yellow ear-tufts and rufous neck and breast in breeding plumage. Lakes and coastal waters.

5 BLACK-NECKED GREBE *Podiceps nigricollis* 28–34 cm
Adult breeding (5a) and non-breeding (5b, 5c). Breeds in Baluchistan; winters mainly in Pakistan, NW India and Nepal. Steep forehead, with crown typically peaking at front or centre. Dusky ear-coverts contrast with white throat and sides of head in non-breeding plumage. Yellow ear-tufts, black neck and breast and rufous flanks in breeding plumage. Reed-edged lakes; also coastal waters in winter.

6 RED-THROATED LOON *Gavia stellata* 53–69 cm
Adult breeding (6a) and non-breeding (6b, 6c). Vagrant. Pakistan. Upturned-looking bill and rounded head. In non-breeding plumage, paler grey and whiter than Black-throated. Grey of crown and hindneck is paler and less extensive compared with Black-throated and does not contrast so strongly with white of ear-coverts and foreneck. Red throat and uniform grey-brown upperparts in breeding plumage. Coastal waters and lakes.

7 BLACK-THROATED LOON *Gavia arctica* 58–73 cm
Adult breeding (7a) and non-breeding (7b, 7c). Vagrant. India. Straight bill and square-shaped head. Black-and-white appearance in non-breeding plumage, and typically shows white flank patch. Black throat and black-and-white chequered upperparts in breeding plumage. Flooded land, lakes and coastal waters.

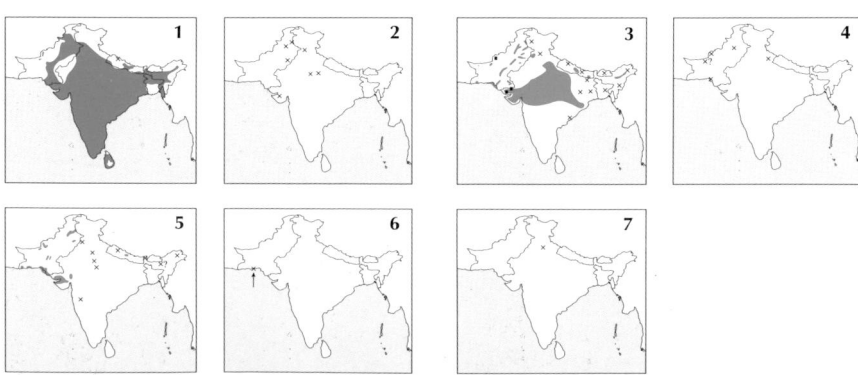

PLATE 76: TROPICBIRDS AND BOOBIES

1 RED-BILLED TROPICBIRD *Phaethon aethereus* 48 cm
Adult (1a, 1b) and juvenile (1c). Visitor to coastal waters. Adult has red bill, white tail-streamers, black barring on mantle and scapulars, and much black on primaries. Juvenile has yellow bill with black tip, and black band across nape; shows more black on primaries than juvenile Red-tailed. Pelagic.

2 RED-TAILED TROPICBIRD *Phaethon rubricauda* 46 cm
Adult (2a, 2b) and juvenile (2c). Breeds in Nicobars. Adult has red bill and red tail-streamers; lacks black barring on mantle, back and rump; wings largely white (with black primary shafts and markings on tertials). Juvenile has grey or black bill, and lacks black nape band; shows less black on primaries than juvenile Red-billed and White-tailed. Pelagic.

3 WHITE-TAILED TROPICBIRD *Phaethon lepturus* 39 cm
Adult (3a, 3b) and juvenile (3c). Resident on Maldives; visitor to coasts of India and Sri Lanka. Smaller and more graceful than other tropicbirds. Adult has yellow or orange bill, black diagonal bar across inner upperwing, and white tail-streamers. Juvenile has yellow bill, and lacks black band across nape; shows more black on primaries than juvenile Red-tailed. Pelagic.

4 MASKED BOOBY *Sula dactylatra* 81–92 cm
Adult (4a), immature (4b) and juvenile (4c, 4d). Breeds on Maldives and Lakshadweep?; visitor to W coastal waters. Large and robust booby. Adult largely white, with black mask and black flight feathers and tail. Juvenile has brown head, neck and upperparts, with whitish collar and whitish scaling on upperparts; underbody white, and shows much white on underwing-coverts. Head, upperbody and upperwing-coverts of immature become increasingly white with age. Pelagic.

5 RED-FOOTED BOOBY *Sula sula* 66–77 cm
Adult white morph (5a, 5b), intermediate morph (5c), immature (5d, 5e) and juvenile (5f). Breeds on Maldives and Lakshadweep?; visitor to coastal waters. Small and graceful booby. Adult has bluish bill, pinkish facial skin and red feet. White, brown and intermediate morphs occur; white morph most likely to be encountered in Indian Ocean. Juvenile has greyish legs and dark bill; underwing uniformly dark. Immature variable; immature white morph has diffuse breast-band. Pelagic.

6 BROWN BOOBY *Sula leucogaster* 64–74 cm
Adult (6a) and immature (6b). Breeds on Lakshadweep?; visitor to coasts and coastal waters. Dark brown, with sharply demarcated white underbody and underwing-coverts. Juvenile has dusky brown underbody, with pale panel across underwing-coverts, but overall appearance is similar to adult. Pelagic.

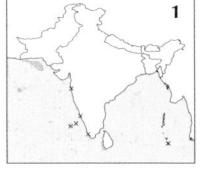 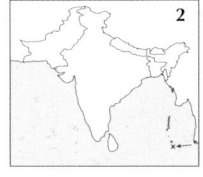 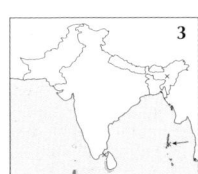 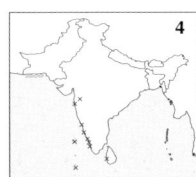

 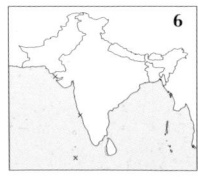

PLATE 77: DARTER AND CORMORANTS

1 DARTER *Anhinga melanogaster* 85–97 cm
Adult male breeding (1a, 1b, 1c) and immature (1d). Widespread resident; unrecorded in parts of the northwest, northeast and Himalayas. Long, slim head and neck, dagger-like bill, and long tail. Often swims with most of body submerged. Adult has white stripe down side of neck, lanceolate white scapular streaks, and white streaking on wing-coverts. Juvenile buffish-white below, with buff fringes to coverts forming pale panel on upper-wing. Mainly inland waters, also coastal waters.

2 PYGMY CORMORANT *Phalacrocorax pygmeus* 45–55 cm
Adult breeding (2a, 2b), non-breeding (2c) and immature (2d). Vagrant. Pakistan. Averages larger and bulkier than Little. Adult breeding has chestnut head and upper neck (becoming nearly black prior to breeding) with more profuse white plumes than breeding Little. Non-breeding and immature very similar to Little, although tend to be browner on body and with more extensive whitish mottling on breast and belly; in non-breeding chin and throat whitish, gradually merging into brown of foreneck (on Little, chin more clearly demarcated). Inland and coastal waters.

3 LITTLE CORMORANT *Phalacrocorax niger* 51 cm
Adult breeding (3a, 3b), non-breeding (3c) and immature (3d). Widespread resident; unrecorded in parts of the northwest, northeast and Himalayas. Smaller than Indian, with shorter bill, rectangular-shaped head and shorter neck. Lacks yellow gular pouch. Adult breeding all black, with a few white plumes on forecrown and sides of head. Non-breeding browner (and lacks white head plumes), with whitish chin. Immature has whitish chin and throat, and foreneck and breast a shade paler than upperparts, with some pale fringes. Inland and coastal waters.

4 INDIAN CORMORANT *Phalacrocorax fuscicollis* 63 cm
Adult breeding (4a, 4b), non-breeding (4c) and immature (4d). Widespread resident; unrecorded in parts of the northwest, northeast and Himalayas. Smaller and slimmer than Great, with thinner neck, slimmer oval-shaped head, finer-looking bill, and proportionately longer tail. In flight, looks lighter, with thinner neck and quicker wing action. Larger than Little, with longer neck, oval-shaped head and longer bill. Adult breeding glossy black, with tuft of white behind eye and scattering of white filoplumes on neck. Non-breeding lacks white plumes; has whitish throat, and browner-looking head, neck and underparts. Immature has brown upperparts and whitish underparts. Inland and coastal waters.

5 GREAT CORMORANT *Phalacrocorax carbo* 80–100 cm
Adult breeding (5a, 5b), non-breeding (5c) and immature (5d). Widespread resident; unrecorded in parts of the northwest, northeast and Western Ghats. Larger and bulkier than Indian, with thicker neck, larger and more angular head, and stouter bill. Adult breeding glossy black, with orange facial skin, white cheeks and throat, white head plumes and white thigh patch. Non-breeding more blackish-brown, and lacks white head plumes and thigh patch. Immature has whitish or pale buff underparts. Inland and coastal waters.

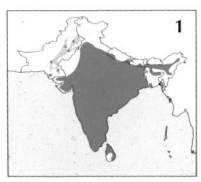 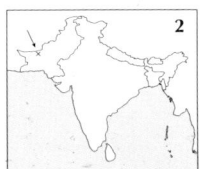 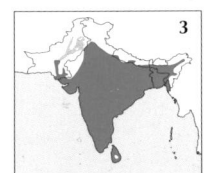 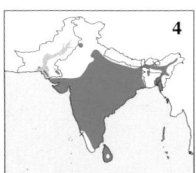

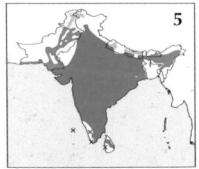

PLATE 78: EGRETS AND POND HERONS

1 LITTLE EGRET *Egretta garzetta* 55–65 cm
Adult breeding (1a) and non-breeding (1b, 1c). Widespread resident; unrecorded in parts of the northwest and northeast. Slim and graceful. Typically, has black bill, black legs with yellow feet, and greyish lores (lores reddish during courtship). Some can be very similar to Western Reef. Bill in non-breeding and immature can be paler and pinkish or greyish at base, and can be dull yellowish on some. Inland and coastal waters.

2 WESTERN REEF EGRET *Egretta gularis* 55–65 cm
Adult white morph breeding (2a) and non-breeding (2b), adult dark morph non-breeding (2c) and intermediate morph (2d). Resident. Mainly W and SE coast. Bill longer and stouter than Little's and usually appearing very slightly downcurved. Legs also slightly shorter and thicker-looking. Bill is usually mainly yellowish or brownish-yellow, but may be black when breeding. Typically has greenish or yellowish lores (although can be greyish as on Little, and Little can, exceptionally, appear to have yellowish tinge to lores). Coastal waters.

3 PACIFIC REEF EGRET *Egretta sacra* 58 cm
Adult white morph breeding (3a) and non-breeding (3b), adult dark morph non-breeding (3c) and juvenile dark morph (3d). Resident. Andamans and Nicobars. Legs shorter and stouter than Western Reef's, and is stockier, with shorter and thicker neck. White throat of dark morph is inconspicuous. Coastal waters.

4 GREAT EGRET *Casmerodius albus* 65–72 cm
Adult breeding (4a, 4b) and non-breeding (4c). Widespread resident; unrecorded in parts of the northwest and northeast. Large size, very long neck and large bill. Black line of gape extends behind eye. Bill is black, lores blue and tibia reddish in breeding plumage. In non-breeding plumage, bill yellow and lores pale green. Inland and coastal waters.

5 INTERMEDIATE EGRET *Mesophoyx intermedia* 65–72 cm
Adult breeding (5a) and non-breeding (5b, 5c). Widespread resident; unrecorded in parts of the northwest and northeast. Smaller than Great, with shorter bill and neck. Black gape-line does not extend beyond eye. Bill is black and lores yellow-green during courtship. Has black-tipped yellow bill and yellow lores outside breeding season. Inland and coastal waters.

6 CATTLE EGRET *Bubulcus ibis* 48–53 cm
Adult breeding (6a, 6b) and non-breeding (6c). Widespread resident; unrecorded in parts of the northwest and northeast. Small and stocky, with short yellow bill and short legs. Has orange-buff on head, neck and mantle in breeding plumage. Damp grassland, paddy-fields and inland waters.

7 INDIAN POND HERON *Ardeola grayii* 42–45 cm
Adult breeding (7a, 7b) and non-breeding (7c). Widespread resident; unrecorded in parts of the northwest and northeast. Whitish wings contrast with dark saddle. Adult breeding has yellowish-buff head and neck and maroon-brown mantle/scapulars. Head, neck and breast streaked/spotted in non-breeding plumage. Inland and coastal wetlands.

8 CHINESE POND HERON *Ardeola bacchus* 52 cm
Adult breeding (8a, 8b) and non-breeding (8c). Resident and winter visitor? Mainly NE India and Andamans. In breeding plumage, has maroon-chestnut head and neck and slaty-black mantle/scapulars. Non-breeding and immature plumages probably not separable from those of Indian Pond Heron. Inland and coastal waters.

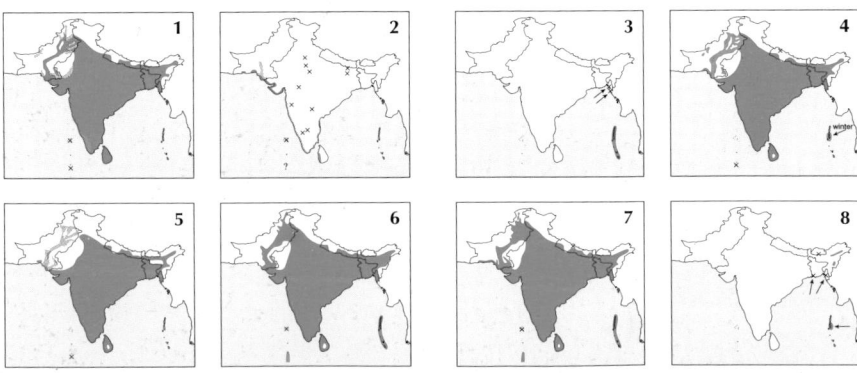

PLATE 79: LARGE HERONS

(1) **GREY HERON** *Ardea cinerea* 90–98 cm
Adult (1a, 1b, 1c) and immature (1d). Resident, passage migrant and winter visitor. Widespread; unrecorded in parts of the northwest and northeast. In flight, black flight feathers contrast with grey upperwing- and underwing-coverts. Adult has yellow bill, whitish head and neck with black head plumes, and black patches on belly. In breeding season, has whitish scapular plumes and bill and legs become orange or reddish. Immature has dark cap with variable crest, and greyer neck; lacks or has reduced black on belly. Inland and coastal waters.

2 **GOLIATH HERON** *Ardea goliath* 135–150 cm
Adult (2a, 2b). Visitor or resident? Mainly NE India. Huge size and large, dark bill. Black legs and feet. Rufous on head and neck. Adult has purplish-chestnut underparts and underwing-coverts; lacks black head stripes of Purple. Juvenile has black crown, indistinct stripes down foreneck, and rufous fringes to upperparts. Rivers.

3 **WHITE-BELLIED HERON** *Ardea insignis* 127 cm
Adult (3a, 3b). Resident. E Himalayan foothills. Large size and very long neck (much longer than shown on plate). Bill blackish, and legs and feet grey. Grey foreneck and breast contrast with white belly. In flight, has uniform dark grey upperwing, and white underwing-coverts contrasting with dark grey flight feathers. In breeding plumage, has greyish-white nape plumes and elongated grey breast feathers with white centres. Wetlands in tropical and subtropical forest.

4 **GREAT-BILLED HERON** *Ardea sumatrana* 115 cm
Adult (4a, 4b). [Vagrant? Possibly recorded in Nicobars. Large size and large bill. Grey head, neck and underparts, and grey upperwing and underwing. Breeding birds have whitish plumes on nape, scapulars and breast. Habitat unrecorded in region.]

(5) **PURPLE HERON** *Ardea purpurea* 78–90 cm
Adult (5a, 5b) and juvenile (5c, 5d). Resident and winter visitor? Widespread; unrecorded in parts of the northwest and northeast. Rakish, with long, thin neck. In flight, compared with Grey, bulge of recoiled neck is very pronounced, protruding feet large, underwing-coverts purplish (adult) or buff (juvenile) and lacks white leading edge to wing. Adult has chestnut head and neck with black stripes, grey mantle and upperwing-coverts, and dark chestnut belly and underwing-coverts. Juvenile has black crown, buffish neck, and brownish mantle and upperwing-coverts with rufous-buff fringes. Mainly inland waters with tall cover.

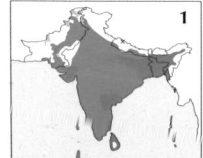 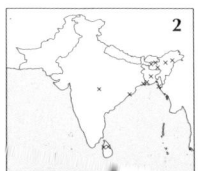 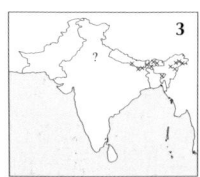 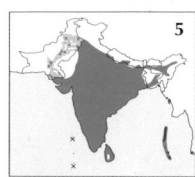

PLATE 80: BITTERNS AND NIGHT HERONS

① LITTLE HERON *Butorides striatus* 40–48 cm
Adult (1a, 1b) and juvenile (1c). Widespread resident; unrecorded in parts of the north-west and northeast. Small, stocky and short-legged. Adult has dark greenish upperparts and greyish underparts. Juvenile has buff streaking on upperparts and dark-streaked underparts. Inland waters with dense shrub cover, and mangroves.

② BLACK-CROWNED NIGHT HERON *Nycticorax nycticorax* 58–65 cm
Adult (2a, 2b) and juvenile (2c). Widespread resident; unrecorded in parts of the north-west and northeast. Stocky, with thick neck. Adult has black crown and mantle contrast-ing with grey wings and whitish underparts. Juvenile boldly streaked and spotted. Immature has unstreaked brown mantle/scapulars. Inland and coastal waters.

3 MALAYAN NIGHT HERON *Gorsachius melanolophus* 51 cm
Adult (3a, 3b) and immature (3c). Resident and partial migrant in Western Ghats, NE India and Nicobars; winter visitor to Sri Lanka. Stocky, with stout bill and short neck. Adult has black crown and crest, rufous sides to head and neck, and rufous-brown upper-parts. Immature finely vermiculated with white, grey and rufous-buff, and with bold white spotting on crown and crest. Streams and marshes in evergreen forest.

4 LITTLE BITTERN *Ixobrychus minutus* 33–38 cm
Adult male (4a, 4b), female (4c) and juvenile (4d). Resident in Kashmir and Assam; wide-ly recorded elsewhere in India and Pakistan. Small size. Buffish wing-coverts contrast with dark flight feathers in all plumages. Male has black crown and mantle/scapulars, and buff neck. Female has brown mantle/scapulars, with brownish-buff streaking on foreneck. Juvenile has warm buff upperparts streaked with dark brown, and brown streaking on underparts; very similar to juvenile Yellow but streaking on foreneck and breast of Yellow is generally more rufous-orange. Reedbeds.

⑤ YELLOW BITTERN *Ixobrychus sinensis* 38 cm
Adult male (5a, 5b) and juvenile (5c). Widespread resident. Small size. Yellowish-buff wing-coverts contrast with dark brown flight feathers. Male has pinkish-brown mantle/scapulars, and face and sides of neck are vinaceous. Female is similar to male, typ-ically with rufous streaking on black crown, variable rufous-orange streaking on foreneck and breast, and diffuse buff edges to rufous-brown mantle and scapulars. Juvenile appears buff with bold dark streaking to upperparts including wing-coverts; foreneck and breast are heavily streaked. Reedbeds and flooded paddy-fields.

6 CINNAMON BITTERN *Ixobrychus cinnamomeus* 38 cm
Adult male (6a, 6b), female (6c) and juvenile (6d). Small size. Widespread resident. Uniform-looking cinnamon-rufous flight feathers and tail in all plumages. Male has cin-namon-rufous crown, hindneck and mantle/scapulars. Female has dark brown crown and mantle, and dark brown streaking on foreneck and breast. Juvenile has buff mottling on dark brown upperparts, and is heavily streaked with dark brown on underparts. Reedbeds and flooded paddy-fields.

⑦ BLACK BITTERN *Dupetor flavicollis* 58 cm
Adult (7a, 7b) and juvenile (7c). Widespread resident. Blackish upperparts, with orange-buff patch on side of neck. Juvenile has rufous fringes to upperparts. Reedbeds.

8 GREAT BITTERN *Botaurus stellaris* 70–80 cm
Adult (8a, 8b). Widespread winter visitor. Stocky. Cryptically patterned. Wet reedbeds.

1a
1c
b
2b
2a
2c
3b
3a
3c
4b
4a
4c
4d
5b
5a
5c
6b
6a
6c
6d
7a
7b
7c
8a
8b

C.D'S

PLATE 81: FLAMINGOS, IBISES AND EURASIAN SPOONBILL

1 GREATER FLAMINGO *Phoenicopterus ruber* 125–145 cm
Adult (1a, 1b), immature (1c) and juvenile (1d). Resident and winter visitor. Breeds in Gujarat; widespread visitor to plains. Larger than Lesser, with longer and thinner neck. Bill larger and less prominently kinked. Adult has pale pink bill with prominent dark tip, and variable amount of pinkish-white on head, neck and body; in flight, crimson-pink upperwing-coverts contrast with whitish body. Immature has greyish-white head and neck, and white body lacking any pink; pink on bill develops with increasing age. Juvenile brownish-grey, with white on coverts; bill grey, tipped with black, and legs grey. Shallow brackish lakes, mudflats and saltpans.

2 LESSER FLAMINGO *Phoenicopterus minor* 80–90 cm
Adult (2a, 2b), immature (2c) and juvenile (2d). Breeds in Gujarat; widespread in Indian and Pakistan plains in non-breeding season. Smaller than Greater Flamingo; neck appears shorter, and bill is smaller and more prominently kinked. Adult has black-tipped dark red bill, dark red iris and facial skin, and deep rose-pink on head, neck and body; blood-red centres to lesser and median upperwing coverts contrast with paler pink of rest of coverts. Immature has greyish-brown head and neck, pale pink body, and mainly pink coverts; bill coloration develops with increasing age. Juvenile mainly grey-brown, with dark-tipped purplish-brown bill and grey legs. Salt and brackish lagoons and saltpans.

3 GLOSSY IBIS *Plegadis falcinellus* 55–65 cm
Adult breeding (3a), non-breeding (3b) and juvenile (3c). Resident and winter visitor. Mainly W and S subcontinent. Small, dark ibis with rather fine downcurved bill. Adult breeding deep chestnut, glossed with purple and green, with metallic green-and-purple wings; has narrow white surround to bare lores. Adult non-breeding duller, with white streaking on dark brown head and neck. Juvenile similar to adult non-breeding, but is dark brown with white mottling on head, and only faint greenish gloss to upperparts. Inland wetlands. WHITE

4 BLACK-HEADED IBIS *Threskiornis melanocephalus* 75 cm
Adult (4a) and immature (4b). Widespread resident; unrecorded in parts of E India and the northwest. Stocky, mainly white ibis with stout downcurved black bill. Adult breeding has naked black head, white lower-neck plumes, variable yellow wash to mantle and breast, and grey on scapulars and elongated tertials. Adult non-breeding has all-white body and lacks neck plumes. Immature has grey feathering on head and neck, and black-tipped wings. Inland and coastal wetlands.

5 BLACK IBIS *Pseudibis papillosa* 68 cm RED-NAPED
Adult. Widespread resident in lowlands of Pakistan, Nepal and India. Stocky, dark ibis with relatively stout downcurved bill. Has white shoulder patch and reddish legs. Adult has naked black head with red patch on rear crown and nape, and is dark brown with green-and-purple gloss. Immature dark brown, including feathered head. Marshes, lakes and fields.

6 EURASIAN SPOONBILL *Platalea leucorodia* 80–90 cm
Adult breeding (6a) and juvenile (6b). Widespread resident; unrecorded in parts of India and the northwest. White, with spatulate-tipped bill. Adult has black bill with yellow tip; has crest and yellow breast patch when breeding. Juvenile has pink bill; in flight, shows black tips to primaries. Mainly inland wetlands.

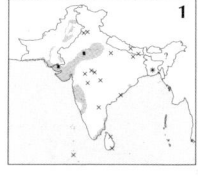 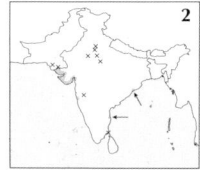 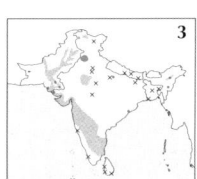 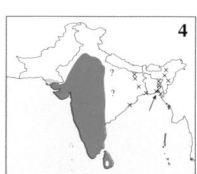

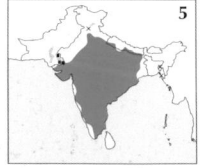 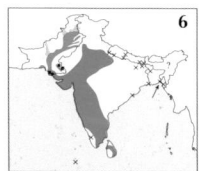

PLATE 82: PELICANS

(1) GREAT WHITE PELICAN *Pelecanus onocrotalus* 140–175 cm
Adult breeding (1a), adult non-breeding (1b, 1c), immature (1d) and juvenile (1e).
Mainly a winter visitor to N subcontinent; breeds in Gujarat. Adult and immature have black underside to primaries and secondaries which contrast strongly with white (or largely white) underwing-coverts. Feathering of forehead narrower than on Dalmatian, and tapers to a point at bill-base (as orbital skin more extensive). Adult breeding has white body and wing-coverts tinged with pink, bright yellow pouch and pinkish skin around eye. Adult non-breeding has duller bare parts and lacks pink tinge and white crest. Immature has variable amounts of brown on wing-coverts and scapulars. Juvenile has largely brown head, neck and upperparts, including upperwing-coverts, and brown flight feathers; upperwing appears more uniform brown, and underwing shows pale central panel contrasting with dark inner coverts and flight feathers; greyish pouch becomes yellower with age. Large lakes and lagoons.

2 DALMATIAN PELICAN *Pelecanus crispus* 160–180 cm
Adult breeding (2a), adult non-breeding (2b, 2c) and immature (2d). Winter visitor. Mainly S Pakistan and NW India. In all plumages, has greyish underside to secondaries and inner primaries (becoming darker on outer primaries) lacking strong contrast with pale underwing-coverts, and often with whiter central panel. Forehead feathering broader across upper mandible (orbital skin more restricted than on White). Legs and feet always dark grey (pinkish on White). Larger than Spot-billed Pelican, with cleaner and whiter appearance at all ages; lacks 'spotting' on upper mandible, and bill usually darker than pouch. Adult breeding has orange pouch and purple skin around eye, and curly or bushy crest. Adult non-breeding more dirty white; pouch and skin around eye paler. Immature dingier than adult non-breeding, with some pale grey-brown on upperwing-coverts and scapulars. Juvenile has pale grey-brown mottling on hindneck and upperparts, including upperwing-coverts; pouch greyish-yellow. Large inland waters and coastal lagoons.

3 SPOT-BILLED PELICAN *Pelecanus philippensis* 140 cm
Adult breeding (3a, 3b), adult non-breeding (3c), immature (3d) and juvenile (3e).
Resident. Breeds in S and NE India and Sri Lanka; widespread in non-breeding season. Much smaller than Great White and Dalmatian, with dingier appearance, rather uniform pinkish bill and pouch (except in breeding condition), and black spotting on upper mandible (except juveniles). Tufted crest/hindneck usually apparent even on young birds. Underwing pattern similar to that of Dalmatian (and quite different from Great White), showing little contrast between wing-coverts and flight feathers and with paler greater coverts producing distinct central panel. Adult breeding has cinnamon-pink rump, underwing-coverts and undertail-coverts; head and neck appear greyish; has purplish skin in front of eye, and pouch is pink to dull purple and blotched with black. Adult non-breeding dirtier greyish-white, with pouch pinkish. Immature has variable grey-brown markings on upperparts. Juvenile has brownish head and neck, brown mantle and upperwing-coverts (fringed with pale buff), and brown flight feathers; spotting on bill initially lacking (and still indistinct at 12 months). Large inland and coastal waters.

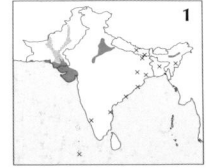 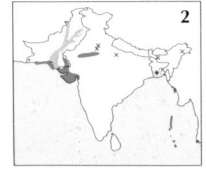 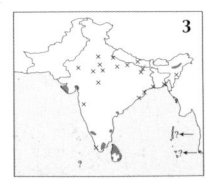

PLATE 83: FRIGATEBIRDS

1 GREAT FRIGATEBIRD *Fregata minor* 85–105 cm
Adult male (1a), adult female (1b), juvenile (1c) and immature (1d). Visitor. Coasts of India, Sri Lanka and Maldives. Adult male is only frigatebird with all-black underparts. Adult female has black cap and pink eye-ring; also has grey throat and black neck sides, and lacks spur of white on underwing. Juvenile and immature have rufous or white head, blackish breast-band and largely white underparts, which are gradually replaced by adult plumage; lack white spur on underwing (shown by all Lesser and some Christmas Island Frigatebirds); inseparable from some juvenile and immature Christmas Island, although any black on belly will indicate Great. Pelagic.

2 LESSER FRIGATEBIRD *Fregata ariel* 70–80 cm
Adult male (2a), adult female (2b), immature male (2c) and juvenile (2d). Visitor to coasts of India, Sri Lanka and Maldives; has bred. Smaller and more finely built than other two frigatebirds. Adult male entirely black except for white spur extending from breast sides onto inner underwing. Adult female has black head and red eye-ring; also black throat, white neck sides, white spur extending from white breast onto inner underwing, and black belly and vent. Juvenile and immature have rufous or white head, blackish breast-band and much white on underparts, which are gradually replaced by adult plumage; always show white spur on underwing (lacking on Great); any black on belly indicates Lesser rather than Christmas Island. Pelagic.

3 CHRISTMAS ISLAND FRIGATEBIRD *Fregata andrewsi* 90–100 cm
Adult male (3a), adult female (3b), immature male (3c) and juvenile (3d). Visitor. Coasts of India and Sri Lanka. Adult male has black underparts except for large white patch on belly. Adult female has black head and pink eye-ring; also black throat, white neck sides, white spur extending from white breast onto inner underwing, black wedge on side of breast, and white belly and vent. Juvenile has buffish to white head, blackish breast-band, and white underparts, with black head of female and black head and breast of male acquired gradually; some show white spur on underwing (always lacking on Great), and lower belly always remains white (gradually becoming black on both Lesser and Great). Pelagic.

  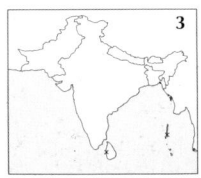

PLATE 84: STORKS

1 PAINTED STORK *Mycteria leucocephala* 93–100 cm
Adult (1a, 1b) and immature (1c, 1d). Widespread resident in plains; unrecorded in parts of the northwest and northeast. Adult has downcurved yellow bill, bare orange-yellow or red face, and red legs; white barring on mainly black upperwing-coverts, pinkish tertials, and black barring across breast. Juvenile dirty greyish-white, with grey-brown (feathered) head and neck and brown lesser coverts; bill and legs duller than adult's. Inland and coastal wetlands.

2 ASIAN OPENBILL *Anastomus oscitans* 68 cm
Adult breeding (2a) and non-breeding (2b, 2c). Widespread resident in plains; unrecorded in parts of the northwest and northeast. Stout, dull-coloured 'open bill'. Largely white (breeding) or greyish-white (non-breeding), with black flight feathers and tail; legs usually dull pink, brighter in breeding condition. Juvenile has brownish-grey head, neck and breast, and brownish mantle and scapulars slightly paler than the blackish flight feathers. Mainly inland wetlands.

3 WOOLLY-NECKED STORK *WHITE-NECKED* *Ciconia episcopus* 75–92 cm
Adult (3a, 3b). Widespread resident; unrecorded in parts of the northwest, northeast and E India. Stocky, largely blackish stork with 'woolly' white neck, black 'skullcap', and white vent and undertail-coverts. Juvenile similarly patterned to adult, but has duller brown body and wings, and feathered forehead. In flight, upperwing and underwing entirely dark. Freshwater wetlands in open wooded country.

4 WHITE STORK *Ciconia ciconia* 100–125 cm
Adult (4a, 4b). Widespread winter visitor and passage migrant. Mainly white stork, with black flight feathers, and striking red bill and legs. Generally has cleaner black-and-white appearance than Asian Openbill; note tail is white (black in Asian Openbill). Juvenile is similar to adult but with brown greater coverts and duller brownish-red bill and legs. Grassland and fields.

5 ORIENTAL STORK *Ciconia boyciana* 110–150 cm
Adult (5a, 5b). Winter visitor. Mainly NE India. Larger than White Stork, with larger, slightly upturned, black bill. Usually shows prominent greyish-white outer webs to secondaries. Lores red (black on White). Wet meadows and marshes.

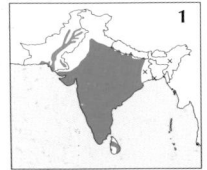 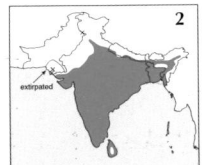 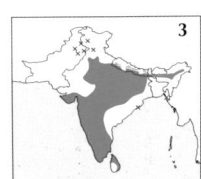 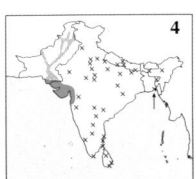

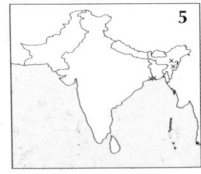

C.D'S

PLATE 85: STORKS

1 BLACK STORK *Ciconia nigra* 90–100 cm
Adult (1a, 1b) and immature (1c). Winter visitor and passage migrant. Mainly N subcontinent. Adult mainly glossy black, with white lower breast and belly, and red bill and legs; in flight, white underparts and axillaries contrast strongly with black neck and underwing. Juvenile has brown head, neck and upperparts flecked with white; bill and legs greyish-green. Inland wetlands.

2 BLACK-NECKED STORK *Ephippiorhynchus asiaticus* 129–150 cm
Adult (2a, 2b) and immature (2c, 2d). Widespread resident in lowlands. Large, black-and-white stork with long red legs and huge black bill. In flight, wings white except for broad black band across coverts, and tail black. Male has brown iris; yellow in female. Juvenile has fawn-brown head, neck and mantle, mainly brown wing-coverts, and mainly blackish-brown flight feathers; legs dark. Mainly inland wetlands.

3 LESSER ADJUTANT *Leptoptilos javanicus* 110–120 cm
Adult breeding (3a) and non-breeding (3b, 3c). Widespread resident in lowlands; unrecorded in Pakistan. Flies with neck retracted, as Greater Adjutant. Smaller than Greater, with slimmer bill that has straighter ridge to culmen. Adult typically shows pale frontal plate on head and denser feathers on head and neck, forming small crest. Adult has glossy black mantle and wings, largely black underwing (with white axillaries), white undertail-coverts, and largely black neck ruff (appearing as black patch on breast sides in flight); in breeding plumage, has narrow white fringes to scapulars and inner greater coverts and copper spots on median coverts. Juvenile similar to adult, but upperparts dull black and head and neck more densely feathered. Inland wetlands.

4 GREATER ADJUTANT *Leptoptilos dubius* 120–150 cm
Adult breeding (4a, 4b, 4c) and immature (4d). Resident. Mainly Assam; rare elsewhere. Larger than Lesser Adjutant, with stouter, conical bill with convex ridge to culmen. Adult breeding has bluish-grey mantle, silvery-grey panel across greater coverts, greyish or brownish underwing-coverts, grey undertail-coverts, and more extensive white neck ruff; further has blackish face and forehead (with appearance of dried blood) and neck pouch (visible only when inflated). Adult non-breeding and immature have darker grey mantle and inner wing-coverts, and brown greater coverts (which barely contrast with rest of wing); immature with brownish, rather than pale, iris. Marshes and lakes.

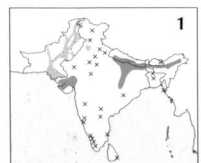 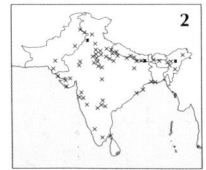 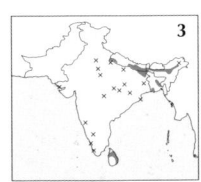 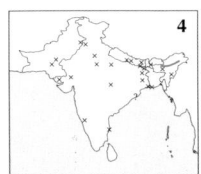

C.D'S

PLATE 86: PETRELS AND STORM-PETRELS

1 **CAPE PETREL** *Daption capense* 38–40 cm
Adult (1a, 1b). Vagrant. Sri Lanka. Black head, white underparts, white-and-black chequered upperparts, and black tail-band. Pelagic.

2 **BARAU'S PETREL** *Pterodroma baraui* 38 cm
Adult (2a, 2b). Visitor. India and Sri Lanka. Whitish forehead and dark grey cap, blackish M-mark across upperwing, dark rump and tail contrasting with grey lower mantle and back, and dark patches on sides of breast. Largely white underwing with black band on leading and trailing edges. Pelagic.

3 **SOFT-PLUMAGED PETREL** *Pterodroma mollis* 34 cm
Adult (3a, 3b). [Vagrant? Possibly recorded in Sri Lanka. Grey breast-band, grey crown, and fairly uniform dark upperwing which may show darker M-mark. Pelagic.]

4 **BULWER'S PETREL** *Bulweria bulwerii* 26–27 cm
Adult (4a, 4b). Vagrant. India, Sri Lanka and Maldives. Small and dark, with long tail. Smaller than Jouanin's, with finer bill, more prominent pale band across greater coverts (although Jouanin's in worn plumage may show this). Has weaker flight, with rapid beats interspersed with twisting glides; becoming shallow arcs in strong wind. Pelagic.

5 **JOUANIN'S PETREL** *Bulweria fallax* 30–32 cm
Adult (5a, 5b). Visitor. India and Sri Lanka. All dark, with long, pointed tail. Larger and broader-winged than Bulwer's, with stouter bill. Flight more powerful, with 'shearing' or long glides interspersed with steady flapping. Smaller and with less languid flight than Wedge-tailed Shearwater. Pelagic.

6 **WILSON'S STORM-PETREL** *Oceanites oceanicus* 15–19 cm
Adult (6a, 6b). Visitor. W and S coastal waters. Dark underparts and underwing. White rump band. Feet project noticeably beyond tail. When fluttering over water, dangling feet show yellow webbing. Pelagic.

7 **WHITE-FACED STORM-PETREL** *Pelagodroma marina* 20 cm
Adult (7a, 7b). Visitor. SW Indian coastal waters. White supercilium and dark mask, white underparts, grey rump, and peculiar bounding flight. Pelagic.

8 **SWINHOE'S STORM-PETREL** *Oceanodroma monorhis* 20 cm
Adult (8a, 8b). Visitor. India and Sri Lanka. All-dark storm-petrel, lacking white rump band. Tail slightly forked, and feet do not project beyond tail. Pelagic and coastal waters.

9 **WHITE-BELLIED STORM-PETREL** *Fregetta grallaria* 20 cm
Adult (9a, 9b). Vagrant. Maldives. Black head, and white underbody. Pelagic.

10 **BLACK-BELLIED STORM-PETREL** *Fregetta tropica* 20 cm
Adult (10a, 10b). Vagrant. India and Sri Lanka. Black head, white flanks, with black line down centre of belly and black undertail coverts. Pelagic.

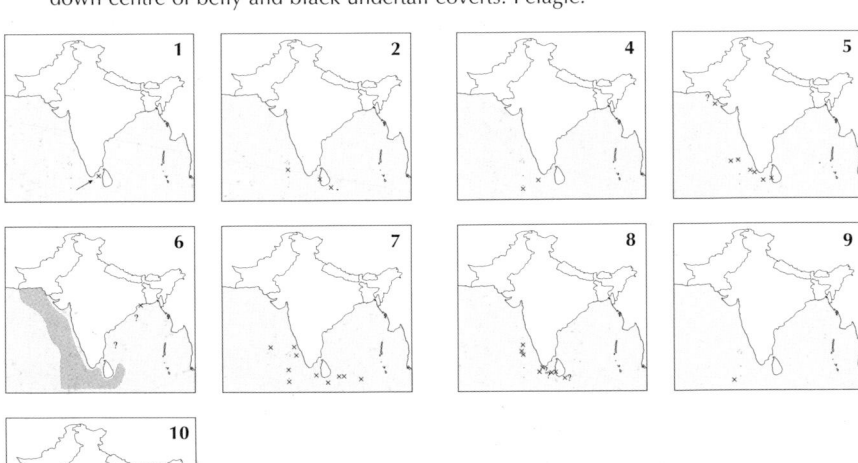

PLATE 87: SHEARWATERS

1 STREAKED SHEARWATER *Calonectris leucomelas* 48 cm
Adult (1a, 1b). Visitor. India and Sri Lanka. White underparts and underwing-coverts and large size. Variable dark streaking on whitish head, and pale bill with dark tip. Flight typically rather relaxed and gull-like with wings slightly angled at carpal joints. Pelagic, inshore waters.

2 WEDGE-TAILED SHEARWATER *Puffinus pacificus* 41–46 cm
Pale morph (2a) and dark morph (2b, 2c). Visitor. India, Sri Lanka and Maldives. Large size, long pointed or wedge-shaped tail, fine greyish bill with dark tip, and pale legs and feet. Comparatively broad rounded wing-tips. In calm conditions, lazy flapping and short glides with wings held forward and bowed; soars in low arcs between short bursts of flapping in strong winds. Two colour morphs; dark morph has all-dark underwing. Pelagic.

3 FLESH-FOOTED SHEARWATER *Puffinus carneipes* 41–45 cm
Adult (3a, 3b). Visitor. India, Sri Lanka and Maldives. Large, dark, broad-winged shearwater. Pink legs and feet. Greyish patch on underside of primaries. Stout pinkish bill with dark tip. Flight typically relaxed with strong flapping interspersed with stiff-winged glides; banks and glides with less flapping in stronger winds. Offshore.

4 SOOTY SHEARWATER *Puffinus griseus* 40–46 cm
Adult (4a, 4b). Vagrant. Sri Lanka. Sooty-brown, with whitish flash on underwing-coverts. Has all-dark bill, and dark legs and feet just extend beyond tail. Slim, pointed wings, and strong, deliberate flight action with stiff flapping and long glides. Offshore and pelagic waters.

5 SHORT-TAILED SHEARWATER *Puffinus tenuirostris* 41–43 cm
Adult (5a, 5b). Vagrant. Pakistan and Sri Lanka. Sooty-brown, with pale grey underwing-coverts. Much as Sooty, but has shorter bill and steeper forehead, shorter extension of rear body and tail behind wings, and pale panel on underwing tends to be less striking. Inshore, offshore and pelagic waters.

6 AUDUBON'S SHEARWATER *Puffinus lherminieri* 30 cm
Adult (6a, 6b). Resident or breeding visitor? India, Sri Lanka and Maldives. Small size. Dark brown upperparts, white underparts with dark on breast sides; white wing-linings, axillaries and flanks, with broad dark margins to underwing. Flies with fairly fast wing-beats interspersed with short glides. Offshore and pelagic waters.

7 PERSIAN SHEARWATER *Puffinus persicus* 30.5–33 cm
Adult (7a, 7b). Visitor. Pakistan and India. Slightly larger than Audubon's, with browner coloration to upperparts, longer bill, less extensive white on underwing, and brownish axillaries and flanks. There may be differences in leg and bill colour. Offshore and pelagic waters.

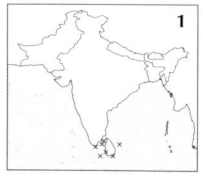 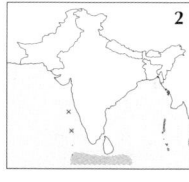 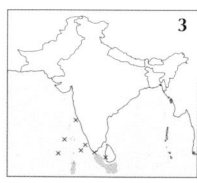 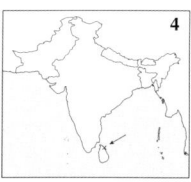

 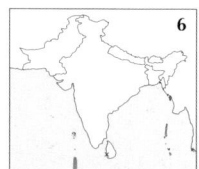 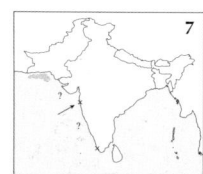

PLATE 88: PITTAS, BROADBILLS, ASIAN FAIRY BLUEBIRD AND LEAFBIRDS

Maps p. 129

1 BLUE-NAPED PITTA *Pitta nipalensis* 25 cm
Male (1a), female (1b) and juvenile (1c). Resident. Himalayas, NE India and Bangladesh. Large and stocky, with fulvous underparts. Male has glistening blue hindcrown and nape. Female has smaller greenish-blue patch on nape. Has powerful double whistle. Broadleaved evergreen forest.

2 BLUE PITTA *Pitta cyanea* 23 cm
Male (2a), female (2b) and juvenile (2c). Resident. NE India and Bangladesh. Pinkish-red hindcrown and black spotting on underparts. Male has blue upperparts. Female has dark olive upperparts. Song is a liquid *pleoow-whit*, the first part falling, the second part sharp and short. Broadleaved evergreen forest.

3 HOODED PITTA *Pitta sordida* 19 cm
Adult (3a) and juvenile (3b). Summer visitor or resident? Himalayas, NE India and Bangladesh. Black head with chestnut crown, green breast and flanks, and black belly patch. Song is an explosive double whistle, *wieuw-wieuw*. Broadleaved evergreen and moist deciduous forest.

4 INDIAN PITTA *Pitta brachyura* 19 cm
Adult (4a) and juvenile (4b). Resident. Breeds in Himalayan foothills and NE India; winters in S India and Sri Lanka. Bold black stripe through eye, white throat and supercilium, buff lateral crown-stripes, and buff breast and flanks. A sharp two-noted whistle, second note descending, *pree-treer*. Mainly broadleaved forest.

5 MANGROVE PITTA *Pitta megarhyncha* 20 cm
Adult (5a) and juvenile (5b). Resident? Sunderbans, Bangladesh. Similar to Indian Pitta, but larger and longer bill, uniform rufous-brown crown with narrow buffish supercilium, and deeper blue wing-coverts and rump. A loud, slurred *tae-laew*. Mangroves.

6 SILVER-BREASTED BROADBILL *Serilophus lunatus* 18 cm
Male (6a) and female (6b). Resident. Himalayan foothills, NE India and Bangladesh. Stout bluish bill, crested head, dusky supercilium, pale chestnut tertials, and white-and-blue on wing. A *ki-uu*, like a rusty hinge. Broadleaved evergreen and semi-evergreen forest.

7 LONG-TAILED BROADBILL *Psarisomus dalhousiae* 28 cm
Adult (7a) and juvenile (7b). Resident. Himalayan foothills, NE India and Bangladesh. Long tail. Green, with black cap, and yellow 'ear' spot and throat. Juvenile has green cap. A loud, piercing *pieu-wieuw-wieuw-wieuw*. Broadleaved and semi-evergreen forest.

8 ASIAN FAIRY BLUEBIRD *Irena puella* 25 cm
Male (8a) and female (8b). Resident. Himalayan foothills, hills of NE, E and S India, Bangladesh and Sri Lanka. Male has glistening violet-blue upperparts and black underparts. Female and first-year male entirely dull blue-green. Evergreen and moist deciduous forest.

9 BLUE-WINGED LEAFBIRD *Chloropsis cochinchinensis* 20 cm
Male (9a), female (9b) and juvenile (9c) *C. c. jerdoni*; **male (9d), female (9e) and juvenile (9f)** *C. c. cochinchinensis*. Resident. Peninsular India and Sri Lanka (*jerdoni*), hills of NE India and Bangladesh (nominate). Nominate has blue wing panel and sides to tail in all plumages (lacking in *jerdoni*). Male has smaller black throat patch than Golden-fronted, with yellowish forehead. Female nominate has bluish-green throat and turquoise moustachial stripe; juvenile has greenish head with hint of turquoise moustachial. Female and juvenile *jerdoni* have yellowish border to turquoise throat. Open forest and well-wooded areas.

10 GOLDEN-FRONTED LEAFBIRD *Chloropsis aurifrons* 19 cm
Adult *C. a. aurifrons* **(10a); adult (10b) and juvenile (10c)** *C. a. frontalis.* Resident. Himalayas, NE, E, S and SW India, Bangladesh and Sri Lanka. Lacks blue on flight feathers and tail. Adult has golden-orange forehead. Nominate, of NE subcontinent, has broader yellow border to black throat than *frontalis* from S India. Juvenile head green, with hint of turquoise moustachial stripe. Broadleaved forest and secondary growth.

11 ORANGE-BELLIED LEAFBIRD *Chloropsis hardwickii* 20 cm
Male (11a), female (11b) and juvenile (11c). Resident. Himalayas, NE India and Bangladesh. Male has orange belly, and black of throat extends to breast. Female has orange belly centre and large blue moustachial stripe. Juvenile has green head; some with touch of orange on belly. Broadleaved forest.

1 **RED-BACKED SHRIKE** *Lanius collurio* 17 cm
   Male (1a), female (1b) and first-winter (1c). Autumn passage migrant. Pakistan and NW
   India. Male lacks broad black forehead, has rufous mantle, and lacks white wing patch.
   Female has grey cast to head and nape, and dark brown tail. First-winter similar to
   female, but has barred upperparts. Bushes and cultivation in dry country.

2 **RUFOUS-TAILED SHRIKE** *Lanius isabellinus* 17 cm
   Male (2a), female (2b) and first-winter (2c) *L. i. phoenicuroides;* **male (2d), female (2e)**
   and first-winter (2f) *L. i. isabellinus.* Breeds in Baluchistan; winters mainly in NW subcontinent. Typically, has paler sandy-brown/grey-brown mantle and warmer rufous
   rump and tail than Brown. Male has small white patch at base of primaries. Female has
   grey-brown ear-coverts. Open dry scrub.

3 **BROWN SHRIKE** *Lanius cristatus* 18–19 cm
   Male (3a) and first-winter (3b) *L. c. cristatus;* **male** *L. c. lucionensis* **(3c).** Widespread
   winter visitor; unrecorded in Pakistan. Compared with Rufous-tailed, typically has darker rufous-brown upperparts (lacking clear contrast between crown and mantle and
   between mantle and tail); also thicker bill and more graduated tail. *L. c. lucionensis* has
   grey cast to crown. Forest edges and scrub.

4 **BURMESE SHRIKE** *Lanius collurioides* 20 cm
   Male (4a), female (4b) and immature (4c). Passage migrant. Mainly NE India. Male has
   dark grey crown and nape, dark chestnut mantle, white tail sides, and chestnut rump.
   Female has whitish forehead, and paler chestnut mantle than male. Immature has brownish-grey crown with indistinct dark and buff barring, rufous mantle with some diffuse
   dark barring, and rufous rump and uppertail-coverts. Secondary growth, and bushes in
   cultivation.

5 **BAY-BACKED SHRIKE** *Lanius vittatus* 17 cm
   Adult (5a), immature (5b) and juvenile (5c). Widespread resident; unrecorded in the
   northeast and Sri Lanka. Adult has black forehead and mask contrasting with pale grey
   crown and nape, deep maroon mantle, whitish rump, and white patch at base of primaries. Juvenile told from juvenile Long-tailed by smaller size and shorter tail, more uniform greyish/buffish base colour to upperparts, pale rump, and more intricately patterned
   wing-coverts and tertials (with buff fringes and dark subterminal crescents and central
   marks), and primary coverts are prominently tipped with buff. First-year like washed-out
   version of adult; lacks black forehead. Open dry scrub, and bushes in cultivation.

6 **LONG-TAILED SHRIKE** *Lanius schach* 25 cm
   Adult (6a) and juvenile (6b) *L. s. erythronotus;* **adult** *L. s. caniceps* **(6c); adult** *L. s. tri-*
   ***color* (6d).** Widespread resident. Adult has grey mantle, rufous scapulars and upper back
   (except *caniceps* of peninsular India and Sri Lanka), narrow black forehead, rufous sides
   to black tail, and small white patch on primaries. Juvenile has (dark-barred) rufous-
   brown scapulars, back and rump; dark greater coverts and tertials fringed rufous.
   Himalayan *tricolor* has black hood. Bushes in cultivation, open forest, gardens.

7 **GREY-BACKED SHRIKE** *Lanius tephronotus* 25 cm
   Adult (7a) and juvenile (7b). Breeds in Himalayas; winters in Himalayas and adjacent
   plains in N and NE India and Bangladesh. Adult has dark grey upperparts (no rufous on
   scapulars and upper back); usually lacks white primary patch. Juvenile has cold grey
   base colour to upperparts. Bushes in cultivation, scrub and secondary growth.

8 **LESSER GREY SHRIKE** *Lanius minor* 20 cm
   Adult (8a) and juvenile (8b). Vagrant. India. Adult has black forehead (lacking on first-
   winter). Smaller than other 'grey shrikes', with mainly black secondaries, and long extension of primaries beyond tertials. Open dry country with bushes.

9 **SOUTHERN GREY SHRIKE** *Lanius meridionalis* 24 cm
   Adult (9a) and juvenile (9b) *L. e. lahtora.* Resident. Mainly N, NW and W subcontinent.
   Adult has pale grey mantle, white scapulars, bold white markings on black wings and
   tail, greyish rump, and all-white underparts. Juvenile has sandy cast to grey upperparts,
   buff tips to tertials and coverts, and grey mask. *L. m. pallidirostris* (not illustrated), which
   breeds in extreme W Pakistan and winters east to Rajasthan, lacks black forehead, has
   restricted dark mask and paler upperparts. Scrub and open forest in dry country.

10 **GREAT GREY SHRIKE** *Lanius excubitor* 25 cm
    Adult *L. e. homeyeri.* Vagrant. Pakistan and India. Lacks black forehead and has pale
    grey mantle. Very similar to *pallidirostris* race of Southern Grey but has broad white
    band at base of secondaries, and white rump.

PLATE 89, p. 206

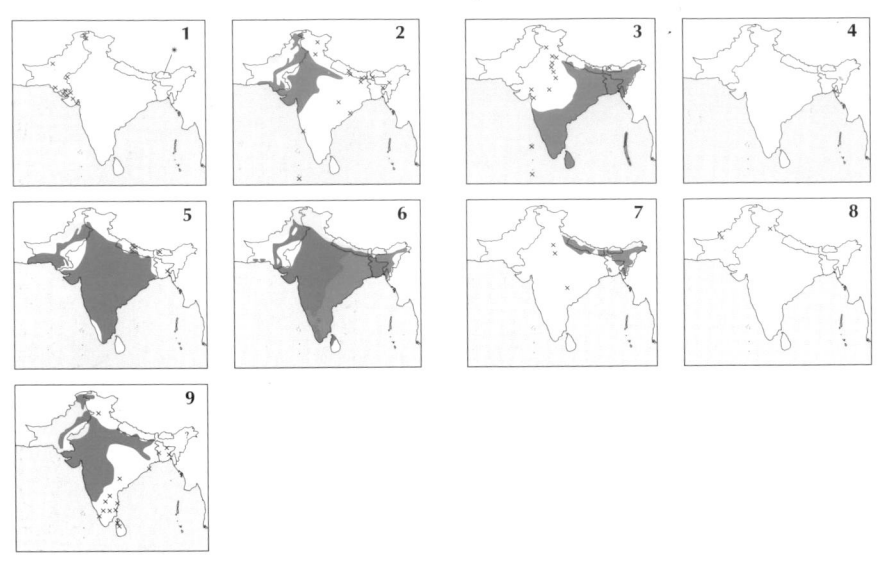

PLATE 90, p. 210

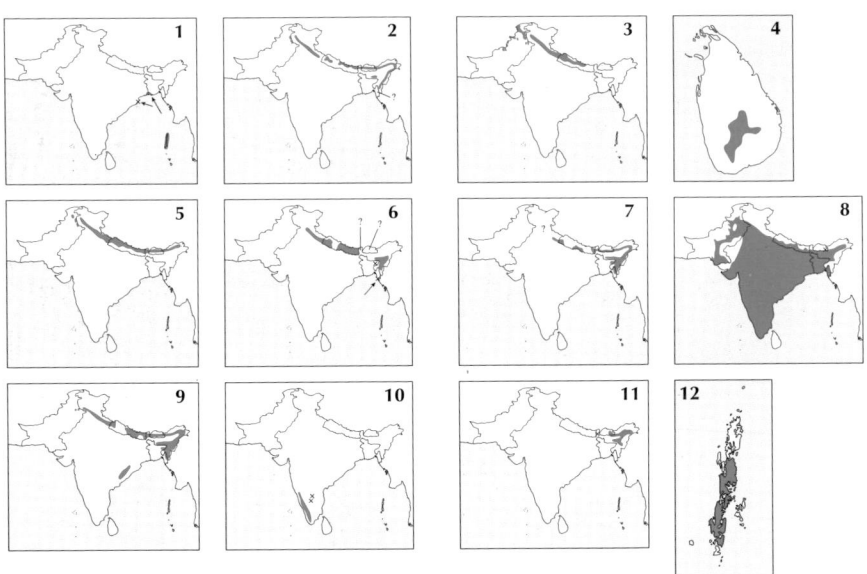

PLATE 91, p. 212

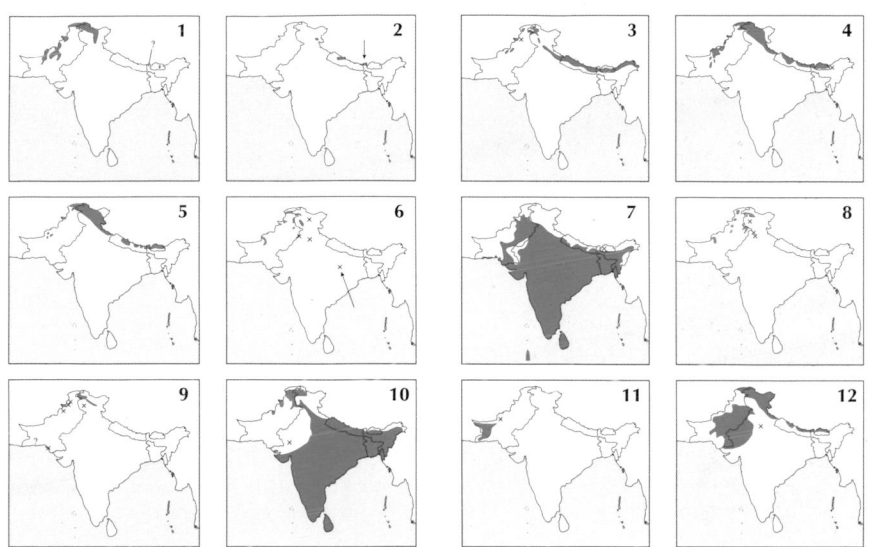

PLATE 92, p. 214

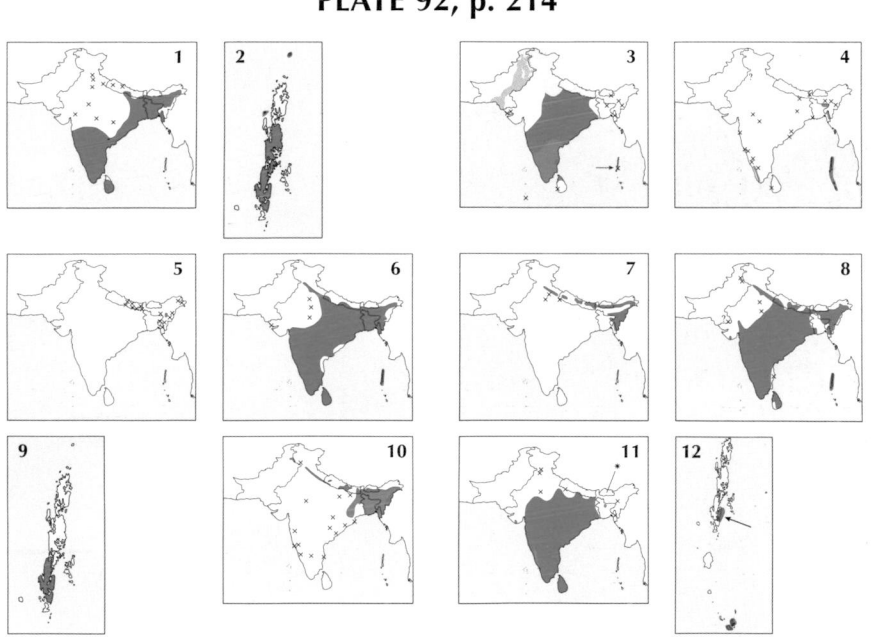

PLATE 90: JAYS, MAGPIES, TREEPIES AND MANGROVE WHISTLER

Maps p. 208

1 **MANGROVE WHISTLER** *Pachycephala grisola* 17 cm
Adult. Resident. Sunderbans in India and Bangladesh, and Andamans. Drab grey-brown upperparts and breast, and thick black bill. Mangroves.

2 **EURASIAN JAY** *Garrulus glandarius* 32–36 cm
Adult. Resident. Himalayas, NE India and Bangladesh. Pinkish- to reddish-brown head and body, black moustachial stripe, and blue barring on wings. White rump contrasts with black tail in flight. Temperate forest, mainly broadleaved.

3 **BLACK-HEADED JAY** *Garrulus lanceolatus* 33 cm
Adult. Resident. NW mountains of Pakistan and Himalayas. Black face and crest, streaked throat, and pinkish-fawn body; blue barring on wings and tail. Mixed temperate forest.

4 **SRI LANKA BLUE MAGPIE** *Urocissa ornata* 42–47 cm
Adult. Resident. Sri Lanka. Chestnut head and wings, blue body, and white-tipped blue tail. Evergreen broadleaved forest.

5 **YELLOW-BILLED BLUE MAGPIE** *Urocissa flavirostris* 61–66 cm
Adult (5a) and juvenile (5b) *U. f. cucullata*; **adult** *U. f. flavirostris* **(5c)**. Resident. Himalayas and NE India. Yellow bill, and white crescent on nape. Nominate eastern race has yellow wash to underparts. Juvenile has olive-yellow bill. Temperate mixed forest.

6 **RED-BILLED BLUE MAGPIE** *Urocissa erythrorhyncha* 65–68 cm
Adult (6a) and juvenile (6b). Resident. Himalayas, NE India and Bangladesh. Red bill, and white hindcrown and nape. Juvenile has more extensive white crown. Broadleaved forest and trees in cultivation.

7 **COMMON GREEN MAGPIE** *Cissa chinensis* 37–39 cm
Adult. Resident. Himalayas, NE India and Bangladesh. Green, with red bill and legs, black mask, chestnut wings, and white tips to tertials and tail feathers. Broadleaved evergreen and moist deciduous forest.

8 **RUFOUS TREEPIE** *Dendrocitta vagabunda* 46–50 cm
Adult (8a) and immature (8b) *D. v. vagabunda*; **adult** *D. v. pallida* **(8c).** Widespread resident; unrecorded in Sri Lanka. Slate-grey hood, buffish underparts and rump, pale grey wing panel, and whitish subterminal tail-band. Juvenile has brown hood. Open wooded country, and gardens with trees and bushes.

9 **GREY TREEPIE** *Dendrocitta formosae* 36–40 cm
Adult (9a) and immature (9b). Resident. Himalayas, NE India, Eastern Ghats and Bangladesh. Dark grey face, grey underparts and rump, and black wings with white patch at base of primaries. Juvenile duller version of adult. Broadleaved forest and secondary growth.

10 **WHITE-BELLIED TREEPIE** *Dendrocitta leucogastra* 48 cm
Adult. Resident. Western Ghats and SE India. Black face, white nape and underparts, white rump, black wings with white patch, and extensive black tip to tail. Evergreen hill forest and secondary growth.

11 **COLLARED TREEPIE** *Dendrocitta frontalis* 38 cm
Adult. Resident. Himalayas and NE India. Black face and throat, grey nape and underparts, rufous lower belly and vent, rufous rump, and black tail. Broadleaved evergreen forest.

12 **ANDAMAN TREEPIE** *Dendrocitta bayleyi* 32 cm
Adult (12a) and immature (12b). Resident. Andamans, where the only treepie. Blue-grey hood, rufous-brown upperparts, bright rufous underparts, blackish tail, and white patch on wing. Juvenile has brownish hood. Dense evergreen forest.

PLATE 91: BLACK-BILLED MAGPIE, HUME'S GROUNDPECKER, SPOTTED NUTCRACKER, CHOUGHS AND CROWS   Maps p. 209

1 **BLACK-BILLED MAGPIE** *Pica pica* 43–50 cm
Adult. Resident. Mountains of N and W Pakistan, and Himalayas in N India and N Bhutan. Black and white, with long metallic green/purple tail. Open cultivated upland valleys.

2 **HUME'S GROUNDPECKER** *Pseudopodoces humilis* 19 cm
Adult. Resident. Himalayas in extreme N India and Nepal. Downcurved black bill. Sandy-brown upperparts, buffish underparts, and white tail sides. Tibetan steppe country.

3 **SPOTTED NUTCRACKER** *Nucifraga caryocatactes* 32–35 cm
Adult *N. c. multipunctata* (3a); adult *N. c. hemispila* (3b). Resident. Mountains of NW Pakistan and Himalayas. Mainly brown, with white spotting on head and body (*multipunctata* of W Himalayas more heavily spotted and with white tips to wing feathers). Coniferous forest.

4 **RED-BILLED CHOUGH** *Pyrrhocorax pyrrhocorax* 36–40 cm
Adult (4a) and juvenile (4b). Resident. Mountains of W Pakistan and Himalayas. Curved red bill (shorter and orange-brown on juvenile). High mountains, alpine pastures and cultivation.

5 **YELLOW-BILLED CHOUGH** *Pyrrhocorax graculus* 37–39 cm
Adult. Resident. Mountains of W Pakistan and Himalayas. Almost straight yellow bill (olive-yellow on juvenile). High mountains, alpine pastures and cultivation.

6 **EURASIAN JACKDAW** *Corvus monedula* 34–39 cm
Adult. Resident. Mountains of W and N Pakistan, and NW Himalayas. Small size. Grey nape and hindneck. Adult has pale grey iris. Open cultivated valleys.

7 **HOUSE CROW** *Corvus splendens* 40 cm
Adult *C. s. splendens* (7a); adult *C. s. zugmayeri* (7b). Widespread resident. Two-toned appearance, with paler nape, neck and breast. Pale collar most pronounced in north-westernmost *zugmayeri*, less prominent in widely distributed nominate, and poorly-defined in races in S India and Sri Lanka (not illustrated). Around human habitation and cultivation.

8 **ROOK** *Corvus frugilegus* 47 cm
Adult (8a, 8b) and juvenile (8c). Winter visitor. Pakistan. Long, pointed bill, steep forehead, and baggy 'trousers'. Adult has bare white skin at base of bill and on throat. Cultivation and pastures.

9 **CARRION CROW** *Corvus corone* 48–56 cm
Adult *C. c. orientalis* (9a, 9b); adult *C. c. sharpii* (9c). Resident (*C. c. orientalis*) and winter visitor (*C. c. sharpii*). Mountains of Pakistan and NW India. Comparatively straight bill and flat crown. Race *sharpii* two-toned like House Crow, but has black head and breast and grey mantle. Open country with cultivation.

10 **LARGE-BILLED CROW** *Corvus macrorhynchos* 46–59 cm
Adult *C. m. intermedius* (10a, 10b); adult *C. m. culminatus* (10c, 10d). Widespread resident. All black, lacking paler collar of House Crow. Domed head, and large bill with arched culmen. The two Himalayan forms (including *intermedius*) are bigger and with heavier bill, wedge-shaped tail, and harsher calls, compared with those in the 'plains' (including *culminatus*). Himalayan forms best told from Raven by absence of throat hackles, shorter and broader wings, less strongly wedge-shaped tail, squarer or domed crown, and dry *kaaa-kaaa* call. Wide range of habitats, except deserts and semi-deserts.

11 **BROWN-NECKED RAVEN** *Corvus ruficollis* 52–56 cm
Adult (11a, 11b). Resident. Pakistan. Brown cast to head, neck and breast; lacks prominent throat hackles. Slimmer than Common Raven, with different call. Desert.

12 **COMMON RAVEN** *Corvus corax* 58–69 cm
Adult *C. c. subcorax* (12a, 12b). Resident. Pakistan and NW India (*C. c. subcorax*), and high Himalayas (*C. c. tibetanus*). Very large; long and angular wings, prominent throat hackles, wedge-shaped tail, and deep resonant, croaking *wock...wock* call. Race *subcorax* in lowland desert and semi-desert; *tibetanus* in dry rocky areas above treeline.

PLATE 92: WOODSWALLOWS, ORIOLES AND CUCKOOSHRIKES
Maps p. 209

1 ASHY WOODSWALLOW *Artamus fuscus* 19 cm
Adult (1a, 1b). Resident. Mainly E, SE and S subcontinent. Slate-grey head, pinkish-grey underparts, and whitish crescent on uppertail-coverts. Open wooded country.

2 WHITE-BREASTED WOODSWALLOW *Artamus leucorynchus* 19 cm
Adult (2a, 2b). Resident. Andamans. Slate-grey head, white underparts, and broad white band across lower rump and uppertail-coverts. Forest clearings.

3 EURASIAN GOLDEN ORIOLE *Oriolus oriolus* 25 cm
Male (3a), female (3b) and immature (3c) *O. o. kundoo*; **male** *O. o. oriolus* (a vagrant) **(3d).** Summer visitor to W Pakistan, Himalayas and N plains; resident in N and C India; winters farther south. Male golden-yellow, with black mask and mainly black wings. Female and immature variable, usually with streaking on underparts and yellowish-green upperparts. Open woodland, and trees in cultivation.

4 BLACK-NAPED ORIOLE *Oriolus chinensis* 27 cm
Male (4a), female (4b) and immature (4c). Winter visitor to Kerala and Bangladesh; resident on Andamans and Nicobars; status elsewhere uncertain. Large, stout bill; nasal call. Black eye-stripe and nape band poorly defined in immature. Male has yellow mantle and wing-coverts concolorous with underparts (brighter than in Slender-billed). Female and immature probably not safely separable from Slender-billed by plumage. Broadleaved forest and well-wooded areas.

5 SLENDER-BILLED ORIOLE *Oriolus tenuirostris* 27 cm
Male (5a), female (5b) and immature (5c). Breeds in E Himalayas and NE India; winters west to C Nepal and Bihar. Long, slender, slightly downcurved bill, and woodpecker-like *kick* call are most reliable features from Black-naped. Adult has black stripe through eye and band across nape which tends to be narrower than in Black-naped (diffuse or indistinct on immature). Well-wooded areas.

6 BLACK-HOODED ORIOLE *Oriolus xanthornus* 25 cm
Male (6a), female (6b) and immature (6c). Widespread resident; unrecorded in Pakistan. Adult has black head and breast. Immature has yellow forehead, black-streaked white throat, and yellow breast. Open broadleaved forest and well-wooded areas.

7 MAROON ORIOLE *Oriolus traillii* 27 cm
Male (7a), female (7b) and immature (7c). Resident. Himalayas, NE India and Bangladesh. Maroon rump and tail. Male has maroon underparts. Female has whitish belly and flanks, streaked with maroon-grey. Immature has browner upperparts and brown-streaked white underparts. Dense broadleaved forest.

8 LARGE CUCKOOSHRIKE *Coracina macei* 30 cm
Male *C. m. nipalensis* **(8a); female (8b) and juvenile (8c)** *C. m. macei.* Widespread resident; unrecorded in northwest. Large. Pale grey upperparts and greyish-white underparts with variable amounts of faint grey barring. Male *macei* (peninsula) and female *nipalensis* (Himalayas and NE subcontinent) (not illustrated) have grey throat and breast and barring on belly. Open woodland, and trees in cultivation.

9 BAR-BELLIED CUCKOOSHRIKE *Coracina striata* 26 cm
Male (9a), female (9b) and immature (9c). Resident. Andamans. Smaller than Large Cuckooshrike, with darker grey upperparts and crimson iris. Female entirely barred below (Andaman race of Large has unbarred grey throat and breast). First-year has rufous cast to throat and breast. Forest.

10 BLACK-WINGED CUCKOOSHRIKE *Coracina melaschistos* 24 cm
Male (10a) and female (10b). Resident. Breeds in Himalayas and NE Indian hills; winters mainly in Himalayan foothills, E and NE India and Bangladesh. Male slate-grey, with black wings and bold white tips to tail feathers. Female paler grey, with faint barring on underparts. Open forest and groves.

11 BLACK-HEADED CUCKOOSHRIKE *Coracina melanoptera* 18 cm
Male (11a) and female (11b). Widespread resident; unrecorded in Pakistan. Male has slate-grey head and breast, and pale grey mantle. Female has whitish supercilium, barred underparts, and pale grey back and rump contrasting with blackish tail; broad white fringes to coverts and tertials. Open broadleaved forest and secondary growth.

12 PIED TRILLER *Lalage nigra* 18 cm
Male (12a) and female (12b). Resident. Nicobars. Male has white supercilium and black upperparts. Female has slate-grey upperparts and faintly barred underparts. Forest edges and secondary growth.

PLATE 93: MINIVETS, BAR-WINGED FLYCATCHER-SHRIKE AND FANTAILS
Maps p. 218

1 ROSY MINIVET *Pericrocotus roseus* 20 cm
Male (1a) and female (1b). Resident. Breeds in Himalayas and NE India; winters mainly in NE and E India and Bangladesh. Male has grey-brown upperparts, white throat, and pinkish underparts and rump. Female has greyish forehead, white throat, pale yellow underparts, and dull olive-yellow rump. Forest.

2 ASHY MINIVET *Pericrocotus divaricatus* 20 cm
Male (2a) and female (2b). Winter visitor. Mainly C and S India. Grey and white, lacking any yellow or red in plumage. Male has black 'hood'. Light forest.

3 SMALL MINIVET *Pericrocotus cinnamomeus* 16 cm
Male (3a) and female (3b) *P. c. malabaricus*; **male (3c) and female (3d)** *P. c. pallidus.* Widespread resident. Small size. Much racial variation. Palest is *pallidus* of NW subcontinent; brightest is *malabaricus* of SW peninsula. Male has dark grey to pale grey upperparts, black to dark grey throat, and deep orange to mainly white underparts. Female's underparts vary from mainly orange-yellow to mainly white. Open wooded areas.

4 WHITE-BELLIED MINIVET *Pericrocotus erythropygius* 15 cm
Male (4a) and female (4b). Resident. Mainly N and C India. White wing patch and orange rump. Male has black head and upperparts, and white underparts with orange breast. Female has brown upperparts and white underparts. Dry open scrub and forest.

5 GREY-CHINNED MINIVET *Pericrocotus solaris* 18 cm
Male (5a) and female (5b). Resident. Himalayas and NE India. Male has grey chin and pale orange throat, grey ear-coverts, slate-grey upperparts, and orange-red underparts and rump. Female has grey forehead, supercilium and ear-coverts, whitish chin and whitish sides to yellow throat. Moist broadleaved forest.

6 LONG-TAILED MINIVET *Pericrocotus ethologus* 20 cm
Male (6a) and female (6b). Resident. Breeds in N Baluchistan, Himalayas, NE India and Bangladesh; winters south to C India. Male has red wing line down secondaries. Female has indistinct yellow forehead and supercilium, grey ear-coverts, and pale yellow throat. Distinctive *pi-ru* whistle. Forest; also well-wooded areas in winter.

7 SHORT-BILLED MINIVET *Pericrocotus brevirostris* 20 cm
Male (7a) and female (7b). Resident. Himalayas and NE India. Male lacks extension of red wing patch down secondaries. Female has yellow forehead and cast to ear-coverts, and deep yellow throat concolorous with rest of underparts. Distinctive monotone whistle. Broadleaved forest and forest edges.

8 SCARLET MINIVET *Pericrocotus flammeus* 20–22 cm
Male (8a) and female (8b). Resident. Himalayas, hills of India, Bangladesh and Sri Lanka. Large. Isolated red (male) or yellow (female) patch on secondaries. Female head pattern closest to Short-billed. Forest.

9 BAR-WINGED FLYCATCHER-SHRIKE *Hemipus picatus* 15 cm
Male (9a) and female (9b) *H. p. picatus*; **male** *H. p. capitalis* of Himalayas **(9c).** Resident. Himalayas, hills of India, Bangladesh and Sri Lanka. Dark cap, white wing patch and white rump. Broadleaved forest and forest edges.

10 YELLOW-BELLIED FANTAIL *Rhipidura hypoxantha* 13 cm
Male. Resident. Himalayas, NE India and Bangladesh. Long fanned tail, yellow supercilium, dark mask, and yellow underparts. Forest.

11 WHITE-THROATED FANTAIL *Rhipidura albicollis* 19 cm
Adult *R. a. canescens* **(11a); adult** *R. a. albogularis* **(11b).** Resident. Himalayas, NE India, Bangladesh and Indian peninsula. Narrow white supercilium and white throat; lacks spotting on wing-coverts. Much racial variation: birds in Himalayas and northeast (e.g. *canescens*) have slate-grey underparts; birds in peninsula (e.g. *albogularis*) have white-spotted grey breast and buff belly. Forest, secondary growth and wooded areas.

12 WHITE-BROWED FANTAIL *Rhipidura aureola* 18 cm
Adult (12a) and juvenile (12b). Widespread resident. Broad white supercilia which meet over forehead, blackish throat, white breast and belly, and white spotting on wing-coverts. Forest and wooded areas.

C.D'S

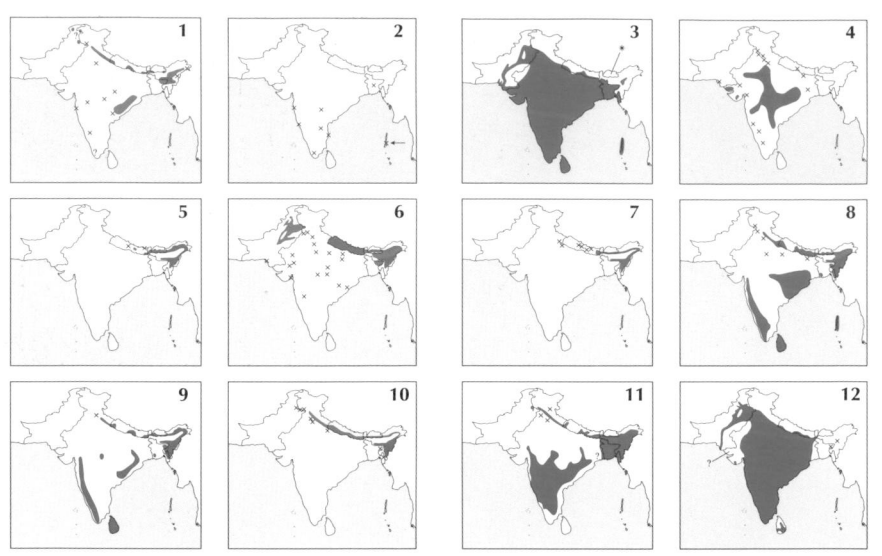

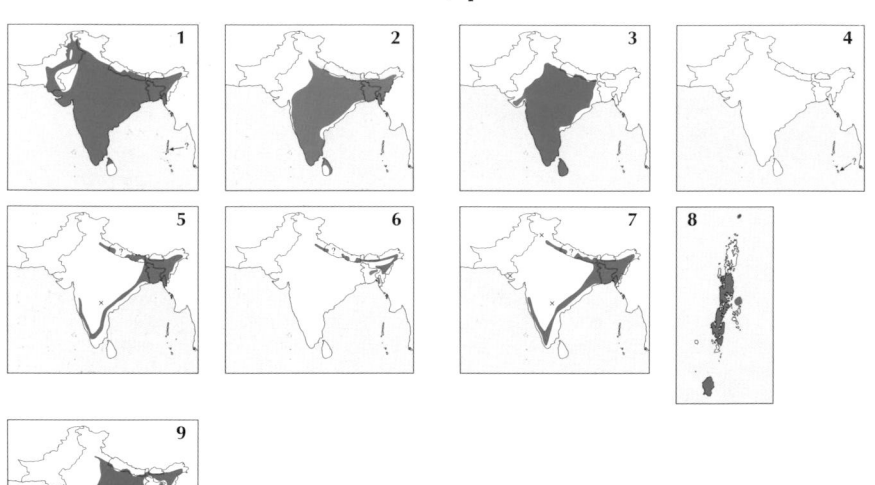

PLATE 95, p. 222

PLATE 97, p. 226

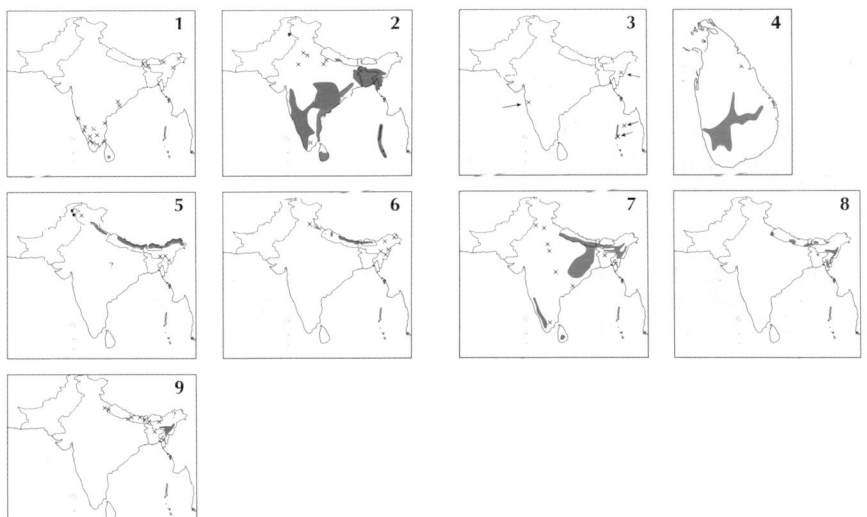

1 BLACK DRONGO *Dicrurus macrocercus* 28 cm
Juvenile (1a), immature (1b) and adult (1c). Widespread resident. Adult has glossy blue-black underparts and white rictal spot. Tail-fork may be lost during moult. First-winter has black underparts with bold whitish fringes. Juvenile has uniform dark brown upperparts and underparts. Around habitation and cultivation.

2 ASHY DRONGO *Dicrurus leucophaeus* 29 cm
Immature (2a) and adult (2b) *D. l. longicaudatus*; **adult** *D. l. hopwoodi* **(2c); adult** *D. l. salangensis* **(2d).** Breeds in Himalayas and NE Indian hills; winters in plains in peninsula and Sri Lanka. Adult has dark grey underparts and slate-grey upperparts with blue-grey gloss; iris bright red. First-winter has brownish-grey underparts with indistinct pale fringes. Juvenile as juvenile Black. E Himalayan *hopwoodi* paler grey. Vagrant *salangensis* has white lores and ear-coverts. Breeds in forest; winters in well-wooded areas.

3 WHITE-BELLIED DRONGO *Dicrurus caerulescens* 24 cm
Immature (3a) and adult (3b) *D. c. caerulescens*; **adult** *D. c. leucopygialis* **(3c).** Widespread resident; unrecorded in Pakistan, the northeast or Sri Lanka. Whitish from belly downwards in all plumages, except in Sri Lanka, where one race (*leucopygialis*) has white restricted to vent and undertail-coverts. Open forest and well-wooded areas.

4 CROW-BILLED DRONGO *Dicrurus annectans* 28 cm
Immature (4a) and adult (4b). Summer visitor/resident? in Himalayan foothills and NE India; winters in NE India and Bangladesh. Adult has stout bill, and widely splayed tail with shallow fork. First-winter has white spotting on breast and belly. Moist broadleaved forest.

5 BRONZED DRONGO *Dicrurus aeneus* 24 cm
Juvenile (5a) and adult (5b). Resident. Himalayan foothills, NE India, Bangladesh and Eastern and Western Ghats. Adult small, with shallow tail-fork, and heavily spangled. Juvenile has brown underparts, and duller and less heavily spangled upperparts. Moist broadleaved forest.

6 LESSER RACKET-TAILED DRONGO *Dicrurus remifer* 25 cm
Immature (6a) and adult (6b). Resident. Himalayan foothills, NE India and Bangladesh. Tufted forehead without crest, square-ended tail, and smaller size and bill than Greater Racket-tailed; has smaller flattened rackets which are webbed on both sides of shaft (rather than longer, twisted and webbed only on one side of shaft). As in Greater, tail streamers and rackets can be missing or broken in adult, and are missing in immature. Moist broadleaved forest.

7 SPANGLED DRONGO *Dicrurus hottentottus* 32 cm
Juvenile (7a) and adult (7b). Resident. Himalayan foothills, NE India, Bangladesh and Eastern and Western Ghats. Broad tail with upward-twisted corners, and long downcurved bill. Adult has extensive spangling, and hair-like crest. Moist broadleaved forest.

8 ANDAMAN DRONGO *Dicrurus andamanensis* 32 cm
Adult. Resident. Andamans. Large bill, and long broad tail with shallow fork twisted inwards at tip. Forest.

9 GREATER RACKET-TAILED DRONGO
Dicrurus paradiseus 32 cm
Immature (9a) and adult (9b) *D. p. ceylonicus*; **adult** *D. p. grandis* **(9c).** Widespread resident; unrecorded in Pakistan. Larger and with larger bill than Lesser Racket-tailed. Typically, has crest and forked tail; crest much reduced in some races and on immatures. *D. p. lophorhinus* of wet zone in Sri Lanka has long, deeply forked tail and lacks terminal rackets of other races. Broadleaved forest and bamboo jungle.

Greater Racket-tailed Drongo D. p. lophorhinus.
Drawing by Nigel Bean

PLATE 95: BLACK-NAPED MONARCH, ASIAN PARADISE-FLY-CATCHER, IORAS, WOODSHRIKES, BOHEMIAN WAXWING AND DIPPERS
Maps p. 219

1 BLACK-NAPED MONARCH *Hypothymis azurea* 16 cm
Male (1a) and female (1b) *H. a. styani*; **male (1c) and female (1d)** *H. a. ceylonensis.* Widespread resident; unrecorded in Pakistan. Male mainly blue, with black nape and gorget (except in Sri Lanka, where black often absent or indistinct). Female duller, with grey-brown mantle and wings. Broadleaved forest and well-wooded areas.

2 ASIAN PARADISE-FLYCATCHER *Terpsiphone paradisi* 20 cm
White male (2a), rufous male (2b) and female (2c). Widespread resident. Male has black head and crest, with white or rufous upperparts and long tail-streamers. Female has reduced crest and lacks streamers. Forest and well-wooded areas.

3 COMMON IORA *Aegithina tiphia* 14 cm
Male breeding (3a), male non-breeding (3b) and female (3c) *A. t. humei*; **male breeding** *A. t. multicolor* **(3d); male breeding** *A. t. tiphia* **(3e).** Widespread resident; unrecorded in the northwest. Lacks white on tail. Very variable. Crown and mantle of breeding males vary from uniformly black (e.g. *multicolor* of S India and Sri Lanka), to black mixed with much yellow on mantle (e.g. *humei* of central peninsula), to mainly yellowish-green (e.g. *tiphia* of Himalayas and northeast). Females very similar to non-breeding males. Open forest and well-wooded areas.

4 MARSHALL'S IORA *WHITE - TAILED* *Aegithina nigrolutea* 14 cm
Male breeding (4a) and female (4b). Resident. N and C peninsular India. Extensive white on black tail. Breeding male has black crown and nape, yellow hind-collar (not usually shown by any race of Common) and blackish mantle with yellowish-green mottling. Scrub and groves.

5 LARGE WOODSHRIKE *Tephrodornis gularis* 23 cm
Male (5a) and female (5b). Resident. Himalayan foothills, NE, E and SW India, and Bangladesh. Larger than Common Woodshrike; lacks white supercilium and white on tail. Female differs from male in having poorly defined brown mask, and brown (rather than grey) crown and mantle. Broadleaved forest and well-wooded areas.

6 COMMON WOODSHRIKE *Tephrodornis pondicerianus* 18 cm
Adult (6a) and juvenile (6b). Widespread resident. Smaller than Large Woodshrike, with broad white supercilium and white tail sides. Open broadleaved forest, secondary growth and well-wooded areas.

7 BOHEMIAN WAXWING *Bombycilla garrulus* 18 cm
Adult male. Vagrant. Pakistan, Nepal, India. Prominent crest, black throat, and waxy red and yellow markings on wings and tail. Open country with fruiting trees and bushes.

8 WHITE-THROATED DIPPER *Cinclus cinclus* 20 cm
Adult (8a) and juvenile (8b) *C. c. cashmeriensis*; **adult** *C. c. leucogaster* **(8c).** Resident. Himalayas. Adult has white throat and breast. Juvenile has dark scaling on grey upperparts and grey scaling on whitish underparts. White-bellied *leucogaster* has been recorded in N Pakistan. Mountain streams.

9 BROWN DIPPER *Cinclus pallasii* 20 cm
Adult (9a) and juvenile (9b). Resident. Himalayas, NE India and Bangladesh. Adult entirely brown. Juvenile has white or rufous-buff spotting on brown upperparts and underparts. Mountain streams and small lakes.

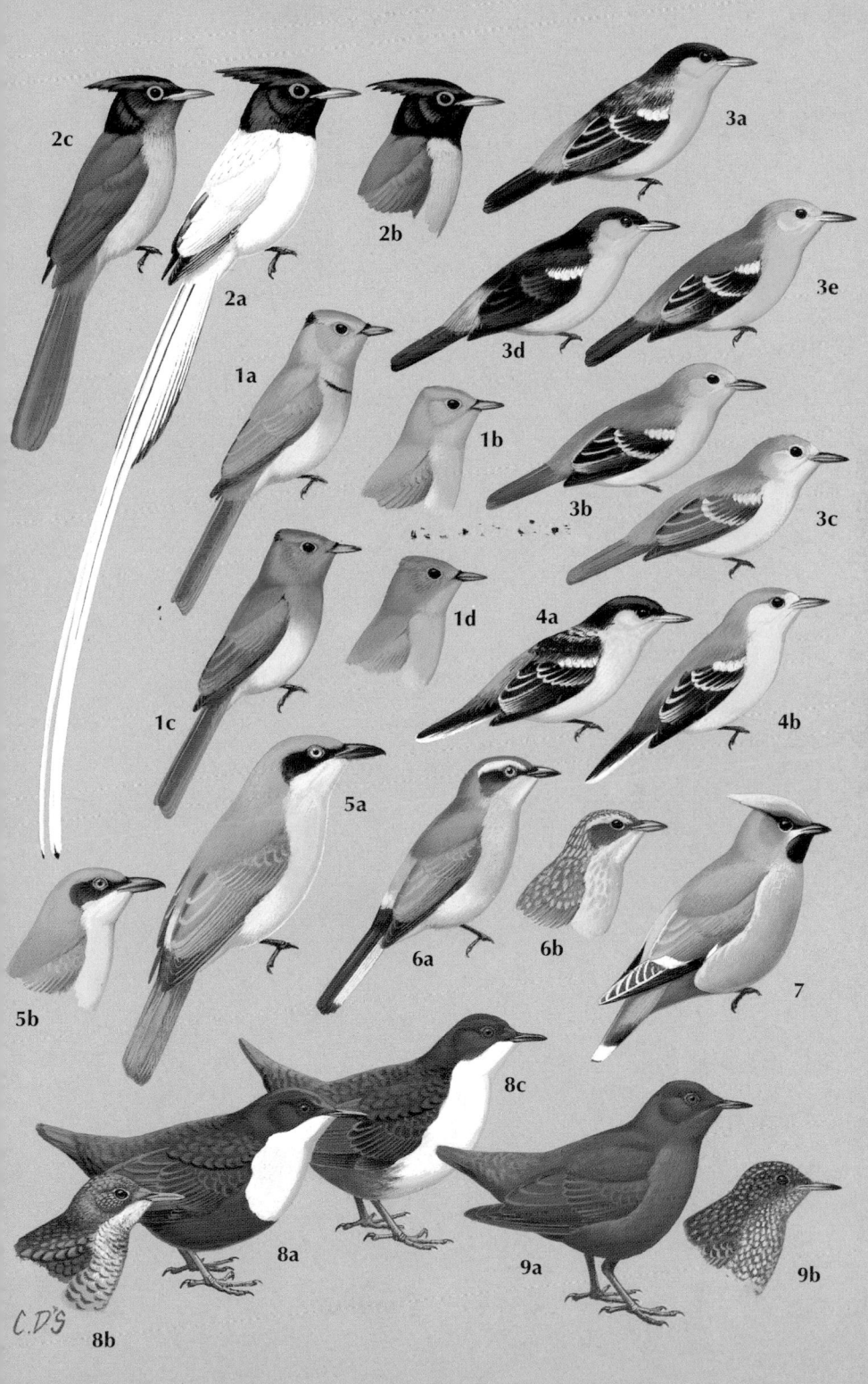

PLATE 96: ROCK THRUSHES AND WHISTLING THRUSHES

1 **RUFOUS-TAILED ROCK THRUSH** *Monticola saxatilis* 20 cm
Male breeding (1a), female (1b) and 1st-winter male (1c). Breeds in Baluchistan; passage migrant in Pakistan and Ladakh. Orange-red uppertail-coverts and tail in all plumages. Male has bluish head/mantle, white back and orange underparts, which are obscured by pale fringes in non-breeding and first-winter plumages. Female has scaling on upperparts, and orange wash to scaled underparts. Open rocky hillsides.

2 **BLUE-CAPPED ROCK THRUSH** *Monticola cinclorhynchus* 17 cm
Male breeding (2a), female (2b) and 1st-winter male (2c). Summer visitor to Himalayas and NE India; winters mainly in Western Ghats and Assam hills. Male has white wing patch and blue-black tail; blue crown and throat and orange underparts, obscured by pale fringes in non-breeding and first-winter plumages. Female has uniform olive-brown upperparts; lacks buff neck patch of Chestnut-bellied and orange-red tail of Rufous-tailed. Summers in open dry forest; winters in moist forest and well-wooded areas.

3 **CHESTNUT-BELLIED ROCK THRUSH** *Monticola rufiventris* 23 cm
Male (3a), female (3b), juvenile male (3c) and juvenile female (3d). Resident. Himalayas and NE India. Male has chestnut-red underparts and blue rump and uppertail-coverts; lacks white on wing. Female has orange-buff neck patch, dark barring on slaty olive-brown upperparts, and heavy scaling on underparts. Non-breeding and first-winter male (not illustrated) are very similar to breeding male but have fine buff fringes to mantle, scapulars and throat. Juvenile has pale spotting on upperparts; male with blue on wing. Open forest on rocky slopes.

4 **BLUE ROCK THRUSH** *Monticola solitarius* 20 cm
Male breeding (4a), female (4b) and 1st-winter male (4c) *M. s. pandoo*; **male** *M. s. philippensis* **(4d).** Resident and winter visitor. Breeds in Baluchistan and Himalayas; widespread in winter. Male indigo-blue, obscured by pale fringes in non-breeding and first-winter plumages. Female has bluish cast to slaty-brown upperparts, and buff scaling on underparts. Vagrant *philippensis* has rufous breast and belly. Breeds on open rocky slopes; winters in dry rocky areas.

5 **SRI LANKA WHISTLING THRUSH** *Myophonus blighi* 20 cm
Male (5a) and female (5b). Resident. Sri Lanka. Male brownish-black, with glistening blue on forehead, supercilium and shoulders. Female brown (with rufescent cast to lores, throat and breast) with blue shoulders. Mountain streams in moist, dense forest.

6 **MALABAR WHISTLING THRUSH** *Myophonus horsfieldii* 25 cm
Adult (6a) and juvenile (6b). Resident. Hills of C and W India. Adult blackish, with blue forehead and shoulders. Juvenile more sooty-brown, and lacks blue forehead. Rocky hill streams in forest and well-wooded areas.

7 **BLUE WHISTLING THRUSH** *Myophonus caeruleus* 33 cm
Adult (7a) and juvenile (7b). Resident. N Baluchistan, Himalayas and NE India. Adult blackish, spangled with glistening blue; yellow bill. Juvenile browner, and lacks blue spangling. Forest and wooded areas, usually close to streams.

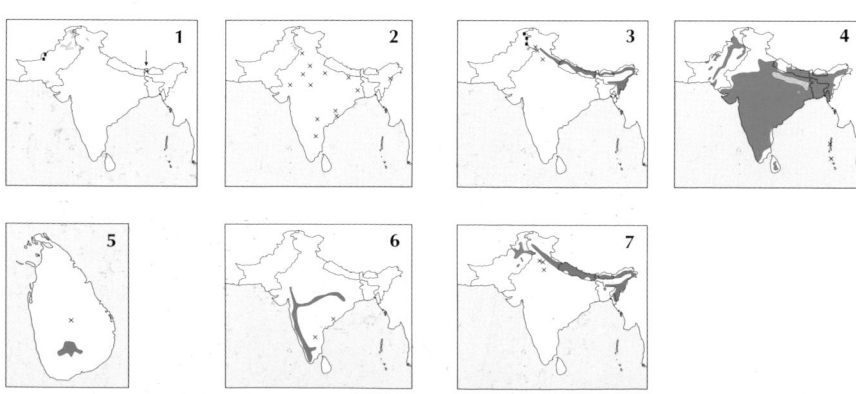

1 PIED THRUSH *Zoothera wardii* 22 cm
Male (1a), female (1b) and juvenile (1c). Resident. Breeds in Himalayas and NE India; winters in Sri Lanka and Tamil Nadu. Male black and white, with white supercilium and wing-bars, and yellow bill. Female has buff supercilium and wing-bars, and scaled underparts. Juvenile has buff streaking on mantle and breast. Open broadleaved forest and secondary growth.

② ORANGE-HEADED THRUSH *Zoothera citrina* 21 cm
Male (2a), female (2b) and juvenile (2c) *Z. c. citrina*; **male** *Z. c. cyanotus* (2d). Widespread resident. Adult has orange head and underparts; male with blue-grey mantle, female with olive-brown wash to mantle. Juvenile has buffish-orange streaking on upperparts and mottled breast. *Z. c. cyanotus*, of the peninsula, has vertical black head stripes. Damp, shady places in forest and well-wooded areas.

3 SIBERIAN THRUSH *Zoothera sibirica* 22 cm
Adult male (3a), female (3b) and 1st-winter male (3c). Winter visitor. Manipur hills and Andamans. Male slate-grey, with white supercilium; buff supercilium, throat and greater-covert bar in first-winter plumage. Female has buff supercilium and scaling on underparts; lacks buff tips to tertials of Pied, wing-bars are much less prominent or non-existent, while scaling on flanks is partly obscured by olive-brown (flanks whiter, and scaling more prominent, in female Pied). Forest.

4 SPOT-WINGED THRUSH *Zoothera spiloptera* 27 cm
Adult (4a) and juvenile (4b). Resident. Sri Lanka. Adult has white wing-bars, black face markings, and black spotting on underparts. Juvenile has diffuse head pattern, buff streaking on mantle, and scaled breast. Moist forest and well-wooded areas.

5 PLAIN-BACKED THRUSH *Zoothera mollissima* 27 cm
Adult (5a) and juvenile (5b). Resident. Himalayas and NE India. Adult lacks (or has indistinct) wing-bars, and has heavy black scaling on belly and flanks. Has more rufescent coloration to upperparts (valid in C and E Himalayas only), less pronounced pale wing panel, and shorter tail. Juvenile has buff streaking on upperparts and heavy black scaling and barring on underparts. Summers on rocky and grassy slopes with bushes; winters in forest and open country with bushes.

6 LONG-TAILED THRUSH *Zoothera dixoni* 27 cm
Adult (6a) and juvenile (6b). Resident. Himalayas and NE India. Adult has prominent wing-bars; belly and flanks more sparsely marked than on Plain-backed, flanks more barred than scaled, and is longer-tailed. Juvenile has buff streaking on upperparts; underparts similar to adult's. Undergrowth in forest; in winter, also open country with bushes.

7 SCALY THRUSH *Zoothera dauma* 26–27 cm
Adult (7a) and juvenile (7b) *Z. d. dauma*; **adult** *Z. d. imbricata* (7c). Breeds in Himalayas, hills of NE and W India and Sri Lanka; N birds winter south to Orissa. Boldly scaled upperparts and underparts. Juvenile has spotted breast. Sri Lankan *imbricata* smaller, with longer bill, and rufous-buff underparts. Forest; also well-wooded areas in winter.

8 LONG-BILLED THRUSH *Zoothera monticola* 28 cm
Adult (8a) and juvenile (8b). Resident. Himalayas and NE India. Huge bill and short tail. Differs from Dark-sided in larger bill with prominent hook, dark lores, dark slate-olive upperparts, darker and more uniform sides of head and underparts, and dark spotting on belly. Moist, dense forest.

9 DARK-SIDED THRUSH *Zoothera marginata* 25 cm
Adult (9a) and juvenile (9b). Resident. Himalayas and NE India. Long bill and short tail. Differs from Long-billed in rufescent-brown upperparts, pale lores, more strongly marked sides of head (dark ear-covert patch with pale crescent behind), paler underparts with more prominent scaling on breast and flanks, and rufous panel on wing. Moist, dense forest near streams.

PLATE 98: *TURDUS* THRUSHES Maps p. 230

1 TICKELL'S THRUSH *Turdus unicolor* 21 cm
Male (1a), female (1b) and 1st-winter male (1c). Resident. Summers in Himalayas; winters mainly farther east and south in India. Small thrush. Male pale bluish-grey, with whitish belly and vent. Female and first-winter male have pale throat and submoustachial stripe and dark malar stripe, and often with spotting on breast. Females of some races of Eurasian Blackbird of peninsula can be quite similar. Tickell's is smaller with finer bill; white throat, dark malar stripe, spotting on breast (if present), and orange-buff wash to breast and flanks are also useful features of Tickell's. Open forest and well-wooded areas.

2 BLACK-BREASTED THRUSH *Turdus dissimilis* 22 cm
Male (2a) and female (2b). Resident in NE India; winters south to Bangladesh. Male has black head and upper breast, and orange lower breast and flanks. Female has plain face, spotted breast, and orange lower breast and flanks. Broadleaved evergreen forest; also scrub and mangroves in winter.

3 WHITE-COLLARED BLACKBIRD *Turdus albocinctus* 27 cm
Male (3a), female (3b) and juvenile (3c). Resident. Himalayas and NE India. Male black, with white collar. Female brown, with variable pale collar. Juvenile has bold spotting on orange-buff underparts. Forest and forest edges.

4 GREY-WINGED BLACKBIRD *Turdus boulboul* 28 cm
Male (4a), female (4b) and juvenile male (4c). Resident. Himalayas and NE India. Male black, with greyish wing panel. Female olive-brown, with pale rufous-brown wing panel. Juvenile has orange-buff streaking on upperparts, and very variable orange-buff markings on underparts; wing panel similar to adult's. Forest and forest edges.

5 EURASIAN BLACKBIRD *Turdus merula* 25–28 cm
Male *T. m. kinnisii* (5a); male (5b) and female (5c) *T. m. nigropileus*; male (5d) and female (5e) *T. m. maximus*. Resident. Himalayas, hills of peninsular India and Sri Lanka. Very variable. Males of Himalayan races (e.g. *maximus*) are black and females mainly dark brown. Races in the peninsula (e.g. *nigropileus*) are smaller, brownish slate-grey above, with variable dark cap, have distinct orange patch behind eye (not shown in plate), and have paler underparts; females are paler than Himalayan races, especially on underparts. In Sri Lanka *kinnisii* is uniform bluish-grey. In Himalayas, summers on grassy and rocky slopes with scrub, winters in junipers; farther south, in moist forest and well-wooded areas.

6 CHESTNUT THRUSH *Turdus rubrocanus* 27 cm
Male (6a) and female (6b) *T. r. rubrocanus*; male *T. r. gouldii* (6c). Resident. Himalayas and NE India. Grey head; chestnut upperparts and underparts. Male *rubrocanus* has pale collar; female has more uniform brownish-grey head/neck. *T. r. gouldii*, a rare visitor to E Himalayas and NE, has darker head/neck and lacks collar. Summers in coniferous and mixed forest; winters in open wooded areas.

7 KESSLER'S THRUSH *Turdus kessleri* 27 cm
Male (7a) and female (7b). Winter visitor. E Himalayas. Male has black head, creamy-white mantle and breast-band, and chestnut back and belly. Female has brownish head, pale mantle and breast-band, and ginger-brown belly. Shrubberies, juniper stands and fields.

8 GREY-SIDED THRUSH *Turdus feae* 24 cm
Male (8a) and female (8b). Winter visitor. NE India. White supercilium and crescent below eye; rufescent-olive upperparts, crown and ear-coverts. Male has grey flanks. Female may have flanks washed with orange-buff, and look similar to dullest Eyebrowed but that species has greyish cast to crown and ear-coverts. Habitat unrecorded in region.

9 EYEBROWED THRUSH *Turdus obscurus* 23 cm
Male (9a) and 1st-winter female (9b). Winter visitor. E Himalayas. White supercilium, greyish crown and ear-coverts, and orange flanks. Open forest.

PLATE 98, p. 228

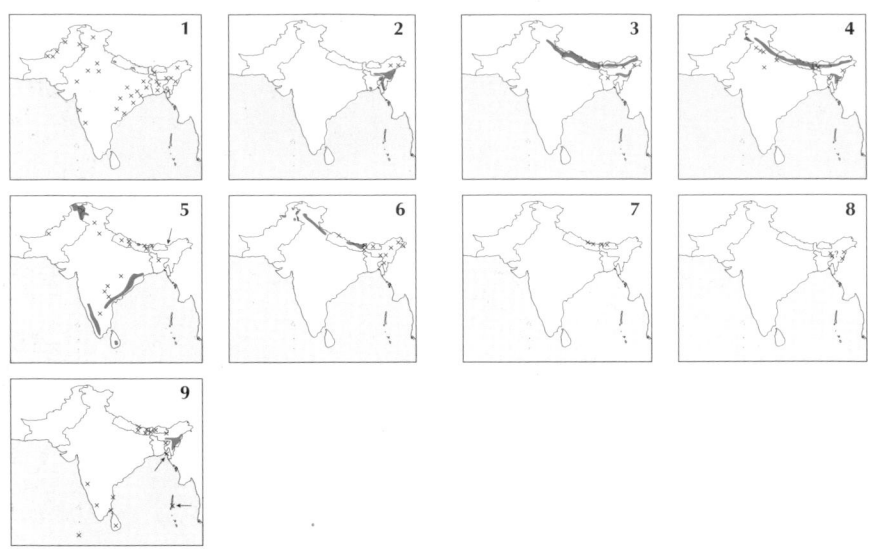

PLATE 99, p. 232

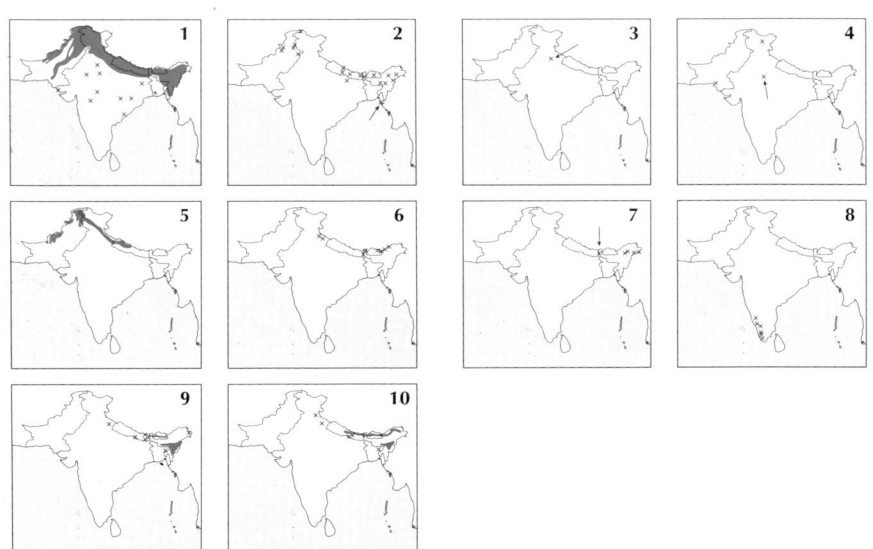

PLATE 100, p. 234

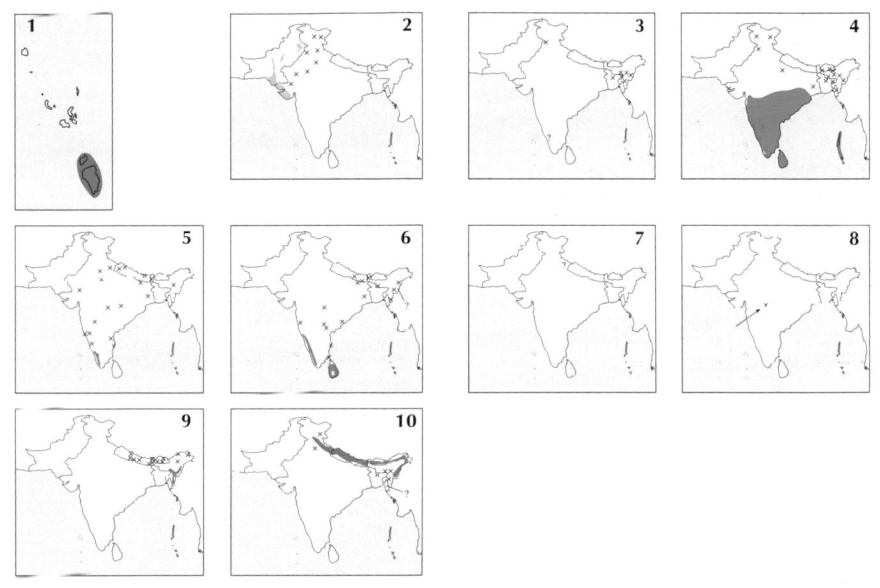

PLATE 102, p. 238

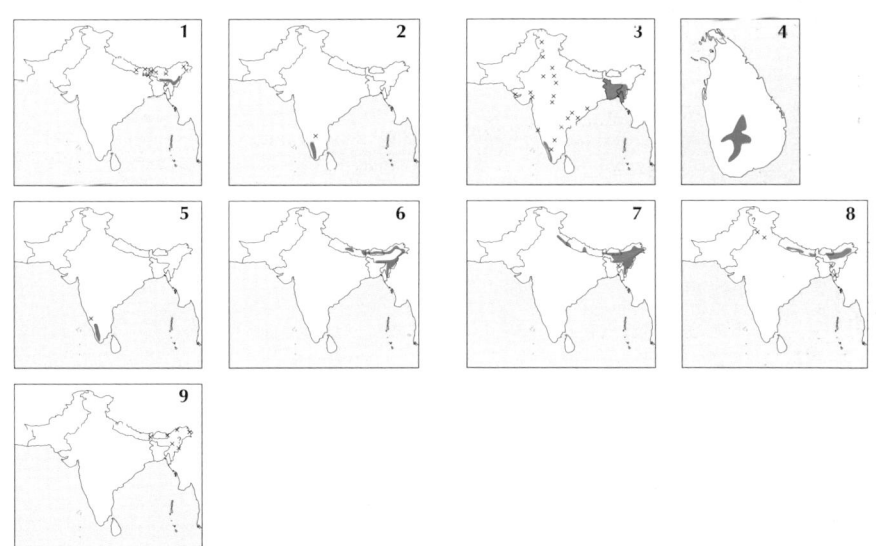

PLATE 99: *TURDUS* THRUSHES AND SHORTWINGS

Maps p. 230

1 DARK-THROATED THRUSH *Turdus ruficollis* 25 cm
Male (1a), female (1b) and 1st-winter female (1c) *T. r. ruficollis*; **male (1d), female (1e) and 1st-winter female (1f)** *T. r. atrogularis.* Winter visitor. N subcontinent. Uniform grey upperparts and wings. *T. r. ruficollis* has red throat and/or breast, and red on tail; first-winter with rufous wash to supercilium and breast. *T. r. atrogularis* has black throat and/or breast; first-winter with grey streaking on breast and flanks. Forest, forest edges, cultivation and pastures with scattered trees.

2 DUSKY THRUSH *Turdus naumanni* 24 cm
Male (2a) and 1st-winter (2b) *T. n. eunomus.* Winter visitor. Himalayas and NE India. Prominent supercilium, double gorget of spotting across breast, and chestnut on wing. First-winter birds can be very dull, with chestnut in wing sometimes not apparent. Broad supercilium and spotting on flanks are best features from Dark-throated. Cultivation and pastures with scattered trees.

3 FIELDFARE *Turdus pilaris* 25 cm
Adult. Vagrant. India. Blue-grey head and rump/uppertail-coverts, chestnut-brown mantle, and orange-buff wash to spotted breast. Fields and orchards.

4 SONG THRUSH *Turdus philomelos* 23 cm
Adult. Vagrant. Pakistan and India. Small size, olive-brown upperparts, and spotted breast. Head rather plain, lacking supercilium. Thorn scrub.

5 MISTLE THRUSH *Turdus viscivorus* 27 cm
Adult (5a) and juvenile (5b). Resident. Baluchistan and W Himalayas. Large size, pale grey-brown upperparts, whitish edges to wing feathers, and spotted breast. Juvenile has buffish-white spotting to upperparts; lacks golden-buff bands on wing of Scaly Thrush. Summers in open coniferous forest, shrubberies; winters on grassy slopes and at forest edges.

6 GOULD'S SHORTWING *Brachypteryx stellata* 13 cm
Adult (6a) and juvenile (6b). Resident. Himalayas. Adult with chestnut upperparts, slate-grey underparts and white star-shaped spotting on belly and flanks. Juvenile streaked rufous on upperparts and breast. Breeds in shrubberies near treeline and among boulders in alpine zone; winters in forest.

7 RUSTY-BELLIED SHORTWING *Brachypteryx hyperythra* 13 cm
Male (7a) and female (7b). Resident. Himalayas. Male has fine white supercilium, blue upperparts, and rufous-orange underparts. Female has olive-brown upperparts and pale rufous-orange underparts. Winters in forest undergrowth and thickets.

8 WHITE-BELLIED SHORTWING *Brachypteryx major* 15 cm
Adult *B. m. major* **(8a); adult** *B. m. albiventris* **(8b).** Resident. Hills of SW India. Slaty-blue upperparts and breast, and white belly. Flanks rufous in nominate *major*. Dense undergrowth in ravines and evergreen forest.

9 LESSER SHORTWING *Brachypteryx leucophrys* 13 cm
'Blue' male (9a) and female (9b). Resident. Himalayas, NE India and Bangladesh. Smaller and shorter-tailed than White-browed, with pinkish legs. Male is pale slaty-blue with white throat and belly. Female is brown with white throat and belly. Both sexes have fine white supercilium which may be obscured. Immature male shows intermediate plumage. Undergrowth in moist broadleaved forest and secondary growth.

10 WHITE-BROWED SHORTWING *Brachypteryx montana* 15 cm
Male (10a), female (10b), immature male (10c) and juvenile (10d). Resident. Himalayas and NE India. Larger than Lesser with longer tail and dark legs. Male dark slaty-blue, with fine white supercilium. Rufous-orange lores and more uniform brownish underparts (lacking white throat and belly) of female and immature male are useful differences from those plumages of Lesser. Immature male has fine white supercilium. Undergrowth in moist forest and thickets in ravines.

1 BROWN-CHESTED JUNGLE FLYCATCHER *Rhinomyias brunneata* 15 cm
Adult. Winter visitor/resident on Nicobars; vagrant to Andamans. Dark brown, with rufescent-brown tail, scaling on throat, brown breast, and long bill. Mainly forest.

2 SPOTTED FLYCATCHER *Muscicapa striata* 15 cm
Adult. Summer visitor to Baluchistan and Himalayas in Pakistan; passage migrant in Pakistan and NW India. Large size, large and mainly dark bill, streaking on forehead and crown, indistinct eye-ring, and streaked throat and breast. Breeds in open conifer forest.

3 DARK-SIDED FLYCATCHER *Muscicapa sibirica* 14 cm
SIBERIAN
Adult (3a) and juvenile (3b). Breeds in Himalayas and NE India; winter quarters poorly known. Small dark bill, and long primary projection (exposed primaries are equal to or distinctly longer, usually by 15–20%, than the tertials). Breast and flanks heavily marked, with narrow white line down centre of belly. Juvenile has spotted upperparts and finely marked breast. Temperate and subalpine forest.

4 ASIAN BROWN FLYCATCHER *Muscicapa dauurica* 13 cm
Fresh-plumaged adult (4a), worn adult (4b) and juvenile (4c). Breeds in Himalayan foothills and hills of C and W India; winters in S, C and E India and Sri Lanka. Large bill with prominent pale base to lower mandible; shorter primary projection than Dark-sided (shorter than tertials, usually 80–90% their length). Pale underparts, with light brownish wash to breast and flanks. Lores are more extensively pale than in Dark-sided. Open forest and wooded areas.

5 RUSTY-TAILED FLYCATCHER *Muscicapa ruficauda* 14 cm
Adult (5a) and juvenile (5b). Breeds in Himalayas; winters mainly in SW India. Rufous uppertail-coverts and tail, rather plain face, and pale orange lower mandible. Forest.

6 BROWN-BREASTED FLYCATCHER *Muscicapa muttui* 14 cm
Adult. Breeds in NE India; winters in SW India and Sri Lanka. Compared with Asian Brown has larger bill with entirely pale lower mandible, pale legs and feet, rufous-buff edges to greater coverts and tertials, and slightly rufescent tone to rump and tail. Dense thickets in evergreen forest.

7 FERRUGINOUS FLYCATCHER *Muscicapa ferruginea* 13 cm
Adult (7a) and juvenile (7b). Probably summer visitor. Breeds in Himalayas and NE India. Rufous-orange uppertail-coverts and tail, rufous-orange flanks and undertail-coverts, and grey cast to head. Moist forest.

8 YELLOW-RUMPED FLYCATCHER *Ficedula zanthopygia* 13 cm
Male (8a), female (8b) and 1st-winter male (8c). Vagrant. India. Yellow rump, and white on wing. Male has black upperparts and yellow underparts. Female and first-winter have greyish-olive upperparts. Undergrowth along rivers and streams.

9 SLATY-BACKED FLYCATCHER *Ficedula hodgsonii* 13 cm
Male (9a) and female (9b). Resident. Himalayas and NE India. Male has orange underparts, deep blue upperparts (lacking any patches of glistening blue as in male *Cyornis* flycatchers) and black tail with white at base. Female has greyish-olive underparts, lacking well-defined white throat, and lacks rufous on tail. Forest.

10 RUFOUS-GORGETED FLYCATCHER *Ficedula strophiata* 14 cm
Male (10a), female (10b) and juvenile (10c). Resident. Himalayas and NE India. Rufous gorget, and white sides to black tail. Female duller than male. Juvenile with orange-buff spotting on upperparts. Forest.

PLATE 101: FLYCATCHERS

1 RED-THROATED FLYCATCHER *Ficedula parva* 11.5–12.5 cm
Male (1a) and female (1b) *F. p. parva;* **male** *F. p. albicilla* **(1c).** Widespread winter visitor and passage migrant; has bred in W Himalayas. White sides to tail. Male has reddish-orange throat. Female and many males have creamy-white to greyish-white underparts. *F. p. albicilla* has grey breast-band; compared with nominate, female has black uppertail-coverts and dark base to bill. Open forest, bushes and wooded areas.

2 KASHMIR FLYCATCHER *Ficedula subrubra* 13 cm
Male (2a), female (2b) and juvenile (2c). Resident. Breeds in NW Himalayas; winters in Sri Lanka and Western Ghats. Male has more extensive and deeper red on underparts than Red-throated, with diffuse black border. Female and first-winter similar to some male Red-throated, but rufous is often more pronounced on breast than throat, and often continues as wash onto belly and/or flanks. Some lack rufous-orange on underparts and are best told by combination of darker grey-brown upperparts, grey wash across breast and pale base to bill. Breeds in deciduous forest; winters in wooded areas.

3 WHITE-GORGETED FLYCATCHER *Ficedula monileger* 13 cm
Adult (3a) and juvenile (3b) *F. m. monileger;* **adult** *F. m. leucops* **(3c).** Resident. Himalayas and NE India. White throat and black gorget. Supercilium whitish (NE sub-continent east and south of Brahmaputra) or orange-buff (E Himalayas). Moist broadleaved forest.

4 SNOWY-BROWED FLYCATCHER *Ficedula hyperythra* 11 cm
Male (4a), female (4b) and juvenile (4c). Resident. Himalayas and NE India. Small size and short tail. Both sexes with rufous-brown wings. Male has short white supercilium, slaty-blue upperparts, and orange throat/breast. Female has orange-buff supercilium and eye-ring. Moist broadleaved forest.

5 LITTLE PIED FLYCATCHER *Ficedula westermanni* 11 cm
Male (5a), female (5b), juvenile male (5c) and juvenile female (5d) *F. w. collini;* **female** *F. w. australorientis* **(5e).** Resident. Himalayas, NE India and Bangladesh. Male black and white, with broad white supercilium. Female has grey-brown upperparts, brownish-grey wash to breast, and rufous cast to rump/uppertail-coverts (more pronounced in eastern race *australorientis*). Breeds in forest; winters in open wooded country.

6 ULTRAMARINE FLYCATCHER *Ficedula superciliaris* 12 cm
Male (6a), female (6b), 1st-summer male (6c) and juvenile (6d) *F. s. superciliaris;* **male** *F. s. aestigma* **(6e).** Resident. Breeds in Himalayas and NE India; winters south to S India. Male has deep blue upperparts and sides of neck/breast, and white underparts; white supercilium in *superciliaris* of W Himalayas. Female has greyish-brown breast-side patches and lacks rufous on rump/uppertail-coverts. First-year males, and some females, show blue on upperparts. Breeds in forest; winters in open woodland and wooded areas.

7 SLATY-BLUE FLYCATCHER *Ficedula tricolor* 13 cm
Male (7a), female (7b) and juvenile (7c) *F. t. tricolor;* **male (7d) and female (7e)** *F. t. cerviniventris.* Resident. Mainly Himalayas and NE India. Male has white throat and white on tail; belly and flanks greyish-white (or orange-buff in *cerviniventris* of NE sub-continent). Female has rufous tail; throat white or orange-buff. Breeds in subalpine shrub-beries and forest undergrowth; winters in forest undergrowth, ravines and tall grass.

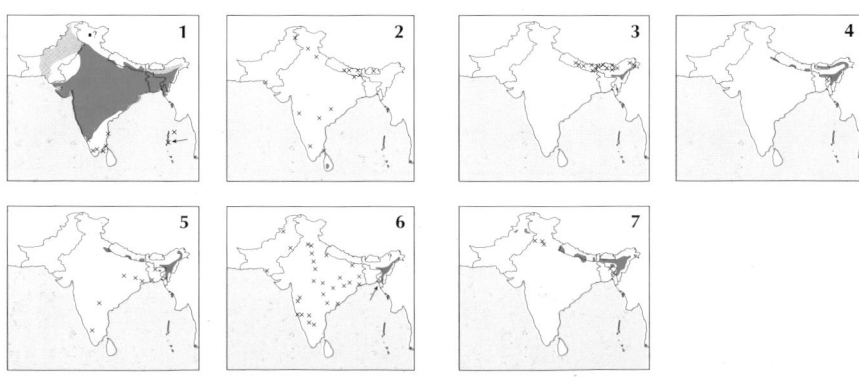

PLATE 102: FLYCATCHERS, INCLUDING NILTAVAS Maps p. 231

1 SAPPHIRE FLYCATCHER *Ficedula sapphira* 11 cm
Male (1a), female (1b), immature male (1c) and juvenile male (1d). Resident. Himalayas
and NE India. Small size, slim appearance and tiny bill. Orange throat and breast contrast
with white belly. Male has blue breast sides and bright blue or brown-and-blue upperparts. Female has rufous uppertail-coverts and tail. Juvenile has buff breast and white belly
and flanks. Evergreen broadleaved forest.

2 BLACK-AND-ORANGE FLYCATCHER *Ficedula nigrorufa* 11 cm
Male (2a) and female (2b). Resident. Western Ghats. Male rufous-orange and black;
female duller. Evergreen sholas and moist thickets in ravines.

3 VERDITER FLYCATCHER *Eumyias thalassina* 16 cm
Male (3a), female (3b) and juvenile male (3c). Resident. Breeds in Himalayas and NE
India; widespread in winter. Male greenish-blue, with black lores. Female duller and greyer, with dusky lores. Juvenile has orange-buff spotting, with turquoise cast to upperparts
and underparts. Open forest and wooded areas.

4 DULL-BLUE FLYCATCHER *Eumyias sordida* 15 cm
Adult (4a) and juvenile (4b). Resident. Sri Lanka. Both sexes ashy-blue, with greyish-white
belly, black lores and cobalt-blue forehead and supercilium. Female slightly duller than
male. Forest and well-wooded areas.

5 NILGIRI FLYCATCHER *Eumyias albicaudata* 15 cm
Male (5a), female (5b) and juvenile male (5c). Resident. Western Ghats. White on tail-
base and diffuse whitish fringes to blue-grey undertail-coverts. Male indigo-blue, with
blue-grey belly, black lores and bright blue forehead and supercilium. Female blue-grey,
paler on underparts. Juvenile has buff spotting on upperparts and blackish scaling on
white underparts. Evergreen biotope in hills.

6 LARGE NILTAVA *Niltava grandis* 21 cm
Male (6a), female (6b) and juvenile male (6c). Resident. Himalayas and NE India. Large
size. Male dark blue, with brilliant blue crown, neck patch and shoulder patch. Female
has rufous-buff forecrown and lores, rufescent wings and tail, and buff throat patch. Has
glistening patch of blue on neck like female Rufous-bellied. Juvenile has rufous underparts
with blackish barring. Moist broadleaved forest.

7 SMALL NILTAVA *Niltava macgrigoriae* 13 cm
Male (7a), female (7b) and juvenile male (7c). Resident. Himalayas and NE India. Small
size. Male dark blue, with brilliant blue forehead and neck patch. Female has indistinct
blue neck patch and rufescent wings and tail; lacks oval throat patch of female Rufous-
bellied. Juvenile has diffuse brown streaking on underparts. Bushes in broadleaved forest;
also reed and grass jungle in plains in winter.

8 RUFOUS-BELLIED NILTAVA *Niltava sundara* 18 cm
Male (8a), female (8b) and juvenile female (8c). Resident. Himalayas and NE India. Male
has brilliant blue crown and neck patch, and orange on underparts extending to vent.
Female and juvenile have oval-shaped throat patch. Undergrowth in forest and secondary
growth.

9 VIVID NILTAVA *Niltava vivida* 17.5 cm
Male (9a) and female (9b). Resident. NE Indian hills. Different head shape from Rufous-
bellied. Male lacks glistening blue crown and nape of Rufous-bellied, and black of throat
is indented by orange wedge. Female has buffish throat, but lacks oval-shaped throat
patch. Lacks blue neck patch of female Large and Rufous-bellied. Undergrowth in
broadleaved evergreen forest.

1 WHITE-TAILED FLYCATCHER *Cyornis concretus* 18 cm
Male (1a) and female (1b). Resident. Breeds in Arunachal Pradesh; winters in Assam and Mizoram. Large size, and white on tail. Male has white belly and undertail-coverts. Female has white patch on lower throat; different shape, blue cast to crown and white in tail are best features from female Rufous-bellied Niltava. Dense forest.

2 WHITE-BELLIED BLUE FLYCATCHER *Cyornis pallipes* 15 cm
Male (2a), female (2b) and juvenile female (2c). Resident. Western Ghats and hills of W Tamil Nadu. Large bill, and lacks white at base of tail. Male indigo-blue, with white belly and unmarked undertail-coverts (compare with Nilgiri Flycatcher). Female has orange-red throat and breast and greyish head; these features more striking than in female Blue-throated; also has more extensive cream lores, brighter chestnut tail, and has longer bill. Juvenile has unmarked buff throat and white belly. Undergrowth in dense evergreen forest.

3 PALE-CHINNED FLYCATCHER *Cyornis poliogenys* 18 cm
Adult (3a) and juvenile (3b) *C. p. poliogenys*; **adult** *C. p. vernayi* **(3c).** Resident. Himalayan foothills, NE and E India, and Bangladesh. Nominate, of Himalayas, has greyish head, well-defined cream throat, and orange-orange breast and flanks which merge with belly. More uniform creamy-orange underparts, thin eye-ring, and pale pinkish legs help separate *vernayi*, of Eastern Ghats, from female Tickell's Blue. Juvenile has diffusely marked upperparts, well-defined buff throat, and barring on flanks. Undergrowth in broadleaved forest.

4 PALE BLUE FLYCATCHER *Cyornis unicolor* 18 cm
Male (4a), female (4b) and juvenile male (4c). Resident. Himalayas and NE India. Male confusable with Verditer but has longer bill, and is pale blue in coloration with distinctly greyer belly. Female very different from Verditer and more like other *Cyornis*; best told by large size and uniform greyish underparts. Juvenile has bold orange-buff spotting on scapulars and heavily scaled underparts. Moist broadleaved forest and secondary growth.

5 BLUE-THROATED FLYCATCHER *Cyornis rubeculoides* 14 cm
Male (5a), female (5b) and juvenile male (5c). Resident. Breeds in Himalayas and NE India; winters in E Himalayan foothills and south to Bangladesh, SW India and Sri Lanka. Male has blue throat (some with orange wedge) and well-defined white belly and flanks. Female has narrow and poorly defined creamy-orange throat, orange breast well demarcated from white belly, and creamy lores (compare with Pale-chinned and female Hill Blue). Olive-brown head and upperparts and rufescent tail are best features from female Tickell's. Juvenile has poorly defined pale throat, prominently spotted scapulars, and barred breast. Open forest and wooded areas.

6 HILL BLUE FLYCATCHER *Cyornis banyumas* 14 cm
Male (6a) and female (6b). Resident. Himalayas and NE India. Long bill and long primary projection. On both sexes, orange of breast and flanks merges gradually with white of belly. Male has blackish ear-coverts. Female has dark lores and sharp demarcation between ear-coverts and creamy-orange throat. Dense, moist broadleaved forest.

7 TICKELL'S BLUE FLYCATCHER *Cyornis tickelliae* 14 cm
Male (7a), female (7b) and juvenile (7c) *C. t. tickelliae.* Resident. Peninsular and NE India, and Sri Lanka. Male has orange throat and breast with clear horizontal division from white flanks and belly (except in Sri Lanka). Female has greyish-blue upperparts (especially rump and tail). Juvenile of both sexes has cerulean-blue on wings and weak scaling on breast. Open dry forest and wooded areas.

8 PYGMY BLUE FLYCATCHER *Muscicapella hodgsoni* 10 cm
Male (8a) and female (8b). Resident. Himalayas and NE India. Small size, short tail, fine bill, and flowerpecker-like appearance and behaviour. Underparts entirely orange on male and orange-buff on female. Dense, moist broadleaved forest.

9 GREY-HEADED CANARY FLYCATCHER *Culicicapa ceylonensis* 13 cm
Adult. Resident. Breeds in Himalayas, hills of India, Bangladesh and Sri Lanka; winters in Himalayan foothills, and plains in Pakistan and E and NE India. Grey head and breast, yellow rest of underparts, and greenish upperparts. Forest and wooded areas.

PLATE 103, p. 240

PLATE 107, p. 250

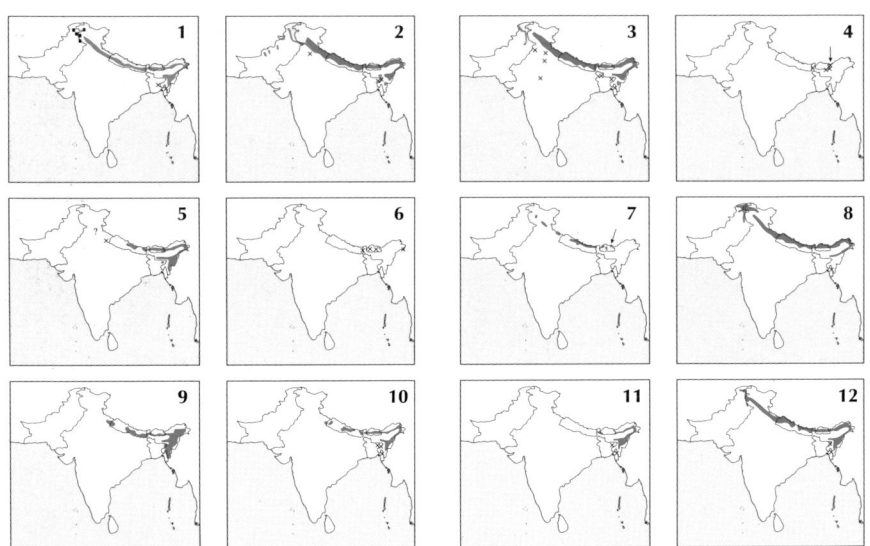

PLATE 108, p. 252

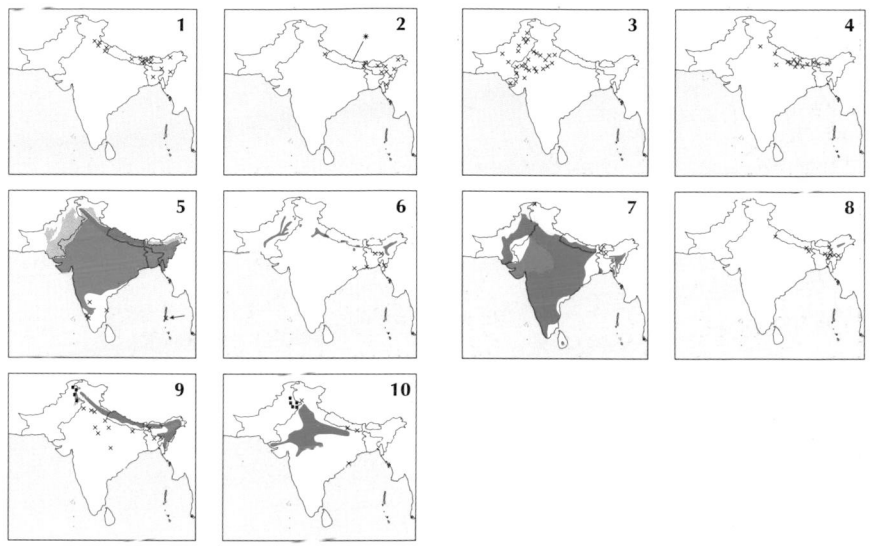

PLATE 109, p. 254

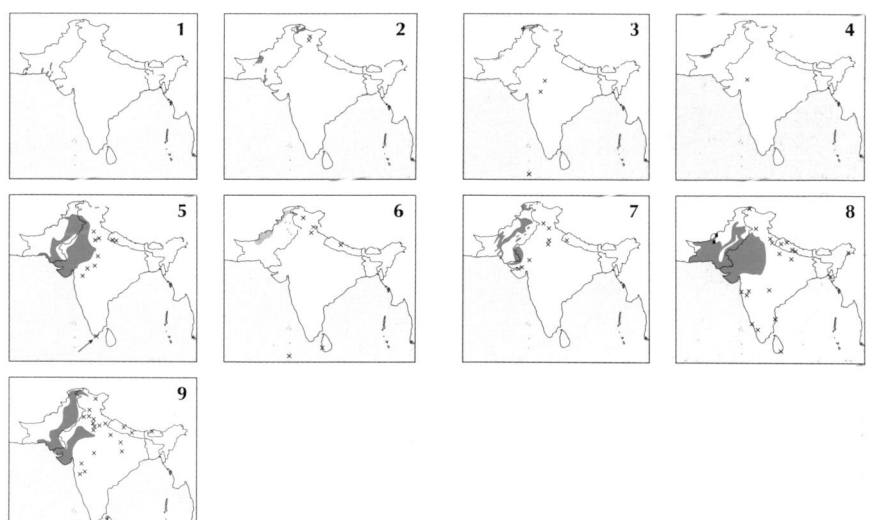

PLATE 104: CHATS

1 COMMON NIGHTINGALE *Luscinia megarhynchos* 16 cm
Adult. Vagrant. Pakistan and India. Rufous uppertail-coverts and long rufous tail, indistinct head markings, and pale fringes to wing-coverts and remiges. Bushes.

2 SIBERIAN RUBYTHROAT *Luscinia calliope* 14 cm
Male (2a) and female (2b). Winter visitor. Himalayan foothills, peninsular and NE India and Bangladesh. Olive-brown upperparts and tail, and white supercilium and moustachial stripe. Male has ruby-red throat and grey breast. Female has olive-buff wash to breast. Legs pale brown. Bushes and thick undergrowth.

3 WHITE-TAILED RUBYTHROAT *Luscinia pectoralis* 14 cm
Male (3a), female (3b) and juvenile female (3c) *L. p. pectoralis*; **male** *L. p. tschebaiewi* **(3d).** Resident. Breeds in Himalayas; winters mainly in Himalayan foothills and NE India. Male has ruby-red throat, black breast-band (fringed with white in fresh plumage) and white on tail. Female has grey upperparts, grey breast-band and white tip to tail. Legs black. Male *tschebaiewi* has white moustachial stripe, sometimes shown also by female. Breeds in subalpine scrub, and on alpine slopes; winters in scrub and tall grass in marshes.

4 BLUETHROAT *Luscinia svecica* 15 cm
Male non-breeding (4a) and 1st-winter female (4b) *L. s. svecica*; **male breeding** *L. s. abbotti* **(4c).** Summer visitor to NW Himalayas; widespread in winter. White supercilium and rufous tail sides. Male has variable blue, black and rufous patterning to throat and breast (patterning obscured by whitish fringes in fresh plumage). Female is less brightly coloured but usually with blue and rufous breast-bands. First-winter female may have just black submoustachial stripe and band of black spotting across breast. Summers in scrub along streams and lakes; winters in scrub and tall grass.

5 FIRETHROAT *Luscinia pectardens* 15 cm
Male (5a), female (5b) and 1st-winter male (5c). Winter visitor? Mainly NE India. Male has white on tail, and flame-orange throat and breast bordered at sides with black. Female has mainly orange-buff underparts; possible features from Indian Blue Robin are orange-buff vent and undertail-coverts and darker legs. First-winter male has blue on back and rump, with tail as male and underparts as female. Dense bushes and woodland.

6 INDIAN BLUE ROBIN *Luscinia brunnea* 15 cm
Male (6a), female (6b) and juvenile (6c). Resident. Breeds in Himalayas and NE Indian hills; winters in Sri Lanka, hills of NE and SW India, and E Himalayan foothills. Male has blue upperparts and orange underparts, with white supercilium and black ear-coverts. Female has olive-brown upperparts, and buffish underparts with white throat and belly. Breeds in forest undergrowth; winters in forest, secondary scrub and plantations.

7 SIBERIAN BLUE ROBIN *Luscinia cyane* 15 cm
Male (7a), female (7b) and 1st-winter male (7c). Vagrant. Nepal and India. Male has blue upperparts and white underparts. Female usually has blue on uppertail-coverts and tail. First-winter male similar to female, but with blue on mantle. Dense bushes.

8 RUFOUS-TAILED SCRUB ROBIN *Cercotrichas galactotes* 15 cm
Adult. Southward passage migrant through Pakistan and NW India; also breeds in Pakistan. Long rufous tail, tipped white and with black subterminal markings. Sandy-grey upperparts and creamy-white underparts, with whitish supercilium and dark eye-stripe and moustachial stripe. Dry scrub jungle.

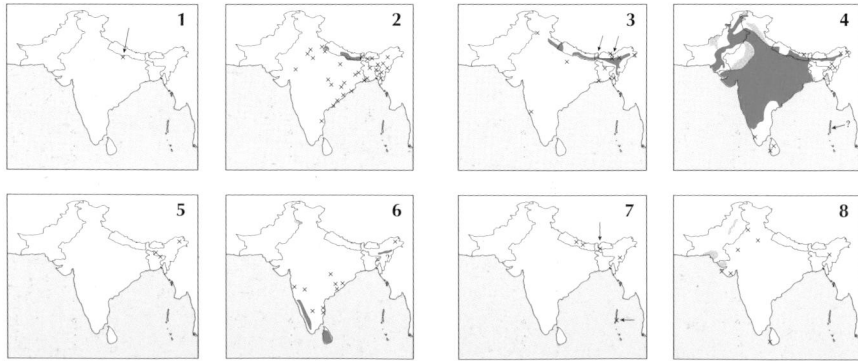

PLATE 105: CHATS

1 ORANGE-FLANKED BUSH ROBIN *Tarsiger cyanurus* 14 cm
Male (1a), female (1b) and juvenile (1c). Resident. Breeds in Himalayas; winters in Himalayas and NE Indian hills. White throat, orange flanks, blue tail, and redstart-like stance. Male has blue upperparts and breast sides. Female has olive-brown upperparts and breast sides. Juvenile has bold spotting on scapulars. Forest understorey.

2 GOLDEN BUSH ROBIN *Tarsiger chrysaeus* 15 cm
Male (2a), female (2b) and juvenile (2c). Resident. Himalayas and NE Indian hills. Orange to orange-buff underparts, with orange tail sides. Male has broad orange supercilium, dark mask, and orange scapulars. Female duller, with less distinct supercilium. Juvenile has adult tail pattern, and pale legs. Summers in subalpine shrubberies and forest undergrowth; winters in forest undergrowth and dense scrub.

3 WHITE-BROWED BUSH ROBIN *Tarsiger indicus* 15 cm
Male (3a), female (3b) and juvenile (3c). Resident. Himalayas and NE Indian hills. Upright stance, long tail, long and fine supercilium which curves down behind eye, and dark legs (good features from Indian Blue Robin). Male has slaty-blue upperparts and rufous-orange underparts. Female has olive-brown upperparts and dirty orange-buff underparts. Forest undergrowth.

4 RUFOUS-BREASTED BUSH ROBIN *Tarsiger hyperythrus* 15 cm
Male (4a), female (4b) and juvenile (4c). Resident. Breeds in Himalayas; winters south to NE Indian hills. Carriage and profile as Orange-flanked. Male has dark blue upperparts, blackish ear-coverts, glistening blue supercilium and shoulders, and rufous-orange underparts. Female has blue tail; compared with female Orange-flanked has orange-buff throat, and browner breast and flanks. Summers in bushes at forest edges; winters in moist forest undergrowth.

5 ORIENTAL MAGPIE ROBIN *Copsychus saularis* 23 cm
Male (5a), female (5b) and juvenile (5c). Widespread resident; unrecorded in most of the northwest. Black/slate-grey and white, with white on wing and at sides of tail. Juvenile scaled with dark brown on throat and breast. Gardens, groves and open broadleaved forest.

6 WHITE-RUMPED SHAMA *Copsychus malabaricus* 22 cm
Male (6a), female (6b) and juvenile (6c) *C. m. malabaricus;* **male** *C. m. albiventris* **(6d).** Resident. Himalayan foothills, NE, E and W India, Bangladesh and Sri Lanka. Long, graduated tail and white rump. Male has glossy blue-black upperparts and breast, and rufous-orange underparts. Female duller, with brownish-grey upperparts. Male *albiventris* of Andamans has white belly. Undergrowth in broadleaved forest.

7 INDIAN ROBIN *Saxicoloides fulicata* 19 cm
Male (7a) and female (7b) *S. f. cambaiensis;* **male** *S. f. fulicata* **(7c).** Widespread resident. Reddish vent and black tail in all plumages. Male has white shoulders and black underparts. Female has greyish underparts. In Sri Lanka and S India (e.g. *fulicata*), upperparts of male glossy blue-black. Dry stony areas with scrub, and cultivation edges.

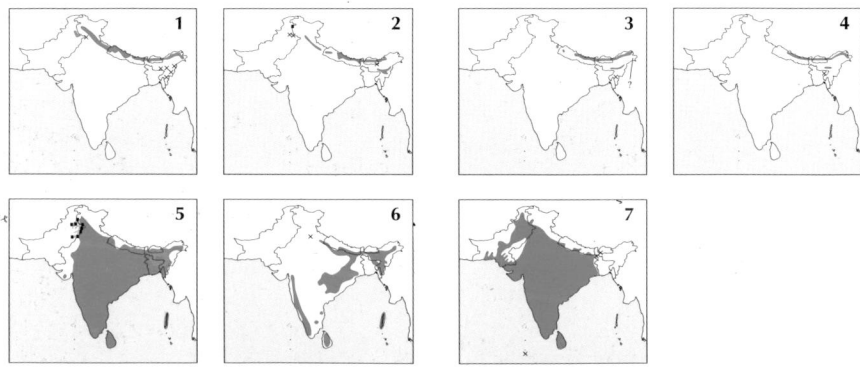

246

PLATE 106: REDSTARTS

1 RUFOUS-BACKED REDSTART *Phoenicurus erythronota* 16 cm
Male breeding (1a), 1st-winter male (1b) and female (1c). Winter visitor. Hills of Pakistan and W Himalayas. Large size. Male has rufous mantle and throat, white on wing, and black mask; heavily obscured by pale fringes in non-breeding and first-winter plumages. Female has double buffish wing-bar. Dry hills and valleys with scrub.

2 BLUE-CAPPED REDSTART *Phoenicurus coeruleocephalus* 15 cm
Male breeding (2a), female (2b), 1st-winter male (2c) and juvenile male (2d). Resident. Himalayas. Male has blue-grey cap, black tail, and white on wing; heavily obscured by pale fringes in non-breeding and first-winter plumages. Female has grey underparts, prominent double wing-bar, blackish tail, and chestnut rump. Summers on rocky slopes with open forest; winters in open forest and secondary growth.

(3) BLACK REDSTART *Phoenicurus ochruros* 15 cm
Male (3a), female (3b) and juvenile (3c) *P. o. phoenicuroides;* **male** *P. o. rufiventris* **(3d).** Resident. Breeds in Pakistan mountains and Himalayas; widespread in winter. Male has black (C and E Himalayas) or dark grey (W Himalayas) upperparts, black breast, and rufous underparts. Female has dusky brown underparts, with orange-buff wash to flanks and vent. Breeds in Tibetan steppe habitat; winters in cultivation and plantations.

4 COMMON REDSTART *Phoenicurus phoenicurus* 15 cm
Male breeding (4a), 1st-winter male (4b) and female (4c). Spring passage migrant. Mainly Pakistan. Male has grey upperparts, white forehead, black throat, and rufous-orange underparts; heavily obscured by pale fringes in non-breeding and first-winter plumages. Female has buff-brown upperparts and buffish underparts (and is paler and more warmly coloured than female Black and Hodgson's). Arid areas.

5 HODGSON'S REDSTART *Phoenicurus hodgsoni* 15 cm
Male breeding (5a) and female (5b). Winter visitor. Himalayas and NE Indian hills. Male (both breeding and non-breeding) has grey upperparts, white wing patch, and black throat and breast. Female has dusky brown upperparts and grey underparts; very similar to Black but with whitish area on belly (and lacks rufous-orange wash to lower flanks and belly of that species). First-winter male as female. Stony river beds with trees, and bushes in cultivation.

6 WHITE-THROATED REDSTART *Phoenicurus schisticeps* 15 cm
Male (6a), female (6b) and juvenile (6c). Resident and winter visitor. Himalayas; unrecorded in Pakistan. Both sexes with white throat, white wing patch, rufous rump and dark tail. Summers in shrubberies on rocky slopes and forest edges; winters in meadows and cultivation and on bush-covered slopes.

7 DAURIAN REDSTART *Phoenicurus auroreus* 15 cm
Male non-breeding (7a) and female (7b). Resident. Himalayas and NE Indian hills. Both sexes have white patch on wing. Mantle of male black (worn) or brown with black mottling (fresh). Summers in open forest and trees in cultivation; winters in bushes and secondary growth.

8 WHITE-WINGED REDSTART *Phoenicurus erythrogaster* 18 cm
Male (8a), female (8b) and juvenile male (8c). Resident and winter visitor. Himalayas. Large size and stocky appearance. Male has white cap and large white patch on wing. Female has buff-brown upperparts and buffish underparts. Breeds in rocky alpine meadows; winters in stony pastures and scrub patches.

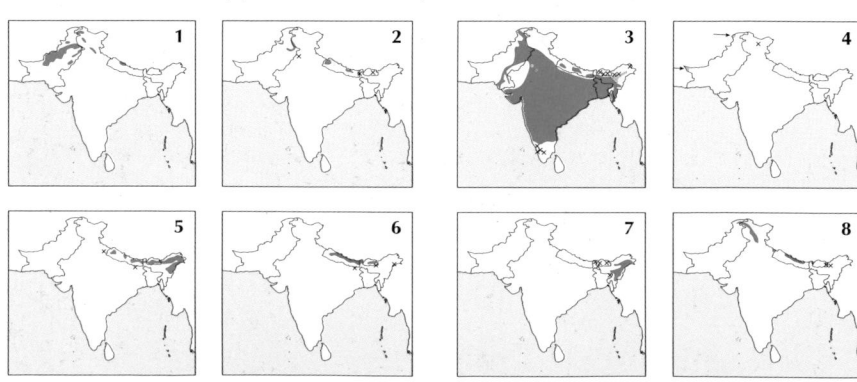

PLATE 107: REDSTARTS, BLUE ROBINS, GRANDALA AND FORKTAILS

Maps p. 242

1 BLUE-FRONTED REDSTART *Phoenicurus frontalis* 15 cm
Male (1a), female (1b) and juvenile (1c). Resident. Breeds in Himalayas; winters in Himalayan foothills, NE India and Bangladesh. Orange rump and tail sides, with black centre and tip to tail. Male has blue head and upperparts and chestnut-orange underparts; heavily obscured by rufous-brown fringes in non-breeding and first-winter plumage. Female has dark brown upperparts and underparts, with orange wash to belly; tail pattern best feature from other female redstarts. Breeds in subalpine shrubberies; winters in bushes and open forest.

2 WHITE-CAPPED WATER REDSTART *Chaimarrornis leucocephalus* 19 cm
Adult (2a) and juvenile (2b). Resident. Breeds in Himalayas and NE Indian hills; winters south to Baluchistan and Bangladesh. White cap, and rufous tail with broad black terminal band. Mainly mountain streams and rivers.

3 PLUMBEOUS WATER REDSTART *Rhyacornis fuliginosus* 12 cm
Male (3a), female (3b) and juvenile (3c). Resident. Breeds in Himalayas and NE Indian hills; winters south to Bangladesh. Male slaty-blue, with rufous-chestnut tail. Female and first-year male have black-and-white tail and white spotting on grey underparts. Mountain streams and rivers.

4 WHITE-BELLIED REDSTART *Hodgsonius phaenicuroides* 18 cm
Male (4a) and female (4b). Resident. Himalayas. Long, graduated tail often held cocked and fanned. Male has white belly, rufous tail sides, and white spots on alula. Female has white throat and belly, and chestnut on tail. Breeds in subalpine shrubberies; winters in thick undergrowth and forest edges at lower levels.

5 WHITE-TAILED ROBIN *Myiomela leucura* 18 cm
Male (5a), female (5b) and juvenile female (5c). Resident. Himalayas and NE Indian hills. White patches on tail. Male blue-black, with glistening blue forehead and shoulders. Female olive-brown, with whitish lower throat. Undergrowth in moist broadleaved forest.

6 BLUE-FRONTED ROBIN *Cinclidium frontale* 19 cm
Male (6a) and female (6b). Resident. Himalayas. Long, graduated tail lacking any white or rufous. Male deep blue, with glistening blue forehead. Female from female White-bellied Redstart by dark brown tail and more uniform brown underparts. Thickly vegetated gullies and dense vegetation at forest edges.

7 GRANDALA *Grandala coelicolor* 23 cm
Male (7a) and female (7b). Resident. Himalayas. Slim and long-winged. Male purple-blue, with black wings and tail. Female and immature male have white patches on wing and streaked head and underparts. Rocky slopes and stony meadows; alpine zone in summer, lower altitudes in winter.

8 LITTLE FORKTAIL *Enicurus scouleri* 12 cm
Adult. Resident. Himalayas and NE Indian hills. Small and plump, with short tail. White forehead. Mountain streams; also slower-moving streams in winter.

9 BLACK-BACKED FORKTAIL *Enicurus immaculatus* 25 cm
Adult. Resident. Himalayan foothills, NE India and Bangladesh. Black crown and mantle, and more white on forehead than Slaty-backed. Fast-flowing streams in moist broadleaved forest.

10 SLATY-BACKED FORKTAIL *Enicurus schistaceus* 25 cm
Adult. Resident. Himalayas and NE India. Slaty-grey crown and mantle; less white on forehead and larger bill than Black-backed. Fast-flowing streams in forest and wooded lake margins.

11 WHITE-CROWNED FORKTAIL *Enicurus leschenaulti* 25 cm
Adult. Resident. E Himalayan foothills and NE Indian hills. Large size; white forehead and forecrown, black breast and black mantle. Fast-flowing waters in tropical evergreen forest.

12 SPOTTED FORKTAIL *Enicurus maculatus* 25 cm
Adult (12a) and juvenile (12b). *E. m. maculatus.* Resident. Himalayas and NE Indian hills. Large size; white forehead, white spotting on mantle, and black breast. Rocky streams in forest.

1 PURPLE COCHOA *Cochoa purpurea* 30 cm
Male (1a), female (1b) and juvenile male (1c). Resident. Himalayas and NE Indian hills. Lilac crown, wing panelling and tail (latter with dark tip). Male purplish-brown. Female has rufous-brown upperparts and brownish-orange underparts. Juvenile with bold orange-buff spotting and scaling; wings and tail adult. Mainly dense moist broadleaved forest.

2 GREEN COCHOA *Cochoa viridis* 28 cm
Male (2a), female (2b) and juvenile female (2c). Resident. Himalayas and NE India. Mainly green, with bluish head, and blue tail with black band. Male has blue wing panelling. Female has green in blue wing panels. Juvenile with bold orange-buff spotting and scaling; wings and tail as adult. Dense broadleaved evergreen forest.

3 STOLICZKA'S BUSHCHAT *Saxicola macrorhyncha* 17 cm
Male breeding (3a), male non-breeding (3b) and female (3c). Resident. Mainly Rajasthan, India. Male has white supercilium, white primary coverts, and much white on tail; upperparts and ear-coverts appear blackish when worn (breeding) and streaked when fresh (non-breeding). Female differs from female Common Stonechat in longer bill and tail, more prominent supercilium, and broad buffish edges and tips to tail feathers. Sandy desert plains with scattered bushes.

4 HODGSON'S BUSHCHAT *Saxicola insignis* 17 cm
Male non-breeding (4a) and female (4b). Winter visitor. N Indian plains and Nepal terai. Large size. Male has white throat extending to form almost complete white collar, and more white on wing than Common Stonechat. Female has broad buffish-white wing-bars and tips to primary coverts. Tall vegetation along river beds and cane fields.

5 COMMON STONECHAT *Saxicola torquata* 17 cm
Male breeding (5a), male non-breeding (5b) and female (5c) *S. t. indica.* Resident and winter visitor. Male has black head, white patch on neck, orange breast, and whitish rump (features obscured in fresh plumage); lacks white in tail. Female has streaked upperparts and orange on breast and rump. Tail darker than in female White-tailed. Summers in open country with bushes, including high-altitude semi-desert; winters in scrub, reedbeds and cultivation.

6 WHITE-TAILED STONECHAT *Saxicola leucura* 12.5–13 cm
Male breeding (6a) and female (6b). Resident. N subcontinent, mainly in plains. Male has largely white inner webs to tail feathers. Female has greyer upperparts than Common, with diffuse streaking, and paler grey-brown tail. Reeds and tall grassland.

7 PIED BUSHCHAT *Saxicola caprata* 13.5 cm
Male breeding (7a), female (7b) and 1st-winter male (7c) *S. c. bicolor.* Widespread resident. Male black, with white rump and wing patch; rufous fringes to body in non-breeding and first-winter plumages. Female has dark brown upperparts and rufous-brown underparts, with rufous-orange rump. Mainly cultivation and open country with scattered bushes or tall grass.

8 JERDON'S BUSHCHAT *Saxicola jerdoni* 15 cm
Male (8a) and female (8b). Resident. Mainly NE Indian plains and Himalayan foothills. Male has black upperparts, including rump and tail, and white underparts. Female similar to female Grey, but lacks prominent supercilium, and has longer, more graduated tail lacking rufous at sides. Tall grassland.

9 GREY BUSHCHAT *Saxicola ferrea* 15 cm
Male (9a), female (9b) and juvenile (9c). Resident. Breeds in Himalayas and NE Indian hills; winters south to N Indian plains. Male has white supercilium and dark mask; upperparts grey to almost black, depending on extent of wear. Female has buff supercilium and rufous rump and tail sides. Bushes and secondary growth.

10 BROWN ROCK-CHAT *Cercomela fusca* 17 cm
Adult. Resident. Mainly Pakistan and N India. Both sexes brown, with more rufescent underparts. Rocky hills, cliffs and old buildings.

PLATE 109: WHEATEARS

1 HOODED WHEATEAR *Oenanthe monacha* 17.5 cm
Adult (1a), 1st-winter male (1b) and female (1c). Resident. S Baluchistan. Long bill. Male has white crown and largely white outer tail feathers; in winter, buffish or greyish wash to crown and pale fringes to upperparts and wings (first-winter male has tail as female). Female has rufous-buff rump and tail, with brown central tail feathers. Barren desert.

2 HUME'S WHEATEAR *Oenanthe alboniger* 17 cm
Adult. Resident. Mainly Pakistan; vagrant to India. All-black head and largely white underparts. Told from *picata* race of Variable by stockier appearance and domed head, larger bill, glossy sheen to black of plumage (except when worn), black of throat does not extend so far down on breast and white of rump extending farther up lower back. Barren stony slopes with boulders.

3 NORTHERN WHEATEAR *Oenanthe oenanthe* 15 cm
Male breeding (3a), female breeding (3b), and 1st-winter (3c). Passage migrant. Mainly Pakistan; vagrant elsewhere. Breeding male has blue-grey upperparts, black mask, and pale orange breast. Breeding female greyish to olive-brown above; lacks rufous patch on ear-coverts of Finsch's and never shows dark grey/black on throat. Compared with Isabelline, adult winter and first-winter have blackish centres to wing-coverts and tertials and show more white at sides of tail. Open stony ground and cultivation.

4 FINSCH'S WHEATEAR *Oenanthe finschii* 14 cm
Male (4a) and female (4b) and 1st-winter female (4c). Winter visitor. Baluchistan. Male has creamy-buff to white mantle. Adult female and first-winter have rufous cast to ear-coverts, rather pale grey-brown upperparts, and broad black terminal band to tail. Dry stony hills and valleys.

5 VARIABLE WHEATEAR *Oenanthe picata* 14.5 cm
Male (5a) and female (5b) *O. p. picata*; **male (5c) and female (5d)** *O. p. capistrata*; **male (5e) and female (5f)** *O. p. opistholeuca*. Breeds in Baluchistan and N Pakistan; winter visitor mainly to Pakistan and NW India. Very variable. Males can be mainly black, have black head with white underparts, or white crown and white underparts. Females can be mainly sooty-brown or have greyish upperparts with variable greyish-white underparts. Breeds in barren valleys and low hills; winters in plains, stony desert foothills and cultivation.

6 PIED WHEATEAR *Oenanthe pleschanka* 14.5 cm
Male (6a), female (6b), 1st-winter male (6c) and 1st-winter female (6d). Breeds in N Pakistan and NW India; also passage migrant in Pakistan. Different tail pattern from Variable: always shows black edge to outer feathers (lacking in Variable) and often has only a narrow and broken terminal black band (broad and even on Variable). On breeding male, white of nape extends to mantle, black of throat does not extend to upper breast, and breast is washed with buff (features from *capistrata* race of Variable). Non-breeding and first-winter male and female have pale fringes to upperparts and wings (not apparent on fresh-plumaged Variable). Open stony country with lowlands.

7 RUFOUS-TAILED WHEATEAR *Oenanthe xanthoprymna* 14.5 cm
Male breeding (7a) and male non-breeding (7b). Breeds in Baluchistan; winter visitor to Pakistan and NW India. Rufous-orange lower back and rump, and rufous tail sides. Male has black lores. Summers on dry rocky slopes; winters in semi-desert.

8 DESERT WHEATEAR *Oenanthe deserti* 14–15 cm
Male breeding (8a), male non-breeding (8b), female breeding (8c) and female non-breeding (8d). Breeds in NW Himalayas; winter visitor mainly to Pakistan and NW India. Sandy-brown upperparts, with largely black tail and contrasting white rump. Male has black throat (partly obscured when fresh). Female has blackish centres to wing-coverts and tertials in fresh plumage and largely black wings when worn (useful distinction from Isabelline). Breeds on barren plateaux; winters in barren semi-desert.

9 ISABELLINE WHEATEAR *Oenanthe isabellina* 16.5 cm
Adult breeding (9a) and non-breeding (9b). Breeds in Pakistan; winters in Pakistan and NW India. Rather plain sandy-brown and buff. Head and bill look rather large, and legs long. Tail shorter than that of Desert with more white at base and sides. Breeds on stony plateaux and in valleys; winters in sandy semi-desert.

1 ASIAN GLOSSY STARLING *Aplonis panayensis* 20 cm
Adult (1a) and juvenile (1b). Resident on Andamans and Nicobars; visitor to the northeast. Adult glossy greenish-black, with bright red iris. Juvenile has blackish-brown upperparts with variable greenish gloss, and streaked underparts. Groves and forest edges.

2 SPOT-WINGED STARLING *Saroglossa spiloptera* 19 cm
Male (2a) and female (2b). Resident? Himalayan foothills and NE India. White wing patch and whitish iris. Male has blackish mask, reddish-chestnut throat, and dark-scalloped greyish upperparts. Female has browner upperparts, and greyish-brown markings on throat and breast. Juvenile has buff wing-bars. Open forest and well-wooded areas.

3 WHITE-FACED STARLING *Sturnus senex* 22 cm
Adult (3a) and juvenile (3b). Resident. Sri Lanka. Adult has whitish face, grey upperparts with slight green gloss, and white-streaked greyish underparts; head can be all white. Juvenile has whitish supercilium and throat, dull brown upperparts, and dark grey underparts. Tall forest.

4 CHESTNUT-TAILED STARLING *Sturnus malabaricus* 20 cm
Adult (4a) and juvenile (4b) *S. m. malabaricus*; **adult** *S. m. blythii* **(4c).** Resident in NE subcontinent and SW Indian hills; winter visitor to C and W India. Adult has grey upperparts, rufous underparts, and chestnut tail; head whiter in southern race *blythii*. Juvenile rather uniform with rufous sides and tips to outer tail feathers. Open wooded areas.

5 WHITE-HEADED STARLING *Sturnus erythropygius* 21 cm
Adult *S. e. andamanensis*. Resident. Andamans and Nicobars. Creamy-white head and underparts, grey mantle and back, and glossy greenish-black wings and tail. Forest clearings and cultivation.

6 BRAHMINY STARLING *Sturnus pagodarum* 21 cm
Adult (6a) and juvenile (6b). Widespread resident; unrecorded in parts of northwest and northeast. Adult has black crest, and rufous-orange sides of head and underparts. Juvenile lacks crest; has grey-brown cap and paler orange-buff underparts. Dry, well-wooded areas and thorn scrub.

7 PURPLE-BACKED STARLING *Sturnus sturninus* 19 cm
Adult male (7a) and female (7b). Vagrant. Pakistan and India. Male has pale grey head and underparts, purplish-black hindcrown patch and mantle, and white tips to median coverts and rear scapulars. Female and juvenile duller; wing-bars and tips to scapulars less prominent in juvenile. Open wooded areas.

8 WHITE-SHOULDERED STARLING *Sturnus sinensis* 20 cm
Male (8a), female (8b) and juvenile (8c). Vagrant. India. Male has silky-grey head and body and white shoulder patch; head and body may have rusty-orange wash. Female and juvenile browner, with less or no white on wing. Coloration of uppertail-coverts and tail help separate from Chestnut-tailed. Habitat unknown in subcontinent.

9 ROSY STARLING *Sturnus roseus* 21 cm
Adult (9a) and juvenile (9b). Passage migrant in Pakistan; winter visitor mainly to India and Sri Lanka. Adult has blackish head with shaggy crest, pinkish mantle and underparts, and blue-green gloss to wings. In non-breeding and first-winter plumage much duller than shown; pink of plumage partly obscured by buff fringes; black by greyish fringes. Juvenile mainly sandy-brown, with stout yellowish bill, and broad pale fringes to wing feathers. Cultivation and damp grassland.

10 COMMON STARLING *Sturnus vulgaris* 21 cm
Adult breeding (10a) and non-breeding (10b) and juvenile (10c). Mainly winter visitor to N subcontinent; also partly resident in Pakistan, and summer visitor to Kashmir. Adult metallic green and purple; heavily marked with buff and white in winter. Juvenile dusky brown with whiter throat. Cultivation and damp grassland.

11 ASIAN PIED STARLING *Sturnus contra* 23 cm
Adult (11a) and juvenile (11b) *S. c. contra*; **adult** *S. c. superciliaris* **(11c).** Resident. Widespread in N and C subcontinent. Adult black and white, with orange orbital skin and large, pointed yellowish bill. Juvenile has black of plumage replaced by brown. *S. c. superciliaris*, occurring in Manipur, has white streaking on forehead. Cultivation, damp grassland and habitation.

PLATE 110, p. 256

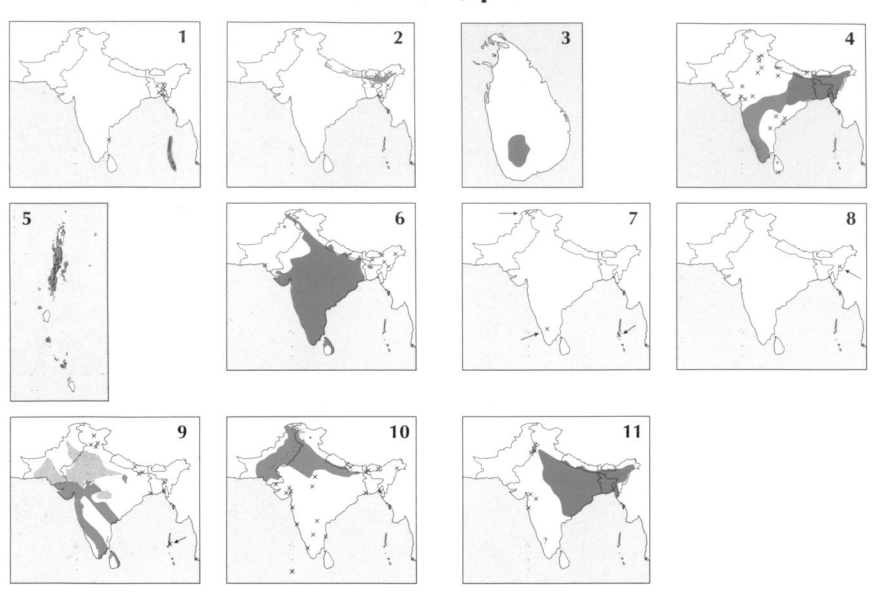

PLATE 112, p. 262

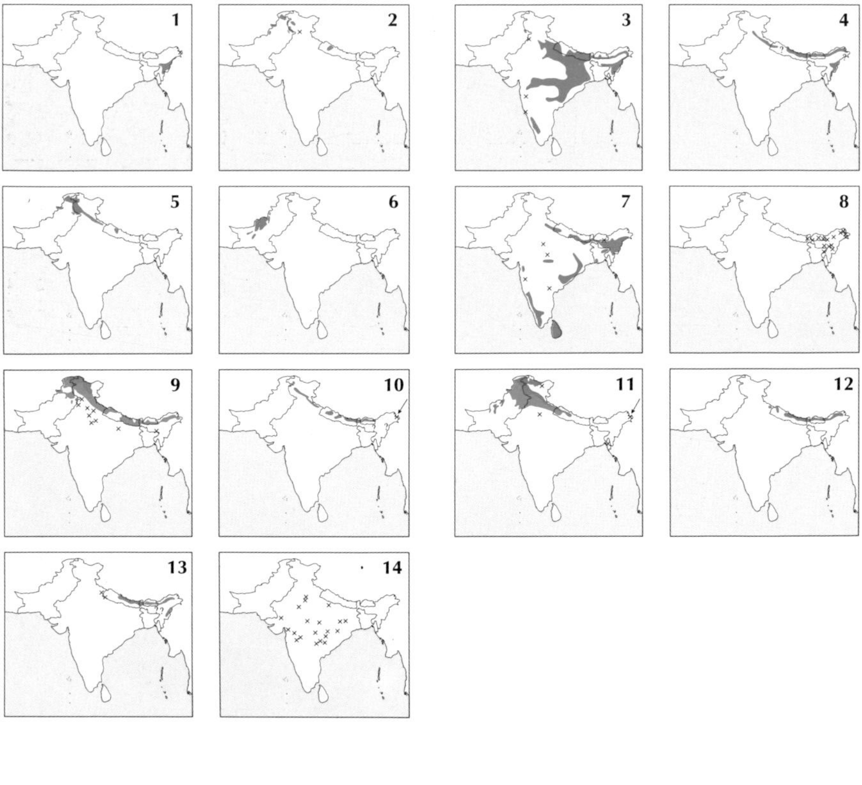

PLATE 114, p. 266

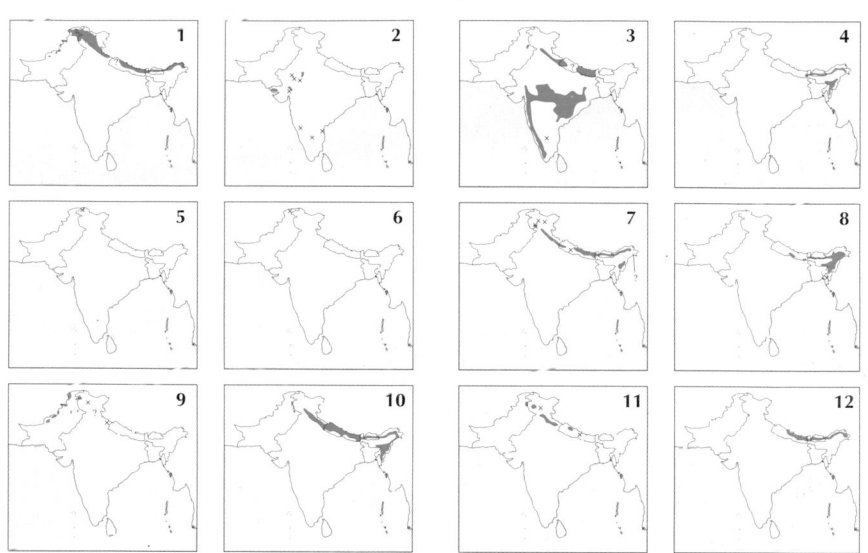

PLATE 115, p. 268

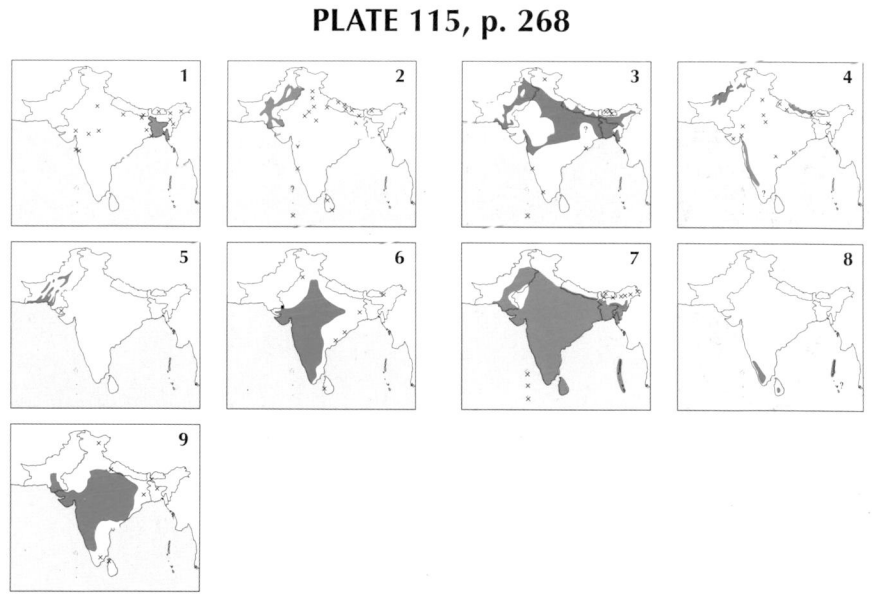

PLATE 111: MYNAS

1 COMMON MYNA *Acridotheres tristis* 25 cm
Adult A. t. tristis (1a, 1b). Widespread resident; unrecorded in parts of the northwest and northeast. Brownish myna with yellow orbital skin, white wing patch and white tail-tip. Juvenile duller. Habitation and cultivation.

2 BANK MYNA *Acridotheres ginginianus* 23 cm
Adult (2a, 2b) and juvenile (2c). Resident. Widespread in N and C subcontinent. Adult is bluish-grey with blackish cap. Orange-red orbital patch, orange-yellow bill, and tufted forehead. Wing patch, underwing-coverts and tail-tip orange-buff. Juvenile duller and browner than adult. Cultivation, damp grassland and habitation.

3 JUNGLE MYNA *Acridotheres fuscus* 23 cm
Adult (3a) and juvenile (3b) A. f. fuscus; adult A. f. mahrattensis (3c). Resident. Himalayas south to Bangladesh and N Orissa, and W India. Tufted forehead, and white wing patch and tail-tip; lacks bare orbital skin. Juvenile browner, with reduced forehead tuft. *A. f. mahrattensis*, of W peninsula, has browner upperparts than nominate and grey or bluish-white (rather than yellow) iris. Cultivation near well-wooded areas, and edges of habitation.

4 WHITE-VENTED MYNA *Acridotheres cinereus* 25 cm
Adult (4a) and juvenile (4b). Resident. NE India and Bangladesh. Similar to Jungle Myna, but has uniform blackish-grey upperparts, uniform dark grey underparts strongly contrasting with white undertail-coverts, all-yellow bill, and reddish to orange-brown iris. Juvenile browner. Cultivation and grassland.

5 COLLARED MYNA *Acridotheres albocinctus* 23 cm
Adult (5a) and juvenile (5b). Resident. Manipur and Assam. Whitish patch on neck sides and has white tips to dark grey undertail-coverts. Neck patch strongly washed with buff in some birds. Neck patch smaller and brownish-white on juvenile. Cultivation and grassland.

6 GOLDEN-CRESTED MYNA *Ampeliceps coronatus* 22 cm
Male (6a), female (6b) and juvenile (6c). Resident. Manipur and Assam. Golden-yellow forehead and crown, yellow throat, naked orange-yellow orbital patch, and yellow patch at base of primaries. Female has less yellow on crown and throat compared with male. Juvenile browner, with less yellow. Open moist forest.

7 SRI LANKA MYNA *Gracula ptilogenys* 25 cm
Adult. Resident. Sri Lanka. Compared with Hill Myna, has stouter orange-red bill with dark blue base, and different shape and positioning of wattles. Forest and well-wooded country.

8 HILL MYNA *Gracula religiosa* 25–29 cm
Adult (8a) and juvenile (8b) G. r. indica; adult G. r. intermedia (8c). Resident. Himalayan foothills, hills of India, Bangladesh and Sri Lanka. Large myna with yellow wattles, large orange to yellow bill, and white wing patches. Juvenile has duller yellowish-orange bill, paler yellow wattles, and less gloss to plumage. *G. r. indica*, of Western Ghats and Sri Lanka, has smaller bill and has the eye wattles separated from those on nape (compare with *intermedia* of N, E, and NE subcontinent). Moist forest and plantations.

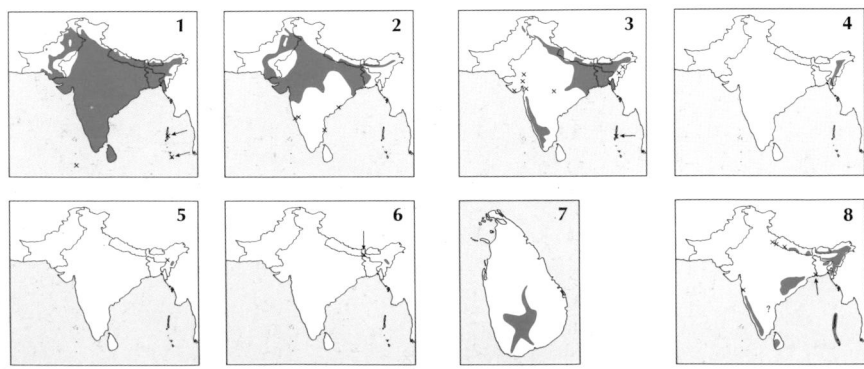

PLATE 112: NUTHATCHES AND TREECREEPERS   Maps p. 258

1 CHESTNUT-VENTED NUTHATCH *Sitta nagaensis* 12 cm
Adult. Resident. NE Indian hills. Whitish underparts with chestnut rear flanks, and chestnut undertail-coverts with white spots. Open forest.

2 KASHMIR NUTHATCH *Sitta cashmirensis* 12 cm
Male (2a) and female (2b). Resident. Himalayas and Indian hills. Compared with female Chestnut-bellied, has uniform undertail-coverts and lacks clearly defined white cheeks. Larger and longer-billed than White-tailed, with more pronounced white cheeks, no white at base of tail, and distinctive rasping, jay-like calls. Forest and groves.

3 CHESTNUT-BELLIED NUTHATCH *Sitta castanea* 12 cm
Male (3a) and female (3b) *S. c. castanea*; **male** *S. c. almorae* **(3c).** Resident. Himalayas and Indian hills. Male has deep chestnut underparts and white cheeks. Female paler cinnamon-brown on underparts, although white cheeks more pronounced than on similar species; has pale fringes to undertail-coverts. *S. c. castanea*, of N and C Indian plains, is relatively small and with grey (rather than white) scalloping on undertail-coverts compared with Himalayan birds (e.g. *almorae*). Calls include an explosive *siditit*. Forest and groves.

4 WHITE-TAILED NUTHATCH *Sitta himalayensis* 12 cm
Adult. Resident. Himalayas and NE Indian hills. Small size with small bill. Calls include a hard *chak'kak* which may be repeated as a rattle. White at base of tail (difficult to see); less distinct white cheek patch than Kashmir; uniform undertail-coverts. Forest.

5 WHITE-CHEEKED NUTHATCH *Sitta leucopsis* 12 cm
Adult. Resident. W Himalayas. Black crown and nape, white face, and whitish underparts with rufous flanks and undertail-coverts. Call likened to bleating of young goat. Coniferous and mixed forest.

6 EASTERN ROCK NUTHATCH *Sitta tephronota* 15 cm
Adult. Resident. Baluchistan. Large, with very large bill. Long black eye-stripe, pale blue-grey upperparts, and whitish underparts. Rocky gorges and ridges.

7 VELVET-FRONTED NUTHATCH *Sitta frontalis* 10 cm
Male (7a) and female (7b). Resident. Himalayas, Indian hills, Bangladesh and Sri Lanka. Violet-blue upperparts, black forehead, black-tipped red bill, and lilac underparts. Male has black eye-stripe. Open broadleaved forest and well-wooded areas.

8 BEAUTIFUL NUTHATCH *Sitta formosa* 15 cm
Adult. Resident. E Himalayas and NE Indian hills. Large; blue-streaked black upperparts, and rufous-orange underparts. Dense forest.

9 WALLCREEPER *Tichodroma muraria* 16 cm
Adult male breeding (9a) and adult non-breeding (9b). Resident. Himalayas; winters down to foothills and plains. Long, downcurved bill. Largely crimson wing-coverts; shows white primary spots in flight. Breeding male has black throat. Rock cliffs and gorges; also ruins and stony river beds in winter.

10 EURASIAN TREECREEPER *Certhia familiaris* 12 cm
Adult *C. f. mandellii* **(10a); adult** *C. f. hodgsoni* **(10b).** Resident. Himalayas, NE India? Dull brown, unbarred tail, and whitish throat and breast. W Himalayan *hodgsoni* comparatively pale and grey above, with pronounced whitish streaking. Forest.

11 BAR-TAILED TREECREEPER *Certhia himalayana* 12 cm
Adult. Resident. Pakistan mountains, W Himalayas and Arunachal Pradesh. Dark barring on tail, white throat, and dull whitish or dirty greyish-buff underparts. Forest; also well-wooded areas in winter.

12 RUSTY-FLANKED TREECREEPER *Certhia nipalensis* 12 cm
Adult. Resident. Himalayas. Buffish supercilium continuing around dark ear-coverts, unbarred tail, white throat, and rufous flanks. Forest.

13 BROWN-THROATED TREECREEPER *Certhia discolor* 12 cm
Adult *C. d. discolor* **(13a); adult** *C. d. manipurensis* **(13b).** Resident. Himalayas and NE India. Brownish-buff (Himalayas) to cinnamon-orange throat and breast (S Manipur); unbarred tail. Forest.

14 SPOTTED CREEPER *Salpornis spilonotus* 13 cm
Adult. Resident. N and C India. Long, downcurved bill, and shortish tail. Plumage spotted with white. Open deciduous forest and groves.

Craig Robson '97

PLATE 113: TITS

1 WHITE-CROWNED PENDULINE TIT *Remiz coronatus* 10 cm
Fresh male (1a), worn male (1b), female (1c) and juvenile (1d). Winter visitor to Pakistan and Punjab, India; breeds in Ladakh? Male has blackish mask and nape, whitish crown and whitish collar. Female has pale grey crown and collar, and lacks black nape band. Juvenile lacks dark mask. Reedbeds and riverain forest.

2 FIRE-CAPPED TIT *Cephalopyrus flammiceps* 10 cm
Male breeding (2a), male non-breeding (2b), female (2c) and immature (2d). Breeds in Himalayas; resident in NE India; winters in Nepal and C India. Flowerpecker-like, with greenish upperparts and yellowish to whitish underparts. Lacks crest. Breeding male has bright orange-scarlet forecrown, chin and throat. Forest.

3 RUFOUS-NAPED TIT *Parus rufonuchalis* 13 cm
Adult (3a) and juvenile (3b). Resident. Baluchistan and W Himalayas. Large size, extensive black bib (to upper belly), and grey belly. Coniferous forest.

4 RUFOUS-VENTED TIT *Parus rubidiventris* 12 cm
Adult (4a) and juvenile (4b) *P. r. rubidiventris*; adult (4c) and juvenile (4d) *P. r. beavani*. Resident. Himalayas and Nagaland. Smaller than Rufous-naped, with smaller black bib, and (where ranges overlap) has rufous belly. E Himalayan *beavani* has greyish belly. Forest.

5 SPOT-WINGED TIT *Parus melanolophus* 11 cm
Adult (5a) and juvenile (5b). Resident. W Himalayas. Small size, white wing-bars, blue-grey mantle, rufous breast sides, and dark grey belly. Coniferous and mixed forest.

6 COAL TIT *Parus ater* 11 cm
Adult (6a) and juvenile (6b). Resident. C and E Himalayas. Small size, whitish wing-bars, olive-grey mantle, and creamy-buff underparts. Coniferous and mixed forest.

7 GREY-CRESTED TIT *Parus dichrous* 12 cm
Adult. Resident. Himalayas. Greyish crest and upperparts, whitish collar, and orange-buff underparts. Broadleaved and mixed forest.

8 GREAT TIT *Parus major* 14 cm
Adult (8a) and juvenile (8b) *P. m. stupae*; adult *P. m. tibetanus* (8c). Resident. Widespread in hills of subcontinent. Black breast centre and line down belly, greyish mantle, greyish-white breast sides and flanks, and white wing-bar. Juvenile has yellowish-white cheeks and underparts, and yellowish-olive wash to mantle. *P. m. tibetanus* (one record from Sikkim) has greenish-olive cast to mantle. Forest and well-wooded country.

9 GREEN-BACKED TIT *Parus monticolus* 12.5 cm
Adult (9a) and juvenile (9b). Resident. Himalayas and NE Indian hills. Green mantle and back, and yellow on underparts. Forest.

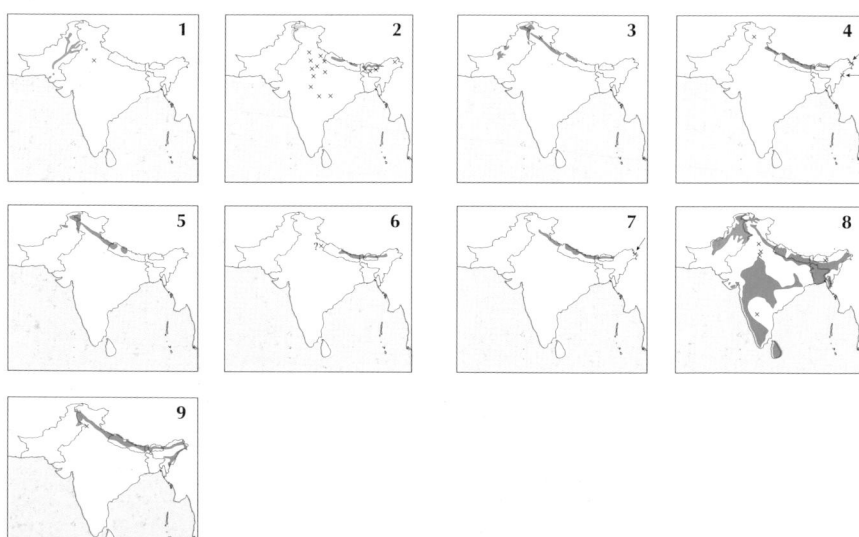

PLATE 114: TITS AND WINTER WREN Maps p. 259

1 WINTER WREN *Troglodytes troglodytes* 9 cm
Adult *T. t. neglectus* (1a); adult *T. t. nipalensis* (1b). Resident. Baluchistan and Himalayas. Small and squat, with stubby tail. Brown, with dark-barred wings, tail and underparts. *T. t. nipalensis*, of C and E Himalayas, is darkest of races in subcontinent. Breeds on high-altitude rocky and bushy slopes; winters around villages and in forest undergrowth.

2 WHITE-NAPED TIT *Parus nuchalis* 12 cm
Adult. Resident. NW and S India. Black mantle and wing-coverts (grey on Great Tit); much white on tertials and at bases of secondaries and primaries. Thorn-scrub forest.

3 BLACK-LORED TIT *Parus xanthogenys* 13 cm
Male (3a) and juvenile (3b) *P. x. xanthogenys*; female *P. x. aplonotus* (3c); female *P. x. travancoreensis* (3d). Resident. Himalayas and peninsular hills. Where ranges overlap in Himalayas (*P. x. xanthogenys*), best told from Yellow-cheeked by black forehead and lores, uniform greenish upperparts with black streaking confined to scapulars, olive rump, and yellowish wing-bars. Two races in the peninsula have white wing-bars (adult) and show sexual variation, most marked in *travancoreensis* where female has greyish-olive crest and mantle. Open forest, forest edges and plantations.

4 YELLOW-CHEEKED TIT *Parus spilonotus* 14 cm
Adult (4a) and juvenile (4b) *P. s. spilonotus*. Resident. E Himalayas and NE Indian hills. Yellow forehead and lores, black streaking on greenish mantle, grey rump and white wing-bars are best features from Black-lored where ranges overlap. Open forest.

5 AZURE TIT *Parus cyanus* 13.5 cm
Adult. Winter visitor? N Pakistan Himalayas. White underparts, lacking yellow on breast; crown and ear-coverts white. River-bed bushes.

6 YELLOW-BREASTED TIT *Parus flavipectus* 13 cm
Adult. Resident? N Pakistan Himalayas. Yellow breast and greyish head; chin and centre of throat greyish (show as faint bib). Dense thickets.

7 YELLOW-BROWED TIT *Sylviparus modestus* 10 cm
Adult *S. m. modestus*. Resident. Himalayas and NE India. Very small, with slight crest and rather stubby bill. Olive-green upperparts, yellowish eye-ring, fine yellow supercilium, and yellowish-buff underparts. Broadleaved forest.

8 SULTAN TIT *Melanochlora sultanea* 20.5 cm
Male (8a) and female (8b). Resident. C and E Himalayas and NE Indian hills. Large, bulbul-like tit. Blue-black (male) or blackish-olive (female), with bright yellow crest and underparts. Mainly evergreen broadleaved forest.

9 WHITE-CHEEKED TIT *Aegithalos leucogenys* 11 cm
Adult (9a) and juvenile (9b). Resident. Baluchistan and W Himalayas. Black throat, cinnamon crown, yellowish iris, and grey-brown mantle. Juvenile has buffish-white throat and streaking on breast. Scrub forest.

10 BLACK-THROATED TIT *Aegithalos concinnus* 10.5 cm
Adult (10a) and juvenile (10b) *A. c. iredalei*; adult *A. c. manipurensis* (10c). Resident. Himalayas and NE Indian hills. Chestnut or rufous crown, white chin and black throat, white cheeks, and grey mantle. Juvenile has white throat and indistinct black-spotted breast-band. Broadleaved and mixed forest and secondary growth.

11 WHITE-THROATED TIT *Aegithalos niveogularis* 11 cm
Adult (11a) and juvenile (11b). Resident. W Himalayas. White forehead and forecrown and whitish throat; iris brownish. Diffuse blackish mask and cinnamon underparts, with darker breast-band. Juvenile has dusky throat, more prominent breast-band, and paler lower breast and belly. Bushes in forest and high-altitude shrubberies.

12 RUFOUS-FRONTED TIT *Aegithalos iouschistos* 11 cm
Adult (12a) and juvenile (12b). Resident. C and E Himalayas. Broad black mask (reaching nape), dusky throat, rufous-buff crown centre and cheeks, and rufous underparts. Juvenile has paler crown-stripe, cheeks and underparts. Forest.

1 SAND MARTIN *Riparia riparia* 13 cm
Adult (1a, 1b, 1c). Breeds in NE India; recorded W to Gujarat. White throat and half-collar and brown breast-band. Very similar to Pale Martin, but upperparts darker brown, breast-band clearly defined and tail-fork deeper. Around large waterbodies; in summer, around rivers and streams.

2 PALE MARTIN *Riparia diluta* 13 cm
Adult (2a, 2b, 2c). Resident. Pakistan (and probably farther east). Upperparts paler and greyer than on Sand and Plain Martins; throat greyish-white; breast-band not clearly defined; tail-fork very shallow. Around large waterbodies.

3 PLAIN MARTIN *Riparia paludicola* 12 cm
Adult (3a, 3b, 3c). Resident. Mainly N and C subcontinent. Pale brownish-grey throat and breast, merging into dingy white rest of underparts; some with suggestion of breast-band. Underwing darker than on Sand and Pale, flight weaker and more fluttering, and has shallower indent to tail. Upperparts darker than on Pale. Around rivers and lakes.

4 EURASIAN CRAG MARTIN *Hirundo rupestris* 15 cm
Adult (4a, 4b, 4c). Resident. Breeds in Pakistan hills and Himalayas; winters in Western Ghats. Larger and darker than Pale Crag Martin. Upperparts and underwing-coverts darker brown; dusky throat, dusky brown flanks and vent, and more distinct pale fringes to undertail-coverts. Rocky cliffs and gorges.

5 ROCK MARTIN *Hirundo fuligula* 13 cm
Adult (5a, 5b, 5c). Resident. C and S Pakistan. Smaller than Eurasian Crag Martin, with paler sandy-grey upperparts (especially rump), buffish-white throat, paler vent and undertail-coverts, and paler underwing-coverts. Rocky gorges and cliffs.

6 DUSKY CRAG MARTIN *Hirundo concolor* 13 cm
Adult (6a, 6b, 6c). Resident. Mainly N and peninsular India. Upperparts and underparts dark brown and rather uniform. Cliffs, gorges and old buildings.

7 BARN SWALLOW *Hirundo rustica* 18 cm
Adult (7a, 7b, 7c) and juvenile (7d) *H. r. rustica*; **adult** *H. r. tytleri* **(7e).** Breeds in Pakistan hills, Himalayas and NE India; widespread farther south in winter. Reddish forehead and throat, long tail-streamers, and blue-black breast-band. Juvenile duller and lacks tail-streamers. *H. r. tytleri*, a winter visitor to NE subcontinent, has rufous underparts. Cultivation, habitation, lakes and rivers.

8 PACIFIC SWALLOW *Hirundo tahitica* 13 cm
Adult (8a, 8b, 8c) and juvenile (8d) *H. t. javanica*; **adult** *H. t. domicola* **(8e, 8f).** Resident. SW Indian hills, Andamans and Sri Lanka. Told from Barn by more extensive rufous on throat, lack of breast-band, dingy underparts and underwing-coverts, and blackish undertail-coverts with whitish fringes; lacks tail-streamers. *H. t. domicola* (SW India and Sri Lanka) has metallic green gloss to upperparts (more purplish-blue in *javanica* of Andamans). Grassy hills, rivers and habitation.

9 WIRE-TAILED SWALLOW *Hirundo smithii* 14 cm
Adult (9a, 9b, 9c) and juvenile (9d). Widespread resident; unrecorded in parts of the northwest, northeast and southeast. Chestnut crown, glistening white underparts and underwing-coverts, and fine filamentous projections to outer tail feathers (often broken or difficult to see). Juvenile has brownish cast to blue upperparts, and dull brownish crown. Open country and cultivation near fresh waters.

PLATE 116: SWALLOWS AND MARTINS

1 RED-RUMPED SWALLOW *Hirundo daurica* 16–17 cm
Adult (1a, 1b, 1c) and juvenile (1d) *H. d. nipalensis*; adult *H. d. hyperythra* (1e, 1f).
Widespread resident; unrecorded in parts of the northwest and northeast. Rufous-orange
neck sides, rufous-orange rump, finely streaked buffish-white underparts, and black
undertail-coverts. Six races in the subcontinent, differing mainly in strength of streaking
on underparts and rump, prominence of collar, and coloration of underparts and rump.
H. d. nipalensis, which breeds in Himalayas, is one of the most heavily streaked. *H. d.
hyperythra*, of Sri Lanka, has unstreaked chestnut underparts and rump. Summers in
upland cultivation and grassy hills; winters in open country and forest clearings.

2 STRIATED SWALLOW *Hirundo striolata* 19 cm
Adult (2a, 2b, 2c) and juvenile (2d). Summer visitor; resident? NE Indian hills and
Bangladesh. Told from Red-rumped by larger size, stronger streaking on underparts and
rump, and lack of or poorly defined rufous collar (although collar can be incomplete in
some races of Red-rumped). Steep cliffs in hills.

3 STREAK-THROATED SWALLOW *Hirundo fluvicola* 11 cm
Adult (3a, 3b, 3c) and juvenile (3d). Resident. Indus plains; widespread in N and C India.
Small and compact, with slight fork to long, broad tail. Chestnut crown, streaked throat
and breast, white mantle streaks, and brownish rump. Juvenile duller, with browner
crown. Cultivation and open country near water.

4 NORTHERN HOUSE MARTIN *Delichon urbica* 13 cm
Adult (4a, 4b, 4c). Summer visitor to W Himalayas; mainly passage migrant elsewhere.
Adult told from Asian House Martin by combination of whiter underparts, longer and
more deeply forked tail, and paler underwing-coverts. Juvenile (not illustrated) has less
glossy upperparts, is rather dingy underneath, and has shallower tail-fork; is more like
Asian. Cliffs and gorges.

5 ASIAN HOUSE MARTIN *Delichon dasypus* 12 cm
Adult (5a, 5b, 5c). Resident. Himalayas. Adult told from Northern by dusky underparts,
shallower fork to shorter tail, darker underwing, and (not always) dusky centres to undertail-coverts; rump patch often looks smaller and dirty white. Juvenile (not illustrated) has
browner upperparts and stronger dusky wash to underparts. Grassy slopes with cliffs, and
forest around mountain villages.

6 NEPAL HOUSE MARTIN *Delichon nipalensis* 13 cm
Adult (6a, 6b, 6c). Resident. Himalayas and NE Indian hills. Square-cut tail (lacking
indentation even when closed), narrow white rump band, blackish underwing-coverts,
black undertail-coverts contrasting sharply with white belly, and blackish throat (only
chin black on some). Mountain ridges with cliffs, forest, and around villages.

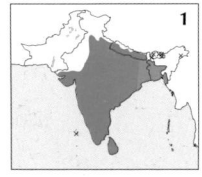 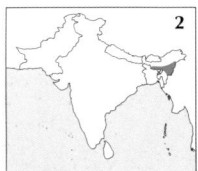 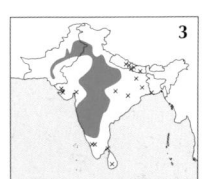 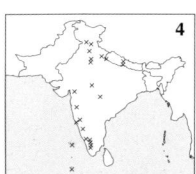

 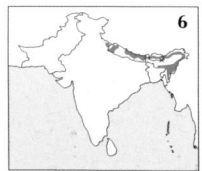

1 CRESTED FINCHBILL *Spizixos canifrons* 22 cm
Adult (1a) and juvenile (1b). Resident. NE Indian hills. Stout, pale bill, and crested appearance. Dark tip to tail. Adult has blackish crest and throat, and grey ear-coverts. Juvenile has blackish-brown crown and pale brown ear-coverts. Broadleaved forest and secondary growth.

2 STRIATED BULBUL *Pycnonotus striatus* 23 cm
Adult. Resident. Himalayas and NE Indian hills. Crested, green bulbul with boldly streaked underparts and finely streaked upperparts. Broadleaved forest.

3 GREY-HEADED BULBUL *Pycnonotus priocephalus* 19 cm
Adult. Resident. SW India. Crestless, grey-and-green bulbul. Greyish head, greenish-yellow forehead, and yellowish bill and iris. Tail appears grey at rest, but in flight shows blackish outer feathers with grey tips. Some birds have olive-green head and greener coloration to rump and tail. Evergreen forest and dense thickets.

4 BLACK-HEADED BULBUL *Pycnonotus atriceps* 18 cm
Adult olive-yellow morph (4a), adult grey morph (4b) and juvenile (4c) *P. a. atriceps*; **adult** *P. a. fuscoflavescens* **(4d).** Resident. NE India, Andamans and Bangladesh. Crestless black head, and yellow wing panel; yellow terminal band and black subterminal band to tail. Grey morph rare. Andaman race *fuscoflavescens* has olive-green crown and ear-coverts and brighter yellow underparts. Open forest.

5 BLACK-CRESTED BULBUL *Pycnonotus melanicterus* 19 cm
Adult (5a) and juvenile (5b) *P. m. flaviventris*; **adult** *P. m. gularis* **(5c); adult** *P. m. melanicterus* **(5d).** Resident. Himalayas, NE, E and SW India, Bangladesh and Sri Lanka. Uniform wings and tail. Nominate race in Himalayas and NE and E India has black crest; other races lack crest and have ruby-red (SW India) or yellow (Sri Lanka) throat. Moist broadleaved forest and thick secondary growth.

6 RED-WHISKERED BULBUL *Pycnonotus jocosus* 20 cm
Adult (6a) and juvenile (6b). Widespread resident; unrecorded in Pakistan, parts of N and NW India and Sri Lanka. Black crest, red 'whiskers', and white underparts with complete or broken breast-band. Red vent. Juvenile duller and lacks 'whiskers'. Open forest and secondary growth.

7 WHITE-EARED BULBUL *Pycnonotus leucotis* 20 cm
Adult *P. l. leucotis* **(7a); adult** *P. l. humii* **(7b).** Resident. Pakistan and NW India. White-cheeked bulbul with black crown and nape, and short (in northwest part of range) or non-existent crest. Thorn scrub and dry, open cultivation.

8 HIMALAYAN BULBUL *Pycnonotus leucogenys* 20 cm
(handwritten: WHITE CHEEKED)
Adult. Resident. N Pakistan hills and Himalayas. Brown crest and nape, and white cheeks with black crescent at rear. Dry scrub and secondary growth.

9 RED-VENTED BULBUL *Pycnonotus cafer* 20 cm
Adult *P. c. humayuni* **(9a); adult** *P. c. bengalensis* **(9b).** Widespread resident. Red vent. Black head with slight crest, and white rump. Mantle and breast vary from pale brown, and heavily scaled, to blackish. Open deciduous forest and secondary growth.

10 YELLOW-THROATED BULBUL *Pycnonotus xantholaemus* 20 cm
Adult. Resident. S Indian hills. Plain yellow-green head, bright yellow throat, grey breast-band, and yellow undertail-coverts and tip to tail. Thorn jungle and moist deciduous habitats in stony hills.

11 YELLOW-EARED BULBUL *Pycnonotus penicillatus* 20 cm
Adult. Resident. Sri Lanka. Blackish crown, yellow ear-tufts and ear-covert patch, and white tufts from lores. Forest.

PLATE 117, p. 272

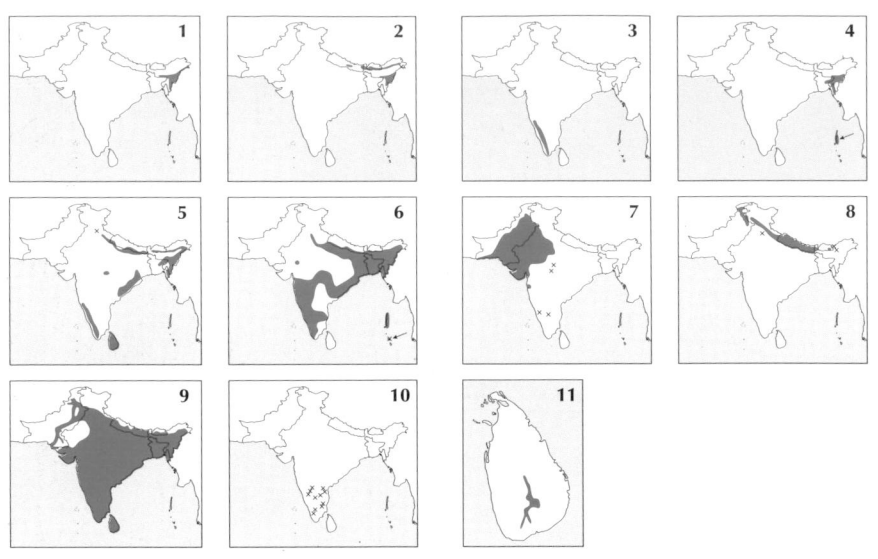

PLATE 118, p. 276

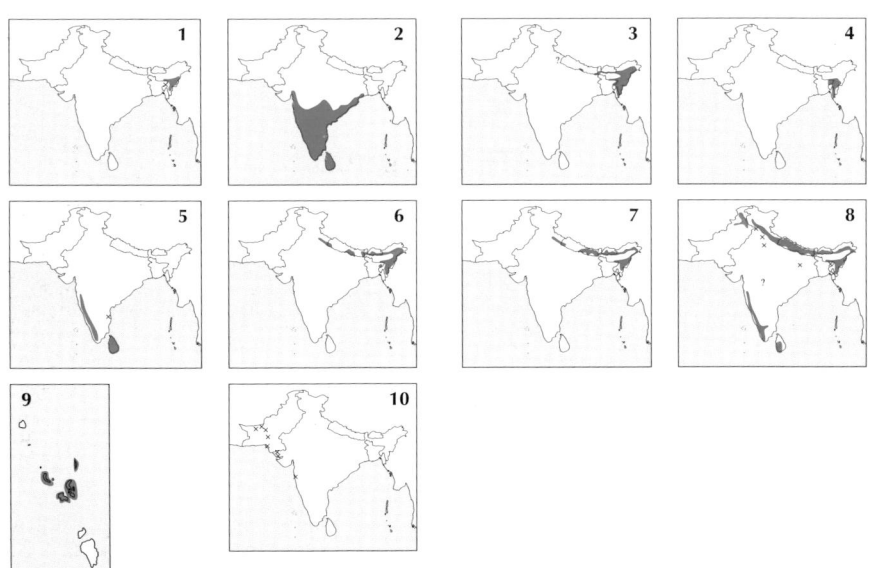

PLATE 120, p. 280

PLATE 121, p. 282

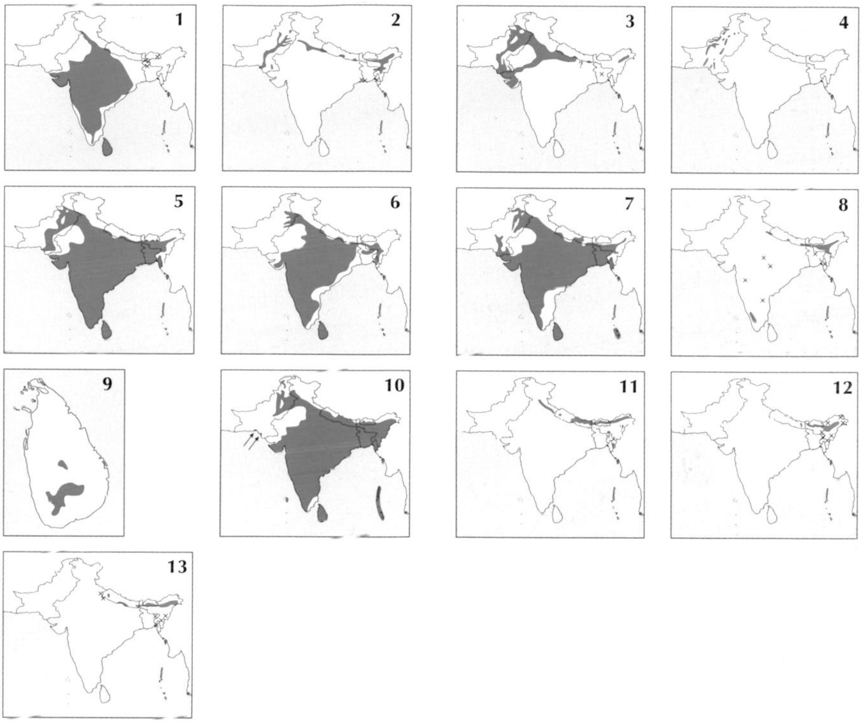

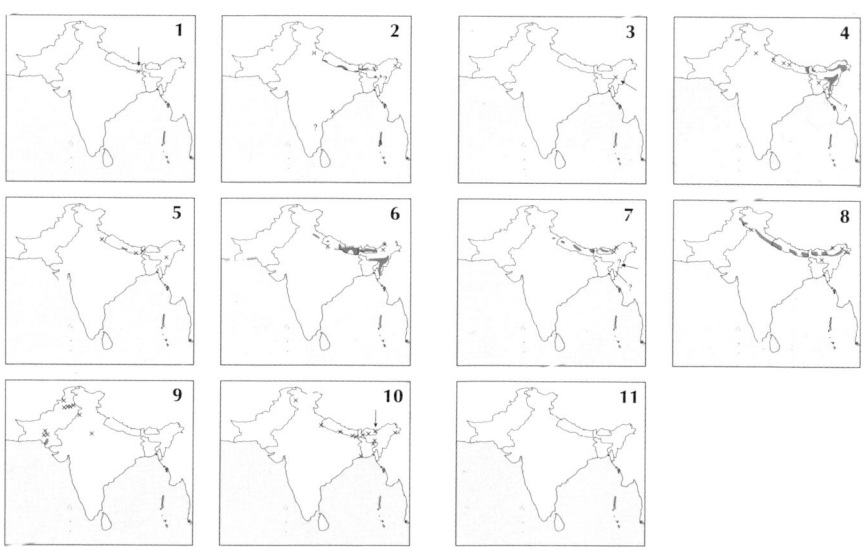

1 FLAVESCENT BULBUL *Pycnonotus flavescens* 22 cm
Adult. Resident. NE Indian hills. Longer tail and stout black bill compared with Olive Bulbul. White supercilium, brownish crest, yellowish undertail-coverts, and greenish uppertail. Forest and secondary growth.

2 WHITE-BROWED BULBUL *Pycnonotus luteolus* 20 cm
Adult. Resident. Peninsular India and Sri Lanka. White supercilium and crescent below eye, and dark eye-stripe and moustachial stripe. Otherwise nondescript. Dry scrub and forest edges.

3 WHITE-THROATED BULBUL *Alophoixus flaveolus* 22 cm
Adult (3a) and juvenile (3b). Resident. Himalayas, NE India and Bangladesh. Brownish crest, white throat, yellow breast and belly, and rufous cast to wings and tail. Juvenile duller, with browner underparts. Undergrowth in evergreen forest and secondary growth.

4 OLIVE BULBUL *Iole virescens* 19 cm
Adult. Resident. NE India and Bangladesh. Longish bill with pale lower mandible, pale olive-yellow underparts, pale rufous undertail-coverts, and rufous-brown tail. Evergreen forest and secondary growth.

5 YELLOW-BROWED BULBUL *Iole indica* 20 cm
Adult (5a) and juvenile (5b). Resident. Western Ghats and Sri Lanka. Yellow supercilium, eye-ring and underparts. Striking black bill and dark eye. Moist forest and secondary growth.

6 ASHY BULBUL *Hemixos flavala* 20 cm
Adult. Resident. Himalayan foothills, NE India and Bangladesh. Grey crest and upperparts, black mask and tawny ear-coverts, and olive-yellow wing patch. Broadleaved forest; also forest edges in winter.

7 MOUNTAIN BULBUL *Hypsipetes mcclellandii* 24 cm
Adult. Resident. Himalayas and NE India. Brown crest, greyish throat with white streaking, cinnamon-brown breast with buff streaking, and greenish upperparts. Forest and secondary growth.

8 BLACK BULBUL *Hypsipetes leucocephalus* 25 cm
Adult (8a) and juvenile (8b) *H. l. psaroides*; **adult** *H. l. ganeesa* **(8c).** Resident. Himalayas, NE and SW India, and Sri Lanka. Slate-grey to blackish bulbul with shallow fork to tail; red bill, legs and feet. Birds in Western Ghats (*H. l. ganeesa*) and Sri Lanka are darker than *H. l. psaroides* which occupies most of Himalayan range. Juvenile lacks crest; has whitish underparts with diffuse grey breast-band, and brownish cast to upperparts. Mainly broadleaved forest and plantations.

9 NICOBAR BULBUL *Hypsipetes nicobariensis* 20 cm
Adult. Resident. Nicobars. Drab bulbul with dark brown crown and nape, and whitish throat and breast merging into yellowish belly and undertail-coverts. Forest and secondary growth.

10 GREY HYPOCOLIUS *Hypocolius ampelinus* 25 cm
Male (10a) and female (10b). Winter visitor. S Pakistan and Gujarat. Crested, with long tail and white on primaries. Male has black mask and tail-band. Female rather uniform sandy-brown. Thorn scrub and date-palm groves in semi-desert.

1

2

3a

3b

4

5b

5a

6

7

8a

8b

10b

9

8c

10a

C.D'S

PLATE 119: PRINIAS

1 HILL PRINIA *Prinia atrogularis* 17 cm
Adult breeding (1a) and non-breeding (1b) P. a. atrogularis; adult breeding (1c) and non-breeding (1d) P. a. khasiana. Resident. E Himalayas and NE Indian hills. Black throat and breast with white spotting in breeding plumage. White supercilium and buffish underparts in non-breeding plumage; compared with Striated Prinia, has finer bill, unstreaked upperparts, and whitish supercilium. *P. a. khasiana* (east and south of Brahmaputra River) differs from nominate in having rufous-brown upperparts (especially crown) and warmer buff flanks in both breeding and non-breeding plumage. Scrub and grass.

2 RUFOUS-VENTED PRINIA *Prinia burnesii* 17 cm
Adult P. b. burnesii (2a); adult P. b. cinerascens (2b). Resident. Indus plains in Pakistan and NW India (nominate); Brahmaputra plains in NE India (*cinerascens*). Large size, streaked upperparts, whitish lores/eye-ring, and broad tail. Nominate race has rufous vent. *P. b. cinerascens* has cold olive-grey coloration to upperparts and greyish flanks and undertail-coverts. Tall grassland and reedbeds.

3 STRIATED PRINIA *Prinia criniger* 16 cm
Adult breeding (3a) and non-breeding (3b) P. c. criniger. Resident. Himalayas, hills of Pakistan and NE India. Large size, streaked upperparts, and stout bill. Dark bill and lores, and indistinct streaking to grey-brown upperparts, in breeding plumage. Prominently streaked rufous-brown upperparts, with buff lores, in non-breeding plumage. Scrubby hillsides, and long grass in open forest.

4 GREY-CROWNED PRINIA *Prinia cinereocapilla* 11 cm
Adult. Resident. Himalayan foothills and Assam. Orange-buff supercilium, dark blue-grey crown and nape, and rufous-brown mantle and back. Bushes at forest edges and secondary growth.

5 RUFOUS-FRONTED PRINIA *Prinia buchanani* 12 cm
Adult (5a) and grey variant (5b). Resident. Pakistan and N and C India. Rufous-brown crown and broad white tips to tail (very prominent in flight). Call is a distinctive rippling trill. Rufous to crown may be difficult to see when worn. Upperparts uniform pale rufous-brown on juvenile. Scrub in semi-desert.

6 RUFESCENT PRINIA *Prinia rufescens* 11 cm
Adult breeding (6a), adult non-breeding (6b) and juvenile (6c). Resident. E Himalayas, hills of NE and E India and Bangladesh. Large bill with paler lower mandible. Grey cast to crown, nape and ear-coverts in summer. In non-breeding plumage has more rufescent mantle and edgings to tertials, and has stronger buffish wash to throat and breast, compared with Grey-breasted. Buzzing call. Tall grassland, grass under forest and secondary growth.

7 GREY-BREASTED PRINIA *Prinia hodgsonii* 11 cm
Adult breeding (7a) and non-breeding (7b) P. h. rufula; non-breeding P. h. hodgsonii (7c); male (7d) and female (7e) P. h. pectoralis. Widespread resident. Small size. Grey breast-band in summer. Where ranges overlap with Rufescent, non-breeding is best distinguished by fine dark bill, grey-brown tail, and greyish wash to sides of neck and breast. Laughing, high-pitched call. Bushes at forest edges, scrub and secondary growth.

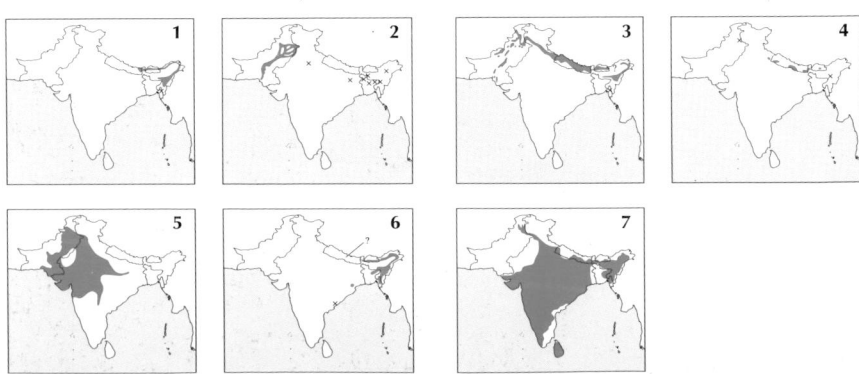

PLATE 120: PRINIAS, CISTICOLAS, WHITE-EYES AND TESIAS
Maps p. 275

1 JUNGLE PRINIA *Prinia sylvatica* 13 cm
Adult breeding (1a) and non-breeding (1b) *P. s. gangetica.* Widespread in lowlands and foothills; unrecorded in Pakistan. Large stout bill, uniform wings. Song is loud, pulsing *zong zee chu*, repeated monotonously; call is a loud *tiu*. Dry scrub and tall grass.

2 YELLOW-BELLIED PRINIA *Prinia flaviventris* 13 cm
Adult breeding (2a) and juvenile *P. f. flaviventris* of NE subcontinent **(2b)**. Resident. Widespread in N subcontinent. White throat and breast and yellow belly. Slate-grey cast to crown and olive-green cast to upperparts. Juvenile has uniform yellowish olive-brown upperparts and yellow underparts. Tall grassland by wetlands.

3 GRACEFUL PRINIA *Prinia gracilis* 11 cm
Adult *P. g. lepida.* Resident. Lowlands in N subcontinent. Small, with fine bill and streaked upperparts. Tall grass and scrub, especially by wetlands.

4 STREAKED SCRUB WARBLER *Scotocerca inquieta* 10 cm
Adult. Resident. Pakistan hills. Vinaceous-buff supercilium and ear-coverts, black throat streaking, greyish upperparts, and boldly streaked crown. Dry stony and scrubby slopes.

5 PLAIN PRINIA *Prinia inornata* 13 cm
Adult breeding (5a) and non-breeding (5b) *P. i. inornata*; breeding *P. i. franklinii* **(5c)**. Widespread resident. Smaller than Jungle, with finer bill. Pale or rufous fringes to tertials. Song is a rapid trill, *tlick tlick tlick*; calls include plaintive *tee-tee-tee* and nasal *beep*. Tall crops, reeds, grassland, scrub and tall grass, and mangroves.

6 ASHY PRINIA *Prinia socialis* 13 cm
Adult breeding (6a) and non-breeding (6b) *P. s. stewarti.* Widespread resident. Slate-grey crown and ear-coverts, red eyes, slate-grey or rufous-brown upperparts, and orange-buff wash to underparts. Sri Lankan race *brevicauda* has very short tail. Tall grass and scrub, open secondary growth and reedbeds.

7 ZITTING CISTICOLA *Cisticola juncidis* 10 cm
Adult breeding (7a) and non-breeding (7b). Widespread resident. Small, with short tail that has prominent white tips. Bold streaking on buff upperparts, including nape, and thin whitish supercilium. Fields and grassland.

8 BRIGHT-HEADED CISTICOLA *Cisticola exilis* 10 cm
Male breeding (8a) and non-breeding (8b) *C. e. tytleri*; **male breeding (8c) and non-breeding (8d)** *C. e. erythrocephala.* Resident. Terai, NE and S Indian hills, and Bangladesh. Breeding males have unstreaked crown. Otherwise, typically unstreaked rufous nape, rufous supercilium and neck sides, and uniformly dark tail except for narrow buff tips. Tall grassland; scrubby hillsides in S India.

9 SRI LANKA WHITE-EYE *Zosterops ceylonensis* 11 cm
Adult. Resident. Sri Lanka. Dull green upperparts, and olive-yellow throat and breast. Dusky lores and white eye-ring. Forest, gardens and plantations.

10 ORIENTAL WHITE-EYE *Zosterops palpebrosus* 10 cm
Adult. Widespread resident; unrecorded in parts of the northwest. White eye-ring, yellow throat and breast, and whitish belly. Open broadleaved forest and wooded areas.

11 CHESTNUT-HEADED TESIA *Tesia castaneocoronata* 8 cm
Adult (11a) and juvenile (11b). Resident. Himalayas and NE Indian hills. Chestnut head and yellow underparts. Thick undergrowth in moist forest.

12 SLATY-BELLIED TESIA *Tesia olivea* 9 cm
Adult. Resident. Himalayas and NE Indian hills. Darker grey underparts than Grey-bellied. Crown often brighter than mantle. Bright orange lower mandible without dark tip. Thick undergrowth in moist, mainly evergreen forest.

13 GREY-BELLIED TESIA *Tesia cyaniventer* 9 cm
Adult (13a) and juvenile (13b). Resident. Himalayas, hills of NE India and Bangladesh. Paler grey underparts than Slaty-bellied, with almost whitish belly. Brighter supercilium than crown, and yellow lower mandible with dark tip. Thick undergrowth in moist forest.

Clive Byers

1 ASIAN STUBTAIL *Urosphena squameiceps* 11 cm
Adult. Vagrant. Nepal, Bangladesh. Very short tail, long supercilium, rufous-brown upper-parts, and white underparts. Pale pinkish legs and feet. Tropical broadleaved forest.

2 PALE-FOOTED BUSH WARBLER *Cettia pallidipes* 11 cm Table p. 366
Adult *C. p. pallidipes* (2a); adult *C. p. osmastoni* (2b). Resident. Himalayas, NE India and S Andamans (*osmastoni*). Rufous-brown upperparts and whiter underparts compared with Brownish-flanked. Pale pinkish legs and feet. Song is loud, explosive *zip..zip-tschuk-o-tschuk*. Tall grass and bushes at forest edges.

3 JAPANESE BUSH WARBLER *Cettia diphone* M 18 cm, F 15 cm Table p. 366
Adult male (3a) and female (3b). Vagrant. India. Large size (especially male) and long tail. Rufous crown, stout bill, prominent supercilium, and buffy underparts. Scrub jungle, and bushes at forest edges.

4 BROWNISH-FLANKED BUSH WARBLER *Cettia fortipes* 12 cm Table p. 366
Adult (4a) and 1st-winter? (4b) *C. f. fortipes*; adult *C. f. pallidus* (4c). Resident. Himalayas and NE India. Duskier underparts than Pale-footed, with brownish legs and feet and more olive-tinged upperparts (especially *pallidus* of NW Himalayas). Some *fortipes* have olive cast to upperparts and yellowish wash on belly (but not so green above and yellow below as Aberrant and with buff flanks). Song is a loud whistle, *weeee*, followed by explosive *chiwiyou*. Open forest and thickets.

5 CHESTNUT-CROWNED BUSH WARBLER *Cettia major* 13 cm Table p. 366
Adult (5a) and juvenile (5b). Resident. Himalayas and NE Indian hills. Chestnut crown. Told from Grey-sided by larger size, rufous-buff on fore supercilium, and whiter underparts. Song has introductory note, followed by 3- or 4-noted explosive warble. Summers in rhododendron shrubberies and bushes in forest; winters in reedbeds.

6 ABERRANT BUSH WARBLER *Cettia flavolivacea* 12 cm Table p. 366
Adult fresh (6a) and worn (6b). Resident. Himalayas and NE Indian hills. Greenish upperparts, and yellowish supercilium and underparts. Can appear rather worn when lacking strong yellow on underparts. Song is a short warble, followed by a long inflected whistle *dir dir-tee teee-weee*. Call is a *brrrt-brrrt*, different from any *Phylloscopus*. Bushes at forest edges, long grass and bushes in pine forest.

7 YELLOWISH-BELLIED BUSH WARBLER *Cettia acanthizoides* 9.5 cm
Table p. 366
Adult. Resident. Himalayas. Small size, pale rufous-brown upperparts, whitish throat and breast, and yellowish belly and flanks. Song is a thin, high-pitched *see-saw see-saw see-saw* etc. Bamboo stands.

8 GREY-SIDED BUSH WARBLER *Cettia brunnifrons* 10 cm Table p. 366
Adult (8a) and juvenile (8b). Resident. Himalayas and NE India. Chestnut crown. Told from Chestnut-crowned by small size, shorter whitish supercilium, and greyer underparts. Song is a loud wheezing *sip ti ti sip*, repeated continually. Summers in high-altitude shrubberies and bushes at forest edges; winters in scrub and forest undergrowth.

9 CETTI'S BUSH WARBLER *Cettia cetti* 14 cm Table p. 366
Adult. Winter visitor and passage migrant. Pakistan and NW India. Large size with big tail; white breast and indistinct supercilium, greyish breast sides and flanks, and whitish tips to undertail-coverts. Song is an explosive *chit..chit..chitity chit...chitity chit*; call is an explosive *chit*. Reedbeds and tamarisks.

10 SPOTTED BUSH WARBLER *Bradypterus thoracicus* 13 cm Table p. 367
Adult *B. t. thoracicus* (10a, 10b); adult *B. t. shanensis* (10c). Breeds in Himalayas; winters in foothills and NE Indian plains. Spotting on throat and breast (can be indistinct). Shortish bill, grey ear-coverts and breast, and olive-brown flanks; boldly patterned undertail-coverts. *B. t. shanensis* (recorded in NE subcontinent) has brownish wash on breast, weaker spotting, whitish supercilium, and pale lower mandible. Song of *thoracicus* is a *trick-i-di* etc. Song of *shanensis* is a buzzing *dzzzzzzr* etc. Summers in high-altitude shrubberies, grass and bushes; winters in reedbeds and tall grass.

11 LONG-BILLED BUSH WARBLER *Bradypterus major* 13 cm Table p. 367
Adult worn (11a, 11b) and fresh (11c). Resident. W Himalayas. Spotting on throat and breast (can be indistinct). Long bill, white underparts and unmarked undertail-coverts. Song is monotonous *pikha-pikha-pikha* etc. Bushy hillsides, and thickets at forest edges.

PLATE 122: BUSH WARBLERS AND *LOCUSTELLA* AND *ACROCEPHALUS* WARBLERS
Maps p. 286

1 **CHINESE BUSH WARBLER** *Bradypterus tacsanowskius* 14 cm Table p. 367
Adult (1a) and 1st-winter? (1b). Vagrant. Nepal and India. Grey-brown upperparts, and pale tips to undertail-coverts; underparts often with yellowish wash. Some have fine spotting on lower throat. Song is a rasping, insect-like *dzzzeep-dzzzeep-dzzzeep* etc. Reedbeds, grass and bushes, and paddy-fields.

2 **BROWN BUSH WARBLER** *Bradypterus luteoventris* 13.5 cm Table p. 367
Adult (2a, 2b). Resident. E Himalayas and NE Indian hills. Rufescent-brown upperparts, rufous-buff breast sides and flanks, rufous-buff supercilium, and lack of prominent pale tips to undertail-coverts. Lacks spotting on throat and breast. Song is a quiet, rapid *tutu-tutututututu...*etc. Grassy hills, and undergrowth in pine forest.

3 **RUSSET BUSH WARBLER** *Bradypterus seebohmi* 13.5 cm Table p. 367
Adult. Resident. E Himalayas. Rich brown upperparts, brown breast sides and flanks, pale fringes to undertail-coverts, and blackish bill. Can have spotted breast. Song is a buzzing *zree-ut zree-ut* etc. Forest edges and secondary growth.

4 **SRI LANKA BUSH WARBLER** *Bradypterus palliseri* 16 cm
Adult (4a) and juvenile (4b). Resident. Sri Lanka. Large *Bradypterus* with dark olive-brown upperparts, orange-buff throat (lacking on juvenile), and olive-grey underparts with olive-yellow wash to belly. Dense forest undergrowth.

5 **LANCEOLATED WARBLER** *Locustella lanceolata* 12 cm
Adult (5a, 5b). Winter visitor. Lowlands, mainly N subcontinent; unrecorded in Pakistan. Streaking on throat, breast and flanks (weak on some). Some can be very similar to Grasshopper: streaking on undertail-coverts is less extensive but blacker and more clear cut, and tertials are darker with clear-cut pale edges. Tall grassland, and bush/grassland.

6 **GRASSHOPPER WARBLER** *Locustella naevia* 13 cm
Adult (6a, 6b). Widespread winter visitor. Olive-brown upperparts, indistinct supercilium, and (usually) unmarked or only lightly streaked throat and breast. Tall grassland, reedbeds and paddy-fields.

7 **RUSTY-RUMPED WARBLER** *Locustella certhiola* 13.5 cm
Adult (7a) and juvenile (7b). Winters locally in subcontinent. Distinct supercilium with greyish crown, rufous rump and uppertail-coverts, rather dark tail with white tips. Juvenile has yellowish wash to underparts, light spotting on breast. Reedbeds and paddy-fields.

8 **MOUSTACHED WARBLER** *Acrocephalus melanopogon* 12.5 cm
Adult. Mainly winter visitor. Pakistan and N and NW Indian plains. Broad white supercilium, blackish eye-stripe, and boldly streaked rufous-brown mantle. Tall reedbeds and tamarisks.

9 **SEDGE WARBLER** *Acrocephalus schoenobaenus* 13 cm
Adult. Vagrant. India. Broad white supercilium and streaked mantle. Head pattern less striking than Moustached's; also has buffish olive-brown coloration to upperparts, well-defined buffy fringes to tertials and greater coverts, and longer primary projection. Tall vegetation at wetland edges.

10 **BLACK-BROWED REED WARBLER** *Acrocephalus bistrigiceps* 13 cm
Table p. 368
Adult. Winter visitor. Mainly NE India and Bangladesh. Broad supercilium and blackish lateral crown-stripes. Short tail and dark grey legs. Tall grass and paddy-fields.

11 **PADDYFIELD WARBLER** *Acrocephalus agricola* 13 cm Table p. 368
Adult fresh (11a) and worn (11b). Widespread winter visitor; unrecorded in Sri Lanka; has bred Baluchistan. Prominent white supercilium behind eye, and stout bill with dark tip. Often shows dark edge to supercilium. Strong rufous cast to upperparts in fresh plumage. Typically shows dark centres and contrastingly paler edges to tertials, which are usually very uniform on Blyth's Reed. Reedbeds, damp grassland and paddy-fields.

12 **BLUNT-WINGED WARBLER** *Acrocephalus concinens* 13 cm Table p. 368
Adult fresh (12a) and worn (12b). Summer visitor to W Himalayas; resident in Assam. Longer and stouter bill than Paddyfield, with pale lower mandible. Supercilium indistinct behind eye. Reedbeds, and tall grass near water.

13 **BLYTH'S REED WARBLER** *Acrocephalus dumetorum* 14 cm Table p. 368
Adult fresh (13a) and worn (13b). Widespread winter visitor and passage migrant. Long bill, olive-brown to olive-grey upperparts and uniform wings. Comparatively indistinct supercilium barely apparent behind eye. Bushes and trees at edges of forest, cultivation and in wooded areas.

PLATE 122, p. 284

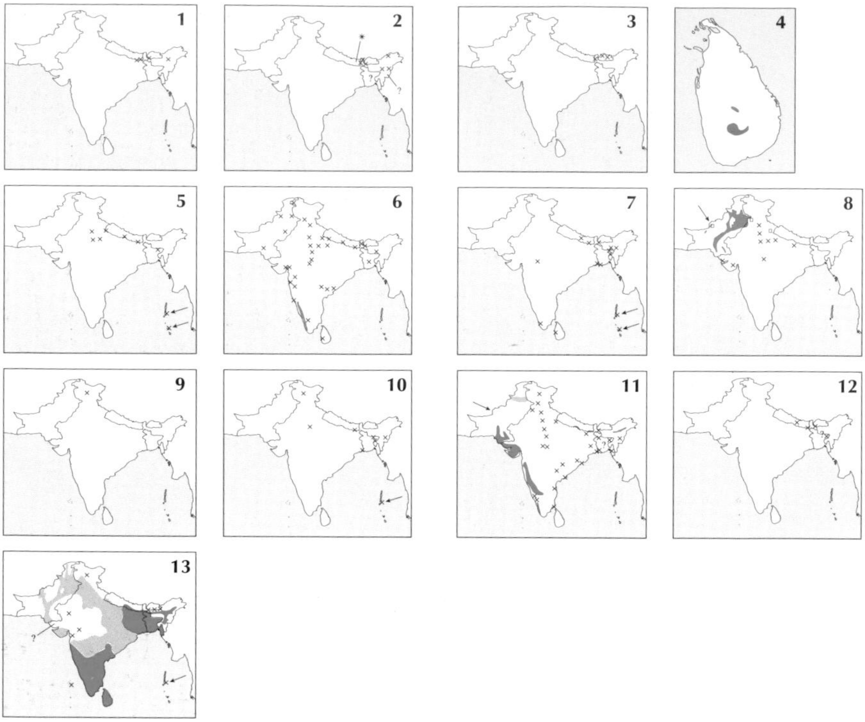

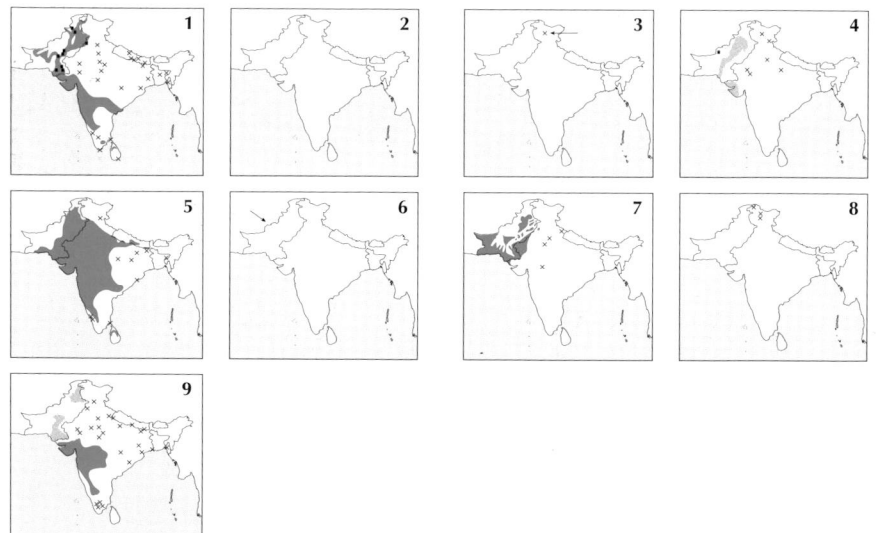

PLATE 124, p. 290

286

PLATE 125, p. 292

PLATE 126, p. 294

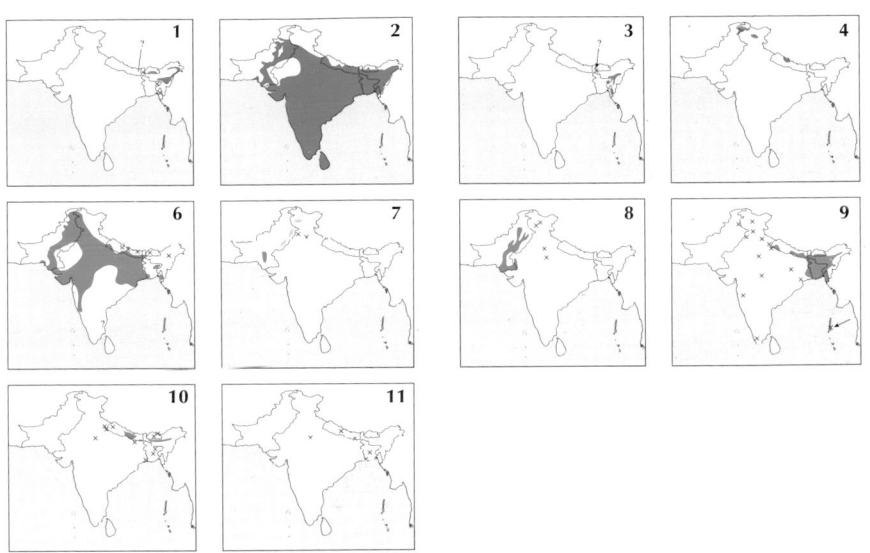

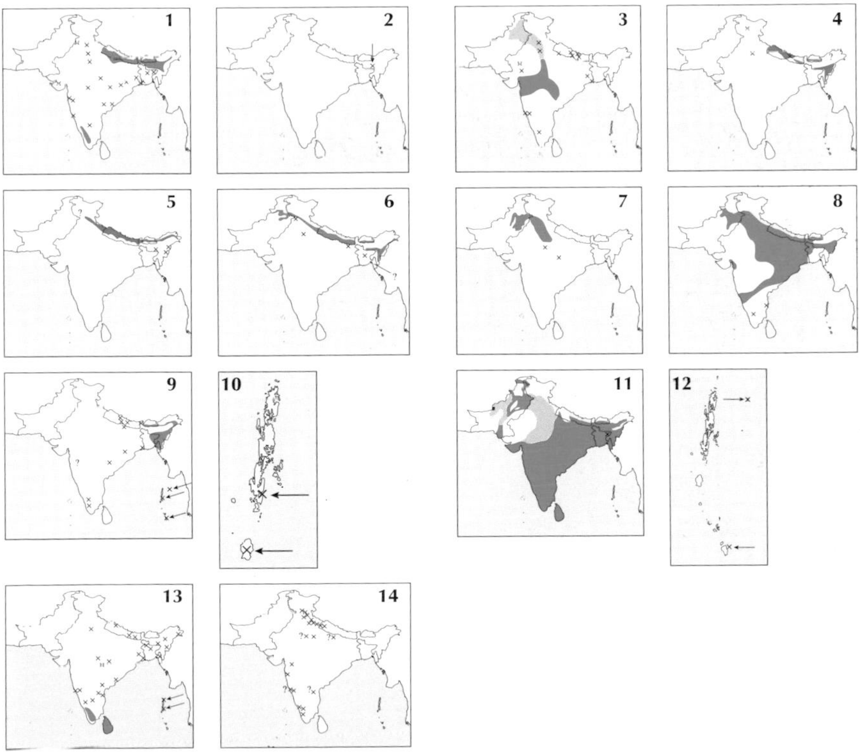

PLATE 123: LARGE *ACROCEPHALUS* WARBLERS AND GRASSBIRDS

1 **GREAT REED WARBLER** *Acrocephalus arundinaceus* 19 cm
Adult. Vagrant. Pakistan and India. Differs from Clamorous Reed in shorter, stouter bill, longer primary projection, and shorter-looking tail. Primary projection is roughly equal to length of tertials, with 8 or 9 exposed primary tips visible beyond the tertials. Lacks whitish tip to tail and (usually) lacks streaking on breast. Reedbeds.

2 **ORIENTAL REED WARBLER** *Acrocephalus orientalis* 18 cm
Adult worn (2a) and fresh (2b). Winter visitor. Mainly NE India. Smaller than Clamorous Reed, with shorter, squarer tail. Primary projection is usually shorter than length of exposed tertials. Often has streaking on sides of neck and breast, and well-defined whitish tips to outer rectrices. Reedbeds.

3 **CLAMOROUS REED WARBLER** *Acrocephalus stentoreus* 19 cm
Adult worn (3a) and fresh (3b) *A. s. brunnescens*; **adult** *A. s. meridionalis* **(3c).** Breeds locally in Pakistan, India and Sri Lanka; widespread in winter. Large size, long bill, short primary projection, whitish supercilium, and lacks white at tip of tail. Primary projection is roughly two-thirds of length of tertials, with 6 or 7 exposed primary tips visible beyond tertials. Sri Lankan *meridionalis* darker brown above, and often smaller. Reedbeds and bushes around wetlands.

4 **THICK-BILLED WARBLER** *Acrocephalus aedon* 19 cm
Adult. Widespread winter visitor; unrecorded in Pakistan and Sri Lanka. Short, stout bill and rounded head. 'Plain-faced' appearance, lacking prominent supercilium or eye-stripe. Tall grass and scrub, reeds and bushes.

5 **STRIATED GRASSBIRD** *Megalurus palustris* 25 cm
Adult worn (5a) and fresh (5b). Resident. Lowlands in N and C subcontinent. Streaked upperparts, finely streaked breast and long, graduated tail. Has longer and finer bill and more prominent supercilium than Bristled. Tall damp grassland, reedbeds and tamarisks.

6 **BRISTLED GRASSBIRD** *Chaetornis striatus* 20 cm
Adult. Local resident. Mainly lowlands in India and Nepal. Streaked upperparts and fine streaking on lower throat. Has shorter, stouter bill and less prominent supercilium than Striated, also shorter and broader tail with buffish-white tips. Tall grassland with bushes, and paddy-fields.

7 **RUFOUS-RUMPED GRASSBIRD** *Graminicola bengalensis* 18 cm
Adult. Resident. Terai and NE plains. Rufous and whitish streaking on black upperparts, white-tipped blackish tail, and white underparts with rufous-buff breast sides and flanks. Tall grass and reeds near water.

8 **BROAD-TAILED GRASSBIRD** *Schoenicola platyura* 18 cm
Adult fresh (8a) and worn (8b). Resident. Western Ghats and Sri Lanka. Stout bill, long and broad tail, unstreaked rufous-brown to greyish-brown upperparts, and whitish underparts. Tail diffusely barred. Tall grass and reeds on open hillsides.

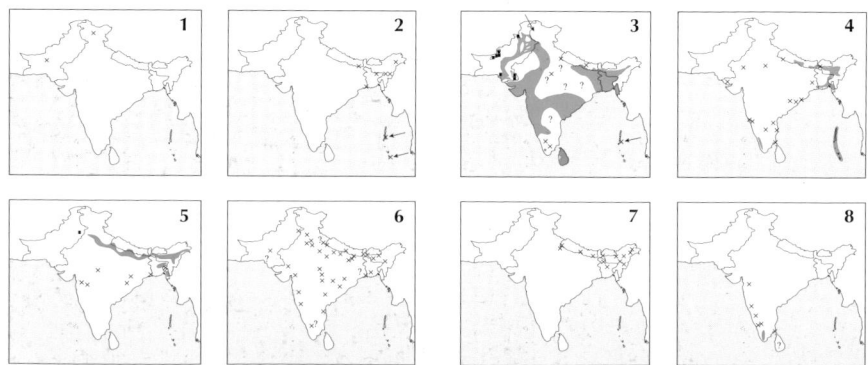

1

2a

2b

3a

3b

3c

4

5a

6

5b

7

8a

8b

Clive Byers

PLATE 124: *HIPPOLAIS* AND *SYLVIA* WARBLERS   Maps p. 286

1 BOOTED WARBLER *Hippolais caligata* 12 cm Table p. 368
Adult *H. c. caligata* (1a); adult *H. c. rama* (1b). Breeds in Pakistan; widespread in winter; unrecorded in parts of the northeast. Small size and *Phylloscopus*-like behaviour (especially *caligata*). Tail looks long and square-ended, and undertail-coverts look short. Often shows faint whitish edges and tip to tail and fringe to tertials. Supercilium usually reasonably distinct. Breeds in tamarisks and reed-grass; winters in scrub and groves in dry habitats.

2 UPCHER'S WARBLER *Hippolais languida* 14 cm Table p. 368
Adult. Summer visitor to Baluchistan. Large size and heavy appearance. Long, full tail is often swayed or flicked downwards. Grey upperparts, often with dark wings and tail. Tail usually shows white sides and tip; usually whitish fringes to wing-coverts and tertials. Open stony and bushy hillsides.

3 GARDEN WARBLER *Sylvia borin* 14 cm
Adult. Vagrant. India. Rather featureless. Stout-billed, stocky appearance and plain face, with just faint suggestion of greyish supercilium, aid separation from *Hippolais* and *Acrocephalus* warblers. Forest undergrowth and bushes.

4 GREATER WHITETHROAT *Sylvia communis* 14 cm
Male (4a) and female (4b). Passage migrant in Pakistan and NW India; has bred in Baluchistan. Larger and longer-tailed than Lesser, with broad, well-defined, sandy-brown to pale rufous-brown fringes to greater coverts and tertials, pale base to lower mandible, and orange-brown to pale brown (not grey) legs and feet. Standing crops and bushes.

5 LESSER WHITETHROAT *Sylvia curruca* 13 cm
Adult *S. c. blythi* (5a); adult *S. c. minula* (5b); adult *S. c. althaea* (5c). Breeds in Pakistan hills and W Himalayas; widespread in winter. Brownish-grey upperparts, grey crown with darker ear-coverts, blackish bill, and dark grey legs and feet. *S. c. althaea* is largest and darkest race; *minula* the most finely built, with pale, sandy grey-brown upperparts. Scrub.

6 MÉNÉTRIES'S WARBLER *Sylvia mystacea* 12 cm
Male (6a) and female (6b). Summer visitor. Baluchistan. Small size, with long tail. Male has blackish hood, reddish-brown eye-ring, and pinkish wash to throat and breast, with white submoustachial line. Female/first-winter has rather uniform sandy grey-brown upperparts (lacking darker mask), dark tail, and pale legs and feet. Scrub in semi-desert.

7 DESERT WARBLER *Sylvia nana* 11.5 cm
Adult. Winter visitor. Pakistan and NW India. Small size, sandy-brown upperparts, rufous rump and tail, yellow iris, and yellowish legs and feet. Scrub in desert and rocky hills.

8 BARRED WARBLER *Sylvia nisoria* 15 cm
Male (8a) and 1st-winter (8b). Vagrant. Pakistan and India. Large size, stout bill, and pale edges and tips to tertials and wing-coverts. Adult has yellow iris and variable barring on underparts. First-winter barred on undertail-coverts and occasionally on flanks. Bushes.

9 ORPHEAN WARBLER *Sylvia hortensis* 15 cm
Adult male (9a), adult female (9b) and 1st-winter (9c). Summer visitor to Pakistan; winters mainly in India. Larger and bigger-billed than Lesser Whitethroat; more ponderous movements, and heavier appearance in flight. Adult has blackish crown, pale grey mantle, blackish tail, and pale iris. First-year has crown concolorous with mantle, with darker grey ear-coverts; very similar to many Lesser Whitethroats (that species has dark iris). Orphean often shows darker-looking uppertail, eye-ring is absent or indistinct, and has greyish centres and pale fringes to undertail-coverts; these features variable and difficult to observe in the field. Breeds on bush-covered hillsides; winters in scrub and groves.

Clive Byers

PLATE 125: TAILORBIRDS, WHITE-BROWED TIT WARBLER AND *PHYLLOSCOPUS* WARBLERS
Maps p. 287

1 MOUNTAIN TAILORBIRD *Orthotomus cuculatus* 13 cm
Adult (1a) and juvenile (1b). Resident. E Himalayas, NE India and Bangladesh. Long bill, yellowish supercilium, greyish throat and breast, and yellow belly. Juvenile has olive-green crown and nape. Evergreen forest and secondary growth.

2 COMMON TAILORBIRD *Orthotomus sutorius* 13 cm
Male (2a) and female (2b) *O. s. guzuratus*; **male** *O. s. sutorius* of Sri Lanka **(2c).** Widespread resident. Rufous forehead, greenish upperparts, and whitish underparts including undertail-coverts. Bushes in gardens, cultivation edges and forest edges.

3 DARK-NECKED TAILORBIRD *Orthotomus atrogularis* 13 cm
Male (3a) and female (3b). Resident. E Himalayas, NE India and Bangladesh. Male has black on throat and breast. Female has yellow at bend of wing and on undertail-coverts. Shows more extensive rufous on crown than Common. Dense scrub and edges of ever-green forest.

4 WHITE-BROWED TIT WARBLER *Leptopoecile sophiae* 10 cm
Male (4a) and female (4b) *L. s. sophiae*; **male (4c) and female (4d)** *L. s. obscura.* Resident. N Himalayas from Pakistan to W Nepal. Whitish supercilium, rufous crown, and lilac and purple in plumage. *L. s. obscura*, of C Himalayas, is brighter in male and darker in female compared with race from W Himalayas. Dwarf scrub in semi-desert.

5 WILLOW WARBLER *Phylloscopus trochilus* 11 cm Table p. 362
Adult. [Two published records, now considered unreliable. Much as Common Chiffchaff, but paler legs, orange at base of bill, and longer primary projection. Often with yellow on supercilium and breast. Bushes and trees.]

6 COMMON CHIFFCHAFF *Phylloscopus collybita* 11 cm Table p. 362
Adult fresh (6a) and worn (6b) *P. c. tristis*; **adult** *P. c. collybita* **(6c).** Winter visitor. N subcontinent. Brownish to greyish upperparts; olive-green edges to wing-coverts, remiges and rectrices. Black bill and legs. No wing-bar. *P. c. collybita*, recorded once in NW, has olive crown and mantle and some yellow in supercilium and underparts. Forest, bushes, crops and reedbeds.

7 MOUNTAIN CHIFFCHAFF *Phylloscopus sindianus* 11 cm Table p. 362
Adult. Pakistan and NW India; breeds in Himalayas, winters in plains and foothills. Much as Common Chiffchaff, but generally lacks olive-green tone to back and to edges of wing-coverts, remiges and rectrices. Different call. Breeds in bushes; winters in riverain trees and bushes.

8 PLAIN LEAF WARBLER *Phylloscopus neglectus* 10 cm Table p. 362
Adult fresh (8a) and worn (8b). Breeds in hills of Baluchistan and Kashmir; winters mainly in Pakistan lowlands. Much as Common Chiffchaff, but smaller, with shorter tail, no olive-green or yellow in plumage, and different call. Breeds in juniper and pine for-est; winters in open wooded areas.

9 DUSKY WARBLER *Phylloscopus fuscatus* 11 cm Table p. 362
Adult. Winter visitor. Himalayan foothills, NE India and Bangladesh. Brown upperparts and whitish underparts, with buff flanks. Prominent supercilium, and hard *chack* call. Bushes and long grass.

10 SMOKY WARBLER *Phylloscopus fuligiventer* 10 cm Table p. 362
Adult *P. f. fuligiventer* **(10a); adult** *P. f. tibetanus* **(10b).** Breeds in C and E Himalayas; winters in adjacent foothills and plains. Very dark, with short yellowish supercilium, and yellowish centre of throat and belly. *P. f. tibetanus*, which occurs in NE in winter, has greyish-white supercilium and belly centre. Breeds in high-altitude shrubberies; winters in dense undergrowth near water.

11 RADDE'S WARBLER *Phylloscopus schwarzi* 12 cm Table p. 362
Fresh autumn (11a) and worn winter (11b). Vagrant. Nepal, India and Bangladesh. Stout bill, long buffish-white supercilium contrasting with dark eye-stripe, orangish legs and feet; call different from Dusky's. In fresh plumage, can show pronounced greenish-olive cast to upperparts and buffish-yellow cast to supercilium and underparts which are dis-tinctive features from Dusky. Bushes and undergrowth.

1 TICKELL'S LEAF WARBLER *Phylloscopus affinis* 11 cm Table p. 362
Fresh. Breeds in Himalayas; widespread in winter; unrecorded in Sri Lanka. Dark greenish to greenish-brown upperparts, and bright yellow supercilium concolorous with throat and breast. Some worn birds paler on supercilium and underparts. Breeds in open country with bushes; winters in bushes at edges of forest and cultivation.

2 BUFF-THROATED WARBLER *Phylloscopus subaffinis* 11 cm Table p. 362
Fresh. Vagrant? to India. Yellowish-buff underparts, buffish-yellow supercilium, and extensive dark tip to lower mandible. Habitat in region unknown.

3 SULPHUR-BELLIED WARBLER *Phylloscopus griseolus* 11 cm Table p. 362
Fresh. Breeds in hills of W Pakistan and W Himalayas; winters mainly in N and C India. Dark greyish upperparts, bright yellow supercilium, and dusky yellow underparts strongly washed with buff. Soft *quip* call. Breeds on stony bushy slopes; winters in rocky areas and around old buildings.

4 BUFF-BARRED WARBLER *Phylloscopus pulcher* 10 cm Table p. 364
Fresh. Resident. Himalayas and NE Indian hills. Buffish-orange wing-bars, yellowish supercilium and wash to underparts, white on tail, and small yellowish rump patch. Breeds in subalpine shrubberies and forest; winters in broadleaved forest.

5 ASHY-THROATED WARBLER *Phylloscopus maculipennis* 9 cm Table p. 364
Fresh. Resident. Himalayas and NE Indian hills. Small size, greyish throat and breast, yellow belly and flanks, white supercilium and crown-stripe, yellow rump, and white on tail. Forest; also secondary growth in winter.

6 LEMON-RUMPED WARBLER *Phylloscopus chloronotus* 9 cm Table p. 364
Fresh *P. c. chloronotus* (6a); fresh *P. c. simlaensis* (6b). Resident. Breeds in Himalayas; winters lower down and in NE Indian hills. Yellowish crown-stripe and rump band, dark lateral crown-stripes. Forest; also secondary growth in winter.

7 BROOKS'S LEAF WARBLER *Phylloscopus subviridis* 9 cm Table p. 364
Fresh (7a) and worn (7b). Breeds in Pakistan Himalayas; winters in plains and hills in Pakistan and N India. Yellow supercilium and ear-coverts; variable yellow wash to throat and breast. Lacks dark lateral crown-stripes and has indistinct pale rump band. Summers in coniferous and mixed forest; winters in bushes and well-wooded areas.

⑧ HUME'S WARBLER *Phylloscopus humei* 10–11 cm Table p. 364
Fresh (8a) and worn (8b). Breeds in Himalayas; winters in plains. Lacks rump band and well-defined crown-stripe. Has buffish or whitish wing-bars and supercilium. Bill appears all-dark, and legs are normally blackish-brown. Breeds in coniferous forest and subalpine shrubberies; winters in forest and secondary growth.

9 YELLOW-BROWED WARBLER *Phylloscopus inornatus* 10–11 cm Table p. 364
Fresh. Winter visitor. E Himalayas, NE and S India, and Bangladesh. Lacks rump band and well-defined crown-stripe. Has yellowish/whitish wing-bars and supercilium. Bill has orange at base. Groves and open forest.

10 ARCTIC WARBLER *Phylloscopus borealis* 12 cm Table p. 363
Fresh. Vagrant. Andamans. Buzzing *dziit* call. Prominent supercilium falls short of forehead; broad eye-stripe reaches bill-base. Mangroves and groves.

⑪ GREENISH WARBLER *Phylloscopus trochiloides* 10–11 cm Table p. 363
Fresh (11a) and worn (11b) *P. t. viridanus*; fresh *P. t. trochiloides* (11c); fresh (11d) and worn (11e) *P. t. nitidus*. Breeds in Himalayas and NE Indian hills; widespread in winter. Slurred, loud *chli-wee* call. No crown-stripe; fine wing-bar (sometimes two). Breeds in forest and subalpine shrubberies; winters in well-wooded areas.

12 PALE-LEGGED LEAF WARBLER *Phylloscopus tenellipes* 10 cm Table p. 363
Fresh. Vagrant. India. Pale legs and feet, pale tip to bill, metallic *pink* call. Often buff wash to ear-coverts and olive-brown cast to upperparts, especially rump. Crown is distinctly greyer and usually contrasts with mantle. Collected on a boat.

⑬ LARGE-BILLED LEAF WARBLER *Phylloscopus magnirostris* 13 cm Table p. 363
Fresh. Breeds in Himalayas; winters in NE and S India, and Sri Lanka. Clear, loud *der-tee* call. Large, with large dark bill. Very bold yellowish-white supercilium and broad dark eye-stripe. Breeds in forest along mountain rivers; winters in evergreen sholas.

14 TYTLER'S LEAF WARBLER *Phylloscopus tytleri* 11 cm Table p. 362
Fresh (14a) and worn (14b). Breeds in W Himalayas; winters mainly in Western Ghats. Slender, mainly dark bill, long fine supercilium, no wing-bars, shortish tail. Breeds in coniferous forest and subalpine shrubberies; winters in broadleaved forest.

1 **WESTERN CROWNED WARBLER** *Phylloscopus occipitalis* 11 cm Table p. 365
Fresh. Breeds in N Pakistan hills and W Himalayas; winters in India, Nepal and Bangladesh. Crown-stripe, large size, greyish-green upperparts, and greyish-white underparts. Head pattern and wing-bars tend to be less striking than on Blyth's Leaf. Forest.

2 **EASTERN CROWNED WARBLER** *Phylloscopus coronatus* 11 cm Table p. 365
Fresh. Winter visitor. E Himalayan foothills and NE Indian hills. Crown-stripe, yellowish undertail-coverts, large size. Darker, purer green upperparts than Western Crowned; more uniform wings with finer wing-bars than Blyth's Leaf. Broadleaved forest.

3 **BLYTH'S LEAF WARBLER** *Phylloscopus reguloides* 11 cm Table p. 365
Fresh *P. r. reguloides* (3a); fresh *P. r. kashmiriensis* (3b). Breeds in Himalayas; winters in foothills and adjacent plains. Crown-stripe, yellowish on underparts, and broad wing-bars with dark panel across greater coverts. Forest.

4 **YELLOW-VENTED WARBLER** *Phylloscopus cantator* 10 cm Table p. 365
Fresh. Resident. E Himalayas and NE Indian hills. Yellow crown-stripe with blackish at sides; yellow throat, white belly, and yellow undertail-coverts. Breeds in evergreen broadleaved forest; winters also in deciduous forest.

5 **GOLDEN-SPECTACLED WARBLER** *Seicercus burkii* 10 cm
Adult. Breeds in Himalayas and NE Indian hills; winters lower down in same hills, also in Bangladesh and E India. Yellow eye-ring, and yellowish-green face. Forest understorey.

6 **GREY-HOODED WARBLER** *Seicercus xanthoschistos* 10 cm
Adult *S. x. xanthoschistos* (6a); adult *S. x. albosuperciliaris* (6b) which has more westerly distribution. Resident. Himalayas and NE Indian hills. *Phylloscopus*-like appearance. Whitish supercilium, and grey crown with pale central stripe; yellow underparts and no wing-bars. Forest and secondary growth.

7 **WHITE-SPECTACLED WARBLER** *Seicercus affinis* 10 cm
Adult. Resident. Mainly E Himalayas and NE Indian hills. White eye-ring, grey crown and supercilium, well-defined blackish lateral crown-stripes; greenish lower ear-coverts, and yellow lores and chin. Forest.

8 **GREY-CHEEKED WARBLER** *Seicercus poliogenys* 10 cm
Adult. Resident. E Himalayas and NE Indian hills. White eye-ring, and dark grey head with poorly defined lateral crown-stripes; grey ear-coverts, grey lores and white chin. Evergreen broadleaved forest.

9 **CHESTNUT-CROWNED WARBLER** *Seicercus castaniceps* 9.5 cm
Adult. Resident. Himalayas and NE Indian hills. Chestnut crown, white eye-ring, and grey ear-coverts; white belly, yellow rump and wing-bars, and white on tail. Mainly oak forest.

10 **BROAD-BILLED WARBLER** *Tickellia hodgsoni* 10 cm
Adult. Resident. E Himalayas and NE Indian hills. Chestnut crown and greyish-white supercilium; grey throat and breast, yellow belly, white on tail, and no wing-bars. Understorey in evergreen broadleaved forest.

11 **RUFOUS-FACED WARBLER** *Abroscopus albogularis* 8 cm
Adult. Resident. E Himalayas and NE Indian hills. Rufous face, and black on throat; yellow breast and white belly, whitish rump, no wing-bars, no white on tail. Bamboo.

12 **BLACK-FACED WARBLER** *Abroscopus schisticeps* 9 cm
Adult *A. s. schisticeps* (12a); adult *A. s. flavimentalis* (12b). Resident. Himalayas and NE Indian hills. Black mask, yellow supercilium and throat, and grey crown. Eastern *A. s. flavimentalis* has yellow restricted to throat. Moist broadleaved forest.

13 **YELLOW-BELLIED WARBLER** *Abroscopus superciliaris* 9 cm
Adult. Resident. Himalayas, hills of NE India and Bangladesh. White supercilium and greyish crown; white throat and breast, yellow underparts, no wing-bars, no white on tail. Bamboo.

14 **GOLDCREST** *Regulus regulus* 9 cm
Adult male (14a) and juvenile (14b). Resident. Himalayas. Small size; yellow centre to crown. Plain face, lacking supercilium, but with dark eye and pale eye-ring. Mainly coniferous forest.

PLATE 127, p. 296

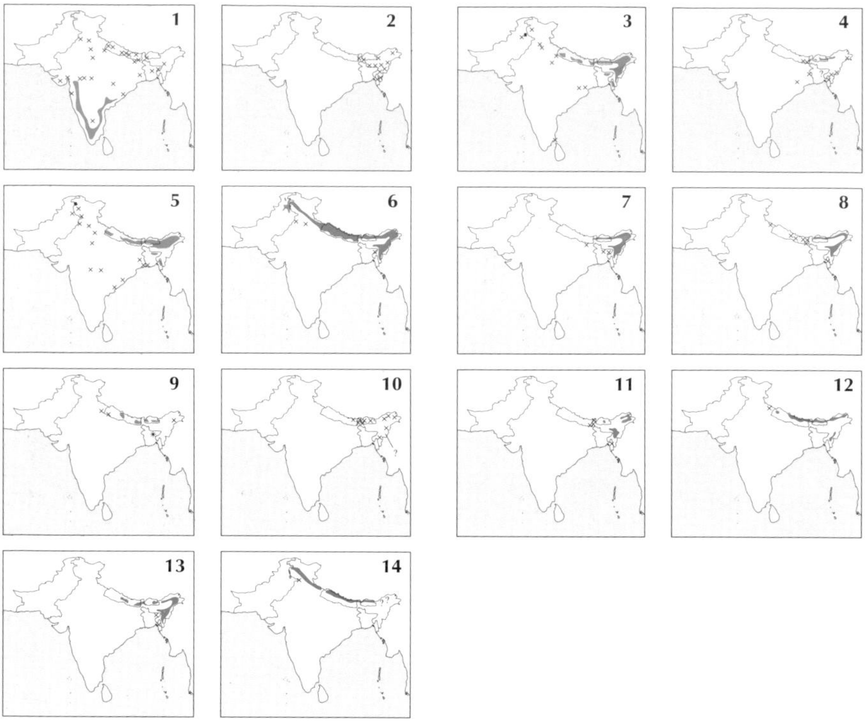

PLATE 128, p. 300

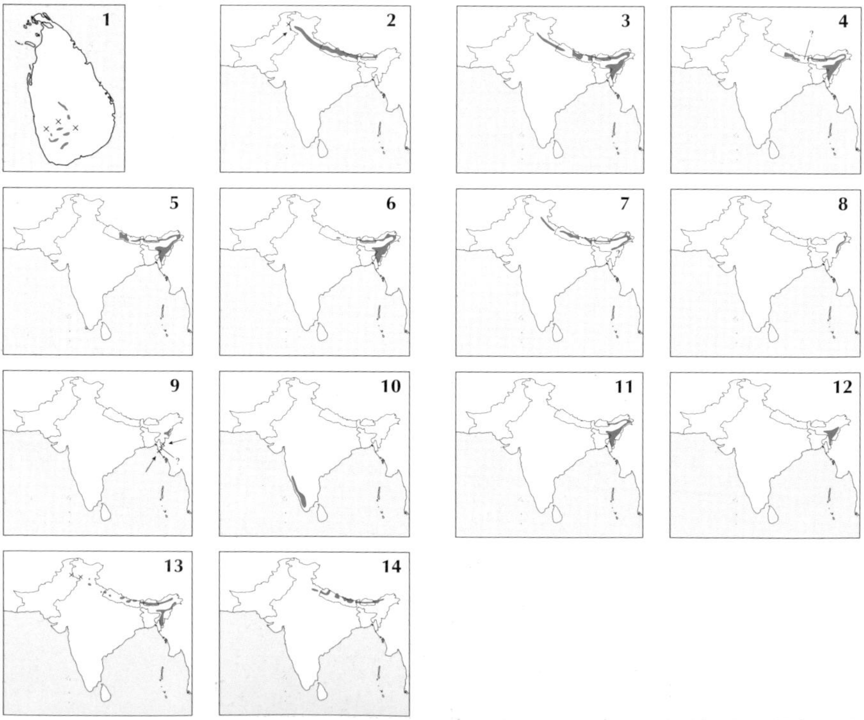

PLATE 129, p. 302

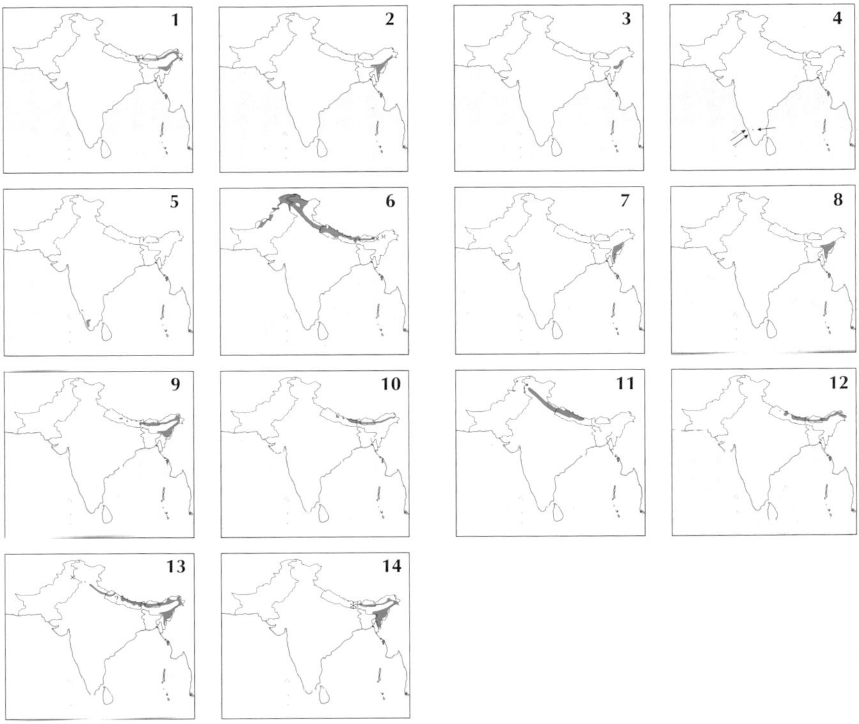

PLATE 130, p. 304

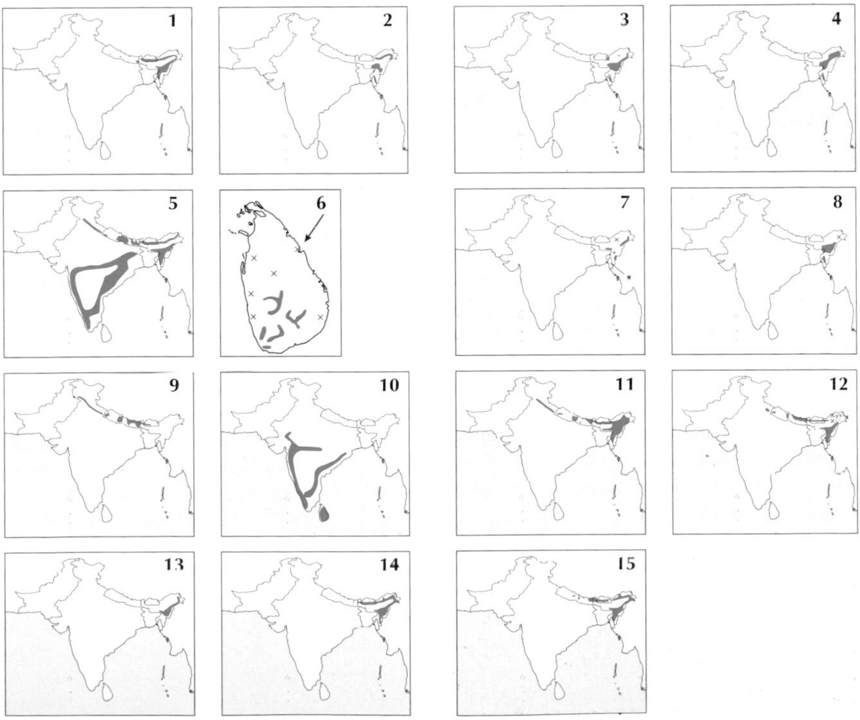

PLATE 128: LAUGHINGTHRUSHES

Maps p. 298

1 **ASHY-HEADED LAUGHINGTHRUSH** *Garrulax cinereifrons* 23 cm
Adult. Resident. Sri Lanka. Greyish head, rufous-brown upperparts, and deep buff underparts with whiter throat. Dense wet forest and bamboo thickets.

2 **WHITE-THROATED LAUGHINGTHRUSH** *Garrulax albogularis* 28 cm
Adult. Resident. Himalayas, and Assam. White throat and upper breast, rufous-orange belly, and broad white tip to tail. Broadleaved and mixed forest and secondary growth.

3 **WHITE-CRESTED LAUGHINGTHRUSH** *Garrulax leucolophus* 28 cm
Adult. Resident. Himalayas, NE India and Bangladesh. White crest and black mask, white throat and upper breast, and chestnut mantle. Broadleaved forest and secondary growth.

4 **LESSER NECKLACED LAUGHINGTHRUSH** *Garrulax monileger* 27 cm
Adult. Resident. Himalayas, NE India and Bangladesh. Smaller than Greater Necklaced. Olive-brown primary coverts, narrow necklace thinning at centre, blackish lores, incomplete lower black border to ear-coverts. Moist broadleaved forest and secondary growth.

5 **GREATER NECKLACED LAUGHINGTHRUSH** *Garrulax pectoralis* 29 cm
Adult. Resident. Himalayas, NE India and Bangladesh. Larger and bigger-billed than Lesser Necklaced. Blackish primary coverts, broad necklace, pale lores, and complete black moustachial stripe bordering white, black or black-and-white ear-coverts. Throat is uniform buff or white without two-toned appearance of Lesser, and legs are slate-grey rather than brownish. Moist broadleaved forest and secondary growth.

6 **RUFOUS-NECKED LAUGHINGTHRUSH** *Garrulax ruficollis* 23 cm
Adult. Resident. Himalayas, NE India and Bangladesh. Black face and throat, rufous patch on neck side, rufous vent. Forest edges, secondary growth and bushes in cultivation.

7 **STRIATED LAUGHINGTHRUSH** *Garrulax striatus* 28 cm
Adult *G. s. vibex* (**7a**); head of *G. s. cranbrooki* of NE (**7b**). Resident. Himalayas and NE India. Crested appearance, white streaking on head and body, stout black bill. Broadleaved forest.

8 **CHESTNUT-BACKED LAUGHINGTHRUSH** *Garrulax nuchalis* 23 cm
Adult. Resident. NE Indian hills. White ear-coverts and sides of throat, black chin and centre of throat, grey crown, and rufous mantle. Scrub-covered ravines.

9 **YELLOW-THROATED LAUGHINGTHRUSH** *Garrulax galbanus* 23 cm
Adult. Resident. Hills of NE India and Bangladesh. Black mask. Yellowish underparts extending onto lower belly and vent, black chin, pale olive-brown upperparts, and mainly grey tail with white tips. Tall grass with trees and bushes, also forest edges.

10 **WYNAAD LAUGHINGTHRUSH** *Garrulax delesserti* 23 cm
Adult. Resident. Western Ghats. Slate-grey crown with blackish ear-coverts, and white throat contrasting with grey breast. Mainly moist evergreen forest.

11 **RUFOUS-VENTED LAUGHINGTHRUSH** *Garrulax gularis* 23 cm
Adult. Resident. Himalayan foothills, hills of NE India and Bangladesh. Black mask. Yellow chin, throat and breast. Rufous flanks and vent, rufous-brown upperparts, and rufous outer tail lacking white tips. Mainly dense evergreen undergrowth.

12 **MOUSTACHED LAUGHINGTHRUSH** *Garrulax cineraceus* 22 cm
Adult. Resident. NE Indian hills. Black moustachial stripe breaking into black streaking on side of throat; grey-buff supercilium, and general greyish-olive coloration. Undergrowth in moist forest and secondary growth.

13 **RUFOUS-CHINNED LAUGHINGTHRUSH** *Garrulax rufogularis* 22 cm
Adult *G. r. rufogularis* (**13a**); adult *G. r. occidentalis* (**13b**). Resident. Himalayas and NE India. Rufous chin and throat, black barring on upperparts, irregular black spotting on underparts, and rufous-orange tips to tail and vent. *G. r. occidentalis*, of W and C Himalayas, has rufous ear-coverts. Undergrowth in broadleaved forest.

14 **SPOTTED LAUGHINGTHRUSH** *Garrulax ocellatus* 32 cm
Adult. Resident. Himalayas. White spotting on chestnut upperparts, black throat and barring on breast, and white tips to chestnut, grey and black tail. Undergrowth in forest and rhododendron shrubberies.

Craig Robson '97

1 **GREY-SIDED LAUGHINGTHRUSH** *Garrulax caerulatus* 25 cm
Adult. Resident. Himalayas and NE India. Black face with blue orbital skin, black scaling on rufous-brown crown, and white underparts. Undergrowth in moist forest and bamboo thickets.

2 **SPOT-BREASTED LAUGHINGTHRUSH** *Garrulax merulinus* 22 cm
Adult. Resident. NE Indian hills. Bold brown spotting on throat and breast; uniform rufescent olive-brown upperparts, wings and tail. Undergrowth in moist forest and bamboo thickets.

3 **WHITE-BROWED LAUGHINGTHRUSH** *Garrulax sannio* 23 cm
Adult. Resident. NE Indian hills. Broad buffish-white supercilium and buffish-white patch on cheeks. Forest undergrowth, secondary growth and bamboo thickets.

4 **NILGIRI LAUGHINGTHRUSH** *Garrulax cachinnans* 20 cm
Adult. Resident. SW Indian hills. Prominent white supercilium, grey crown and black chin, rufous throat and breast, and rufous ear-coverts. Forest undergrowth and scrub.

5 **GREY-BREASTED LAUGHINGTHRUSH** *Garrulax jerdoni* 20 cm
Adult *G. j. fairbanki* (5a); adult *G. j. jerdoni* (5b); adult *G. j. meridionale* (5c). Resident. Western Ghats. White supercilium. Grey or grey-streaked white throat and breast, greyish ear-coverts. Two races lack black chin. Thickets with wild raspberry.

6 **STREAKED LAUGHINGTHRUSH** *Garrulax lineatus* 20 cm
Adult *G. l. lineatus* (6a); adult *G. l. imbricatus* of E Himalayas (6b). Resident. Pakistan hills and Himalayas. Fine white streaking on mantle and underparts; otherwise, rather uniform brown or greyish and brown. Scrub-covered hills, secondary growth and bushes in cultivation.

7 **STRIPED LAUGHINGTHRUSH** *Garrulax virgatus* 25 cm
Adult. Resident. NE hills. Chestnut wing-coverts, white shaft streaking on upperparts and underparts, whitish supercilium and ear-covert patch, chestnut throat. Undergrowth in evergreen forest and secondary growth.

8 **BROWN-CAPPED LAUGHINGTHRUSH** *Garrulax austeni* 22 cm
Adult. Resident. NE Indian hills. Rufous-brown and white scaling on underparts, buff shaft streaking and spotting on rufous-brown head, rufous-brown wings. White tips to tail feathers (except central pair). Bamboo thickets and bushes in cultivation.

9 **BLUE-WINGED LAUGHINGTHRUSH** *Garrulax squamatus* 25 cm
Adult. Resident. Himalayas and NE India. White iris, black supercilium, rufous and bluish wing panels, black rear edge to wing, chestnut uppertail-coverts, and rufous-tipped tail. Undergrowth in moist forest and bamboo thickets.

10 **SCALY LAUGHINGTHRUSH** *Garrulax subunicolor* 23 cm
Adult. Resident. Himalayas. Yellow iris, olive and blue-grey wing panels, olive uppertail-coverts, and white-tipped tail; lacks black supercilium. Undergrowth in moist forest and rhododendron shrubberies.

11 **VARIEGATED LAUGHINGTHRUSH** *Garrulax variegatus* 24 cm
Adult *G. v. variegatus* (11a); adult *G. v. similis* (11b). Resident. W and C Himalayas. Grey or olive, with black patches on greyish wings, rufous-buff forehead and malar stripe, and black throat. W Himalayan *similis* has grey outer webs to primaries, olive-buff in C and E Himalayas. Forest undergrowth and rhododendron shrubberies.

12 **BLACK-FACED LAUGHINGTHRUSH** *Garrulax affinis* 25 cm
Adult. Resident. Himalayas. Black supercilium and ear-coverts, white malar stripe and neck-side patch, and grey-tipped tail. Forest and shrubberies above treeline.

13 **CHESTNUT-CROWNED LAUGHINGTHRUSH** *Garrulax erythrocephalus*
28 cm
Adult *G. e. erythrocephalus* of W Himalayas (13a); adult *G. e. chrysopterus* of Meghalaya **(13b); adult *G. e. nigrimentus* of E Himalayas (13c).** Resident. Himalayas and NE India. Chestnut on head, dark scaling/spotting on mantle and breast, olive-yellow wings, and olive-yellow tail sides. Undergrowth in forest and bushes in cultivation.

14 **RED-FACED LIOCICHLA** *Liocichla phoenicea* 23 cm
Adult. Resident. Himalayas and NE India. Crimson ear-coverts and neck sides, crimson and orange on wing, and rufous-orange tip to black tail. Undergrowth in moist forest and thickets.

PLATE 130: BABBLERS, INCLUDING SCIMITAR BABBLERS
Maps p. 299

1 ABBOTT'S BABBLER *Malacocincla abbotti* 17 cm
Adult. Resident. Himalayan foothills, NE India and Bangladesh. Top heavy, with large bill. Unspotted white throat and breast, grey lores and supercilium, rufous uppertail-coverts and tail, and rufous-buff flanks and vent. Thickets in moist forest.

2 BUFF-BREASTED BABBLER *Pellorneum tickelli* 15 cm
Adult. Resident. NE Indian hills. Buff lores, buff throat and breast (some with brown streaking); longish square-ended tail. Undergrowth in moist forest and bamboo thickets.

3 SPOT-THROATED BABBLER *Pellorneum albiventre* 14 cm
Adult. Resident. E Himalayan foothills, hills of NE India and Bangladesh. White throat with diffuse grey spotting, olive-brown breast and flanks, and grey lores and supercilium; rounded tip to short tail. Scrub and secondary growth.

4 MARSH BABBLER *Pellorneum palustre* 15 cm
Adult. Resident. NE India and Bangladesh. Bold streaking on breast and flanks and grey fore-supercilium. Lacks rufous crown and prominent buff supercilium of Puff-throated. Reedbeds and tall grassland.

5 PUFF-THROATED BABBLER *Pellorneum ruficeps* 15 cm
Adult *P. r. ruficeps* (5a); adult *P. r. mandellii* (5b). Resident. Himalayan foothills, hills of NE India and Bangladesh. Rufous-brown to chestnut crown, prominent buff supercilium, white throat (often puffed-out) and bold brown spotting on breast. Forest undergrowth and secondary growth.

6 BROWN-CAPPED BABBLER *Pellorneum fuscocapillum* 16 cm
Adult. Resident. Sri Lanka. Brown cap, and deep cinnamon to pale cinnamon-buff sides of head and underparts. Forest undergrowth and thick scrub.

7 LARGE SCIMITAR BABBLER *Pomatorhinus hypoleucos* 28 cm
Adult. Resident. Hills of NE India and Bangladesh. Large; dull bill. Grey ear-coverts, breast sides and flanks, rufous on neck sides. Reeds, tall grass and forest undergrowth.

8 SPOT-BREASTED SCIMITAR BABBLER *Pomatorhinus erythrocnemis* 25 cm
Adult. Resident. Hills of NE India and Bangladesh. White throat, well-defined brown spotting on breast, rufous lores and ear-coverts, and olive-brown breast sides and flanks. Forest undergrowth and secondary growth.

9 RUSTY-CHEEKED SCIMITAR BABBLER *Pomatorhinus erythrogenys* 25 cm
Adult. Resident. Himalayas. Rufous lores and ear-coverts. Rufous down sides of neck, breast and flanks. E Himalayan birds can have noticeably grey or grey-streaked throat and breast. Forest undergrowth and thick scrub.

10 INDIAN SCIMITAR BABBLER *Pomatorhinus horsfieldii* 22 cm
Adult *P. h. horsfieldii* (10a); adult *P. h. melanurus* (10b). Resident. Hills of peninsular India, Sri Lanka. Yellow bill, white supercilium. Breast sides and flanks grey to blackish in peninsular India, olive- to chestnut-brown in Sri Lanka. Forest and secondary growth.

11 WHITE-BROWED SCIMITAR BABBLER *Pomatorhinus schisticeps* 22 cm
Adult. Resident. Himalayan foothills, hills of NE India and Bangladesh. Yellow bill and white supercilium. White centre to breast and belly, chestnut sides to neck and breast, and usually has slate-grey crown. Forest and secondary growth.

12 STREAK-BREASTED SCIMITAR BABBLER *Pomatorhinus ruficollis* 19 cm
Adult. Resident. Himalayas and NE India. Yellow bill and white supercilium. Olive-brown streaking on breast and belly, distinct rufous neck patch extending diffusely across nape. Smaller and smaller-billed than White-browed, with olive-brown crown. Forest undergrowth and dense scrub.

13 RED-BILLED SCIMITAR BABBLER *Pomatorhinus ochraceiceps* 23 cm
Adult. Resident. NE Indian hills. Fine orange-red bill, white throat and white/pale buff breast, uniform buffish olive-brown crown. Forest undergrowth and bamboo thickets.

14 CORAL-BILLED SCIMITAR BABBLER *Pomatorhinus ferruginosus* 22 cm
Adult *P. f. ferruginosus* (14a); adult *P. f. formosus* (14b). Resident. E Himalayas and NE India. Stout red bill, rufous/rich buff underparts, white malar stripe and upper throat. Nominate race, of E Himalayas, has blackish crown. Undergrowth in moist forest and bamboo thickets.

15 SLENDER-BILLED SCIMITAR BABBLER *Xiphirhynchus superciliaris* 20 cm
Adult. Resident. Himalayas and NE India. Long, downcurved black bill, feathery white supercilium, deep rufous underparts. Undergrowth in moist forest and bamboo thickets.

Craig Robson '97

1 **LONG-BILLED WREN BABBLER** *Rimator malacoptilus* 12 cm
Adult. Resident. E Himalayas and NE Indian hills. Downcurved bill, dark moustachial stripe, fine buff shaft streaking on upperparts, broad buff streaking on underparts. Forest undergrowth and ravines.

2 **STREAKED WREN BABBLER** *Napothera brevicaudata* 12 cm
Adult. Resident. NE Indian hills. Comparatively long tail. Grey face, diffuse grey throat streaks, rufous-brown underparts, untidily streaked upperparts. Moist forest on rocky ground and ravines.

3 **EYEBROWED WREN BABBLER** *Napothera epilepidota* 10 cm
Adult *N. e. roberti* of NE Indian hills (**3a**); adult ***N. e. guttaticollis*** of E Himalayas (**3b**). Resident. Prominent supercilium and dark eye-stripe, dark spotting on throat and breast, white spots on wing-coverts. Moss-covered boulders and logs in dense forest.

4 **SCALY-BREASTED WREN BABBLER** *Pnoepyga albiventer* 10 cm
Adult white (4a) and fulvous morph (4b) ***P. a. albiventer;*** **adult *P. a. pallidior* (4c).** Resident. Himalayas and NE Indian hills. 'Tail-less'. Larger than Winter Wren (Plate 114). Buff spotting on crown and sides of neck (occasionally on entire mantle). Song is a strong warble, *tzee-tze-zit-tzu-stu-tzit*, rising then ending abruptly. Tall herbage in moist forest.

5 **NEPAL WREN BABBLER** *Pnoepyga immaculata* 10 cm
Adult white (5a) and fulvous morph (5b). Resident. Nepal Himalayas. 'Tail-less'. Narrow black centres to underpart feathers; lack of buff spotting on crown, neck sides and wings. Upperparts are a paler olive-brown than those of nominate Scaly-breasted (where ranges overlap). Eight high-pitched piercing notes, fairly quickly delivered, *si-su-si-si-swi-si-si-si*. Tall herbage in dense forest.

6 **PYGMY WREN BABBLER** *Pnoepyga pusilla* 9 cm
Adult white (6a) and fulvous morph (6b). Resident. Himalayas and NE India. 'Tail-less'. Same size as Winter Wren (Plate 114). Lacks buff spotting on crown and neck sides. Song is a loud, slowly drawn-out *see-saw*, repeated monotonously. Tall herbage in moist forest.

7 **RUFOUS-THROATED WREN BABBLER** *Spelaeornis caudatus* 9 cm
Adult. Resident. E Himalayas. Rufous-orange throat and breast, and barring on flanks; grey ear-coverts. Mossy rocks and ferns in denser forest.

8 **RUSTY-THROATED WREN BABBLER** *Spelaeornis badeigularis* 9 cm
Adult. Resident. Mishmi Hills, E Arunachal Pradesh. Rusty-chestnut throat, white and black bars/spots on breast and flanks, olive-brown ear-coverts. Moist subtropical forest.

9 **BAR-WINGED WREN BABBLER** *Spelaeornis troglodytoides* 10 cm
Adult. Resident. E Himalayas. Finely barred wings and long barred tail, white spotting on crown and sides of neck, and white throat and breast with diffuse dark spotting. Undergrowth in moist forest.

10 **SPOTTED WREN BABBLER** *Spelaeornis formosus* 10 cm
Adult. Resident. E Himalayas, hills of NE India and Bangladesh. Broad, dark brown barring on rufous-brown wings and tail, irregular white flecking on grey-brown upperparts. Denser undergrowth in moist forest.

11 **LONG-TAILED WREN BABBLER** *Spelaeornis chocolatinus* 10 cm
Adult *S. c. chocolatinus* (11a); adult *S. c. oatesi* (11b). Resident. NE Indian hills. Long tail with scaly appearance to brown upperparts. *S. c. chocolatinus*, of S Assam and Manipur hills, has rufous-buff throat, breast and flanks, with brown and buff spotting. *S. c. oatesi*, of Mizoram hills, has rufous buff replaced by white with black spotting. Dense undergrowth in forest and hillsides with moss-covered rocks.

12 **TAWNY-BREASTED WREN BABBLER** *Spelaeornis longicaudatus* 10 cm
Adult. Resident. NE Indian hills. Long tail with scaly appearance to brown upperparts. Grey lores and ear-coverts, orange-buff underparts without prominent black or white spotting. Thick undergrowth in moist forest.

13 **WEDGE-BILLED WREN BABBLER** *Sphenocichla humei* 18 cm
Adult *S. h. humei* (13a); adult *S. h. roberti* (13b). Resident. Indian E Himalayas and NE Indian hills. Conical yellow bill. Blackish underparts with white shaft streaking in *humei*, of Sikkkim and Arunachal Pradesh; white scaling on underparts in *roberti*, of hills south of Brahmaputra River. Evergreen forest with bamboo.

Craig Robson '97

PLATE 131, p. 306

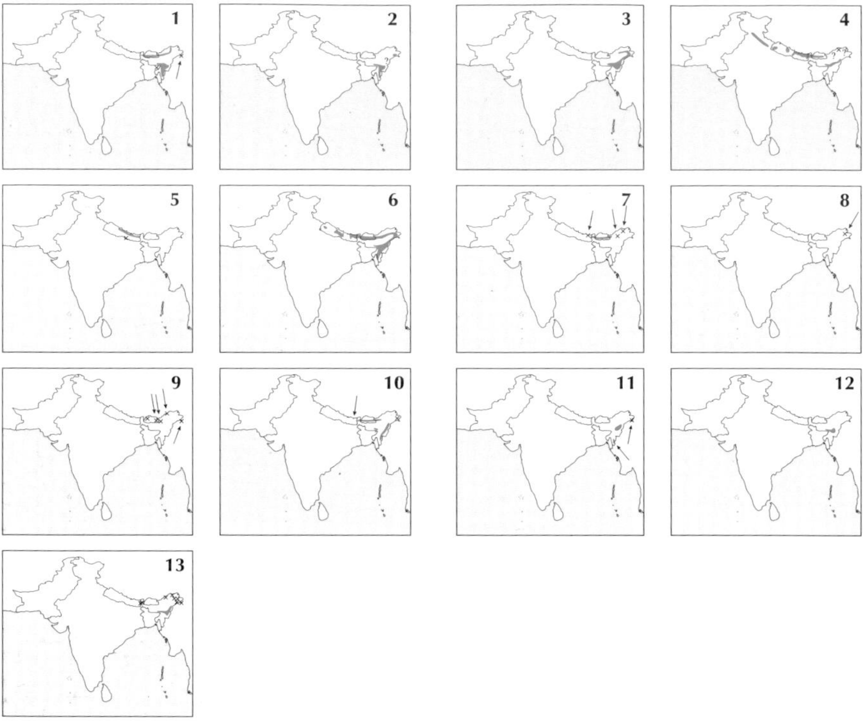

PLATE 132, p. 310

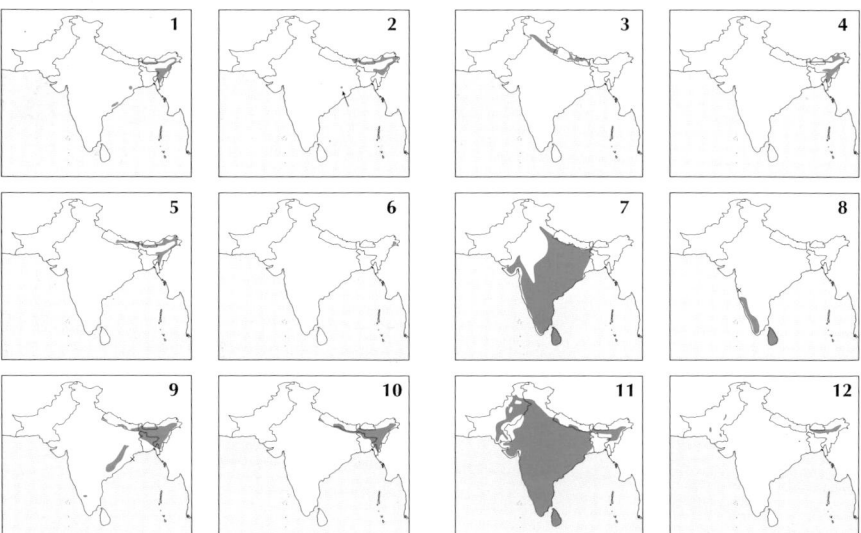

PLATE 133, p. 312

PLATE 134, p. 314

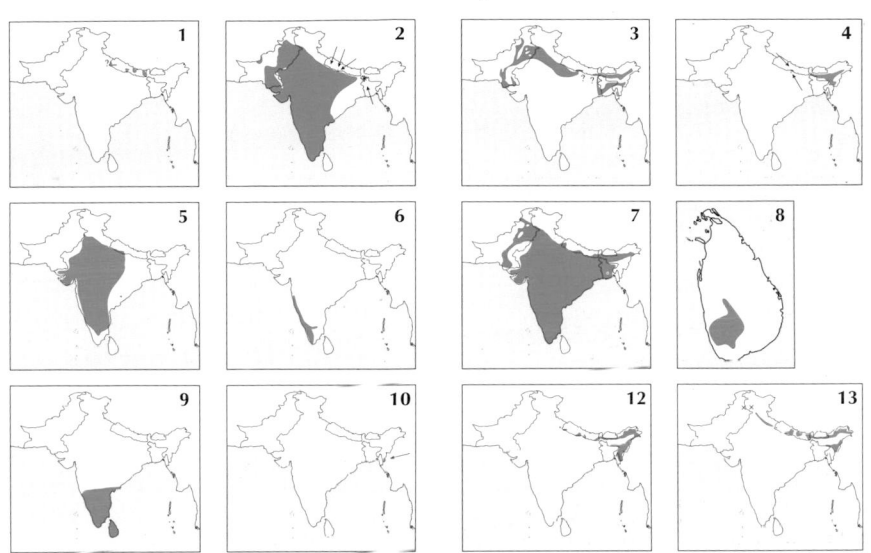

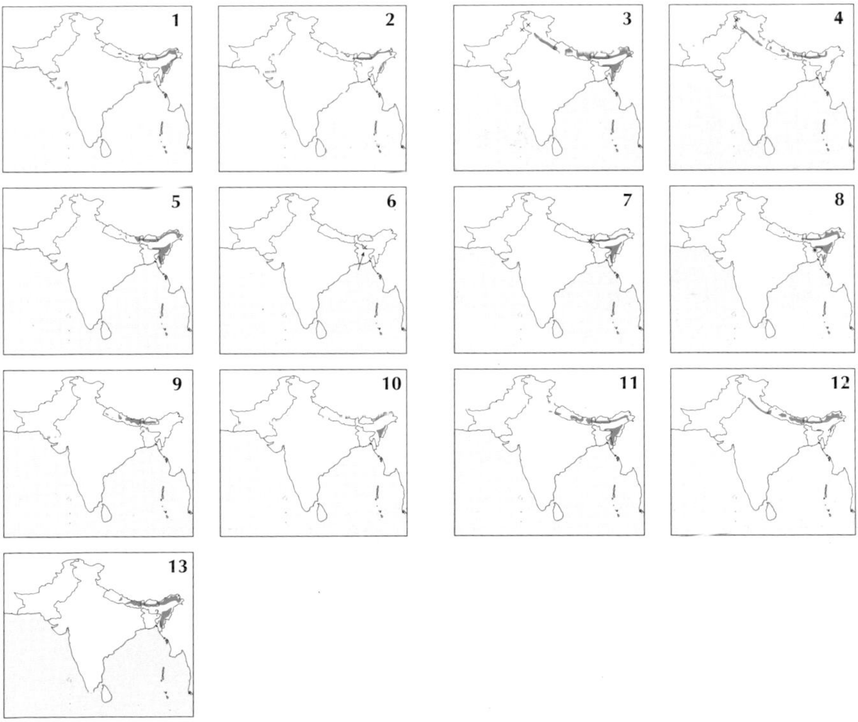

1 RUFOUS-FRONTED BABBLER *Stachyris rufifrons* 12 cm
Adult. Resident. E Himalayan foothills, NE and E Indian hills, and Bangladesh. Grey supercilium, olive-brown ear-coverts concolorous with nape, white throat and buff underparts. Thick undergrowth in open forest and ravines.

2 RUFOUS-CAPPED BABBLER *Stachyris ruficeps* 12 cm
Adult. Resident. E Himalayas and NE and E Indian hills. Yellowish-buff supercilium and ear-coverts which contrast with nape, pale yellow throat, and yellowish-buff underparts. Dense undergrowth in moist forest.

3 BLACK-CHINNED BABBLER *Stachyris pyrrhops* 10 cm
Adult. Resident. Himalayas. Black chin and lores, and orange-buff underparts. Undergrowth in open forest and secondary growth.

4 GOLDEN BABBLER *Stachyris chrysaea* 10 cm
Adult *S. c. chrysaea* (4a); **adult** *S. c. binghami* (4b). Resident. Himalayas, hills of NE India and Bangladesh. Yellow crown with black streaking, black mask, and yellow underparts. *S. c. binghami*, of Mizoram south to Bangladesh, has greener upperparts and duller underparts than nominate. Dense undergrowth in moist forest.

5 GREY-THROATED BABBLER *Stachyris nigriceps* 12 cm
Adult *S. n. nigriceps* (5a); **adult** *S. n. coltarti* (5b). Resident. Himalayas, hills of NE India and Bangladesh. Blackish crown with white streaking, whitish supercilium, and grey or black-and-white throat. Racial differences are mainly in the coloration of underparts and patterning of throat. Forest undergrowth and secondary growth.

6 SNOWY-THROATED BABBLER *Stachyris oglei* 13 cm
Adult. Resident. Arunachal Pradesh hills. Broad white supercilium and throat, black eye-stripe, and white spotting on neck sides. Dense scrub in rocky ravines; evergreen forest in winter.

7 TAWNY-BELLIED BABBLER *Dumetia hyperythra* 13 cm
Adult *D. h. hyperythra* (7a); **adult** *D. h. albogularis* (7b). Resident. Peninsular India, S Nepal and Sri Lanka. Rufous-brown forehead and forecrown and orange-buff underparts. Three races have white throat; *D. h. hyperythra*, of E peninsular India, has throat concolorous with underparts. Tall grass and scrub.

8 DARK-FRONTED BABBLER *Rhopocichla atriceps* 13 cm
Adult *R. a. atriceps* (8a); **adult** *R. a. nigrifrons* (8b). Resident. Western Ghats and Sri Lanka. Stocky, brown upperparts, and whitish underparts. Two races in Western Ghats (including *atriceps*) have dark hood, whilst two races in Sri Lanka (including *nigrifrons*) have dark mask. Dense undergrowth in evergreen biotope.

9 STRIPED TIT BABBLER *Macronous gularis* 11 cm
Adult. Resident. Himalayan foothills, hills of NE, E and S India, and Bangladesh. Rufous-brown cap, pale yellow supercilium, and finely streaked pale yellow throat and breast. Forest undergrowth.

10 CHESTNUT-CAPPED BABBLER *Timalia pileata* 17 cm
Adult. Resident. Himalayan terai and foothills, and N and NE Indian plains. Chestnut cap and black mask contrasting with white forehead and supercilium. Tall grass, reedbeds and scrub.

11 YELLOW-EYED BABBLER *Chrysomma sinense* 18 cm
Adult *C. s. sinense* (11a); **adult** *C. s. hypoleucum* (11b). Widespread resident; unrecorded in parts of the northwest and northeast. Yellow iris and orange eye-ring, white lores and supercilium, and white throat and breast. Tall grass, bushes and reeds.

12 JERDON'S BABBLER *Chrysomma altirostre* 17 cm
Adult *C. a. altirostre* (12a); **adult** *C. a. griseigulare* (12b). Resident. Plains of Pakistan and the northeast, and C Nepal terai. Brown iris, grey lores and supercilium, and grey throat and breast. Eastern race, *C. a. griseigulare*, has richer chestnut-brown upperparts and darker grey throat and breast compared with nominate. Reedbeds and tall grassland.

Craig Robson '97

PLATE 133: *TURDOIDES* BABBLERS, BABAXES AND MESIAS
Maps p. 309

1 SPINY BABBLER *Turdoides nipalensis* 25 cm
Adult (1a, 1b). Resident. Nepal Himalayas. White patterning on face, and black shaft streaking on white or buff throat and breast. Dense scrub.

2 COMMON BABBLER *Turdoides caudatus* 23 cm
Adult. Widespread resident; unrecorded in most of NE and E India, W Pakistan and Sri Lanka. Unstreaked whitish throat and breast centre. Legs and feet are yellowish. Dry scrub in plains and low hills.

3 STRIATED BABBLER *Turdoides earlei* 21 cm
Adult. Resident. Plains of N subcontinent. Brown mottling on fulvous throat and breast. Legs and feet are greyish to olive-brown. In flight, outer tail feathers appear greyish-buff (not so apparent in Common). Reedbeds and tall grass in wet habitats.

4 SLENDER-BILLED BABBLER *Turdoides longirostris* 23 cm
Adult. Resident. Lowlands of C Nepal and NE subcontinent. Unstreaked dark rufous-brown upperparts, white throat and buff underparts, and curved black bill. Tall grass and reeds.

5 LARGE GREY BABBLER *Turdoides malcolmi* 28 cm
Adult. Resident. Pakistan, W Nepal and Indian peninsula. Whitish sides to long, graduated tail; unmottled pinkish-grey throat and breast, pale grey forehead and dark grey lores. Open dry scrub and cultivation.

6 RUFOUS BABBLER *Turdoides subrufus* 25 cm
Adult. Resident. SW Indian hills. Grey forehead and forecrown, black-and-yellow bill, blackish lores, unstreaked rufous underparts. Tall grass and bamboo at forest edges.

7 JUNGLE BABBLER *Turdoides striatus* 25 cm
Adult *T. s. striatus* (7a); adult *T. s. orientalis* (7b); adult *T. s. somervillei* (7c). Widespread resident; unrecorded in parts of the northwest and northeast. Uniform tail; variable dark mottling and streaking on throat and breast. *T. s. somervillei*, of Maharashtra, is a very distinctive race with orange-brown tail and dark primaries. Deciduous forest and cultivation.

8 ORANGE-BILLED BABBLER *Turdoides rufescens* 25 cm
Adult. Resident. Sri Lanka. Orange bill, cinnamon-rufous underparts, and greyish crown and nape. Wet-zone forest.

9 YELLOW-BILLED BABBLER *Turdoides affinis* 23 cm
Adult *T. a. affinis* (9a); adult *T. a. taprobanus* (9b, 9c). Resident. Peninsular India and Sri Lanka. Creamy-white crown, dark mottling on throat and breast, and pale rump and tail-base (although juvenile more similar to Jungle). *T. a. taprobanus* also more similar to Jungle Babbler, although that species does not occur in Sri Lanka. Variant *taprobanus* from near Colombo has blackish on throat and breast. Scrub.

10 CHINESE BABAX *Babax lanceolatus* 28 cm
Adult. Resident. Mizoram. Rufous-brown crown, dark chestnut submoustachial stripe, and broad chestnut streaking on breast sides and flanks, with buffish-white underparts. Open forest and thick vegetation on hillsides.

11 GIANT BABAX *Babax waddelli* 31 cm
Adult. [Doubtful resident in NE Sikkim. Submoustachial stripe diffuse or absent; greyish underparts and upperparts, with diffuse dark brown streaking evenly across breast and belly. Dry high-altitude scrub.]

12 SILVER-EARED MESIA *Leiothrix argentauris* 15 cm
Male (12a) and juvenile female (12b). Resident. Himalayas and NE Indian hills. Black crown, grey ear-coverts, orange-yellow throat and breast, and crimson wing panel. Bushes and forest undergrowth in evergreen biotope.

13 RED-BILLED LEIOTHRIX *Leiothrix lutea* 13 cm
Male (13a) and juvenile female (13b). Resident. Himalayas and NE Indian hills. Red bill, yellowish-olive crown, yellow throat and orange breast, and forked black tail. Juvenile duller, but with striking wing pattern like adult. Forest undergrowth.

PLATE 134: CUTIA, SHRIKE BABBLERS, BARWINGS AND MINLAS
Maps p. 309

1 **CUTIA** *Cutia nipalensis* 20 cm
Male (1a) and female (1b). Resident. Himalayas and NE Indian hills. Grey crown and dark mask, and black barring on flanks. Female has spotted mantle. Mossy broadleaved forest.

2 **BLACK-HEADED SHRIKE BABBLER** *Pteruthius rufiventer* 17 cm
Male (2a) and female (2b). Resident. Himalayas and NE Indian hills. Male has grey throat and breast, black head without white supercilium, and rufous-brown mantle. Female has black on nape, olive mantle, and rufous rump and tip to tail. Dense, moist broadleaved forest.

3 **WHITE-BROWED SHRIKE BABBLER** *Pteruthius flaviscapis* 16 cm
Male (3a) and female (3b). Resident. Himalayas and NE Indian hills. Male has rufous tertials, black head with white supercilium, and grey mantle. Female has grey crown and ear-coverts, and olive mantle. Larger size and rufous tertials are best features of female from Green Shrike Babbler. Mainly broadleaved forest.

4 **GREEN SHRIKE BABBLER** *Pteruthius xanthochlorus* 13 cm
Male *P. x. occidentalis* (4a); male *P. x. xanthochlorus* (4b); male *P. x. hybridus* (4c). Resident. Himalayas and NE Indian hills. Grey crown and nape, white wing-bar, and greyish-white throat and breast and pale yellow belly. *P. x. hybridus*, of hills south of Brahmaputra River, has prominent white eye-ring. Forest.

5 **BLACK-EARED SHRIKE BABBLER** *Pteruthius melanotis* 11 cm
Male (5a) and female (5b). Resident. Himalayas and NE Indian hills. Black patch on ear-coverts and no chestnut on forehead are best features from Chestnut-fronted. Male has chestnut throat and breast and white wing-bars. Female has chestnut reduced to malar region, and has buff wing-bars. Moist broadleaved forest.

6 **CHESTNUT-FRONTED SHRIKE BABBLER** *Pteruthius aenobarbus* 11 cm
Male *P. a. aenobarbulus* (6a); adult female *P. a. intermedius* (6b). Resident. Meghalaya. Chestnut forehead; lacks black patch on ear-coverts. Female of race recorded in subcontinent never described; race from Myanmar illustrated here. Edges of evergreen forest.

7 **WHITE-HOODED BABBLER** *Gampsorhynchus rufulus* 23 cm
Adult (7a) and juvenile (7b). Resident. E Himalayas and NE Indian hills. Adult has white head and underparts. Juvenile has rufous-orange crown; bill finer than that of Greater Rufous-headed Parrotbill. Bamboo jungle and forest undergrowth.

8 **RUSTY-FRONTED BARWING** *Actinodura egertoni* 23 cm
Adult *A. e. egertoni* (8a); adult *A. e. lewisi* (8b). Resident. Himalayas and NE Indian hills. Rufous front to head, unstreaked grey crown and nape. Four races in subcontinent vary in colour of mantle. Undergrowth in moist forest and secondary growth.

9 **HOARY-THROATED BARWING** *Actinodura nipalensis* 20 cm
Adult. Resident. Himalayas. Prominent buffish-white shaft streaking on crown and nape, black moustachial stripe, and greyish throat and breast. Mossy forest.

10 **STREAK-THROATED BARWING** *Actinodura waldeni* 20 cm
Adult *A. w. waldeni* (10a); adult *A. w. daflaensis* (10b). Resident. NE Indian hills. Diffuse streaking on tawny-brown or greyish underparts. *A. w. daflaensis*, of E Himalayas, rather similar to Hoary-throated, but has diffuse brownish-grey streaking on underparts, lacks bold buff shaft streaking to crown and prominent moustachial, and has uniform mantle (note also no known overlap in range). Mossy forest.

11 **BLUE-WINGED MINLA** *Minla cyanouroptera* 15 cm
Adult. Resident. Himalayas and NE Indian hills. Blue on crown and on wings and tail; vinaceous-grey underparts. Bushes in forest and well-wooded country.

12 **CHESTNUT-TAILED MINLA** *Minla strigula* 14 cm
Adult. Resident. Himalayas and NE Indian hills. Orange crown, black-and-white barring on throat, orange-yellow panel in wing, and yellow sides to tail. Forest.

13 **RED-TAILED MINLA** *Minla ignotincta* 14 cm
Male (13a) and female (13b). Resident. Himalayas and NE Indian hills. White supercilium contrasting with dark crown and ear-coverts. Male has maroon-brown (rather than olive-brown) mantle, and brighter red panel in wing and in sides to tail (more orange in female). Moist forest.

PLATE 135: FULVETTAS, YUHINAS AND FIRE-TAILED MYZORNIS
Maps p. 318

Maps p. 318

1 GOLDEN-BREASTED FULVETTA *Alcippe chrysotis* 11 cm
Adult *A. c. chrysotis* (1a); adult *A. c. albilineata* (1b). Resident. Himalayas and NE Indian hills. Blue-grey and yellow fulvetta with silvery-grey ear-coverts. Bamboo.

2 YELLOW-THROATED FULVETTA *Alcippe cinerea* 10 cm
Adult. Resident. Himalayas and NE Indian hills. Yellow supercilium, black lateral crown-stripes, greyish crown, yellow throat and breast. Undergrowth in moist subtropical forest.

3 RUFOUS-WINGED FULVETTA *Alcippe castaneceps* 10 cm
Adult. Resident. Himalayas and NE Indian hills. Chestnut crown streaked with buffish-white, black wing-bar, and white supercilium. Undergrowth in moist forest.

4 WHITE-BROWED FULVETTA *Alcippe vinipectus* 11 cm
Adult *A. v. kangrae* (4a); adult *A. v. austeni* (4b); adult *A. v. chumbiensis* (4c). Resident. Himalayas and NE Indian hills. Broad white supercilium and black panel in primaries. Subalpine shrubberies and bushes in temperate and subalpine forest.

5 BROWN-THROATED FULVETTA *Alcippe ludlowi* 11 cm
Adult. Resident. E Himalayas. No white supercilium or dark lateral crown-stripe; has prominent rufous-brown streaking on throat. Undergrowth in rhododendron forest.

6 STREAK-THROATED FULVETTA *Alcippe cinereiceps* 11 cm
Adult. Resident. NE Indian hills. Lacks white supercilium; has brownish-buff crown and mantle, and greyish ear-coverts. Dense scrub and bamboo.

7 RUFOUS-THROATED FULVETTA *Alcippe rufogularis* 12 cm
Adult. Resident. E Himalayas and NE Indian hills. Rufous collar, broad white supercilium, blackish lateral crown-stripes, uniform brown wings. Bamboo stands and undergrowth in moist tropical forest.

8 RUSTY-CAPPED FULVETTA *Alcippe dubia* 13 cm
Adult. Resident. NE Indian hills. Rufous forehead, white supercilium, prominent buff streaking on neck sides, uniform brown wings. Dense undergrowth in forest.

9 BROWN-CHEEKED FULVETTA *Alcippe poioicephala* 15 cm
Adult. Resident. Hills of India and Bangladesh. Nondescript, lacking any patterning to head or wings. Undergrowth in moist forest and secondary growth.

10 NEPAL FULVETTA *Alcippe nipalensis* 12 cm
Adult. Resident. Himalayas, hills of NE India and Bangladesh. Grey head with black lateral crown-stripes. Undergrowth in moist forest.

11 STRIATED YUHINA *Yuhina castaniceps* 13 cm
Adult *Y. c. rufigenis* (11a); adult *Y. c. castaniceps* (11b). Resident. Himalayas and NE Indian hills. White-tipped tail, grey (or rufous in SE of range) crown with pale scaling, and rufous ear-coverts. Broadleaved forest.

12 WHITE-NAPED YUHINA *Yuhina bakeri* 13 cm
Adult. Resident. Himalayas and NE Indian hills. Rufous crest, white nape, and white streaking on ear-coverts. Evergreen subtropical forest.

13 WHISKERED YUHINA *Yuhina flavicollis* 13 cm
Adult *Y. f. flavicollis* (13a); adult *Y. f. albicollis* (13b). Resident. Himalayas and NE Indian hills. Rufous (or yellowish in W Himalayas) hindcollar, black moustachial stripe. Broadleaved forest and secondary growth.

14 STRIPE-THROATED YUHINA *Yuhina gularis* 14 cm
Adult. Resident. Himalayas and NE Indian hills. Streaked throat, and black and orange wing panels. Temperate forest.

15 RUFOUS-VENTED YUHINA *Yuhina occipitalis* 13 cm
Adult. Resident. Himalayas. Grey crest, rufous lores and nape patch, and rufous vent. Temperate and subalpine forest.

16 BLACK-CHINNED YUHINA *Yuhina nigrimenta* 11 cm
Adult. Resident. Himalayas and NE Indian hills. Black lores and chin, black crest with grey streaking, and red lower mandible. Moist subtropical forest.

17 WHITE-BELLIED YUHINA *Yuhina zantholeuca* 11 cm
Adult. Resident. Himalayas, NE India and Bangladesh. Olive-yellow upperparts and white underparts. Broadleaved forest.

18 FIRE-TAILED MYZORNIS *Myzornis pyrrhoura* 12 cm
Male (18a) and female (18b). Resident. Himalayas. Emerald-green. Subalpine shrubberies, mossy forest and bamboo.

Craig Robson '97

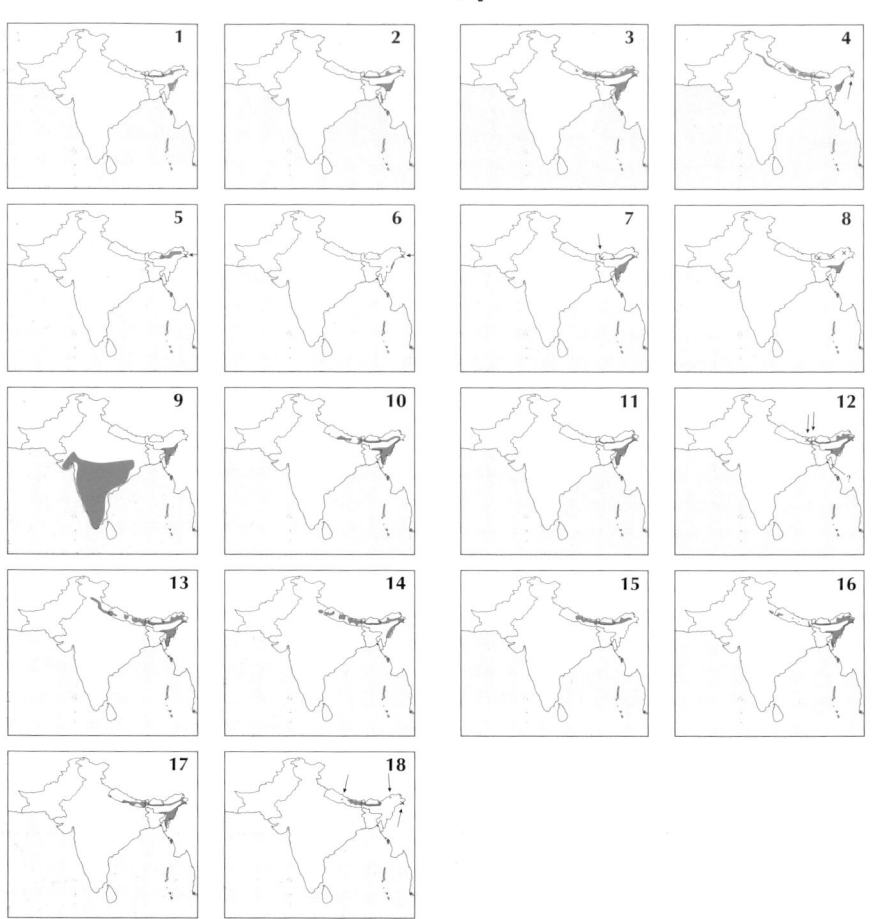

PLATE 136, p. 320

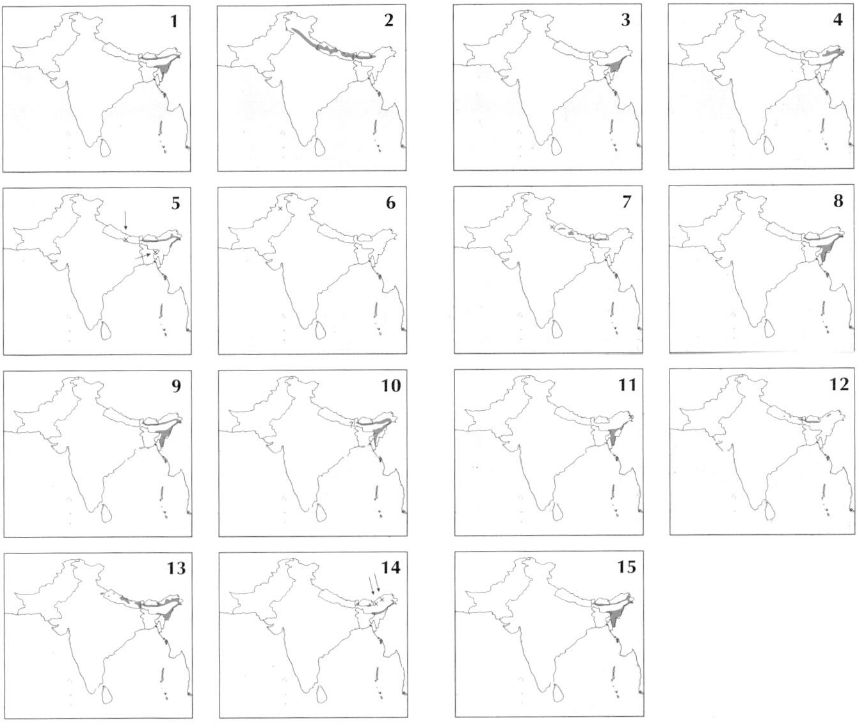

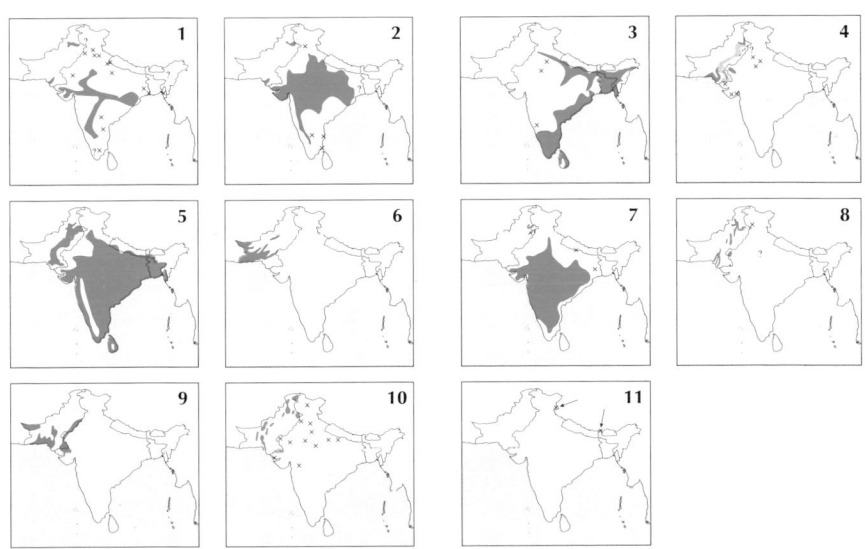

PLATE 137, p. 322

1 RUFOUS-BACKED SIBIA *Heterophasia annectans* 18 cm
Adult. Resident. E Himalayas and NE Indian hills. Black cap, white throat and breast, white and black streaking on nape, rufous back and rump, and black tail with white tips. Broadleaved evergreen forest.

2 RUFOUS SIBIA *Heterophasia capistrata* 21 cm
Adult *H. c. capistrata* (2a); adult *H. c. nigriceps* (2b). Resident. Himalayas. Black cap, and rufous or cinnamon-buff nape and underparts; black and grey bands on rufous tail. Mainly broadleaved forest.

3 GREY SIBIA *Heterophasia gracilis* 21 cm
Adult. Resident. NE Indian hills. Black cap, grey mantle, white underparts, and grey tail with black subterminal band. Mainly broadleaved forest.

4 BEAUTIFUL SIBIA *Heterophasia pulchella* 22 cm
Adult *H. p. pulchella* (4a); adult *H. p. nigroaurita* (4b). Resident. NE Indian hills. Blue-grey crown, slate-grey upperparts and underparts, chestnut-brown tertials. Has black ear-coverts in race north of Brahmaputra River. Moist broadleaved forest.

5 LONG-TAILED SIBIA *Heterophasia picaoides* 30 cm
Adult. Resident. E Himalayas and NE Indian hills. Long tail with white tips, and white patch on secondaries. Broadleaved forest.

6 BEARDED PARROTBILL *Panurus biarmicus* 16–17 cm
Male (6a) and female (6b). Vagrant. Pakistan. Black and white on wings. Male has grey head with black moustache. Female and juvenile have plain buff head. Reedbeds.

7 GREAT PARROTBILL *Conostoma oemodium* 28 cm
Adult. Resident. Himalayas. Huge conical yellow bill, greyish-white forehead, dark brown lores. Bamboo stands in forest.

8 BROWN PARROTBILL *Paradoxornis unicolor* 21 cm
Adult. Resident. Himalayas. Stout yellowish bill, blackish lateral crown-stripes, dusky grey underparts. Bamboo stands and bushes.

9 GREY-HEADED PARROTBILL *Paradoxornis gularis* 21 cm
Adult. Resident. Himalayas and NE Indian hills. Black lateral crown-stripes, black throat, grey crown and ear-coverts, whitish underparts. Forest, bushes and bamboo.

10 BLACK-BREASTED PARROTBILL *Paradoxornis flavirostris* 19 cm
Adult. Resident. Assam. Black patch on breast, and rufous-buff underparts. Reedbeds and tall grass.

11 SPOT-BREASTED PARROTBILL *Paradoxornis guttaticollis* 19 cm
Adult. Resident. NE Indian hills. Arrowhead-shaped spotting on breast, and pale buff underparts. Grass and scrub, also bushes and bamboo.

12 FULVOUS PARROTBILL *Paradoxornis fulvifrons* 12 cm
Adult. Resident. Himalayas. Fulvous and olive-brown head markings, and fulvous throat and breast. Bamboo stands.

13 BLACK-THROATED PARROTBILL *Paradoxornis nipalensis* 10 cm
Adult *P. n. nipalensis* (13a); *P. n. humii* (13b), *P. n. crocotius* (13c) and *P. n. poliotis* (13d). Resident. Himalayas and NE Indian hills. Crown is grey in C Himalayas, and orange in races of E Himalayas and NE. Blackish lateral crown-stripes and throat, white malar patch. Bamboo and dense forest undergrowth.

14 LESSER RUFOUS-HEADED PARROTBILL *Paradoxornis atrosuperciliaris* 15 cm
Adult *P. a. atrosuperciliaris* (14a); adult *P. a. oatesi* (14b). Resident. E Himalayas and NE Indian hills. Small, with stouter bill than Greater Rufous-headed Parrotbill. Black eye-brow in *atrosuperciliaris* (indistinct in *oatesi*), whitish lores and buffish-orange ear-coverts. Bamboo stands, tall grass and scrub jungle.

15 GREATER RUFOUS-HEADED PARROTBILL *Paradoxornis ruficeps* 18 cm
Adult *P. r. ruficeps* (15a); adult *P. r. bakeri* (15b). Resident. E Himalayas and NE Indian hills. Larger and longer-billed than Lesser. No black supercilium. Lores and ear-coverts deep rufous-orange. Bamboo stands and undergrowth in moist broadleaved forest.

raig Robson '97

1 **SINGING BUSHLARK** *Mirafra cantillans* 14 cm Table p. 369
Adult. Resident. Plains and foothills in Pakistan, India and Bangladesh. Stout bill, and rufous on wing; white outer tail feathers, weak and rather restricted spotting on upper breast, and whitish throat with brownish to rufous-buff breast-band. Song is sweet and full with much mimicry, and similar to Oriental Skylark. Open dry scrub, fallow cultivation and grassland.

2 **INDIAN BUSHLARK** *Mirafra erythroptera* 14 cm Table p. 369
RED-WINGED
Adult. Resident. Plains and plateaux in Pakistan and India; unrecorded in the northeast. Stout bill, and rufous on wing; rufous-buff on outer tail feathers, pronounced dark spotting on breast, dark spotting on ear-coverts and malar region, and more uniform whitish underparts. Shows more rufous on wing than other bushlarks. Song is a *tit-tit-tit*, followed by long, drawn-out *tsweeeih-tsweeeih-tsweeeih*. Stony scrub and fallow cultivation.

3 **RUFOUS-WINGED BUSHLARK** *Mirafra assamica* 15 cm Table p. 369
Adult *M. a. assamica* (3a); adult *M. a. affinis* (3b). Resident. Mainly plains and plateaux of N, E and S subcontinent. Stout bill, short tail, and rufous on wing; rufous-buff on outer tail feathers, pronounced dark spotting on breast, dark spotting on ear-coverts and malar region, and pale rufous-buff wash to underparts. Upperparts grey and underparts more rufous in *assamica* of N subcontinent. Song of *assamica* is a repetition of a series of thin, high-pitched disyllabic notes, usually delivered in prolonged song flight; *affinis* has a dry metallic rattle delivered from a perch or during short song flight. Stony scrub and fallow cultivation.

4 **BLACK-CROWNED SPARROW LARK** *Eremopterix nigriceps* 13 cm
Male (4a) and female (4b, 4c). Resident. Pakistan and NW India. Male has brownish-black crown, nape and underparts. Female has stout bill, rather uniform head and upperparts, and dark grey underwing-coverts; probably inseparable from female Ashy-crowned. Sandy deserts.

5 **ASHY-CROWNED SPARROW LARK** *Eremopterix grisea* 12 cm
Male. Widespread resident. Male has grey crown and nape, and brownish-black underparts. Female has stout greyish bill, rather uniform head and upperparts, and dark grey underwing-coverts; probably inseparable from female Black-crowned. Open dry scrub and dry cultivation.

6 **BAR-TAILED LARK** *Ammomanes cincturus* 15 cm
Adult. Resident. Baluchistan. Blackish terminal bar to rufous tail; tertials orangey-buff and contrast with blackish primaries. Smaller and stockier than Desert, with shorter and finer bill. Low stony hills and gravelly plains.

7 **RUFOUS-TAILED LARK** *Ammomanes phoenicurus* 16 cm
Adult. Resident. Plains in N Pakistan, S Nepal and India. Dusky grey-brown upperparts, rufous-orange underparts, prominent dark streaking on throat and breast, and rufous orange uppertail-coverts and tail, with dark terminal bar. Cultivation, open dry scrub.

8 **DESERT LARK** *Ammomanes deserti* 17 cm
Adult. Resident. Pakistan and NW India. Tail largely grey-brown with rufous at sides; tertials grey-brown and contrast little with primaries. Larger and slimmer than Bar-tailed, with longer and broader bill. Low, dry rocky hills.

9 **GREATER HOOPOE LARK** *Alaemon alaudipes* 19 cm
Adult (9a, 9b). Resident. Pakistan and Rann of Kutch. Longish downcurved bill and long legs. Black-and-white wing patterning prominent in flight. Desert.

10 **BIMACULATED LARK** *Melanocorypha bimaculata* 17 cm
Adult (10a, 10b). Winter visitor. Pakistan and N and NW India. Large, with stout bill and short tail. Prominent white supercilium, black patch on side of breast, and white tip to tail. Semi-desert and fallow cultivation.

11 **TIBETAN LARK** *Melanocorypha maxima* 21 cm
Adult (11a, 11b). Resident? Ladakh and Sikkim, India. Large, with long bill. Rather uniform head, blackish breast-side patch, white trailing edge to secondaries and tip to tail; crown, ear-coverts and rump can be rufous. Marshes around high-altitude bogs.

1 GREATER SHORT-TOED LARK *Calandrella brachydactyla* 14 cm Table p. 370
Adult *C. b. dukhunensis* (1a); adult *C. b. longipennis* (1b, 1c). Widespread winter visitor; unrecorded in Sri Lanka and parts of India. Stouter bill than Hume's, with more prominent supercilium and eye-stripe; upperparts warmer, with more prominent streaking; dark breast-side patches often apparent. Breast of *dukhunensis* has warm rufous-buff wash, especially at sides. Open stony grassland, fallow cultivation and semi-desert.

2 HUME'S SHORT-TOED LARK *Calandrella acutirostris* 14 cm Table p. 370
Adult. Summer visitor to Baluchistan and Himalayas; winters mainly in S Nepal and N India. Greyer and less heavily streaked upperparts than Greater, with pinkish uppertail-coverts; dark breast-side patch usually apparent, with greyish-buff breast-band. Head pattern less pronounced than Greater's, with rather uniform ear-coverts. Breeds in high-altitude semi-desert; winters in fallow cultivation.

3 LESSER SHORT-TOED LARK *Calandrella rufescens* 13 cm Table p. 370
Adult *C. r. persica.* Winter visitor. Pakistan and India. Primaries extend beyond tertials. Bill large, short and stout. Broad gorget of fine streaking on breast, fine but clear streaking on upperparts, streaked ear-coverts; whitish supercilia appear to join across bill. Stony foothills.

4 ASIAN SHORT-TOED LARK *Calandrella cheleensis* 13 cm Table p. 370
Adult *C. c. leucophaea.* Vagrant. Pakistan. Primaries extend beyond tertials (more prominently than illustrated). Bill small, short, stout. Broad gorget of diffuse streaking on breast, diffuse streaking on upperparts. Open stony grassland, fallow cultivation, semi-desert.

5 SAND LARK *Calandrella raytal* 12 cm Table p. 370
Adult *C. r. raytal* (5a); adult *C. r. adamsi* (5b). Resident. Widespread in N subcontinent. Fine bill. Small size, short tail, cold sandy-grey upperparts, and whitish underparts with fine sparse streaking on breast. Bill of *adamsi*, of NW, is especially fine. Banks of lakes, rivers, tidal creeks and coastal dunes.

6 CRESTED LARK *Galerida cristata* 18 cm
Adult. Resident. Widespread in N subcontinent. Large size and very prominent crest. Sandy upperparts and well-streaked breast; broad, rounded wings, rufous-buff underwing-coverts and outer tail feathers. Desert, semi-desert, dry cultivation and coastal mudflats.

7 MALABAR LARK *Galerida malabarica* 16 cm
Adult. Resident. Plains and hills in W peninsular India. Prominent crest, heavily streaked rufous upperparts, rufous-buff breast with heavy black spotting, and pale rufous outer tail feathers and underwing-coverts. Bill longer than Sykes's, and has buffish-white belly and flanks. Cultivation, grass-covered hills and open scrub.

8 SYKES'S LARK *Galerida deva* 14 cm
Adult. Resident. Mainly C India. Prominent crest and pale rufous outer tail feathers. Smaller than Malabar, with pale rufous underparts and finer and less extensive breast streaking. Stony, scrubby areas and dry cultivation.

9 EURASIAN SKYLARK *Alauda arvensis* 18 cm
Adult. Winter visitor. Pakistan and N India. Large, with long tail; primaries extend beyond tertials. Pronounced whitish trailing edge to secondaries. Underparts whiter than on Oriental, has white outer tail feathers, lacks rufous wing panel. Cultivation and grassland.

10 ORIENTAL SKYLARK *Alauda gulgula* 16 cm
Adult *A. g. australis* (10a); adult *A. g. inconspicua* (10b). Widespread resident and winter visitor. Variable in coloration and prominence of streaking on upperparts and underparts. Fine bill, buffish-white outer tail feathers, and indistinct rufous wing panel. Race of W peninsula and Sri Lanka, *australis,* is warmer buff compared with other races; note smaller bill and shorter crest and *bazz bazz* flight call which are useful differences from Malabar Lark. Grassland, cultivation and coastal mudflats.

11 HORNED LARK *Eremophila alpestris* 18 cm
Male (11a) and female (11b) *E. a. longirostris;* male *E. a. albigula* (11c). Resident. High Himalayas. Male has black-and-white head pattern and black breast-band. Breeds on stony ground and alpine pastures; winters in fallow cultivation, and on stony and sandy ground.

PLATE 138, p. 324

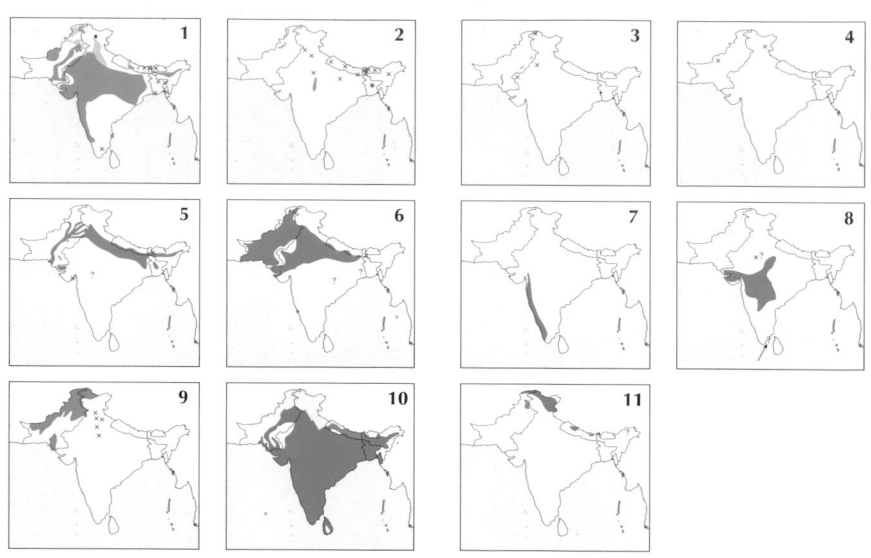

PLATE 139, p. 328

PLATE 140, p. 330

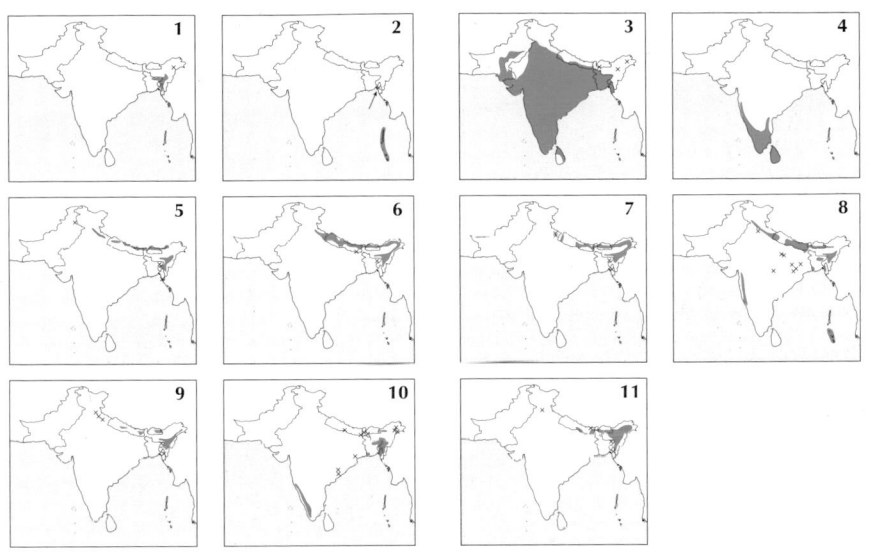

PLATE 141, p. 332

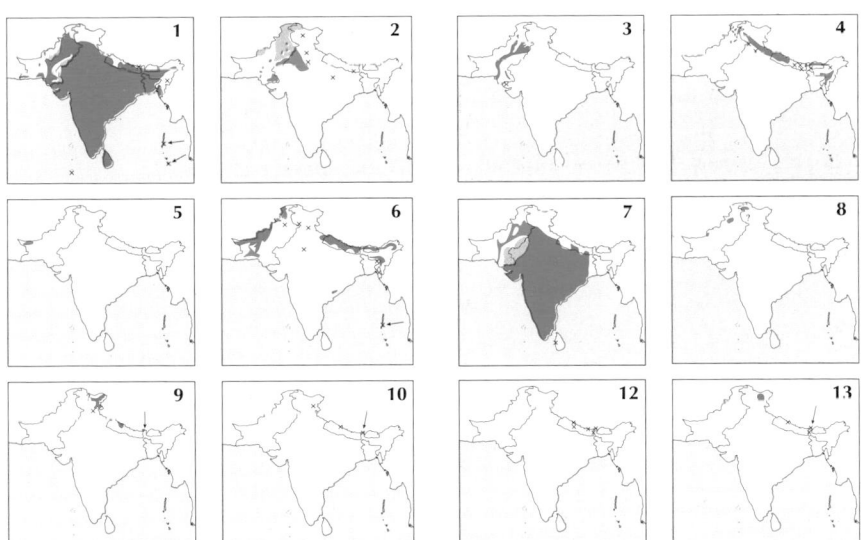

1 THICK-BILLED FLOWERPECKER *Dicaeum agile* 10 cm
Adult. Widespread resident; unrecorded in parts of NE, NW and E subcontinent. Thick bill; diffuse malar stripe, streaking on breast, and indistinct white tip to tail. Forest and well-wooded country.

2 YELLOW-VENTED FLOWERPECKER *Dicaeum chrysorrheum* 10 cm
Adult. Resident. Himalayas, hills of NE India and Bangladesh. Fine, downcurved bill; dark malar stripe and breast streaking, and orange-yellow vent. Open forest and forest edges.

3 YELLOW-BELLIED FLOWERPECKER *Dicaeum melanoxanthum* 13 cm
Male (3a) and female (3b). Resident. Himalayas and NE Indian hills. Large size and stout bill; white centre of throat and breast, dark breast sides, and yellow belly and vent. Broadleaved forest.

4 LEGGE'S FLOWERPECKER *Dicaeum vincens* 10 cm
Male (4a), female (4b) and juvenile (4c). Resident. Sri Lanka. Stout bill; white throat, yellow lower breast and belly. Male has bluish-black upperparts. Female has dark olive mantle and back. Forest and wooded gardens.

5 ORANGE-BELLIED FLOWERPECKER *Dicaeum trigonostigma* 9 cm
Male (5a), female (5b) and juvenile male (5c). Resident. NE Indian hills and Bangladesh. Grey throat, orange rump contrasting with dark tail, orange on underparts. Juvenile has olive-yellow rump and belly centre. Edges of evergreen forest and mangroves.

6 PALE-BILLED FLOWERPECKER *Dicaeum erythrorynchos* 8 cm
Adult. Widespread resident; unrecorded in parts of NE and NW subcontinent. Pale bill, greyish-olive upperparts, pale grey underparts. Open broadleaved forest and well-wooded areas.

7 PLAIN FLOWERPECKER *Dicaeum concolor* 9 cm
Adult *D. c. concolor* (7a); adult *D. c. virescens* (7b); adult *D. c. olivaceum* (7c). Resident. Mainly Himalayan foothills, hills of NE and SW India and Bangladesh. Dark bill. Nominate SW Indian race has darker olive-brown upperparts and paler greyish-white underparts than Pale-billed. Andaman *virescens* has yellowish lower belly. Himalayan *olivaceum* has olive-green upperparts. Edges of broadleaved forest and well-wooded areas.

8 FIRE-BREASTED FLOWERPECKER *Dicaeum ignipectus* 9 cm
Male (8a), female (8b) and juvenile (8c). Resident. Himalayas and NE Indian hills. Male has metallic blue/green upperparts, and buff underparts with red breast. Female has olive-green upperparts and orange-buff throat and breast. Juvenile has duller upperparts and greyer underparts. Broadleaved forest and secondary growth.

9 SCARLET-BACKED FLOWERPECKER *Dicaeum cruentatum* 9 cm
Male (9a), female (9b) and juvenile (9c). Resident. E Himalayan foothills, NE India and Bangladesh. Male has scarlet upperparts and black 'sides'. Female has scarlet rump contrasting with dark tail. Juvenile lacks scarlet rump, and has orange-red bill. Broadleaved forest and secondary growth.

10 RUBY-CHEEKED SUNBIRD *Anthreptes singalensis* 11 cm
Male (10a), female (10b) and juvenile (10c). Resident. C and E Himalayan foothills, NE India and Bangladesh. Rufous-orange throat, yellow underparts. Male has metallic green upperparts and 'ruby' cheeks. Juvenile uniform yellow below. Open forest and forest edges.

11 PURPLE-RUMPED SUNBIRD *Nectarinia zeylonica* 10 cm
Male (11a), female (11b) and juvenile (11c). Resident. Widespread in C and S India, Bangladesh and Sri Lanka. Male has narrow maroon breast-band, maroon head sides and mantle, and greyish-white flanks. Female has greyish-white throat, yellow breast, whitish flanks, and rufous-brown on wing. Juvenile uniform yellow below, with rufous-brown on wing. Calls include a high-pitched *ptsee-ptsee*, and a metallic *chit*. Cultivation and secondary growth.

12 CRIMSON-BACKED SUNBIRD *Nectarinia minima* 8 cm
Male (12a), female (12b) and eclipse male (12c). Resident. Hills of W India. Smaller and finer-billed than Purple-rumped. Male has broad crimson breast-band and mantle. Female has crimson rump. Eclipse male has crimson back and purple rump. Calls include a flowerpecker-like *thlick-thlick*. Evergreen forest and plantations.

C.D'S

PLATE 140: SUNBIRDS

Maps p. 327

1 PURPLE-THROATED SUNBIRD *Nectarinia sperata* 10 cm
Male (1a) and female (1b). Resident. Plains of NE India and Bangladesh. Male has purple throat and maroon breast and belly. Female similar to female Purple, but smaller, with shorter bill. Open forest and gardens.

2 OLIVE-BACKED SUNBIRD *Nectarinia jugularis* 11 cm
Male (2a), female (2b) and eclipse male (2c) *N. j. andamanica*; **male** *N. j. klossi* of Nicobars **(2d).** Resident. Andamans and Nicobars. Male has olive-green upperparts and metallic purple-and-green throat. Female similar to female Purple, but brighter yellow below. Forest and scrub.

3 PURPLE SUNBIRD *Nectarinia asiatica* 10 cm
Male (3a), female (3b, 3c) and eclipse male (3d). Widespread resident; unrecorded in parts of NE and NW subcontinent. Male metallic purple. Female has uniform yellowish underparts, with faint supercilium and darker mask (some greyer and whiter). Call is buzzing *zit* and high-pitched, wheezy *swee*. Open deciduous forest and gardens.

4 LOTEN'S SUNBIRD *Nectarinia lotenia* 13 cm
Male (4a), female (4b) and eclipse male (4c). Resident. C and S Indian peninsula and Sri Lanka. Sickle-shaped bill. Male has dusky-brown belly and vent. Female dark olive-green on upperparts; lacks supercilium and masked appearance of Purple. Call is a hard *chit chit*, lacking buzzing quality of Purple. Well-wooded country.

5 MRS GOULD'S SUNBIRD *Aethopyga gouldiae* 10 cm
Male (5a) and female (5b) *A. g. gouldiae*; **male** *A. g. dabryii* **(5c).** Resident. Himalayas and NE Indian hills. Male has metallic purplish-blue crown, ear-coverts and throat, crimson mantle and back (reaching yellow rump), yellow belly, and blue tail. Female has pale yellow rump, yellow belly, short bill, and prominent white on tail. *A. g. dabryii* race, with scarlet breast, has been recorded in NE. Forest.

6 GREEN-TAILED SUNBIRD *Aethopyga nipalensis* 11 cm
Male (6a) and female (6b). Resident. Himalayas and NE India. Male has metallic blue-green crown, throat and tail, maroon mantle, and olive-green back. Female lacks prominent yellow rump; has long, graduated tail with white tips. Forest and secondary growth.

7 BLACK-THROATED SUNBIRD *Aethopyga saturata* 11 cm
Male (7a) and female (7b). Resident. Himalayas and NE India. Male has black throat and breast, greyish-olive underparts, and crimson mantle. Female has dusky olive-green underparts, yellow rump and longish bill. Bushes in forest and secondary growth.

8 CRIMSON SUNBIRD *Aethopyga siparaja* 11 cm
Male (8a) and female (8f) *A. s. seheriae*; **male (8b), eclipse male? (8c) and female (8d)** *A. s. vigorsii*; **male (8e)** *A. s. nicobarica*. Resident. Himalayas, hills of India and Bangladesh; also N and NE plains in winter. Male has crimson mantle, scarlet throat and breast, and grey or yellowish-olive belly. Female has yellowish-olive to grey underparts; lacks yellow rump and prominent white on tail. Eclipse male/female can show red throat and breast. Males of *vigorsii* (Western Ghats) and *nicobarica* (Nicobars) lack greatly elongated central tail feathers. Bushes in forest, and groves.

9 FIRE-TAILED SUNBIRD *Aethopyga ignicauda* 12 cm
Male (9a), eclipse male (9b) and female (9c). Resident. Himalayas and NE Indian hills. Male has red uppertail-coverts and red on tail. Female has yellowish belly, yellowish wash to rump, brownish-orange tail sides (which lack white at tip). Breeds in rhododendron shrubberies; winters in broadleaved and mixed forest.

10 LITTLE SPIDERHUNTER *Arachnothera longirostra* 16 cm
Adult. Resident. E Himalayan foothills, hills of India and Bangladesh and adjacent plains. Very long downcurved bill, unstreaked upperparts, yellowish underparts. Wild bananas in moist broadleaved forest.

11 STREAKED SPIDERHUNTER *Arachnothera magna* 19 cm
Adult. Resident. Mainly Himalayas and NE India. Very long downcurved bill, and boldly streaked upperparts and underparts. Moist broadleaved forest.

1 HOUSE SPARROW *Passer domesticus* 15 cm
Male (1a) and female (1b). Widespread resident, except in parts of NE and NW sub-continent. Male has grey crown, black throat and upper breast, chestnut nape, and brownish mantle. Female has buffish supercilium and unstreaked greyish-white under-parts. Breeds in habitation; also cultivation in winter.

2 SPANISH SPARROW *Passer hispaniolensis* 15.5 cm
Male breeding (2a), male non-breeding (2b) and female (2c). Winter visitor. Pakistan, Nepal and N India. Male has chestnut crown, black breast and streaking on flanks, and blackish mantle with pale 'braces'; pattern obscured by pale fringes in non-breeding season. Female told from female House Sparrow by longer whitish supercilium, fine streaking on underparts, and pale 'braces'. Cultivation, semi-desert and reedbeds.

3 SIND SPARROW *Passer pyrrhonotus* 13 cm
Male (3a) and female (3b). Resident. Pakistan and NW India. Smaller and slimmer than House, with finer bill. Male told from male House by chestnut on head restricted to crescent around ear-coverts; also grey ear-coverts, and small black throat patch. Female from female House by more prominent buffish-white supercilium, greyish ear-coverts, and warmer buffish-brown lower back and rump. Trees close to water.

4 RUSSET SPARROW *Passer rutilans* 14.5 cm
Male (4a) and female (4b). Resident. Himalayas and NE Indian hills. Male lacks black cheek patch; has bright chestnut mantle, and yellowish wash to underparts. Female has prominent supercilium and dark eye-stripe, rufous-brown scapulars and rump, and yellowish wash to underparts. Open forest, forest edges and cultivation.

5 DEAD SEA SPARROW *Passer moabiticus* 12.25 cm
Male (5a) and female (5b). Winter visitor. Baluchistan. Male has grey head with prominent buff supercilium and white submoustachial stripe; wing-coverts largely chestnut, and has yellow wash to underparts. Female has indistinct yellowish patch on neck, sandy-buff upperparts and yellow wash to underparts. Bushes near streams.

6 EURASIAN TREE SPARROW *Passer montanus* 14 cm
Adult *P. m. malaccensis* (6a); adult *P. m. dilutus* (6b). Resident. Baluchistan, Himalayas, NE India, Eastern Ghats and Bangladesh. Chestnut crown, and black spot on ear-coverts. Sexes similar. Birds in NW are paler than those in NE. Habitation and cultivation.

YELLOW THROATED

7 CHESTNUT-SHOULDERED PETRONIA *Petronia xanthocollis* 13.5 cm
Male (7a) and female (7b). Resident. Pakistan, Nepal and Indian peninsula. Unstreaked brownish-grey head and upperparts, and prominent wing-bars. Male and some females have yellow on throat. Male with chestnut lesser coverts and white wing-bars; lesser coverts brown and wing-bars buff in female. Open dry forest and scrub.

8 ROCK SPARROW *Petronia petronia* 17 cm
Adult (8a) and juvenile (8b). Winter visitor. Pakistan. Striking head pattern, including pale crown-stripe. Has whitish patch at base of primaries and tip to tail. Dry stony ground in mountains.

9 TIBETAN SNOWFINCH *Montifringilla adamsi* 17 cm
Adult (9a) and juvenile (9b). Resident. N Himalayas. Largely white or buffish-white wing-coverts. Adult has black throat, but head otherwise rather plain grey-brown. Rocky high-altitude semi-desert.

10 WHITE-RUMPED SNOWFINCH *Pyrgilauda taczanowskii* 17 cm
Adult. Resident? and winter visitor. N Himalayas. White rump, black lores, white supercilium and throat, and streaked greyish upperparts. Rocky high-altitude semi-desert.

11 SMALL SNOWFINCH *Pyrgilauda davidiana* 15 cm
Adult. [One published record, now considered doubtful. Small size, black forehead and throat, sandy-brown nape, white patch on primary coverts, and streaked mantle. High-altitude semi-desert.]

12 RUFOUS-NECKED SNOWFINCH *Pyrgilauda ruficollis* 15 cm
Adult. Resident? N Himalayas. Cinnamon nape and neck sides, rufous patch at rear of ear-coverts, black malar stripe and white throat, and prominent wing-bars. High-altitude semi-desert and grassy plateaux.

13 PLAIN-BACKED SNOWFINCH *Pyrgilauda blanfordi* 15 cm
Adult. Resident? and winter visitor. N Himalayas. Cinnamon nape and neck sides, black 'spur' dividing white supercilium, black throat; lacks wing-bars. High-altitude semi-desert.

PLATE 142: WAGTAILS

1 FOREST WAGTAIL *Dendronanthus indicus* 18 cm
Adult. Mainly a winter visitor to NE and SW India, Bangladesh and Sri Lanka; breeds in Assam. Broad yellowish-white wing-bars, double black breast-band, olive upperparts, white supercilium, and whitish underparts. Paths and clearings in forest.

2 WHITE WAGTAIL *Motacilla alba* 19 cm Table p. 371
Male breeding (2a), male non-breeding (2b) and juvenile (2c) *M. a. alboides*; **male breeding (2d) and 1st-winter (2e)** *M. a. personata*; **male** *M. a. leucopsis* **(2f)**; **male** *M. a. ocularis* **(2g)**; **male** *M. a. baicalensis* **(2h)**; **male** *M. a. dukhunensis* **(2i).** Breeds in Himalayas; widespread in winter. Extremely variable. Head pattern and mantle colour (grey or black) indicate racial identification of breeding males. Non-breeding and first-winter birds often not racially distinguishable. Never has head pattern of adult White-browed. Breeds by running waters in open country; winters near water in open country.

3 WHITE-BROWED WAGTAIL *Motacilla maderaspatensis* 21 cm
LARGE PIED **Adult (3a) and juvenile (3b).** Widespread resident. Large black-and-white wagtail. Head black with white supercilium, and has black mantle. Juvenile has brownish-grey head, mantle and breast, with white supercilium. Freshwater wetlands.

4 CITRINE WAGTAIL *Motacilla citreola* 19 cm
Male breeding (4a), adult female (4b), juvenile (4c) and 1st-winter (4d, 4e) *M. c. calcarata*; **male breeding** *M. c. citreola* **(4f).** Breeds in Baluchistan and Himalayas; widespread in winter. Broad white wing-bars in all plumages. Male breeding has yellow head and underparts, and black or grey mantle. Female breeding and adult non-breeding have broad yellow supercilium continuing around ear-coverts, grey upperparts, and mainly yellow underparts. Juvenile lacks yellow; has brownish upperparts, buffish supercilium (with dark upper edge) and ear-covert surround, and spotted black gorget. First-winter has grey upperparts; white surround to ear-coverts, dark border to supercilium, pale brown forehead, pale lores, all-dark bill, and white undertail-coverts are good features from first-winter Yellow; by early November, has yellowish supercilium, ear-covert surround and throat. Breeds in high-altitude wet grassland; winters at freshwater wetlands.

5 YELLOW WAGTAIL *Motacilla flava* 18 cm Table p. 371
Male breeding (5a), adult female (5b), juvenile (5c) and 1st-winter (5d) *M. f. beema*; **male** *M. f. leucocephala* **(5e)**; **male (5f) and 1st-winter (5g)** *M. f. lutea*; **male** *M. f. melanogrisea* **(5h)**; **male** *M. f. superciliaris* **(5i)**; **male** *M. f. zaissanensis* **(5j)**; **male** *M. f. plexa* **(5k)**; **male** *M. f. taivana* **(5l)**; **male (5m) and 1st-winter (5n)** *M. f. thunbergi.* Breeds in W Himalayas; widespread in winter. Male breeding has olive-green upperparts and yellow underparts, with considerable variation in coloration of head depending on race. Female extremely variable, but often some features of breeding male. First-winter birds typically have brownish-olive upperparts, and whitish underparts with variable yellowish wash; some can closely resemble Citrine, but have narrower white supercilium which does not continue around ear-coverts. See above for other differences. Damp grasslands.

6 GREY WAGTAIL *Motacilla cinerea* 19 cm
Male breeding (6a), adult female (6b) and juvenile (6c). Breeds in Baluchistan and Himalayas; widespread in winter. Longer-tailed than other wagtails. White supercilium, grey upperparts, and yellow vent and undertail-coverts. Male has black throat when breeding. Breeds by mountain streams; winters by slower streams in lowlands and foothills.

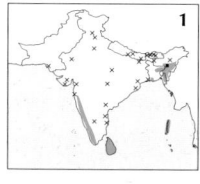 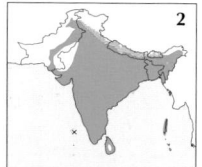 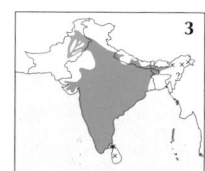 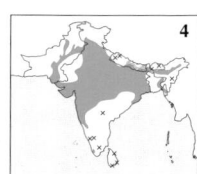

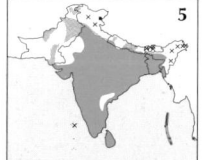 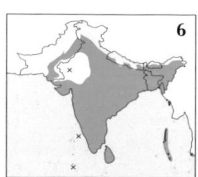

PLATE 143: LARGE PIPITS

1 RICHARD'S PIPIT *Anthus richardi* 17 cm
Adult (1a) and juvenile (1b). Widespread winter visitor. Large size and loud, explosive *schreep* call. Well-streaked upperparts and breast, pale lores, long and stout bill, and long hindclaw. When flushed, typically gains height and distance with deep undulations (compare with Paddyfield). Moist grassland and cultivation.

2 PADDYFIELD PIPIT *Anthus rufulus* 15 cm
Adult *A. r. waitei* (2a); adult (2b) and juvenile (2c) *A. r. rufulus.* Widespread resident, except in parts of NE and NW subcontinent. Smaller than Richard's, with *chip-chip-chip* call. Well-streaked breast; lores usually look pale. When flushed, has comparatively weak, rather fluttering flight. Short grassland and cultivation.

3 TAWNY PIPIT *Anthus campestris* 16 cm
Adult (3a), 1st-winter (3b) and juvenile (3c). Winter visitor. Mainly Pakistan and NW India. Loud *tchilip* or *chep* call. Adult and first-winter have plain or faintly streaked upperparts and breast. Juvenile more heavily streaked; useful features are dark lores, comparatively fine bill, rather horizontal stance, and wagtail-like behaviour. Stony semi-desert and fallow cultivation.

4 BLYTH'S PIPIT *Anthus godlewskii* 16.5 cm
Adult (4a) and 1st-winter (4b). Widespread winter visitor. Call a wheezy *spzeeu.* Smaller than Richard's, with shorter tail and shorter and more pointed bill. Shape of centres to adult median coverts distinctive if seen well, but this feature of no use in first-winter and juvenile plumage; have square-shaped, well-defined black centres with broad pale tips; centres to median coverts more triangular in shape, and more diffuse in Richard's. Pale lores and well-streaked breast useful distinctions from Tawny. Grassland and cultivation.

5 LONG-BILLED PIPIT *Anthus similis* 20 cm
Adult *A. s. jerdoni* (5a); adult *A. s. travancoriensis* (5b). Resident. Hills of Pakistan and India, and W Himalayan foothills; also N plains in winter. Call is a deep *chup*, and loud ringing *che-vlee*. Considerably larger than Tawny, with very large bill and shorter-looking legs. Dark lores. Marked racial variation. Northern races (e.g. *jerdoni*) have greyish upperparts and warm buff colour to unstreaked or only lightly streaked underparts. Southern races (e.g. *travancoriensis*) darker grey-brown on upperparts and warm rufous-buff on underparts, with breast more heavily streaked/spotted. Breeds on rocky or scrubby slopes; winters in dry cultivation and scrub.

6 UPLAND PIPIT *Anthus sylvanus* 17 cm
Adult (6a, 6b). Resident. Pakistan hills and Himalayas. Large, heavily streaked pipit with short and broad bill, and rather narrow, pointed tail feathers. Fine black streaking on underparts, whitish supercilium; ground colour of underparts varies from warm buff to rather cold and grey. Call is a sparrow-like *chirp.* Rocky and grassy slopes, and abandoned cultivation.

7 NILGIRI PIPIT *Anthus nilghiriensis* 17 cm
Adult. Resident. SW Indian hills. Large, heavily streaked pipit. Compared with Paddyfield, has shorter tail, more heavily streaked upperparts, and streaked upper belly and flanks, and lacks malar stripe and patch. Call a weak *see-see*, quite unlike Paddyfield's. Grassy slopes.

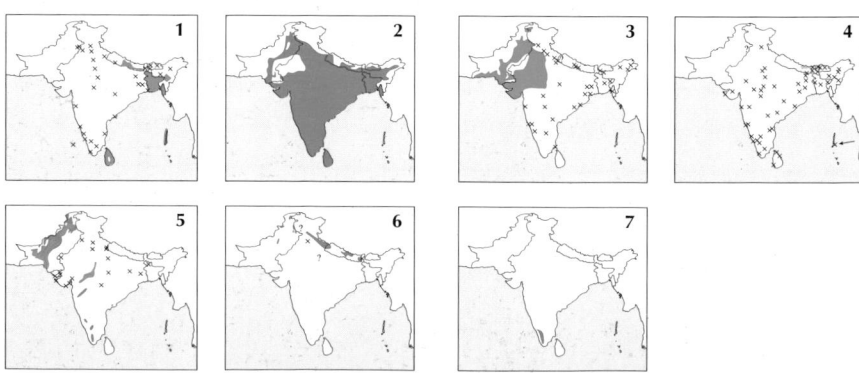

PLATE 144: PIPITS

1 TREE PIPIT *Anthus trivialis* 15 cm
Adult A. t. trivialis (1a); adult A. t haringtoni (1b). Resident and winter visitor. Breeds in NW Himalayas; widespread in winter; unrecorded in Sri Lanka. Buffish-brown to greyish ground colour to upperparts (lacking greenish-olive cast), and buffish fringes to greater coverts, tertials and secondaries. *A. t. haringtoni*, which breeds in NW, generally colder and greyer than nominate. Breeds on grassy slopes at treeline; winters in fallow cultivation and open country.

2 OLIVE-BACKED PIPIT *Anthus hodgsoni* 15 cm
Adult fresh (2a) and worn (2b) A. h. hodgsoni; adult A. h. yunnanensis (2c). Resident and winter visitor. Breeds in Himalayas; widespread in winter, except NW and SE subcontinent. Greenish-olive cast to upperparts, and greenish-olive fringes to greater coverts, tertials and secondaries. Typically, has more striking head pattern than Tree Pipit. *A .h. yunnanensis*, a widespread winter visitor, much less heavily streaked on upperparts than nominate race (and even less so than Tree). Open forest and shrubberies.

3 MEADOW PIPIT *Anthus pratensis* 15 cm
Adult. Vagrant. Pakistan. Call a soft *sip-sip-sip*. Subtle differences from Tree are slimmer build, slimmer and weaker bill, and less boldly streaked breast but more boldly streaked flanks. Lacks prominent white supercilium, broad white wing-bars and distinct greenish edges to tertials and secondaries of Rosy Pipit. Open grassy areas.

4 RED-THROATED PIPIT *Anthus cervinus* 15 cm
Adult male breeding (4a) and 1st-year (4b). Winter visitor. Mainly N subcontinent. Adult has reddish throat and upper breast, which tend to be paler on female and on autumn/winter birds. First-year has heavily streaked upperparts, pale 'braces', well-defined white wing-bars, strongly contrasting blackish centres and whitish fringes to tertials, pronounced dark malar patch, and more boldly streaked breast and (especially) flanks. Call a drawn-out *seeeeee*. Marshes, grassland and stubble.

5 ROSY PIPIT *Anthus roseatus* 15 cm
Adult breeding (5a, 5b) and non-breeding (5c). Breeds in high Himalayas; winters in plains and foothills in N subcontinent. Always has boldly streaked upperparts, olive cast to mantle, and olive to olive-green edges to greater coverts, secondaries and tertials. Adult breeding has mauve-pink wash to underparts. Heavily streaked underparts and dark lores in non-breeding plumage. Call a weak *seep-seep*. Breeds on slopes above treeline; winters in marshes, damp grassland and cultivation.

6 WATER PIPIT *Anthus spinoletta* 15 cm
Adult breeding (6a) and non-breeding (6b). Winter visitor. Pakistan, N India and Nepal. In all plumages, has lightly streaked upperparts, lacks olive-green on wing, has dark legs, and usually has pale lores; underparts less heavily marked than on Rosy and Buff-bellied Pipits. Orange-buff wash to supercilium and underparts in breeding plumage. Marshes, wet grassland and cultivation.

7 BUFF-BELLIED PIPIT *Anthus rubescens* 15 cm
Adult breeding (7a) and non-breeding (7b). Winter visitor. Pakistan, N India and Nepal. In all plumages, has lightly streaked upperparts, lacks olive-green on wing, and has pale lores; underparts more heavily streaked, has pronounced malar, and upperparts darker and legs paler compared with Water Pipit. Marshes, wet grassland and cultivation.

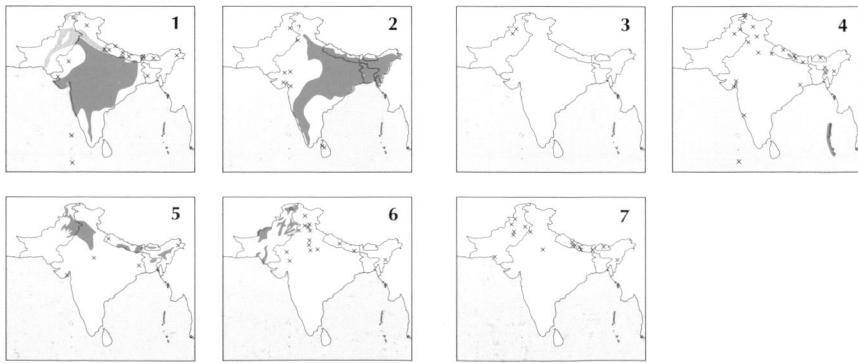

PLATE 145: ACCENTORS

1 **ALPINE ACCENTOR** *Prunella collaris* 15.5–17 cm
Adult (1a) and juvenile (1b). Resident. Himalayas. Black barring on throat, grey breast and belly, and black band across greater coverts. Open stony slopes and rocky pastures.

2 **ALTAI ACCENTOR** *Prunella himalayana* 15–15.5 cm
Adult. Winter visitor. Himalayas. White throat, with black gorget and spotting in malar region; white underparts, with rufous mottling on breast and flanks. Grassy and stony slopes and plateaux.

3 **ROBIN ACCENTOR** *Prunella rubeculoides* 16–17 cm
Adult (3a) and juvenile (3b). Resident. Himalayas. Uniform grey head, rusty-orange band across breast, and whitish belly. Juvenile similar to juvenile Rufous-breasted, but lacks streaking on belly. Breeds in dwarf scrub and sedge clumps; winters around upland villages.

4 **RUFOUS-BREASTED ACCENTOR** *Prunella strophiata* 15 cm
Adult (4a), 1st-winter? (4b) and juvenile (4c). Resident. Himalayas. Rufous band across breast, white-and-rufous supercilium, blackish ear-coverts, and streaking on neck sides and underparts. Juvenile similar to juvenile Robin Accentor, but has streaked belly. Breeds on high-altitude slopes; winters in bushes in cultivation and scrub.

5 **SIBERIAN ACCENTOR** *Prunella montanella* 15 cm
Adult. [One published record, now considered doubtful. Orange-buff supercilium and throat, rufous streaking on mantle and often on flanks. Scrub.]

6 **BROWN ACCENTOR** *Prunella fulvescens* 14.5–15 cm
Adult (6a) and juvenile (6b). Resident. N Himalayas. White supercilium, faintly streaked upperparts, and pale orange-buff underparts which are usually unstreaked. Dry scrubby and rocky slopes; also around upland villages in winter.

7 **BLACK-THROATED ACCENTOR** *Prunella atrogularis* 14.5–15 cm
Adult (7a) and 1st-winter female (7b). Winter visitor. W Himalayas. Orange-buff supercilium and submoustachial stripe, and black throat. Some have indistinct (or lack) black on throat, which instead is whitish; note heavily streaked mantle. Bushes near cultivation and dry scrub.

8 **RADDE'S ACCENTOR** *Prunella ocularis* 15–16 cm
Adult. Vagrant. Pakistan. Whitish supercilium, dark brown crown, heavily streaked mantle, spotted malar stripe, buffish breast-band, and streaked flanks. Some show no dark markings on malar and flanks. Shrubs by mountain streams.

9 **MAROON-BACKED ACCENTOR** *Prunella immaculata* 16 cm
Adult (9a) and juvenile (9b). Resident. C and E Himalayas. Grey head and breast, maroon-brown mantle, yellow iris, and grey panel across wing. Moist forest.

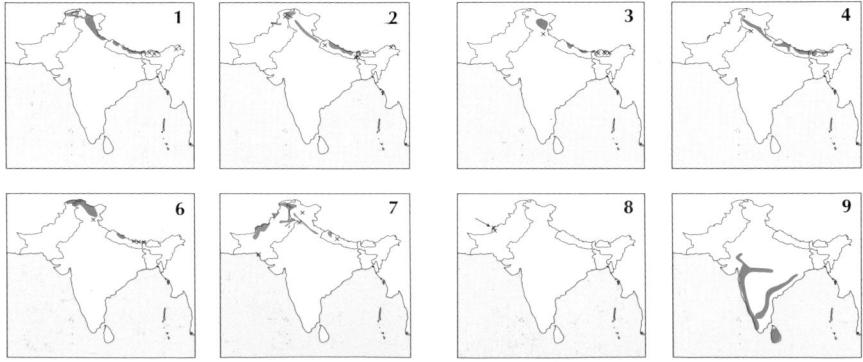

1a

2

1b

4a

3b

3a

4b

5

4c

7b

8

6a

6b

7a

9a

9b

Clive Byers

PLATE 146: WEAVERS AND AVADAVATS

1 **BLACK-BREASTED WEAVER** *Ploceus benghalensis* 14 cm
Male breeding (1a, 1b) and non-breeding (1c, 1d). Resident. Mainly Indus and Gangetic plains. Breeding male has yellow crown and black breast-band; interesting variant has white ear-coverts and throat. In female and non-breeding plumages, breast-band can be broken by whitish fringes or restricted to small patches at sides, and may show indistinct, diffuse streaking on lower breast and flanks; head pattern as on female/non-breeding Streaked, except crown, nape and ear-coverts more uniform; rump also indistinctly streaked and, like nape, contrasts with heavily streaked mantle/back. Tall moist grassland and reedy marshes.

2 **STREAKED WEAVER** *Ploceus manyar* 14 cm
Male breeding (2a), male non-breeding (2b) and female (2c). Widespread local resident. Breeding male has yellow crown, dark brown head sides and throat, and heavily streaked breast and flanks. Other plumages typically show boldly streaked underparts; can be only lightly streaked on underparts, when best told from Baya by combination of yellow supercilium and neck patch, heavily streaked crown, dark or heavily streaked ear-coverts, and pronounced dark malar and moustachial stripes. Reedbeds.

3 **BAYA WEAVER** *Ploceus philippinus* 15 cm
Male breeding (3a), male non-breeding (3b) and female (3c) *P. p. philippinus*; **male breeding (3d) and female (3e)** *P. p. burmanicus*. Widespread resident; unrecorded in parts of NE and NW subcontinent. Breeding male *P. p. philippinus* has yellow crown, dark brown ear-coverts and throat, unstreaked yellow breast, and yellow on mantle and scapulars. Breeding male *burmanicus*, of NE subcontinent, has buff breast, and buff or pale grey throat. Female/non-breeding birds usually have unstreaked buff to pale yellowish underparts; can show streaking as prominent as on some poorly marked Streaked, but generally has less distinct and buffish supercilium, lacks yellow neck patch, and lacks pronounced dark moustachial and malar stripes. Head pattern of some (non-breeding males?) can, however, be rather similar to Streaked. Female *burmanicus* more rufous-buff on supercilium and underparts. Cultivation and grassland.

4 **FINN'S WEAVER** *Ploceus megarhynchus* 17 cm
Male breeding (4a), female breeding (4b) and adult non-breeding (4c). Resident. N India and SE Nepal. Large size and bill. Breeding male has yellow underparts and rump, and dark patches on breast (can show as complete breast-band). Breeding female has pale yellow to yellowish-brown head, and pale yellow to buffish-white underparts. Adult non-breeding and immature very similar to non-breeding Baya. Mainly grassland.

5 **RED AVADAVAT** *Amandava amandava* 10 cm
Male breeding (5a), female (5b) and juvenile (5c). Widespread resident, except in parts of NE, NW and E subcontinent. Breeding male mainly red with white spotting. Non-breeding male and female have red bill, red rump and uppertail-coverts, and white tips to wing-coverts and tertials. Juvenile lacks red in plumage; has buff wing-bars, pink bill-base, and pink legs and feet. Tall wet grassland and reedbeds.

6 **GREEN AVADAVAT** *Amandava formosa* 10 cm
Male (6a) and female (6b). Resident. Widespread in C India. Breeding male green and yellow, with red bill and barred flanks. Female much duller, with weak flank barring. Grass and low bushes, also tall grassland.

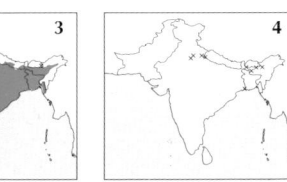
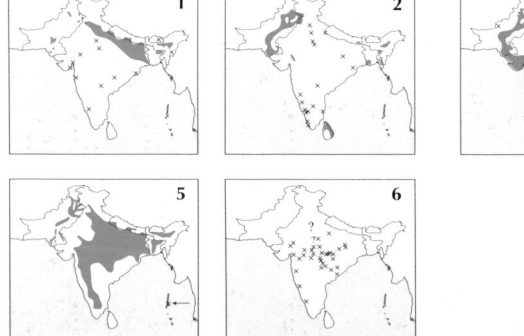

342

PLATE 147: MUNIAS AND FINCHES

1 INDIAN SILVERBILL *Lonchura malabarica* 11–11.5 cm
Adult (1a) and juvenile (1b). Widespread resident, except in NW and NE subcontinent and Himalayas. Adult has white rump and uppertail-coverts, black tail with elongated central feathers, and rufous-buff barring on flanks. Juvenile has buffish underparts, lacks flank barring, and has shorter tail. Dry cultivation, grassland and thorn scrub.

2 WHITE-RUMPED MUNIA *Lonchura striata* 10–11 cm
Adult *L. s. striata* (2a); adult *L. s. acuticauda* (2b). Resident. Himalayan foothills, NE India and Bangladesh, and C and S India and Sri Lanka. Dark breast and white rump. Southern *L. s. striata* has clean black throat and breast, and unstreaked creamy-white or white belly. Northern *acuticauda* has pale streaking on ear-coverts, rufous-brown to whitish fringes to brown breast, and dingy underparts with faint streaking. Open wooded areas and scrub.

3 BLACK-THROATED MUNIA *Lonchura kelaarti* 12 cm
Adult (3a) and immature (3b) *L. k. kelaarti*; adult *L. k. jerdoni* (3c). Resident. Hills of SW and E India, and Sri Lanka. Blackish face, throat and upper breast, and pinkish-cinnamon sides of neck and breast; underparts pinkish-cinnamon (*jerdoni*) or barred white and dark brown (*kelaarti* of Sri Lanka). Juvenile lacks black on head and breast and has uniform upperparts. Forest clearings, scrub and grassland.

4 SCALY-BREASTED MUNIA *Lonchura punctulata* 10.7–12 cm
Adult (4a) and juvenile (4b) *L. p. punctulata*. Widespread resident; unrecorded in parts of the northwest. Adult has chestnut throat and upper breast, and whitish underparts with dark scaling. Juvenile has brown upperparts and buffish underparts; bill black. Open forest, bushes and cultivation.

5 BLACK-HEADED MUNIA *Lonchura malacca* 11.5 cm
Adult (5a) and juvenile (5b) *L. m. malacca*; adult *L. m. atricapilla* (5c). Widespread resident in NE, E, C and S subcontinent. Black head, neck and upper breast, rufous-brown upperparts, and black belly centre and undertail-coverts. Lower breast and flanks are white in nominate of peninsula and Sri Lanka, chestnut in races of N and NE. Juvenile has uniform brown upperparts and buff to whitish underparts; bill blue-grey. Cultivation, marshes and tall grassland.

6 JAVA SPARROW *Lonchura oryzivora* 12.5–13 cm
Adult (6a) and juvenile (6b). Introduced resident. Mainly around Colombo, Sri Lanka. Adult mainly grey, with pinkish-red bill, and black crown and throat contrasting with white cheeks. Juvenile much duller, with dusky white cheeks and pink base to grey bill. Cultivation and reedbeds.

7 CHAFFINCH *Fringilla coelebs* 16 cm
Male non-breeding (7a) and female (7b). Winter visitor. Pakistan hills and N Himalayas. White wing-bars; lacks white rump. Male has blue-grey crown and nape, orange-pink face and underparts, and maroon-brown mantle. Female dull, with greyish-brown mantle and greyish-buff underparts. Upland fields with nearby bushes and forest.

8 BRAMBLING *Fringilla montifringilla* 16 cm
Male breeding (8a), male non-breeding (8b) and female (8c). Winter visitor. Pakistan hills and N Himalayas. White rump and belly, and orange scapulars, breast and flanks. Patterning of head and mantle vary with sex and wear. Upland fields and nearby bushes and forest.

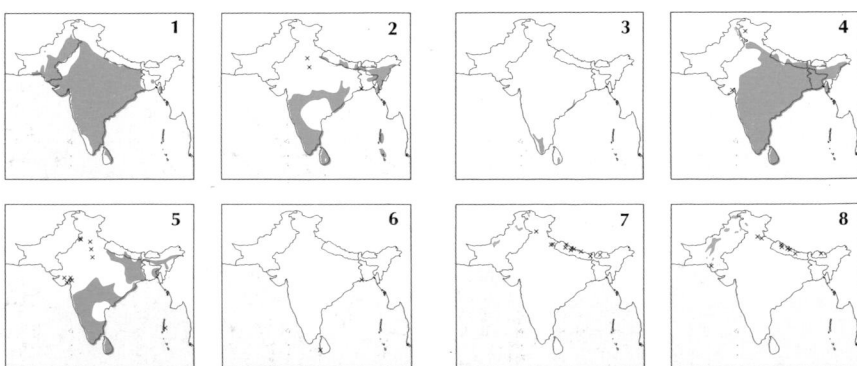

PLATE 148: FINCHES, INCLUDING MOUNTAIN FINCHES
Maps p. 348

1 FIRE-FRONTED SERIN *Serinus pusillus* 12.5 cm
Male (1a), female (1b) and juvenile (1c). Baluchistan mountains and W and C Himalayas. Adult has blackish head with scarlet forehead. Juvenile has cinnamon-brown head. Breeds in Tibetan steppe habitat; winters on stony and bushy slopes.

2 TIBETAN SISKIN *Carduelis thibetana* 12 cm
Male (2a) and female (2b). Breeds in E Himalayas?; winters in C and E Himalayas. Lacks large yellow patches on wing. Male mainly olive-green, with yellowish supercilium and underparts. Female heavily streaked, with indistinct yellowish wing-bars. Summers in mixed forest; winters in alders.

3 YELLOW-BREASTED GREENFINCH *Carduelis spinoides* 14 cm
Male (3a), female (3b) and juvenile (3c) *C. s. spinoides.* Resident. Himalayas and NE India. Yellow supercilium and underparts, dark ear-coverts and malar stripe, and yellow patches on wing. Juvenile heavily streaked. Open forest, shrubberies and cultivation with nearby trees.

4 BLACK-HEADED GREENFINCH *Carduelis ambigua* 12.5–14 cm
Male (4a) and female (4b). Resident? N Arunachal Pradesh. Yellow wing patches and tail sides, greenish mantle, greyish-white greater-covert bar, and greyish underparts. Male has dull black head. Open forest and shrubberies.

5 EURASIAN SISKIN *Carduelis spinus* 11–12 cm
Male (5a) and female (5b). Vagrant. Nepal and India. Male has black crown and chin, and black-and-yellow wings. Female differs from female Tibetan Siskin in wing pattern and brighter yellow rump. Forest.

6 EUROPEAN GOLDFINCH *Carduelis carduelis* 13–15.5 cm
Male (6a) and juvenile (6b) *C. c. caniceps*; **male** *C. c. major* **(6c).** Resident and winter visitor. Pakistan hills and W and C Himalayas. Red face (lacking on juvenile), and black-and-yellow wings with white tertial markings. Head pattern distinct in larger *major*, which has been reported as a vagrant. Upland cultivation, shrubberies and open forest.

7 TWITE *Carduelis flavirostris* 13–13.5 cm
Male (7a) and female (7b) *C. f. rufostrigata*; **male** *C. f. montanella* **(7c).** Resident. N Himalayas. Rather plain and heavily streaked, with small yellowish bill, buff wing-bars, and white edges to remiges and rectrices. Male has pinkish rump. *C. f. montanella*, from westernmost Himalayas, is sandy-buff, and only lightly streaked below. High-altitude semi-desert.

8 EURASIAN LINNET *Carduelis cannabina* 13–14 cm
Male breeding (8a), male non-breeding (8b) and female (8c). Winter visitor. Mainly Pakistan Himalayas. Told from Twite by greyish crown and nape contrasting with browner mantle, whitish lower rump and uppertail-coverts, and larger greyish bill. Forehead and breast crimson on breeding male. Open stony slopes and upland meadows.

9 PLAIN MOUNTAIN FINCH *Leucosticte nemoricola* 15 cm
Adult breeding (9a) and juvenile (9b). Resident. Himalayas. Told from Brandt's by boldly streaked mantle with pale 'braces', and distinct patterning on wing-coverts (dark-centred, with well-defined wing-bars). Juvenile warmer rufous-buff than adult. Breeds on alpine slopes; winters in open forest and upland cultivation.

10 BRANDT'S MOUNTAIN FINCH *Leucosticte brandti* 16.5–19 cm
Male breeding (10a) and 1st-summer (10b). Resident. Himalayas. Unstreaked to lightly streaked mantle, and rather uniform wing-coverts. More striking white panel on wing and more prominent white edges to tail compared with Plain. Adult breeding has sooty-black head and nape, and brownish-grey mantle with poorly defined streaking. Male has pink on rump. Alpine slopes.

PLATE 148, p. 346

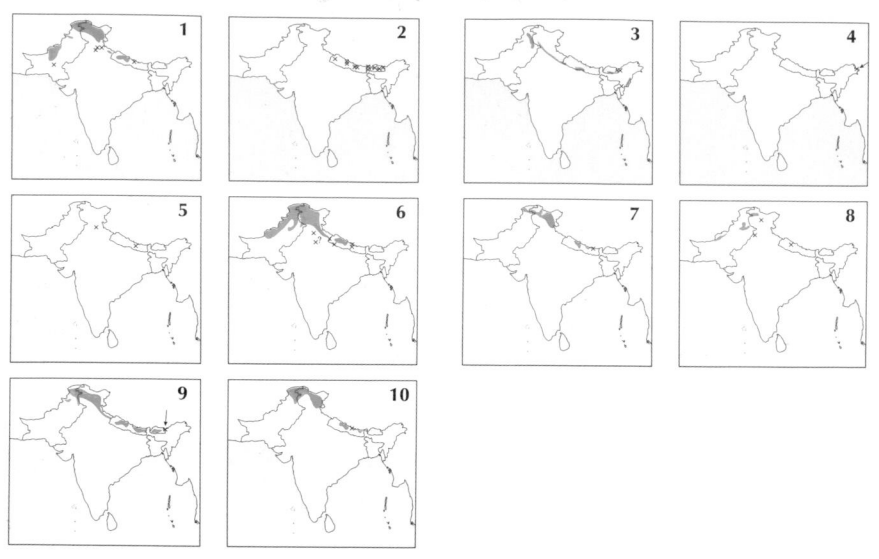

PLATE 149, p. 350

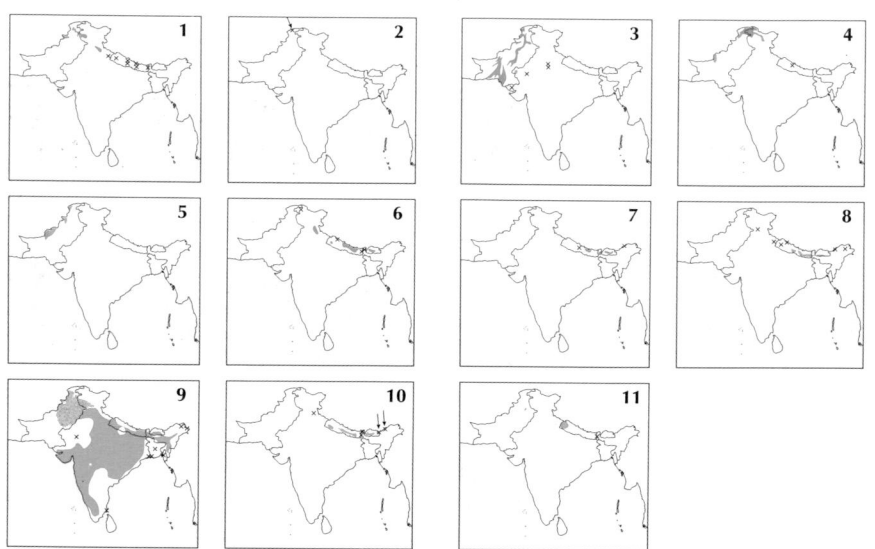

PLATE 150, p. 352

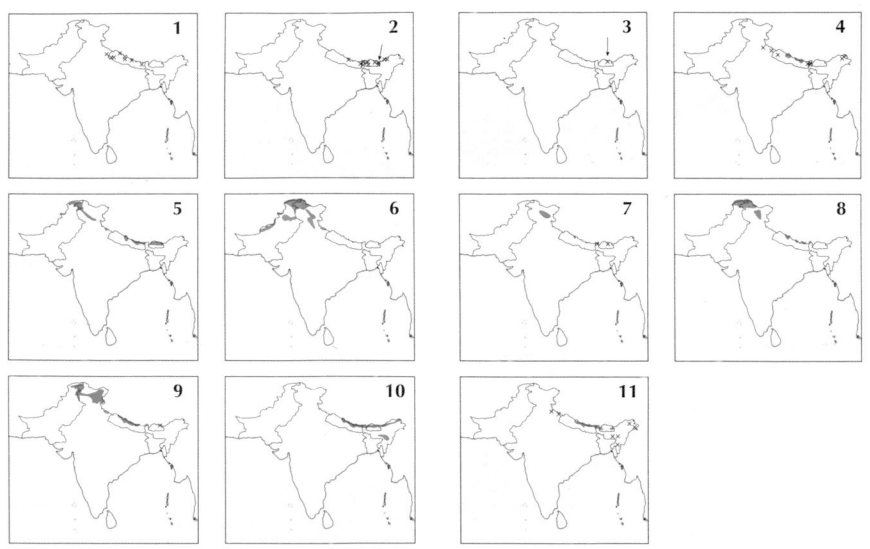

PLATE 151, p. 354

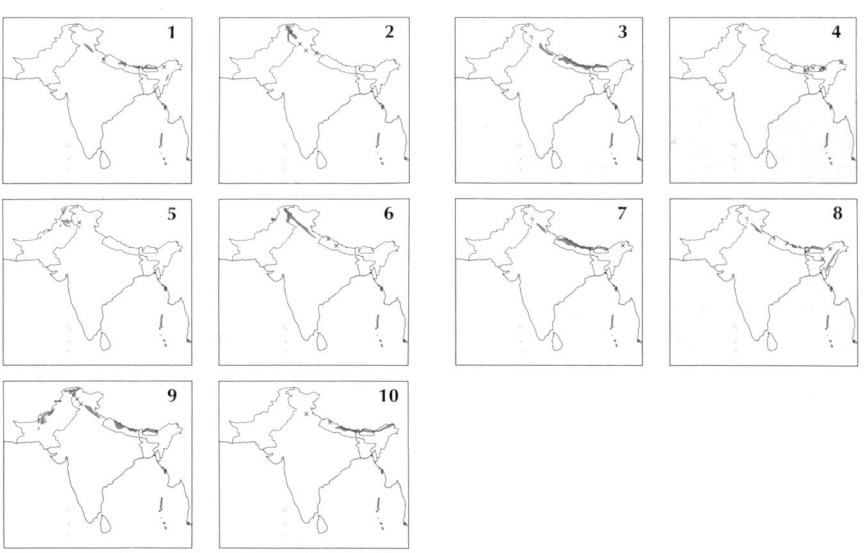

PLATE 149: FINCHES, INCLUDING ROSEFINCHES   Maps p. 348

1 **SPECTACLED FINCH** *Callacanthis burtoni* 17–18 cm
Male (1a) and female (1b). Resident. Himalayas. Black wings with white tips to feathers. Blackish head with red (male) or orange-yellow (female) 'spectacles'. Juvenile has browner head with buff eye-patch, and buffish wing-bars. Open mixed forest.

2 **CRIMSON-WINGED FINCH** *Rhodopechys sanguinea* 15–18 cm
Male (2a) and female (2b). Vagrant. Pakistan. Stout yellowish bill, pink on wing, dark cap, streaked brown mantle, and brown breast and white belly. Vagrants found in alpine grassland.

3 **TRUMPETER FINCH** *Bucanetes githagineus* 14–15 cm
Male (3a) and juvenile (3b). Resident in Pakistan; winter visitor to NW India. Stocky, with very stout pinkish or yellow bill. Comparatively uniform wings and tail show traces of pink (except on juvenile). Dry rocky hills and semi-desert.

4 **MONGOLIAN FINCH** *Bucanetes mongolicus* 14–15 cm
Male (4a) and female (4b). Resident in Pakistan and Ladakh; winter visitor to Baluchistan and Nepal. Whitish panels at bases of greater coverts and secondaries (which can be rather indistinct), whitish outer edges to tail, and bill is less stout than Trumpeter's. Dry stony slopes.

5 **DESERT FINCH** *Rhodospiza obsoleta* 14.5–15 cm
Male breeding (5a) and female (5b). Resident. Baluchistan. Pink edges to wing-coverts and secondaries, white edges to remiges and outer edges to tail, and black centres to tertials. Adult breeding has black bill. Male has black lores. Dry steppe with scattered forest.

6 **RED CROSSBILL** *Loxia curvirostra* 16–17 cm
Male (6a), female (6b) and juvenile (6c). Resident. Himalayas. Dark bill with crossed mandibles. Male rusty-red. Female olive-green, with brighter rump. Juvenile heavily streaked; mandibles initially not crossed. Coniferous forest.

7 **BLANFORD'S ROSEFINCH** *Carpodacus rubescens* 15 cm Table p. 372–3
Male (7a) and female (7b). Resident. C and E Himalayas. Slimmer bill than Common; male has more uniform head, duller crimson crown, and often distinct greyish cast to underparts. Female plain, lacks supercilium, has uniform wings and upperparts, and reddish or bright olive cast to rump and uppertail-coverts. Glades in coniferous and mixed forest.

8 **DARK-BREASTED ROSEFINCH** *Carpodacus nipalensis* 15–16 cm
Table p. 372–3
Male (8a) and female (8b). Resident. Himalayas. Slim, with slender bill. Male has maroon-brown breast-band, dark eye-stripe, and maroon-brown upperparts with indistinct dark streaking. Female has unstreaked underparts, lacks supercilium, and has streaked mantle, buffish wing-bars and tips to tertials, and olive-brown rump and uppertail-coverts. Breeds in high-altitude shrubberies; winters in forest clearings.

9 **COMMON ROSEFINCH** *Carpodacus erythrinus* 14.5–15 cm Table p. 372–3
Male (9a) and female (9b) *C. e. roseatus*; **male (9c) and female (9d)** *C. e. erythrinus.*
Breeds in Baluchistan and Himalayas; widespread in winter; unrecorded in Sri Lanka. Compact, with short, stout bill. Male has red head, breast and rump. Female has streaked upperparts and underparts, and double wing-bar. Migrant nominate race has less red in male, and female is less heavily streaked compared with resident race. Breeds in high-altitude shrubberies and open forest; winters in cultivation with bushes.

10 **BEAUTIFUL ROSEFINCH** *Carpodacus pulcherrimus* 15 cm Table p. 372–3
Male (10a) and female (10b) *C. p. pulcherrimus.* Resident. Himalayas. Male has pale lilac-pink supercilium, rump and underparts; upperparts grey-brown and heavily streaked. Female has poorly defined supercilium and heavily streaked underparts. Breeds in high-altitude shrubberies; winters on bush-covered slopes and cultivation with bushes.

11 **PINK-BROWED ROSEFINCH** *Carpodacus rodochrous* 14–15 cm
Table p. 372–3
Male (11a) and female (11b). Resident. Himalayas. Male has deep pink supercilium and underparts, and crimson crown. Female has buff supercilium and fulvous ground colour to rump, belly and flanks. Breeds in high-altitude shrubberies and open forest; winters in oak forest and on bushy slopes.

1 **VINACEOUS ROSEFINCH** *Carpodacus vinaceus* 13–16 cm Table p. 372–3
Male (1a) and female (1b). Resident? Nepal and Indian Himalayas. Male dark crimson, with pink supercilium and pinkish-white tips to tertials. Female lacks supercilium; has whitish tips to tertials, and streaked underparts. Understorey in moist forest.

2 **DARK-RUMPED ROSEFINCH** *Carpodacus edwardsii* 16–17 cm Table p. 372–3
Male (2a) and female (2b). Resident. C and E Himalayas. Male has pink supercilium and dark rump; maroon breast and flanks contrast with pink throat and belly. Female has narrow buff supercilium, pale tips to tertials, and brownish-buff underparts with lightly streaked throat and breast. High-altitude shrubberies and open forest; favours rhododendron.

3 **THREE-BANDED ROSEFINCH** *Carpodacus trifasciatus* 17–19.5 cm
Table p. 372–3
Male (3a) and female (3b). Vagrant. Bhutan. Both sexes have broad double wing-bars and white band down scapulars. Crimson of male's plumage replaced by orange-yellow on male. Upland village fields.

4 **SPOT-WINGED ROSEFINCH** *Carpodacus rodopeplus* 15 cm Table p. 372–3
Male (4a) and female (4b). Resident. Nepal and Indian Himalayas. Male has pink supercilium and underparts, maroon upperparts, and pinkish tips to wing-coverts and tertials. Female has prominent buff supercilium, buff tips to tertials, and fulvous underparts with bold streaking on throat and breast. Supercilium more prominent than in female Dark-rumped, with dark ear-coverts, paler and more heavily streaked throat, and more prominent wing-bars. Breeds in rhododendron shrubberies; winters in forest understorey.

5 **WHITE-BROWED ROSEFINCH** *Carpodacus thura* 17 cm Table p. 372–3
Male (5a) and female (5b) *C. t. thura*; **female** *C. t. feminus* **(5c).** Resident. Himalayas. Large size. Male has pink-and-white supercilium, pink rump and underparts, and heavily streaked brown upperparts. Female has prominent supercilium with dark eye-stripe, ginger-brown throat and breast (except northeastern *feminus*), and olive-yellow rump. Breeds in high-altitude shrubberies and open forest; winters on bushy hills.

6 **RED-MANTLED ROSEFINCH** *Carpodacus rhodochlamys* 18 cm Table p. 372–3
Male (6a) and female (6b). Resident. Pakistan mountains and W Himalayas. Large size and large bill. Male has pink supercilium and underparts, and pale grey-brown upperparts with pinkish wash. Female pale grey and heavily streaked, with indistinct supercilium. Breeds in dry high-altitude shrubberies and forest; winters in well-wooded areas.

7 **STREAKED ROSEFINCH** *Carpodacus rubicilloides* 19 cm Table p. 372–3
Male (7a) and female (7b). Resident. N Himalayas. Large size and long tail. Male has crimson-pink head and underparts and heavily streaked upperparts. Female lacks supercilium and has streaked upperparts. High-altitude semi-desert.

8 **GREAT ROSEFINCH** *Carpodacus rubicilla* 19–20 cm Table p. 372–3
Male (8a) and female (8b). Resident. N Himalayas. Large size and long tail. Male has pale pink head and underparts, and pale sandy-grey and lightly streaked upperparts. Female lacks supercilium, and has lightly streaked pale sandy-brown upperparts; centres to wing-coverts and tertials pale grey-brown (much darker brownish-black on female Streaked). High-altitude semi-desert.

9 **RED-FRONTED ROSEFINCH** *Carpodacus puniceus* 20 cm Table p. 372–3
Male (9a) and female (9b). Resident. N Himalayas. Large size, conical bill and short tail. On male, red of plumage contrasts with brown crown, eye-stripe and upperparts. Female lacks supercilium, is heavily streaked, and may show yellow/olive rump. High-altitude rocky slopes.

10 **CRIMSON-BROWED FINCH** *Propyrrhula subhimachala* 19–20 cm
Table p. 372–3
Male (10a) and female (10b). Resident. Himalayas and NE India. Short, stubby bill. Male has red forehead, throat and upper breast, greenish coloration to upperparts, and greyish underparts. Female has olive-yellow forehead and supercilium, greyish belly and greenish-olive upperparts. Breeds in high-altitude shrubberies; winters in forest undergrowth.

11 **SCARLET FINCH** *Haematospiza sipahi* 18 cm
Male (11a), female (11b) and immature male (11c). Resident. Himalayas and NE India. Male scarlet. Female olive-green, with yellow rump. First-summer male has orange rump. Broadleaved forest.

PLATE 151: BULLFINCHES AND GROSBEAKS   Maps p. 349

1 BROWN BULLFINCH *Pyrrhula nipalensis* 16–17 cm
Adult (1a) and juvenile (1b). Resident. Himalayas and NE India. Adult has grey-brown mantle, grey underparts, narrow white rump, and long tail. Juvenile has brownish-buff upperparts and warm buff underparts, and lacks adult head pattern. Dense moist forest.

2 ORANGE BULLFINCH *Pyrrhula aurantiaca* 14 cm
Male (2a), female (2b) and juvenile (2c). Resident. W Himalayas. Male has orange head and body and orange-buff wing-bars. Female has grey crown and nape. Juvenile similar to female, but lacks grey on head. Open coniferous and mixed forest.

3 RED-HEADED BULLFINCH *Pyrrhula erythrocephala* 17 cm
Male (3a), female (3b) and 1st-summer male (3c). Resident. Himalayas. Male has orange crown, nape and breast, and grey mantle. Female has yellow crown and nape. First-summer male has yellow breast. Mainly broadleaved forest.

4 GREY-HEADED BULLFINCH *Pyrrhula erythaca* 17 cm
Male (4a) and female (4b). Resident. E Himalayas. Male has grey crown and nape (con-colorous with mantle) and orange-red underparts. Female has grey crown and nape and brown mantle. Mixed forest and willow thickets.

5 HAWFINCH *Coccothraustes coccothraustes* 16–18 cm
Adult male. Winter visitor. Mainly Pakistan, also Jammu. Stocky, short-tailed and huge-billed. Mainly orange-brown, with pale wing-covert band and black chin. Wild olive forest and orchards.

6 BLACK-AND-YELLOW GROSBEAK *Mycerobas icterioides* 22 cm
Male (6a), female (6b) and juvenile male (6c). Resident. W Himalayas. Male usually lacks orange cast to mantle and rump; black of plumage duller than on Collared, and has black thighs. Female has pale grey head, mantle and breast, and peachy-orange rump and belly. Juvenile male has black wings and yellow rump. Coniferous forest.

7 COLLARED GROSBEAK *Mycerobas affinis* 22 cm
Male (7a), female (7b) and juvenile male (7c). Resident. Himalayas. Male has orange cast to mantle; black of plumage strongly glossed, and thighs yellow. Female has olive-yellow underparts and rump and greyish-olive mantle. Juvenile male duller than adult, with black mottling on mantle. Mixed forest.

8 SPOT-WINGED GROSBEAK *Mycerobas melanozanthos* 22 cm
Male (8a) and female (8b). Resident. Himalayas and NE India. Male has black rump and white markings on wings. Female yellow, boldly streaked with black; wing pattern similar to male's. Breeds in mixed forest; winters in broadleaved forest.

9 WHITE-WINGED GROSBEAK *Mycerobas carnipes* 22 cm
Male (9a) and female (9b). Resident. Pakistan mountains and Himalayas. White patch in wing. Male dull black and olive-yellow, with yellowish tips to greater coverts and ter-tials. Female similar, but black of plumage replaced by sooty-grey. Juniper shrubberies, and forest with junipers.

10 GOLD-NAPED FINCH *Pyrrhoplectes epauletta* 15 cm
Male (10a) and female (10b). Resident. Himalayas. Small, with fine bill. White 'stripe' down tertials. Male black, with orange crown and nape. Female has olive-green on head, grey mantle, and rufous-brown wing-coverts and underparts. Undergrowth in oak–rhododendron forest and rhododendron shrubberies.

1 CRESTED BUNTING *Melophus lathami* 17 cm
Male (1a), female (1b) and 1st-winter male (1c). Resident. Himalayan foothills and hills of NE and C India. Always has crest and chestnut on wing and tail; tail lacks white. Male has bluish-black head and body. Female and first-winter male streaked on upperparts and breast; first-winter male darker and more heavily streaked than female, with olive-grey ground colour to underparts. Dry rocky and grassy hillsides, and terraced cultivation.

2 YELLOWHAMMER *Emberiza citrinella* 16.5 cm
Male breeding (2a), male non-breeding (2b) and female (2c). Winter visitor. Nepal and Indian Himalayas. Chestnut rump and long tail. Most show yellow on head and underparts. Some first-winter females lack yellow, and are then very difficult to separate from female Pine, but belly never white, has less prominently streaked malar stripe and breast, and has yellowish (rather than whitish) edges to primaries and tail feathers. (Note that hybrids with Pine Bunting can show variety of intermediate characters.) Upland cultivation.

3 PINE BUNTING *Emberiza leucocephalos* 17 cm
Male breeding (3a), male non-breeding (3b) and female (3c). Winter visitor. Pakistan hills and Himalayas. Chestnut rump and long tail. Male has chestnut supercilium and throat, and whitish crown and ear-covert spot; pattern obscured in winter. Female has greyish supercilium and nape/neck sides, dark border to ear-coverts, usually some rufous on breast/flanks, and white belly. Fallow fields.

4 ROCK BUNTING *Emberiza cia* 16 cm
Male (4a) and female (4b) *E. c. stracheyi;* **male** *E. c. par* **(4c).** Resident. Breeds in Pakistan mountains and W Himalayas; winters down to adjacent plains. Male has grey head, black lateral crown-stripes and border to ear-coverts, and rufous underparts. Female duller. *E. c. par*, of extreme NW, paler than *stracheyi*. Breeds on dry grassy and rocky slopes; winters in lowland fallow cultivation.

5 GODLEWSKI'S BUNTING *Emberiza godlewskii* 17 cm
Male breeding (5a), male non-breeding (5b) and juvenile (5c). Resident. N Arunachal Pradesh. Greyish head with chestnut lateral crown-stripes and stripe behind eye. Wing-bars white. Dry rocky and bushy slopes.

6 GREY-NECKED BUNTING *Emberiza buchanani* 15 cm
Male (6a), female (6b) and 1st-winter (6c). Breeds in Baluchistan; winters mainly in Pakistan and C and W India. Pinkish-orange bill, plain head and whitish eye-ring. Adult has blue-grey head, buffish submoustachial stripe and throat, and rusty-pink underparts. First-winter and juvenile often with only slight greyish cast to head and buffish underparts; light streaking on breast. Dry rocky and bushy hills.

7 ORTOLAN BUNTING *Emberiza hortulana* 16 cm
Male (7a), female (7b) and 1st-winter (7c). Vagrant. Pakistan and India. Pinkish-orange bill, plain head and prominent eye-ring. Adult has olive-grey head and breast, and yellow submoustachial stripe and throat. Female streaked on crown and breast. First-winter and juvenile more heavily streaked on mantle, malar region and breast than Grey-necked; submoustachial stripe and throat are buffish, but often with touch of yellow which helps separate from Grey-necked. Orchards and open woodland.

8 WHITE-CAPPED BUNTING *Emberiza stewarti* 15 cm
Male breeding (8a), male non-breeding (8b) and female (8c). Breeds in Pakistan mountains and W Himalayas; winters in foothills and valleys of Pakistan and NC India. Male has grey head, black supercilium and throat, and chestnut breast-band; pattern obscured in winter. Female has rather plain head with pale supercilium; crown and mantle uniformly and diffusely streaked, and underparts finely streaked and washed with buff. Dry grassy and rocky slopes; also fallow fields in winter.

9 HOUSE BUNTING *Emberiza striolata* 13–14 cm
Male (9a) and female (9b). Resident. Pakistan and NW India. Has black eye-stripe and moustachial stripe, white supercilium and submoustachial stripe; throat and breast streaked, and underparts brownish-buff with variable rufous tinge. Female duller than male, with less striking head pattern. Lacks prominent white on tail (Rock has much white on outer tail feathers), and has orange lower mandible (bill all grey on Rock). Dry rocky hills; also sandy plains in winter.

PLATE 153: BUNTINGS

Maps p. 360

1 CHESTNUT-EARED BUNTING *Emberiza fucata* 16 cm
Male (1a), female (1b) and 1st-winter (1c). Resident and winter visitor. Breeds in W Himalayas; winters east to NE India and Bangladesh. Adult has chestnut ear-coverts, black breast streaking, and usually some chestnut on breast sides. Some first-winter birds rather nondescript, but plain head with warm brown ear-coverts and prominent eye-ring distinctive. Dry rocky and bushy hills.

2 LITTLE BUNTING *Emberiza pusilla* 13 cm
Adult (2a) and 1st-winter (2b). Winter visitor. Himalayas, NE India and Bangladesh. Small size. Chestnut ear-coverts (and often supercilium and crown-stripe), and lacks dark moustachial stripe. Fallow cultivation and meadows.

3 RUSTIC BUNTING *Emberiza rustica* 14–15 cm
Male breeding (3a) and 1st-winter (3b). Vagrant. Nepal. Striking head pattern, rufous streaking on breast, white belly, rufous on nape, and prominent white median-covert bar. Damp grassland.

4 YELLOW-BREASTED BUNTING *Emberiza aureola* 15 cm
Male breeding (4a), male non-breeding (4b), female (4c) and juvenile (4d). Winter visitor. Mainly Nepal, NE India and Bangladesh. Male has black face and chestnut breast-band (obscured when fresh), and white inner wing-coverts. Female has striking head pattern, boldly streaked mantle, and prominent white median-covert bar. Juvenile streaked on breast and flanks. Cultivation and grassland.

5 CHESTNUT BUNTING *Emberiza rutila* 14 cm
Male non-breeding (5a), female (5b) and 1st-winter male (5c). Winter visitor. Mainly NE India. Small size, chestnut rump, and little or no white on tail. Male has chestnut head and breast, which may be barely apparent in first-winter plumage. Female has buff throat and yellow underparts; head pattern less striking than on Yellow-breasted. Bushes near cultivation and forest clearings.

6 BLACK-HEADED BUNTING *Emberiza melanocephala* 16–18 cm
Male breeding (6a), male non-breeding (6b), worn female (6c) and immature (6d). Winter visitor to N, W and WC India and SE Nepal; passage migrant in Pakistan. Larger than Red-headed with longer bill. Male has black on head and chestnut on mantle. Female when worn may show ghost pattern of male; fresh female almost identical to Red-headed, but indicative features (although not always apparent) include rufous fringes to mantle and/or back, slight contrast between throat and greyish ear-coverts, and more uniform yellowish underparts. Immature with buff underparts and yellow undertail-coverts. Cereal crops.

7 RED-HEADED BUNTING *Emberiza bruniceps* 16 cm
Male breeding (7a), male non-breeding (7b), fresh female (7c) and immature (7d). Winter visitor, mainly to NW and WC India; passage migrant in Pakistan. Smaller than Black-headed, with shorter, more conical bill. Male has rufous on head and yellowish-green mantle. Female when worn may show rufous on head and breast, and yellowish to crown and mantle, and are distinguishable from female Black-headed. Fresh female has throat paler than breast, with suggestion of buffish breast-band; forehead and crown often virtually unstreaked (indicative features from Black-headed). Immature often not separable from Black-headed but may exhibit some features of fresh female. Cultivation.

8 BLACK-FACED BUNTING *Emberiza spodocephala* 15 cm
Male breeding (8a), male non-breeding (8b) and female (8c). Winter visitor. Mainly Nepal and NE India. Male has greenish-grey head with blackish lores and chin, and yellow underparts. Non-breeding male with yellow submoustachial stripe and throat. Female has yellowish supercilium, yellow throat, olive rump, and white on tail (compare with Chestnut Bunting). Long grass, paddy-fields and marsh edges.

9 REED BUNTING *Emberiza schoeniclus* 14–15 cm
Adult male breeding (9a) and female (9b) *E. s. pallidior;* **adult male non-breeding *E. s. pyrrhuloides* (9c).** Winter visitor. Pakistan and NW India. Male has black head and white submoustachial stripe; obscured by fringes when fresh. Female has buff supercilium, brown ear-coverts, and dark moustachial stripe. Reedbeds and irrigated crops.

10 CORN BUNTING *Miliaria calandra* 18 cm
Adult. Vagrant. Pakistan and India. Stocky and heavily streaked. Cultivation.

PLATE 152, p. 356

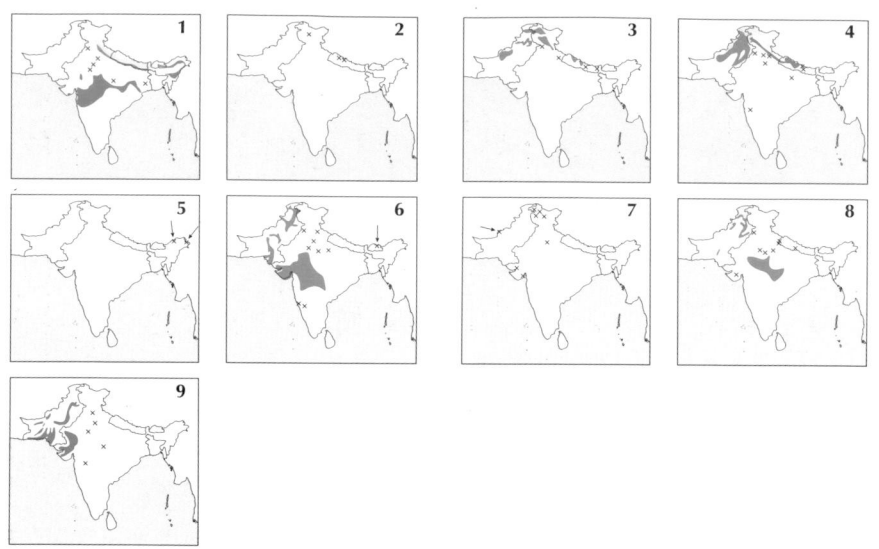

PLATE 153, p. 358

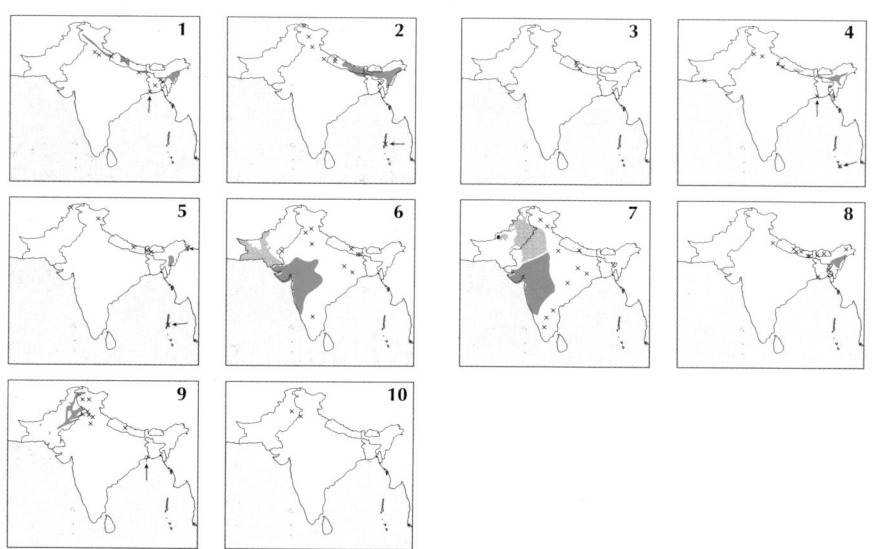

IDENTIFICATION OF NIGHTJARS

Species	Size and structure	General coloration	Crown/nape	Scapulars/wing-coverts	Primaries	Tail	White throat patch
Grey Nightjar I = *C. i. indicus* H = *C. i. hazarae*	Medium. Well-proportioned, longish wings and tail, and large head	I – Uniform cold grey to grey-brown, heavily marked with black. H – Dark grey-brown, heavily marked with black	Variable. Heavily to very heavily marked with black drop-shaped streaks; some with irregular patches of rufous on nape. Streaking less regular and more extensive than on Large-tailed	Scapulars heavily but irregularly marked with black, usually lacking well-defined buff or white edges (although pronounced pale edges may be prominent on some). Coverts with variable greyish-white to buffish spotting, usually poorly defined (I) or more rufous (H)	Male has small white spots on three or four primaries. On female, spots either lacking or small and rufous	I – Male variable, usually with white at tips of all but central tail feathers and with diffuse greyish margin at end. H – Male has more distinct blackish margin to white tips. Females of both races lack white on tail	Large central white spot on male, or buff in female
Eurasian Nightjar	Medium. Long wings and tail, and small head	Grey, neat lanceolate streaking	Regular, bold, black lanceolate streaking	Bold lanceolate streaking or scapulars, with buff outer edge. Well-defined, regular pale buff spots on coverts	Male has large white spots on three primaries, and female has no spots	Outermost two tail feathers have broad white tips on male. No white tips on female	Indistinct, but generally complete white throat crescent
Egyptian Nightjar	Medium. Long wings and tail, and large head	Sandy with fine dark vermiculations and buff mottling	Relatively unmarked with fine dark streaking and irregular mottling	Scapulars relatively poorly patterned with buff and with black inverted 'anchor-shaped' marks. Coverts with prominent irregular buff mottling	Male and female have no white spots	Tips on male are buff, but with no white tips	Generally has unbroken narrow white crescent
Sykes's Nightjar	Small. Shortish wings and tail, and large head	Grey, with buff mottling and restricted dark vermiculations. Some are as sandy as Egyptian	Variable, small dark arrowhead markings, more extensive than on Egyptian. Irregular buff spotting on nape gives suggestion of collar	Scapulars relatively unmarked (with a few black inverted 'anchor-shaped' marks). Coverts with irregular and small buff markings	Male has large white spots on three or four primaries. Female's primary spots are buffish	On male, two outermost pairs have broad white tips. On female, tail is unmarked or has buffish tip to outer tail	Broken, large white patches at sides; some have complete crescent
Indian Nightjar	Small. Short wings and tail, and small head	Grey, with bold buff, black and some rufous markings	Bold, broad, black streaking on crown. Nape marked with rufous-buff, forming distinct collar	Bold triangular black centres and broad rufous-buff fringes to scapulars. Coverts with bold buff- or rufous-buff spotting	Both sexes have small white or buffish spots on four primaries	Both sexes have broad white tips to outer two tail feathers	Generally broken. Large white patches at sides, lacking on some
Large-tailed Nightjar	Large. Long-winged with long broad tail, and large head	More warmly coloured than Grey, with buff-brown tones, heavily marked with black and buff	Brownish-grey, with bold black streaks down centre. Diffuse pale rufous-brown band across nape	Scapulars have well-defined buff edges with bold wedge-shaped black centres. Coverts boldly tipped buff	Male has white spots on four primaries. Female lacks these or has smaller buff spots	Male has extensive white tips to two outermost feathers. Female has less extensive buff tips to outer two feathers	Large central white throat patch on both sexes
Jerdon's Nightjar	Medium. Relatively short-winged and short-tailed, and large head	Warmly coloured, as Large-tailed, though generally darker	As Large-tailed. More extensive rufous-brown coloration to nape and upper mantle	Much as Large-tailed	As Large-tailed	As Large-tailed	As Large-tailed
Savanna Nightjar	Medium. Shortish wings and tail, and large head	Dark brownish-grey, intricately patterned (without bold, dark streaking), but with variable rufous-buff markings	Variable. Some only finely vermiculated, others with black, arrowhead markings and others with irregular-shaped black markings	Scapulars variably marked, but most show rufous-buff outer web. Coverts variably marked with rufous-buff, showing as distinct spotting on some	Male shows white spots on four primaries, with buff to rufous-buff wash on female	Outer two tail feathers are mainly white on male, but not on female	Large white patches at sides

SMALL TO MEDIUM-SIZED *PHYLLOSCOPUS* WARBLERS, LACKING WING-BARS AND CROWN STRIPE (+ = vagrant)

Species	Head pattern	Upperparts including wings	Underparts	Call	Additional features
Common Chiffchaff (excluding vagrant *P. c. collybita*)	Whitish or buffish supercilium, and prominent crescent below eye	Greyish to brownish with olive-green cast to rump and edges of remiges and rectrices	Whitish with variable buffish or greyish cast to breast sides and flanks	Plaintive *peu*, more disyllabic *sie-u*	Blackish bill and legs (compare with Willow, Greenish, and Dusky)
Mountain Chiffchaff	Whitish or buffish supercilium	Brownish to greyish-brown. Lacks olive-green tinge to rump, and to edges of remiges and rectrices (edges buffish)	Mainly whitish, often with warm buff coloration to ear-coverts, breast sides and flanks (usually more pronounced than in Common Chiffchaff)	Distinctly disyllabic *swe-eet*, or *tiss-yip*; sometimes almost three-noted *tiss-yuit*	Bend of wing whitish (usually brighter yellowish in Common Chiffchaff)
Plain Leaf Warbler	Whitish supercilium	Greyish-brown. Lacks greenish to upperparts; edges to remiges buffish	Whitish; buff to ear-coverts, breast sides and flanks less apparent than in Mountain Chiffchaff	A hard *tak-tak*, low-pitched *churr* or *chiip* and a *twissa-twissa*	Very small; short-looking tail
Willow Warbler+	Supercilium more prominent than in chiffchaffs, and pale crescent below eye less prominent; may show yellow to supercilium	Variable, olive-brown with yellowish-green tinge, to brownish grey and lacking greenish tinge	With yellowish wash, or whitish	Disyllabic *who-eet*	Legs/feet brownish or orangish; bill with orange on lower mandible (black in chiffchaffs)
Dusky Warbler	Broad, buffish-white supercilium with strong dark eye-stripe	Dark brown to paler greyish-brown; never shows any greenish in plumage	White with buff to sides of breast and flanks	Hard *chack chack*	Pale brown legs, and orangish base to lower mandible. Typically skulking
Smoky Warbler	Comparatively short and indistinct yellowish supercilium with prominent white eye crescent	Dark sooty-olive, with greenish tinge in fresh plumage	Mainly dusky-olive, almost concolorous with upperparts, with oily yellow centre to throat, breast and belly (lacking in *P. f. tibetanus*)	Throaty *thrup thrup*	Skulking
Tickell's Leaf Warbler	Prominent yellow supercilium concolorous with throat, well-defined eye-stripe	Dark greenish to greenish-brown upperparts, with greenish edges to remiges	Bright lemon-yellow underparts, lacking strong buff tones	A *chit*, or *sit*; not so hard as Dusky	
Buff-throated Warbler+?	Less prominent, buffish-yellow supercilium compared with Tickell's (and more uniform; often becomes paler toward rear in Tickell's). Eye-stripe is less distinct and contrasts less with ear-coverts	Greenish-brown	More yellowish-buff (paler on centre of belly) than Tickell's	Soft, rather weak *trrup* or *tripp*	Tip of lower mandible extensively dark; Tickell's has little or no dark tip
Sulphur-bellied Warbler	Prominent, bright sulphur-yellow supercilium, distinctly brighter than throat	Cold brown to brownish-grey lacking greenish tones, and with greyish edges to remiges	Yellowish-buff with strong buff tones to breast and flanks, and sulphur-yellow belly	Soft *quip* or *dip*	Climbs about rocks, or nuthatch-like on tree trunks
Radde's Warbler+	Long buffish-white supercilium, contrasting with dark eye-stripe. In fresh plumage, supercilium is buffish-yellow	Olive-brown. In fresh plumage can have pronounced greenish-olive cast	Whitish with buff wash to breast sides and flanks. In fresh plumage, can have buffish-yellow wash to entire underparts	A nervous *twit-twit*, and sharp *chuck chuck*	Long tail, sometimes cocked; stout and rather pale bill; thick and strong-looking orangish legs and feet
Tytler's Leaf Warbler	Prominent, fine white to yellowish-white supercilium, with broad dark olive eye-stripe	Greenish, becoming greyer when worn	Whitish, with variable yellowish wash when fresh	A double *y-it*	Long, slender mainly dark bill; shortish tail

MEDIUM-SIZED TO LARGE *PHYLLOSCOPUS* WARBLERS, WITH NARROW WING-BARS, AND LACKING CROWN STRIPE (+ – vagrant)

Note wing-bars may be missing when plumage is worn (when confusion possible with species in table on page 362)

Species	Head pattern	Upperparts including wings	Underparts	Bill	Call	Other features
Arctic Warbler+	Very prominent supercilium, which typically falls short of forehead; eye-stripe broad and dark and usually extends to base of bill	Greyish-green, generally lacking darker crown. One or two whitish wing-bars	Whitish, frequently with greyish wash, or diffuse grey streaking, to breast sides and flanks	Orangish lower mandible with distinct dark tip	A buzzing *dziit* or *dziip*	Legs and feet paler than those of Greenish and Large-billed, sometimes orangish
Greenish Warbler *P. t. viridanus / P. t. ludlowi*	Prominent yellowish-white supercilium, usually wide in front of eye and extends to forehead; eye-stripe, usually falls short of base of bill	Olive-green, becoming duller and greyer when worn; generally lacking darker crown. Single narrow but well-defined white wing-bar	Whitish with faint yellowish suffusion	Lower mandible orangish, usually lacking prominent dark tip	Loud, slurred *chit-wee*	
Greenish Warbler *P. t. nitidus*	Prominent yellowish supercilium, and yellow wash to cheeks	Upperparts brighter and purer green than those of *viridanus*, with one or two slightly broader and yellower wing-bars	Strongly suffused with yellow, which can still be apparent in worn plumage	As *viridanus*	More trisyllabic than that of *viridanus*, a *chis-ru-weet*	
Greenish Warbler *P. t. trochiloides*	Prominent whitish or yellowish-white supercilium, broad, dark eye-stripe and dusky mottling to cheeks	Dark oily green upperparts, with darker olive crown; one or two whitish or yellowish-white wing-bars	Greyish cast to underparts. Often with diffuse oily yellow wash to breast, belly and under-tail-coverts	Dark bill, with orange at base, or basal two-thirds, of lower mandible	*Chis-weet*	Very similar to Large-billed; best distinguished by call
Pale-legged Leaf Warbler+	Prominent buff or white supercilium, which contrasts strongly with broad, dark eye-stripe; ear-coverts frequently washed with buff	Vary from olive-green to olive-brown some with bronze cast, with darker and greyer crown; double whitish wing-bar	Whitish (lacking yellow) and may show buffish wash to flanks	Mainly dark with whitish tip	High-pitched metallic *pink* or *peet*	Very pale pinkish legs and feet
Large-billed Leaf Warbler	Striking yellowish-white supercilium contrasting with broad, dark eye-stripe, with greyish mottling on ear-coverts	Dark oily green with noticeably darker crown; one or two yellowish-white wing-bars	Dirty, often with diffuse streaking on breast and flanks and oily yellow wash to breast and belly; can, however, appear whitish	Large and mainly dark, with orange at base of lower mandible; often with pronounced hooked tip	Loud, clear whistled, upward-inflected *der-tee*	Large

SMALL *PHYLLOSCOPUS* WARBLERS WITH BROAD, GENERALLY DOUBLE, WING-BARS; MOST HAVING PALE CROWN STRIPE

Species	Head pattern	Wing bars	Rump and Tail	Underparts	Call	Other features
Buff-barred Warbler	Poorly defined dull yellowish crown stripe; yellowish supercilium	Double buffish-orange wing-bars, although median-covert wing-bar often not apparent	White on tail; small yellowish rump patch	Sullied with grey and can be washed with yellow	Short, sharp *swit*	
Ashy-throated Warbler	Greyish-white crown stripe, contrasting with dark grey sides to crown; greyish-white supercilium	Double yellowish wing-bars	White on tail; prominent yellow rump	Greyish throat and breast and yellow belly, flanks and undertail-coverts	Short *swit*	
Lemon-rumped Warbler	Yellowish crown stripe contrasting with dark olive sides to crown; yellowish-white supercilium	Double yellowish-white wing-bars	No white on tail; well-defined yellowish (sometimes almost whitish) rump	Uniform whitish or yellowish-white	High-pitched *uist*	
Brooks's Leaf Warbler	Narrow, usually poorly defined yellowish crown stripe; sides to crown barely darker than mantle; yellowish supercilium and wash to ear-coverts	Double-yellowish wing-bars; bases of median and greater coverts do not form dark panel across wing as they do in Lemon-rumped	No white on tail; ill-defined yellowish rump, often barely apparent	Yellowish throat; entire underparts washed with buffish-yellow in fresh plumage	Monosyllabic loud and piercing *chwee* or *pseo* or *psee*	Brighter yellowish-olive upperparts compared with similar species. Yellowish-horn basal half of lower mandible (bill mainly dark in Hume's)
Yellow-browed Warbler	Lacks well-defined crown stripe, although can show diffuse paler line; broad yellowish-white supercilium and cheeks	Broad, yellowish or whitish wing bars; median-covert wing-bar is prominent	Lacks pale rump patch and does not have white in tail	White with variable amounts of yellow	A loud *chee-weest*, with distinct rising inflection	Brighter greenish-olive upperparts (in fresh plumage) compared with Hume's. Bill has extensive pale (usually orangish) base to lower mandible, and legs are paler (compared with Hume's)
Hume's Warbler *P. h. humei*	Lacks well-defined crown stripe, although can show diffuse paler line; broad buffish-white supercilium and cheeks	Broad, buffish or whitish greater-covert wing-bar; median-covert wing-bar tends to be poorly defined, but can be prominent	Lacks pale rump patch and does not have white in tail	White, often sullied with grey	A rolling, disyllabic *whit-hoo* or *visu-visu*, and a flat *chwee*	Greyish-olive upperparts, with variable yellowish-green suffusion, and browner crown. Bill appears all dark and legs are normally blackish-brown
Hume's Warbler *P. h. mandellii*	Shows more distinct (but still diffuse) pale crown stripe compared with *P. h. humei*; dirty yellowish-white supercilium; sides of crown darker than mantle	As *humei*, but wing-bar(s) dirty yellowish-white	As *P. h. humei*	Dirty yellowish-white	Strikingly disyllabic *tjis-ip*	Upperparts darker olive-green than those of *P. h. humei*

LARGE *PHYLLOSCOPUS* WARBLERS WITH CROWN STRIPE, PROMINENT WING-BARS, AND LARGE BILL WITH ORANGE LOWER MANDIBLE

Species	Head pattern	Upperparts including wings	Underparts	Call	Additional features
Western Crowned Warbler	Greyish-white to pale yellow crown stripe, contrasting with dusky olive sides to crown, which may be darker towards nape; prominent dull yellow supercilium	Generally duller greyish-green compared with Blyth's, with stronger grey cast to nape; wing-bars narrower and less prominent than those of Blyth's, because bases not so dark	Whitish, strongly suffused with grey, especially on throat and breast; can show traces of yellow on breast and belly	A repeated *chit-weei*	Larger and more elongated than Blyth's, with larger and longer bill
Eastern Crowned Warbler	Yellowish-white crown stripe, contrasting with uniform dark olive sides to crown; supercilium is typically yellow in front of eye, and white behind	Darker and purer green than those of Western Crowned; usually only a single greater-covert wing-bar apparent and tends to lack dark panel across greater coverts which is shown by Blyth's	Whitish with yellow wash to undertail-coverts (although this can be difficult to see)	An occasional harsh, buzzy nasal *dwee*	Larger and more elongated than Blyth's, with larger and longer bill
Blyth's Leaf Warbler	Tends to be more striking than Western Crowned with yellow supercilium and crown stripe contrasting with darker sides to crown	Usually darker and purer green than those of Western Crowned, although may be similar. Wing-bars are more prominent than those of Western and Eastern Crowned, being broader and often divided by dark panel across greater coverts	Generally has distinct yellowish wash, especially to cheeks and breast	Constantly repeated *kee-kew-i*	
Yellow-vented Warbler	Brighter yellow crown stripe and supercilium than those of similar species, contrasting with darker sides to crown	Bright yellowish-green with yellow wing-bars	Yellow throat, upper breast and undertail-coverts contrasting with white belly	A double note	

CETTIA BUSH WARBLERS
See plate caption text for description of song

Species	Head pattern	Upperparts	Underparts	Additional features
Pale-footed Bush Warbler	Pale buff supercilium and dark brown eye-stripe; more prominent than that of Brownish-flanked	Rufescent brown	White throat, centre of breast and belly, strongly contrasting with brownish-olive breast sides and flanks	Shorter, square-ended tail compared with Brownish-flanked. Pale pinkish legs and feet
Japanese Bush Warbler	Rufous-brown forehead and forecrown; prominent whitish supercilium which is buffier in front of eye	Olive-brown	Strong buff or olive-buff wash to underparts, with whiter belly	Large with large stout bill, with long tail that is slightly notched
Brownish-flanked Bush Warbler *C. f. pallidus* (W Himalayas)	Greyish-white supercilium, less prominent than that of Pale-footed	Olive-brown	Pale buffish-grey with brownish-olive flanks with only a small area of off-white on belly	Longer, rounded tail compared with Pale-footed. Brownish legs and feet
Brownish-flanked Bush Warbler *C. f. fortipes* (E Himalayas and NE)	Buffish supercilium, less prominent than that of Pale-footed	Warmer, rufous-brown upperparts compared with *C. f. pallidus* and close to coloration of Pale-footed. First-year? with olive cast	Brownish-buff coloration to throat and breast; olive-buff flanks; duskier underparts than those of Pale-footed. First-year? with yellow wash to belly	As *C. f. pallidus*
Chestnut-crowned Bush Warbler	Chestnut on forehead and crown; supercilium indistinct and rufous-buff in front of eye and buffish-white behind	Dark brown	Whitish with greyish-olive sides to breast and brownish-olive flanks; whiter, particularly on throat and centre of breast, than Grey-sided	Larger than Grey-sided
Aberrant Bush Warbler	Yellowish supercilium	Yellowish-green cast to olive upperparts	Buffish-yellow to olive-yellow, becoming darker olive on sides of breast and flanks. Some worn? birds have less yellow on throat and upper breast and are duller on rest of underparts	
Yellowish-bellied Bush Warbler	Crown is rufous-brown, as mantle; buffish-white supercilium	Pale rufous-brown with strong olive cast, especially to lower back and rump; noticeable rufous fringes to remiges (especially tertials)	Yellowish belly and flanks	Small with small, fine bill
Grey-sided Bush Warbler	Chestnut forehead and crown; short, whitish-buff supercilium is well defined in front of eye (compared with Chestnut-crowned)	Dark brown	Greyish-white with grey sides to breast and brownish-olive flanks	Smaller than Chestnut-crowned
Cetti's Bush Warbler	White supercilium, lacking bold dark stripe through eye	Rufous-brown	White on breast with greyish breast sides and flanks; dull white tips to greyish-brown undertail-coverts	Larger than Pale-footed with longer tail

BRADYPTERUS BUSH WARBLERS

Note none of the following species has streaked upperparts; see plate caption text for description of song

Species	Head	Bill	Throat and Breast	Undertail-coverts	General appearance
Spotted Bush Warbler *B. t. kashmirensis* and *B. t. thoracicus*	Greyish supercilium, less distinct than that of Long-billed	Shorter all-dark bill than that of Long-billed	Usually has bold spotting; some only show fine spotting	Boldly patterned with dark brown centres and sharply-defined white tips	Dark olive-brown with rufescent cast; grey ear-coverts and sides of breast, and olive-brown flanks
Spotted Bush Warbler *B. t. shanensis*	Whitish supercilium	Pale lower mandible	Weaker and browner spotting	As above	Paler brown upperparts than those of *kashmirensis* and *thoracicus*; brownish wash to sides of neck and across breast
Long-billed Bush Warbler	White supercilium	Much longer and finer bill than that of Spotted	Spotting is finer than in Spotted, but more clearly defined against white base colour of breast; in some, spotting almost entirely lacking	Unmarked	Upperparts vary from warm olive-brown when fresh to greyish-olive when worn. Whitish underparts with buffish flanks
Chinese Bush Warbler	Yellowish-white to buffish white supercilium		Unspotted or with fine spotting on lower throat	Pale tips	Greyer-brown upperparts than those of Brown with olive cast; olive grey-brown ear-coverts and sides of breast, and olive-buff flanks; often with yellowish wash to underparts
Brown Bush Warbler	Indistinct rufous-buff supercilium, which barely extends beyond eye and is concolorous with the lores	Pale pinkish-orange lower mandible	Lacks spotting	Lack of prominent pale tips	Warm brown upperparts with slight rufescent cast; warm rufous-buff ear-coverts, sides of neck and breast, and flanks, contrasting with silky-white of rest of underparts
Russet Bush Warbler	Indistinct and off-white supercilium (which does not extend noticeably beyond eye, as it does in Spotted)	Blackish	Unspotted or with brown spotting on lower throat and upper breast	Diffuse pale tips	Rich brown upperparts (darker and more rufescent than those of Chinese and Brown); brown ear-coverts, sides of breast and flanks which are concolorous with upperparts

Species	Bill/feet	Head pattern	Upperparts	Underparts	Additional features
Black-browed Reed Warbler	Dark grey legs and feet	Square-ended buffish-white supercilium, broader and more prominent than that of Paddyfield; broad black lateral crown stripes	Rufous-brown in fresh plumage; more olive-brown when worn	Warm buff sides to breast and flanks when fresh	Shorter-looking tail, and longer projection of primaries beyond tertials, compared with Paddyfield
Paddyfield Warbler	Shorter bill than that of Blyth's Reed, usually with well-defined dark tip to pale lower mandible. Yellowish-brown to pinkish-brown legs and feet	Prominent white supercilium, often broadening behind eye, becoming almost square-ended, with dark eye-stripe; supercilium can appear to be bordered above by diffuse dark line. Supercilium less distinct on some	More rufescent than those of Blyth's Reed. Typically shows dark centres and pale fringes to tertials. Greyer or sandier when worn but usually retains rufous cast to rump	Warm buff flanks; underparts whiter when worn. Often shows whitish sides to neck	Typically looks longer-tailed than Blyth's Reed, with tail often held cocked
Blunt-winged Warbler	Longer and stouter bill than that of Paddyfield, with uniformly pale lower mandible or with dark shadow at tip	Shorter and less distinct supercilium than that of Paddyfield, which typically barely extends beyond eye (occasionally on worn birds may extend as thin line behind eye); lacks dark border above supercilium and lacks prominent dark eye-stripe	As Paddyfield, but more olive-toned when fresh. Colder olive-brown when worn, but with more rufescent rump and uppertail-coverts. Shows more prominent tertial fringes than does Blyth's Reed	Breast and flanks washed with buff when fresh	Longer tail, and shorter primary projection, compared with Paddyfield
Blyth's Reed Warbler	Bill longer than that of Paddyfield. Lower mandible either entirely pale or has diffuse dark tip	Comparatively indistinct supercilium; often does not extend beyond eye, or barely does so, and never reaches rear of ear-coverts. Lacks dark upper border to supercilium and dark eye-stripe	Generally colder olive-grey to olive-brown than Paddyfield. Noticeable warm olive cast to upperparts when fresh (more rufescent in first-winter). Tertials rather uniform	Can have light buffish wash to flanks when fresh; otherwise cold whitish	Can appear similar to *rama* race of Booted. Shorter looking, more rounded tail than that of Booted, and longer upper- and undertail-coverts; more skulking and lethargic than that species
Booted Warbler *H. c. rama*	Longer-billed than *caligata*. Legs and feet paler and browner than those of Blyth's Reed	Supercilium more distinct than that of Blyth's Reed and lores can appear pale	Paler and greyer than *caligata* and all *Acrocephalus* (although can be rather similar to Blyth's Reed)	Off-white	More arboreal than *caligata*; behaviour often *Phylloscopus*-like compared with *Acrocephalus*. Longer-looking square-ended tail than that of *Acrocephalus* with shorter undertail-coverts
Booted Warbler *H. c. caligata*	Comparatively short and fine bill	Supercilium more prominent than that of *rama*; can appear to have dark border	Warmer brown than *rama*. Fine whitish fringes to remiges and edges of outer tail feathers often apparent (also shown by *rama*)	Off-white	Rather *Phylloscopus*-like in appearance, often feeding on ground. Squarer-tail and short undertail-coverts compared with *Acrocephalus*
Upcher's Warbler	Large and long bill	Supercilium short and barely extends beyond eye	Greyer than those of *Acrocephalus* and Booted, and flight feathers and tail often look noticeably darker. White edges and tips to outer rectrices, and prominent pale fringes to remiges and wing-coverts	Whitish	Larger than Booted with broader and fuller tail and longer primary projection. Has habit of flicking tail downwards

IDENTIFICATION OF LARKS

Species	Structural features	Head pattern	Upperpart pattern and coloration	Breast markings	Underpart coloration	Outer tail feathers	Wings	Hindclaw
Singing Bushlark *Mirafra cantillans*	Well proportioned, with moderately long tail. Bill short and stout. Smallest of the bushlarks	Strong buffish-white supercilium. Ear-coverts comparatively uniform brownish-buff (some with diffuse and indistinct dark border at rear and with indistinct spotting in malar region)	Generally more diffusely streaked than Singing, with colder grey-brown coloration to upperparts	Comparatively weak, diffuse and small brown spotting, indistinct or almost lacking on some	Typically, white throat, brownish-buff breast and buffish rest of underparts	Outer tail feathers mainly whitish, some with buffish tinge. Per ultimate feathers with whitish outer webs	Comparatively weak rufous panel. Rufous fringes to primary coverts, and narrow rufous edges to outer webs of primaries and secondaries, with only a small amount of rufous on inner webs of these feathers	Shorter than or roughly equal in length to hindtoe
Indian Bushlark *M. e. erythroptera* *M. e. sindiana*	Much as Singing. Bill looks slightly larger and tail shorter	Supercilium possibly not so prominent as on Singing. Spotted ear-coverts and malar region, with variable, diffuse dark border at rear of ear-coverts	More clearly and heavily streaked than Singing. Crown with slight rufous cast. Upperparts warm sandy-buff (*sindiana*) to rufous-buff (*erythroptera*)	Strong, clearly defined blackish crop-shaped spots	Uniform whitish to buffish-white, some with stronger buff wash to breast	Rufous-buff outer web to outer tail feathers. Penultimate pair with narrow rufous-buff edge to outer webs	Extensive and prominent panel, showing much rufous in flight. Primary coverts rufous except for dark line along shaft. Almost whole of outer webs of primaries and secondaries rufous; most for inner webs rufous except tips	Shorter than or roughly equal in length to hindtoe
Rufous-winged Bushlark *M. a. assamica*	Stocky and comparatively short-tailed. Bill large and stout	Buffish to rufous-buff supercilium. Ear-coverts with variable rufous tinge. Ear-coverts and malar region with bold, diffuse blackish spotting and barring, with diffuse dark border to ear-coverts	Brownish-grey and diffusely streaked (streaking strongest on crown and back)	Large, diffuse spotting, not so bold as in *affinis*	Dirty rufous-buff, with paler throat and grey on flanks	Diffuse rufous edges to outer webs of outer tail feathers	Less extensive and prominent panel than on Indian. Primary coverts with diffuse rufous fringes. Primaries and secondaries with rufous edges to outer webs; broad diffuse edges to inner webs (except primary tips). Black centres to tertials contras markedly with rufous-buff fringes	Long, usually distinctly longer than hindtoe
Rufous-winged Bushlark *M. a. affinis*	Stocky and comparatively short-tailed. Bill large and long; larger than Indian Bushlark's	Buffish supercilium. Boldly spotted ear-coverts and malar region, with prominent dark border to ear-coverts	Heavily streaked crown with slight rufous cast. Upperparts rufous-buff (similar in overall appearance to *M. e. erythroptera*). Often shows prominent buffish (and heavily streaked) nape	Very strong, bold blackish drop-shaped spots	Uniform whitish to buff, with variable rufous-buff wash to breast, belly and flanks	Rufous-buff outer web to outer tail feathers. Rest of tail feathers with narrow rufous-buff fringe	Less extensive and prominent panel than on Indian. Primary coverts with rufous fringe. Primaries and secondaries with rufous edges to outer webs; broad diffuse edge to inner webs (except primary tips)	Long, usually distinctly longer than hindtoe

continued overleaf

IDENTIFICATION OF LARKS continued

Species	Primary projection	Bill	Upperparts and wings	Underparts	Head pattern
Greater Short-toed Lark C. brachydactyla dukhunensis/ C. b. longipennis	Tertials reach or almost reach tip of primaries	Proportionately shorter and broader than Hume's. Usually pale pinkish, with indistinct dark culmen and tip to lower mandible	Warm sandy-buff and heavily streaked. Dark centres to median coverts strongly defined. Race longipennis is a shade colder and greyer on upperparts	Variable dark patch on side of upper breast (lacking on some); some with a few streaks on upper breast. C. b. dukhunensis has buffish-white underparts with variable rufous-buff breast-band (often strongest, and distinctly rufous, on breast sides). C. b. longipennis has breast washed with brownish-buff (again, often strongest on breast sides). Flanks often buffish	Crown heavily streaked, some with distinct rufous cast. Broader supercilium than on Hume's and Lesser and lores usually appear pale. Typically, shows dark eye-stripe and patch on rear ear-coverts, with pale patch on lower ear-coverts and crescent below eye
Hume's Short-toed Lark C. a. acutirostris/ C. a. tibetana	Tertials reach (or almost reach) tip of primaries	Proportionately slightly longer and slimmer than in Greater's. Usually brownish-yellow, with distinct dark culmen and tip	Pale brownish-grey, and less heavily streaked than Greater. Streaking can be very poorly defined in fresh plumage. Uppertail-coverts usually have warm rufous-pink coloration. Dark centres to median coverts less pronounced than on Greater	Variable diffuse dark patch on breast side, some with a few diffuse streaks. Breast washed with cold greyish-buff, although breast warmer and buffier on some. Rest of underparts whitish	Compared with Greater Short-toed: crown less heavily streaked, often appearing almost unstreaked; supercilium narrower and more poorly defined in front of eye; ear-coverts more uniform, usually without prominent dark eye-stripe. Lores usually show dark stripe
Lesser Short-toed Lark C. rufescens persica	3–4 primary tips clearly visible beyond longest tertial	Shorter and stouter than in Greater's, more distinctly curved on both mandibles	Paler, sandy-buff (almost pinkish-buff), compared with Greater, and generally more finely and sparsely streaked. Dark centres to median coverts usually less pronounced than on Greater	Relatively broad band of fine dark streaking. Lacking dark patches on sides of breast and with variable buffish wash. Some with streaking on flanks, streaking continuing onto lower throat on some	Crown strongly streaked, but more finely so than on Greater. Less striking head pattern than Greater, with less prominent supercilium and streaked ear-coverts. Typically, white supercilium continues across forehead (broken at culmen base on Greater)
Asian Short-toed Lark	3–4 primary tips clearly visible beyond longest tertial	Short and stout, but distinctly smaller than that of persica race of Lesser	Generally even paler than Lesser, and streaking more diffuse. Base colour of some cream. Dark centres to median coverts usually less pronounced than on Greater	As Lesser, although streaking generally more diffuse	Much as Lesser
Sand Lark C. r. raytal/ C. r. adamsi	3 primary tips clearly visible beyond longest tertial	Finer than in Greater's. Bill of adamsi is distinctly longer and finer than that of nominate	Cold sandy-grey and diffusely streaked (streaking really distinct only on scapulars). Wings rather uniform, lacking pronounced dark centres to median coverts	Fine, sparse dark streaking on otherwise rather uniform white or creamy-white underparts	Crown more strongly streaked than rest of upperparts. Prominent whitish supercilium and broad crescent below eye-stripe, with whitish patch on ear-coverts

WHITE WAGTAILS (BREEDING MALES ONLY)

Subspecies	Distribution and status	Mantle coloration	Head pattern
M. a. dukhunensis	Widespread winter visitor	Grey	Black chin; white forehead and face
M. a. personata	Breeding NW subcontinent and widespread winter visitor	Grey	Black chin; white forehead and mask
M. a. alboides	Breeding N subcontinent and wintering more widely in N and NE	Black	Black chin; white forehead and mask
M. a. leucopsis	Winter visitor to N and NE	Black	White chin and throat; white forehead and face
M. a. ocularis	Uncommon to rare winter visitor to N and NE	Grey	As *dukhunensis*, but with black eye-stripe
M. a. baicalensis	Passage migrant in Nepal	Grey	White chin, forehead and face

YELLOW WAGTAILS (BREEDING MALES ONLY)

Subspecies	Head pattern
M. f. beema	Pale bluish-grey head, complete and distinct white supercilium, white chin, and usually a white submoustachial stripe contrasting with yellow throat; ear-coverts are grey or brown, usually with some white feathers
M. f. leucocephala	Whole head to nape white, with a variable blue-grey cast on the ear-coverts and rear crown; chin is white, and throat yellow as rest of underparts
M. f. melanogrisea	Black head, lacking any supercilium, and white chin and poorly defined submoustachial stripe contrasting with yellow throat.
M. f. taivana	Differs from all other races in having olive-green crown, concolorous with mantle, and broad yellow supercilium contrasting with blackish lores and ear-coverts
M. f. plexa	Dark blue-grey crown and nape (darker than *beema*), and narrow white supercilium contrasting with blackish lores and dark grey ear-coverts; chin is white
M. f. thunbergi	Dark slate-grey crown with darker ear-coverts, lacking supercilium (although may show faint trace behind eye)
M. f. lutea	Mainly yellow head, with variable amounts of yellowish-green on crown and nape and ear-coverts (concolorous with mantle)
M. f. zaissanensis	Head slate-grey, with narrow white supercilium
M. f. superciliaris	Probably a hybrid between *beema* and *melanogrisea* and looks like the latter, but with a white supercilium

IDENTIFICATION OF FEMALE ROSEFINCHES

Species	Most likely confusion species	Size/structure	Supercilium	Wing-coverts and tertials	Underparts	Upperparts	Other features
Blandford's	Dark-breasted and Vinaceous	Small and compact	Lacking	Relatively uniform, with indistinct pale fringing	Unstreaked, pale greyish-brown	Uniform grey-brown, unstreaked but for indistinct crown streaking	Reddish or bright olive cast to rump and uppertail-coverts
Dark-breasted	Blandford's and Vinaceous	Relatively small, slim-bodied, with slender bill	Lacking	Variable, broad buffish wing-bars and tips to tertials	Unstreaked, dark greyish-brown	Relatively uniform dark greyish-brown, with diffuse mantle streaking	Dark greyish olive-brown rump
Common	Beautiful	Small and compact, with stout, stubby bill	Lacking	Narrow, whitish or buff tips to coverts, forming narrow double wing-bar	Whitish, with variable, bold, dark streaking	Grey-brown with some dark streaking	Beady-eyed appearance
Beautiful	Common	Small and compact	Whitish, but very poorly defined	Indistinct pale tips to median and greater coverts	Whitish, quite heavily streaked	Buffish-grey, heavily-streaked darker	
Pink-browed	Dark-rumped, Spot-winged and White-browed	Relatively small and compact	Prominent buff supercilium, contrasting with dark ear-coverts	Relatively uniform, lacking wing-barred effect	Heavily streaked, with strong fulvous wash from breast to undertail-coverts	Warm brownish-buff with heavy dark streaking	Fulvous coloration on rump
Vinaceous	Blandford's and Dark-breasted	Relatively small and compact	Lacking	Uniform wing-coverts, but conspicuous whitish tips to tertials	Warm brownish-buff, lightly streaked	Warm brown, almost concolorous with underparts, with diffuse streaking	Plain-faced appearance
Dark-rumped	Pink-browed, Spot-winged and White-browed	Medium-sized	Prominent buff supercilium	Buffish tips to greater coverts and outer edge of tertials	Brownish-fulvous, heavily streaked	Rather dark brown with heavy dark streaking	Lacks well-defined dark ear-coverts
Three-banded	Unmistakable	Medium-large	Lacking	Broad, double white wing-bars and scapular line, and prominent white tips to tertials	Dull orange-yellow, extensively mixed with whitish belly to undertail-coverts; some faint flank streaking	Dull orange-yellow, extensively mixed with whitish on mantle and streaked darker	Short, whitish streaks on grey ear-coverts and throat
Spot-winged	Pink-browed, Dark-rumped and White-browed	Medium-sized and rather stocky	Prominent, very broad, buff, supercilium	Prominent pale buff tips to greater coverts and outer edge of tertials	Brownish-fulvous, very heavily streaked, including on throat	Rather dark brown with heavy dark streaking	Well-defined dark ear-coverts contrasting with supercilium
White-browed	Pink-browed, Dark-rumped and Spot-winged	Medium-large	Prominent, long, white supercilium, contrasting with dark lower border and rear of ear-coverts	Whitish to buff tips to median and greater coverts, forming narrow double wing-bar	White, heavily streaked, with racially variable ginger-buff wash to throat and breast	Mid to dark brown with heavy dark streaking	Deep olive-yellow rump, heavily streaked
Red-mantled	Streaked and Great	Large, with stout, heavy bill and long tail	Rather faint whitish supercilium, weakly offset against greyish eye-stripe	Lacks wing-bars, but has indistinct paler tips to median and coverts	Whitish underparts, heavily streaked	Pale grey, heavily streaked	
Streaked	Great and Red-mantled	Large, with stout bill	Lacking	Lacks prominent wing-bars but has dark centres to median and greater coverts and tertials	Whitish underparts, heavily streaked	Dark grey, rather heavily streaked	
Great	Streaked and Red-mantled	Large, with stout bill	Lacking	Relatively uniform, pale grey-brown	Whitish, heavily streaked	Sandy-brown with faint streaking	
Red-fronted	Streaked	Very large, with rather long, conical bill	Lacking	Lacks wing-bars or obvious tertial contact	Greyish, very heavily streaked, with variable pale yellow wash on breast	Very dark grey with bold, heavy dark streaking	Rump and uppertail-coverts more olive than black, or yellow
Crimson-browed Finch	Unmistakable	Large grosbeak-like shape with heavy, stout, stubby bill	Bright olive-yellow, extending across forehead	Relatively uniform	Grey, with olive-yellow breast	Greenish-olive with some diffuse streaking	Often shows olive-yellow rump

IDENTIFICATION OF MALE ROSEFINCHES

Species	Most likely confusion species	Size/structure	General coloration	Supercilium	Wing-coverts and tertials	Underparts	Upperparts	Rump
Blandford's	Common	Small and compact with relatively slender bill	Pinkish-crimson	Lacking	Lacks wing-bars and contrasting tertial fringes	Dull pinkish-crimson, unstreaked, often with greyish cast	Unstreaked, dull crimson	Unstreaked, dull crimson
Dark-breasted	Dark-rumped	Relatively small, slim-bodied, with long, slender bill	Dark maroon-pink and brown	Quite prominent, reddish-pink, contrasting with dark maroon eye-stripe	Uniform; lacks wing-bars and contrasting tertial fringes	Maroon-brown breast band contrasting with rosy-pink throat and belly	Maroon-brown, with indistinct darker streaks, and reddish-brown forecrown	Maroon-brown, concolorous with rest of upperparts
Common	Blandford's	Small and compact, with short, stubby bill	Bright geranium-red	Lacking	Rather indistinct bright red fringes to wing-coverts and tertials	Bright geranium-red, especially on throat and breast	Diffusely streaked bright geranium-red	Unstreaked, bright red
Beautiful	Pink-browed	Small and compact	Cold greyish-pink	Rather indistinct, pale lilac-pink	Indistinct paler fringes to wing-coverts and tertials	Cold greyish-pink with pronounced dark shaft streaks, especially on flanks	Cold pinkish-grey, with conspicuous dark crown and mantle streaking	Contrasting, unstreaked pale lilac-pink
Pink-browed	Beautiful	Smallish and compact	Deep, warm pink	Prominent, deep pink contrasting with dark maroon-pink eye-stripe	Rather uniform; lacks prominent paler fringing to wing-coverts and tertials	Unstreaked, warm pink	Pinkish-brown mantle and back streaked darker; unstreaked or lightly streaked maroon-pink crown	Unstreaked, deep pink
Vinaceous	Unmistakable	Relatively small and compact	Dark crimson	Prominent, pale pink	Uniform coverts; lacks wing-bars but has prominent pinkish-white tertial tips	Uniform dark crimson	Dark crimson, with diffuse dark mantle streaking	Paler, dull crimson, contrasting with rest of upperparts
Dark-rumped	Dark-breasted and Spot-winged	Medium-sized	Brownish-maroon	Prominent, bright pink, contrasting with pinkish-maroon ear-coverts	Rather indistinct pinkish tips to coverts and buffish tips to tertials	Indistinctly streaked, with brownish-maroon breast and flanks	Pink-tinged brown and broad diffuse streaks	Pinkish-brown, concolorous with rest of upperparts
Three-banded	Unmistakable	Medium-large	Pinkish-crimson, white and blackish	Lacking	Broad, double white wing-bars and scapular line, bold white outer edges to tertials	Pinkish-crimson breast contrasting with white belly and lower flanks	Pinkish-crimson crown and nape, with greyish mantle	Pinkish-crimson
Spot-winged	Dark-rumped	Medium-sized and rather stocky	Maroon and pink	Prominent, pale pink, contrasting with crown and ear-coverts	Very prominent pink tips to median and greater coverts and tertials	Rather uniform pink, with some darker mottling	Rather uniform maroon, indistinctly streaked, with irregular pink splashes	Maroon, prominently splashed with pink
White-browed	Red-mantled and Pink-browed	Medium-large	Brownish and pale pink	Prominent, long, pinkish with splashes of white, extends across forehead	Pronounced pale tips to greater and median coverts forming narrow wing-bars	Pink, with some white streaking	Brown, with conspicuous darker streaking	Pink, well defined contrasting with rest of upperparts
Red-mantled	White-browed	Large, with stout, heavy bill and long tail	Pink and pale brownish-grey	Prominent, pink	Very indistinct paler fringing	Pink, with some streaking	Brownish-grey, with pink tinge, streaked darker	Uniform pink
Streaked	Great	Large, with stout bill	Crimson-pink	Lacking	Very indistinct paler fringing	Crimson-pink, with clearly defined white spotting	Grey-brown, washed pink, and with conspicuous darker streaking	Uniform deep pink
Great	Streaked	Large with stout bill	Rose-pink and sandy-grey	Lacking	Very indistinct paler fringing	Rose-pink, with large diffuse white spots	Sandy-grey, washed pink, with narrow streaking	Uniform rose-pink
Red-fronted	Streaked	Very large, with rather long, conical bill	Red and dark grey-brown	Short and red, extending across forehead	Very indistinct paler fringing	Red throat and breast, contrasting with dark streaked grey-brown remainder of underside	Grey-brown, with bold dark streaks	Deep pink, contrasting with rest of upperparts
Crimson-browed Finch	Confusion very unlikely	Grosbeak-like shape with large, stout, stubby bill	Red and brownish-green	Red, extending across forehead	Very indistinct paler fringing	Red throat and upper breast, contrasting with pale olive-grey remainder of underparts	Warm olive-brown, tinged with red, and diffusely streaked	Quite bright red, uniform

INDEX OF ENGLISH NAMES

Figures in **bold** are plate numbers

INDEX OF SCIENTIFIC NAMES

Figures in **bold** are plate numbers